The Criminal Process

THE CRIMINAL PROCESS

An Evaluative Study

Andrew Ashworth

Second Edition

Oxford University Press
1998

Oxford University Press, Great Clarendon Street, Oxford OX2 6DP
Oxford New York
Athens Auckland Bangkok Bogotá Buenos Aires Calcutta
Cape Town Chennai Dar es Salaam Delhi Florence Hong Kong Istanbul
Karachi Kuala Lumpur Madrid Melbourne Mexico City Mumbai
Nairobi Paris São Paulo Singapore Taipei Tokyo Toronto Warsaw
and associated companies in
Berlin Ibadan

Oxford is a registered trade mark of Oxford University Press

Published in the United States
by Oxford University Press Inc., New York

British Library Cataloguing in Publication Data
Data available

Library of Congress Cataloging in Publication Data
Ashworth, Andrew.
The criminal process: an evaluative study / Andrew Ashworth.—2nd ed.
p. cm.
Includes bibliographical references and index.
1. Criminal justice, Administration of—Great Britain.
2. Criminal investigation—Great Britain.
3. Sentences (Criminal procedure)—Great Britain.
I. Title.
HV9960.G7A74 1998 364.941—dc21 98–20507
ISBN 0–19–876537–1
ISBN 0–19–876536–3 (Pbk.)

1 3 5 7 9 10 8 6 4 2

Typeset by Hope Services (Abingdon) Ltd.
Printed in Great Britain
on acid-free paper by
Biddles Ltd., Guildford and King's Lynn

Preface

In the four years since the first edition of this work was published, debates about the pre-trial process have intensified. The Royal Commission on Criminal Justice has now faded into the past—in many respects a lost opportunity for reform and reorientation. As the Human Rights Bill of 1998 passes through its parliamentary stages, it seems staggering that in 1993 the Royal Commission could have presented a report that never once mentioned the European Convention on Human Rights. Yet the increasing references to the advent of a 'rights culture' seem, so far, to have left criminal justice virtually untouched. Many of the legislative and other changes introduced since 1993 have paid scant regard to rights-based arguments, and it remains to be seen whether the new Government, with its ostensible commitment to 'bringing rights home', will set about the alteration of pre-trial procedures that will be necessary if rights are to be brought home to this part of criminal justice.

The aim of the book remains that of providing an integrated treatment of questions of principle and practice in pre-trial processes and procedures, drawing on arguments from the law, research, policy, and principle. It does not purport to be a textbook; it focuses, rather, on a number of key issues for deeper examination than would be possible if the book were to aim for wider coverage. A theoretical framework is advanced in Chapters 2 and 3, which have been re-organized and re-written. They retain the emphasis on the European Convention on Human Rights and supplement it with analysis of other relevant perspectives. Chapter 3 focuses on occupational cultures in the pre-trial process and on questions of legal ethics that arise at various stages.

The second part of the book contains six chapters on particular stages in decision-making; integrating and commenting upon the latest developments in law and practice. Thus Chapter 4 deals with a range of issues arising at the investigative stage, from surveillance and entrapment through to disclosure and identification. Particular emphasis is placed on the 1994 provisions allowing courts to draw adverse inferences from a suspect–defendant's silence, looking at the implications in law, in practice, and under the European Convention on Human Rights. Chapter 5 examines the initial decision whether a suspect should be prosecuted or diverted from the formal criminal process, in the light of recent and proposed changes to the practice of police cautioning. Chapter 6 discusses prosecutorial review, with detailed consideration of the functions and performance of the Crown Prosecution Service. In Chapter 7 there is an analysis of remand decisions, scrutinizing the justifications for taking away liberty before trial. Chapter 8 turns to the relatively under-discussed question of determining whether a case should be heard in a magistrates' court or the Crown Court, with special reference to the 'plea before venue' system introduced in 1997. In Chapter 9 the law and practice on plea negotiation is examined in the light of the 'fair trial' guarantees of the European Convention and other principles. The book closes with a final chapter in which general conclusions about the pre-trial process are elaborated.

I wish to record my gratitude to all those friends and colleagues who have assisted, many willingly and others unwittingly, in the preparation of the two editions of this book.

A.J.A.
Oxford, March 1998

Contents

Abbreviations

ABA	American Bar Association
BJ Crim.	*British Journal of Criminology*
Camb. LJ	*Cambridge Law Journal*
CLP	*Current Legal Problems*
CPS	Crown Prosecution Service
Crim. LR	*Criminal Law Review*
HORS	Home Office Research Study
Howard JCJ	*Howard Journal of Criminal Justice*
ICLQ	*International and Comparative Law Quarterly*
LJ	*Law Journal*
LQR	*Law Quarterly Review*
LR	*Law Review*
MLR	*Modern Law Review*
NILQ	*Northern Ireland Law Quarterly*
New LJ	*New Law Journal*
Oxford JLS	*Oxford Journal of Legal Studies*
PACE	Police and Criminal Evidence Act 1984
PAS Supp.	*Proceedings of the Aristotelian Society Supplement*
PICA	Public Interest Case Assessment
PL	*Public Law*
PSI	Policy Studies institute
RCCJ	Royal Commission on Criminal Justice
RCCP	Royal Commission on Criminal Procedure
SFO	Serious Fraud Office
U. Chi. LR	*University of Chicago Law Review*
U. Pa. LR	*University of Pennsylvania Law Review*

Table of Cases

Table of Statutes

Table of Treaties and Conventions

Part I

General

1 Decisions

THE subject-matter of this book is the criminal process from the first official engagement with a suspected offence or offender through to trial. The treatment is selective rather than comprehensive, focusing on pre-trial procedures and devoting little discussion to trials, sentences, or appeal mechanisms. The selection of issues here is not intended as a comment on their relative importance. The legal and social significance of appeal mechanisms and procedures for correcting miscarriages of justice has been placed beyond doubt by several notorious cases: to what extent the Criminal Appeal Act 1995 alters practice remains to be seen. The principles and practice of sentencing retain a high public profile, and have been examined extensively elsewhere.[1] But it has long been true that the amount of public and academic discussion devoted to criminal trials, particularly trials by jury, far outweighs their numerical significance within the criminal process. The vast majority of defendants are dealt with in magistrates' courts, and the vast majority of defendants in all courts plead guilty. It makes sense, therefore, to focus on the processes and procedures that lead to guilty pleas. For most defendants this is the reality of criminal justice. Speaking statistically, a trial of guilt is most unlikely, and a trial by jury in the Crown Court is highly unlikely. The pre-trial stages are far more important than their low visibility would suggest. Issues relating to the trial and post-trial stages will be mentioned wherever the context requires.

This chapter contains a discursive survey of the English criminal process, designed to provide a context in which readers can place the theoretical discussions and the examination of particular stages in the later chapters. It begins with a brief description of the key decisions taken in respect of suspected offences that come to the notice of the authorities. Many of these decisions are discussed in later chapters, and therefore detailed references are not given at this stage, but it is necessary to have an overall view before we go on to explore issues of policy and principle in Chapters 2 and 3. Consideration is then given to the possibility of classifying the different *types* of decision taken at the pre-trial stage, and also to some of the differences in processing crimes

---

[1] A. Ashworth, *Sentencing and Criminal Justice* (2nd edn. 1995).

of various kinds. There is then some discussion of ways of dealing with errors. This is followed by brief outlines of the decision-making personnel and of recent landmarks in English policy in respect of the pre-trial process. The aim is to provide readers with a short overview of procedures and issues.

1. Key Stages in Decision-Making

In most cases the first decision is that of a member of the public—victim, bystander, employer, etc.—to report an offence-like incident to the police or other authorities. In a minority of cases the authorities might learn about a suspected offence through their own activities. The police might be conducting an undercover operation into drug-dealing, for example, or they may be on duty at a public meeting or procession. The Inland Revenue might discover an offence through their checking procedures, or the Pollution Inspectorate may discover an offence through routine inquiries. If the authorities believe that an offence has been committed, they may seek the offender. In some cases the identity of the probable offender is readily apparent: there might be an identification or even a naming by the person who reported the offence, or there may be a high probability that the person to seek is the victim's husband, or the owner of a certain factory, etc.

Once the authorities begin questioning members of the public, issues of rights and procedures are raised.[2] In general a police officer is free to put any questions to any citizen, but there is no general duty to answer the questions of the police or to remain where the police wish him or her to remain.[3] Many citizens will answer questions, and this may result in the police officer terminating the inquiry, or informing the suspect that a summons will be issued in respect of the offence, or deciding to arrest the suspect. Whether or not the person answers questions, a police officer is entitled to arrest any person whom he or she has reasonable grounds to suspect of having committed or being about to commit an 'arrestable offence'.[4] When the suspect is brought to the police station, the custody officer has to decide whether the suspect should be released without charge, charged, or (if it is thought necessary to obtain further evidence by questioning) detained for questioning.[5] That detention may be for up to six hours in the first place, and there are pro-

---

[2] For an accessible and detailed treatment of the relevant law, see *Emmins on Criminal Procedure* (7th edn. by John Sprack, 1997). For a more critical review of police powers, see K. Ewing and C. Gearty, *Freedom under Thatcher* (1991).

[3] *Rice* v. *Connelly* [1966] 2 QB 414.   [4] PACE, s. 24.   [5] PACE, s. 37.

cedures for renewal.[6] The custody officer must record these and other decisions on a custody sheet, and the suspect must be informed of the right to free
and confidential legal advice. The Codes of Practice issued under the Police
and Criminal Evidence Act 1984 set out standards for the conduct of police
investigations. For example, they impose restrictions on the manner in which
the police may question a suspect,[7] and on the handling of identification procedures. Many details of these procedures will be examined in Chapter 4,
where actual practice as well as the letter of the law will be discussed. The
police will seek to question the victim at an early stage, and should inform victims of violent offences of the existence of the Criminal Injuries
Compensation Board. The police may also put the victim in touch with
Victim Support or other similar agencies. Inquiries in a case may be completed quickly or may spread over a considerable time, in which case the
police have a duty to keep the victim informed of the progress of the case.

The outline in the previous paragraph focused on police procedures. Other
investigating agencies, such as HM Customs and Excise, are subject to the
Codes of Practice, although there is much less legal regulation of inquiries by
the many so-called 'regulatory' agencies. The general principle throughout,
however, is that a person may only be questioned before charge and not after
charge. Once there is sufficient evidence, the suspect should be charged. On
the other hand, it must not be thought that charging is the only way of commencing a prosecution. The alternative method is for a police officer to lay an
information before a magistrate or justices' clerk, as a result of which a summons will be issued and served on the defendant. The summons procedure is
more commonly used for minor offences: the power of arrest, which places
considerable discretion and power in the hands of the police, is typically used
for more serious offences, but can also be deployed for relatively minor
offences against public order.

In the early stages before charge there are also various powers of search. The
police have been given powers to stop and search persons and vehicles in public places, and PACE Code A sets out guidance on these matters.[8] There are
detailed provisions for searches of premises, differentiated according to the
seriousness of the alleged offence and excluding certain kinds of material.[9]
The 1984 Act also provides for the search of arrested persons, and the powers
of the police to carry out non-intimate and intimate searches were considerably expanded by the Criminal Justice and Public Order Act 1994.[10] It should
be added that several regulatory agencies have special powers to search

---

[6] PACE, ss. 40–4. [7] Taken in conjunction with ss. 76, 78, and 67(1) of PACE.
[8] PACE, ss. 1–3. [9] See generally PACE, ss. 8–22.
[10] Recent research on the use of these powers is reported by T. Bucke and D. Brown, *In Police Custody* (1997).

premises in connection with inquiries into particular forms of offence. Indeed, the powers of HM Customs and Excise far exceed those of the police.

It has been assumed so far that the progression from sufficient evidence to charge or summons is natural or inevitable, but that is far from being true. An authority with the power to prosecute may decide to take no formal action at all, perhaps believing that the experience of detection or an informal warning is sufficient, or it may decide that a formal caution or warning is appropriate. The police have developed the practice of issuing a formal caution to certain offenders, particularly the young, the elderly, and those whose offences are very minor. (The practice is currently extra-statutory, but a new system of reprimands and final warnings is to be introduced by the Crime and Disorder Bill 1998, for young offenders only.) The police are supposed to consult the victim of the crime before deciding to caution, although the victim's wishes should not be conclusive. Many regulatory agencies have powers to issue formal warnings to employers, companies, farmers, and others in respect of offences, and they may prefer to adopt this approach in the hope of maximizing compliance with the law. Some agencies have powers to exact financial penalties from offenders without bringing a prosecution: the Inland Revenue may offer citizens the opportunity to pay, say, double the amount of tax evaded as a condition of non-prosecution.

If the prosecution proceeds by way of summons, the defendant will be given a date for first appearance in a magistrates' court. If it proceeds by arrest and charge, the custody officer must decide what course to take after the defendant has been charged. There is a duty to ensure that a defendant is brought before a court as soon as practicable, which is often the morning after arrest (or on Monday morning, if the arrest takes place on a Saturday). The defendant may be bailed to appear in court or, if there are reasonable grounds for believing that detention is necessary for certain purposes, the police may keep the defendant in custody until the first court appearance.[11] At first appearance the magistrates' court must either dispose of the case or, if not (and particularly in serious cases which will be committed to the Crown Court for trial), the court must decide whether to release the defendant on bail or to make a custodial remand. The Bail Act 1976 (as amended) proclaims a presumption in favour of bail, but also sets out various reasons for the refusal of bail.

Legal assistance is available at several stages in the process. Not only is there a right to free legal advice at the police station, but there are duty solicitor schemes to facilitate this and to advise on representation in court. The Legal Aid Act 1988 provides, in effect, that magistrates' courts must grant legal aid

---

[11] PACE, s. 38.

to defendants who are going to the Crown Court, and they have a discretion to grant legal aid for summary trials. Defendants with means are expected to make contributions, but a majority of defendants are unemployed or otherwise in receipt of State assistance. The discretionary grant of legal aid shows considerable variation between courts.[12]

In cases investigated by the police, they take the decision whether or not to charge the defendant, although they may seek advice from the Crown Prosecution Service before doing so. The papers are then passed to the Crown Prosecution Service. Their function is to review the evidence, to consider the 'public interest', and then to decide how to proceed. They have the power to discontinue prosecutions in magistrates' courts,[13] and may drop a case when it is called on in the Crown Court. They may decide to continue with the prosecution on the charges preferred by the police, or may alter the charges. If it is a Crown Court case it will be necessary to draft the indictment.[14] If the defendant has been remanded in custody, there are now time-limits which apply to the period between first appearance in the magistrates' court and committal (seventy days), and between committal to the Crown Court and trial (112 days).[15] The prosecution may apply for an extension, but if there are insufficient grounds the accused must be released on bail until the trial.

The choice of charge determines the mode of trial. Most minor offences are triable summarily only, in the magistrates' courts. Most serious offences are triable only on indictment, in the Crown Court. The intermediate category of offences triable either way may be tried in a magistrates' court or at the Crown Court. The Criminal Procedure and Investigations Act 1996 introduced a new order of events for either-way cases, in which the defendant first indicates what plea is intended. If the defendant states that a guilty plea is intended, the magistrates' court becomes seised of the case and may proceed to pass sentence or, if it believes that its sentencing powers are inadequate, it may commit the case to the Crown Court for sentence. If the defendant states that a not guilty plea is intended, then mode of trial is determined as before. The first decision is that of magistrates, having heard representations, but the defendant has an unfettered right to elect Crown Court trial even if the magistrates regard an 'either-way' case as suitable for summary trial. When a case is committed to the Crown Court for trial, this should not be taken to mean that committal proceedings are held. The vast majority of cases are committed on paper, but both the defendant and the prosecution have the power to insist on

---

[12]   R. Young and D. Wall, *Access to Criminal Justice* (1996), esp. ch. 7.
[13]   Prosecution of Offences Act 1985, s. 23.
[14]   For full discussion, see *Emmins on Criminal Procedure*, ch. 6.
[15]   Prosecution of Offences Act 1985, s.22, on which see A.Samuels, 'Custody Time Limits' [1997] *Crim. LR* 260. The Crime and Disorder Bill 1998 proposes some tightening of the regulations.

full committal proceedings before a magistrates' court to test the strength of the prosecution case, although under the 1996 Act no oral evidence may be heard at committal.

If a defendant indicates an intention to plead not guilty, there may be various exchanges between prosecution and defence before the date set for trial. In some cases there will be a form of preparatory hearing: in some magistrates' courts there may be a pre-trial review, and in the Crown Court a 'Plea and Directions' hearing will be held. In serious or complex cases the Crown Court judge has a power to order a preparatory hearing, where rulings on the admissibility of evidence can be made in advance of the trial.[16] In many cases there will be discussion between prosecuting counsel and defence counsel on the day before, or the very day of, the Crown Court trial. In some cases there may be a preliminary discussion with the judge. Defence counsel may then discuss the case with the defendant, and a change of plea to guilty may take place. This part of the process, sometimes described as 'plea bargaining', is unregulated by statute and little regulated by the Court of Appeal.

A defendant who pleads guilty will be sentenced by the magistrates or by the Crown Court judge, after hearing a statement of facts from the prosecution and a plea in mitigation from the defence, and in non-minor cases after receiving a pre-sentence report. A defendant who pleads not guilty will be tried in the appropriate court. Magistrates' courts tend to be less formal, with less strict adherence to the laws of evidence but also with a greater sense of briskness. In the Crown Court the trial will be before judge and jury, and matters are unfolded in greater detail.

A defendant convicted by a magistrates' court may appeal against conviction or sentence to the Crown Court, where the appeal takes the form of a rehearing. If either the defence or the prosecution wishes to appeal on a point of law, the magistrates may be asked to state a case to the Divisional Court. A defendant convicted in the Crown Court may appeal against conviction and/or sentence to the Court of Appeal (Criminal Division), whose powers have been altered somewhat by the Criminal Appeal Act 1995. That Act also established the Criminal Cases Review Commission, which has powers to review convictions alleged to involve a miscarriage of justice and to refer appropriate cases back to the Court of Appeal.[17] These changes follow the report of the Royal Commission on Criminal Justice, and are designed to

---

[16] Criminal Procedure and Investigations Act 1996, discussed by A. Edwards, 'The Procedural Aspects' [1997] *Crim. LR* 321.

[17] For the history of the Court's exercise of its powers, see R. Pattenden, *English Criminal Appeals 1844–1994* (1995), esp. ch. 10, and the articles on the 1995 Act by D. Schiff and R. Nobles, 'Criminal Appeal Act 1995: The Semantics of Jurisdiction' (1996) 59 *MLR* 573, J.C. Smith, 'The Criminal Appeal Act 1995: Appeals against Conviction' [1995] *Crim. LR* 920, and K. Malleson, 'The Criminal Cases Review Commission: How will it Work?' [1995] *Crim. LR* 929.

introduce a more independent and systematic review of convictions than that which took so long to deal with the notorious cases of miscarriage of justice uncovered in the late 1980s and early 1990s.

The various stages in decision-making outlined above apply generally, although reference was made to differences between the powers and practices of the police and of the regulatory agencies. However, there are differences of approach to cases involving certain types of suspect or defendant and certain types of alleged offence. Where the suspect or defendant is a juvenile, aged between 10 and 18, there are special procedures and safeguards. There is also special provision for mentally disordered suspects and defendants. Persons requiring interpreters or suffering from deafness, etc., should also be treated differently. As for types of offence, brief mention may be made of the different legal regimes for motoring offences and for persons suspected of terrorist offences or of serious fraud. Many motoring offences may be dealt with by a fixed penalty without a court appearance, and some of those that have to be brought to court do not require the appearance of the defendant. There are also several other differences of procedure, including particular time-limits for commencing a prosecution. The Prevention of Terrorism Acts give greater powers to the police when questioning persons suspected of involvement in terrorist offences, including the power to detain such persons without charge for up to seven days. The Criminal Justice Act 1987 gives enhanced powers to the Serious Fraud Office when investigating persons suspected of involvement in frauds involving millions of pounds. The Act authorizes the SFO to require a defendant to furnish documents and to answer questions, and institutes a special procedure for bringing cases of serious fraud to trial.

Before leaving this outline of decisions, their context within a system needs to be emphasized. They are not discrete individual decisions taken in laboratory conditions. Rather, they should be viewed as decisions taken either by individuals or by courts, working within a given professional context. The individual police officer or Crown Prosecutor is likely to be influenced, for example, not only by the working practices and expectations of colleagues, but also by decisions taken by others beforehand and decisions likely to be taken at subsequent stages. The factual basis for the decision may well have been constructed by others, in a way that depends partly on selection and interpretation. This point is developed in the last section of the chapter, but it is important to avoid from the outset the dominance of a 'rationalist' notion of decisions taken by individuals independently and based on objective information.[18]

[18] Cf. R. Baldwin and K. Hawkins, 'Discretionary Justice: Davis Reconsidered' [1984] *PL* 570, at 581.

2. Distinguishing Types of Decision

The various legal procedures and practices described in the previous section combine to affect the ways in which particular suspects and defendants are processed by officials. Formal procedures do not determine that treatment, since the working practices of officials are what suspects and defendants actually experience. Those practices may be more or less faithful to the rules, and in some instances the law may leave discretion rather than imposing rules.

It is noticeable, however, that the various decisions outlined above are not all of the same kind. Most of them might be described as 'processual', in that they are decisions about the processing of the case from initial charge through to trial. But there are two or three decisions that may be described more accurately as 'dispositive', in that they are concerned more with the disposal of the case. One strong example of this is the decision either to give a formal caution or warning or to take no formal action, rather than to prosecute. This decision, whether taken by the police or by a regulatory agency, may be regarded as analogous to sentencing. It disposes of the case, which goes no further in the system, with some form of censure. The weakness of the analogy is that no court is involved. Diversion is premised on the belief that the case does not warrant full processing and a court appearance. A second example is the review of a case by the Crown Prosecution Service, followed by a decision to discontinue the prosecution on grounds of insufficient public interest. A third possible example is the prosecutor's decision to accept a bargain which involves the dropping or reduction of one or more charges—a decision which will usually have implications for sentence, and may therefore be described as dispositive to some extent. Decisions on mode of trial may also have this dimension.

The point of making this distinction is that different considerations will apply to processual decisions and to dispositive decisions—as is clear from the analogy between dispositive decisions and sentencing, which has no application to decisions on the processing of cases. None the less, in practice questions of evidential sufficiency and of the seriousness of the offence often intermingle in the minds of decision-makers, and so the distinction may be less sharp in practice than in theory. Moreover, there is at least one type of decision that is neither processual nor dispositive: the remand decision, whether on bail or in custody. This has no direct bearing on whether the prosecution will be continued or discontinued, nor on mode of trial or plea, although in practice it may be affected by these other decisions. Nor is it a means of taking a case out of the system and dealing with it otherwise. It is *sui generis*, and is perhaps best described as a temporizing decision, in that it arises solely if and when a case cannot be dealt with at the first court appearance. The adjective temporizing refers only to why this decision arises rather than to the nature of the issues involved, but in view of the discussion in Chapter 7 below, this neutrality is probably wise.

3. Miscarriages of Justice

In a number of well-publicized cases, errors have been discovered in the investigations and trials which led to convictions followed by defendants spending long years in prison for serious crimes. It was in the aftermath of these cases that the Government decided in 1991 to appoint a Royal Commission on Criminal Justice. Yet in its report the Royal Commission gave neither an analysis nor even a description of these catalytic cases.[19] It seems that the Commission decided that such an exercise ran a considerable risk of provoking 'further unprofitable controversy', which was taken to outweigh any benefits.[20] However, these cases now form an essential part of the context of criminal justice reform, and it is important to include here a brief survey of the problems they brought to light.[21]

In the case of the 'Guildford Four', the defendants had been convicted in 1976 of murder by causing an explosion at a public house in Guildford. Their appeal against conviction was turned down. In 1989 their case was referred to the Court of Appeal by the Home Secretary. The Director of Public Prosecutions stated that he no longer sought to support the convictions, and the Court quashed them. The primary ground was that tests on police documents undermined the evidence of police officers that the crucial interviews were recorded contemporaneously, since the handwritten notes had evidently been written after the typed 'records' of the interviews.[22]

In the case of the 'Maguire Seven', the defendants, most of whom were members of the Maguire family, had been convicted in 1976 of an offence of possessing explosive substances, the substances being linked by the prosecution to bombings in London and Guildford. Their application for leave to appeal was refused in 1977. After the convictions of the 'Guildford Four' had been quashed, the Home Secretary asked the May Inquiry to consider this case but then referred the case to the Court of Appeal. The Court quashed the

---

[19] Royal Commission on Criminal Justice, *Report*, Cmnd. 2263 (1993).

[20] Michael Zander, 'Where the Critics got it Wrong' [1993] *NLJ* 1338, at 1339.

[21] For a more detailed survey, see Joshua Rozenberg, 'Miscarriages of Justice', in E. Stockdale and S. Casale (eds.), *Criminal Justice under Stress* (1993).

[22] *Armstrong, Conlon, Hill and Richardson*, 19 Oct. 1989, discussed *ibid.* 92–4.

convictions in 1992.[23] There were two main grounds. First, the prosecution had failed to disclose to the defence certain scientific evidence, which amounted to a material irregularity. Secondly, the scientific evidence left open the possibility that the traces of nitro-glycerine found on the defendants and in their house came from an innocent source, which rendered the verdicts unsafe and unsatisfactory. The defendants had spent some thirteen years in prison, and one of them had died there.

In the case of the 'Birmingham Six', the defendants had been convicted in 1975 of murder by causing an explosion at a public house in the centre of Birmingham. Their appeal against conviction was dismissed. In 1987 the Home Secretary used his power to refer the case back to the Court of Appeal, on the grounds of fresh scientific evidence and fresh evidence that the defendants had been beaten following their arrest. The appeal was dismissed. In 1990 the Home Secretary referred the case to the Court of Appeal again as a result of further fresh evidence. In 1991 the Court of Appeal quashed the convictions.[24] The defendants had maintained from the outset that they were beaten and that the so-called confessions were false. Among the reasons given by the Court of Appeal were the finding that all the notes of an alleged interview could not have been written contemporaneously (this was established by electrostatic analysis, the so-called ESDA test), and the finding that the Forensic Science Service had not disclosed the possibility that alleged traces of explosives could have come from innocent contamination or even from smoking cigarettes. The defendants had served over sixteen years in prison. The Crown Prosecution Service decided that there was sufficient evidence to justify prosecuting three police officers involved in the investigation for perjury and conspiracy to pervert the course of justice, but the judge stayed the prosecution on the ground that the publicity surrounding the Birmingham Six case made it impossible for the three former policemen to receive a fair trial on the specific charges alleged.[25]

In the case of the M62 bombing, Judith Ward had been convicted in 1974 of murder and causing an explosion. She did not appeal. In 1991 the Home Secretary referred her case to the Court of Appeal, and in 1992 her convictions were quashed.[26] The first ground was that the Forensic Science Service had failed to disclose the results of tests that were favourable to the defendant, and there were other failures of disclosure by the police, the Director of Public Prosecutions, and prosecuting counsel. The second ground was that the

[23] *Maguire et al.* (1992) 94 Cr.App.R. 133. For the May Inquiry, see *Return to an Address of the Honourable House of Commons Dated 12 July 1990 for the Inquiry into the Circumstances Surrounding the Convictions Arising out of the Bomb Attacks in Guildford and Woolwich in 1974*, HC 556 (1990).
[24] *McIlkenny et al.* (1991) 93 Cr.App.R. 287.   [25] (1992) *The Times* 16 Oct.
[26] *Ward* (1993) 96 Cr.App.R. 1; cf. also *Kiszko* (1992) *The Times* 19 Feb.

defendant's mental condition, a form of personality disorder, rendered her alleged confessions unreliable. Medical evidence available at the time of the trial had not been disclosed, and there was fresh medical evidence. Since the prosecution's case rested chiefly on statements by the defendant, the convictions were unsafe and unsatisfactory. Ms Ward had been in prison for eighteen years.

In the case of the 'Tottenham Three' the defendants were convicted in 1986 of the murder of a police officer during disturbances on the Broadwater Farm estate. Their appeals were unsuccessful, but in 1991 the Home Secretary referred their cases back to the Court of Appeal and the convictions were quashed. The principal ground was that ESDA tests on the 'notes of interview' showed that some parts of the alleged records had been written at different times from others. Although much is sometimes made of the fact that the investigation of all the earlier cases took place before the controls introduced by the Police and Criminal Evidence Act, it is noteworthy that the provisions of that Act were being tested in late 1985 in the police division where the three defendants were questioned.[27]

In one way the most significant case is that of the 'Cardiff Three', convicted in 1990 of the murder of a Cardiff prostitute. Their convictions were quashed by the Court of Appeal on the ground that the tenor and length of the police interviews were such that they should have been excluded from evidence. The Lord Chief Justice held that the techniques of interrogation used by the police amounted to 'oppression' within the meaning of section $76(2)(a)$ of the Police and Criminal Evidence Act 1984. On playing one of the tapes recording the interview, the appeal judges were 'horrified'.

> Miller was bullied and hectored. The officers, particularly Detective Constable Greenwood, were not questioning him so much as shouting at him . . . Short of physical violence, it is hard to conceive of a more hostile and intimidating approach by officers to a suspect. It is impossible to convey on the printed page the pace, force and menace of the officer's delivery.[28]

The particular significance of this case is that one defensive comment on most of the previous miscarriages of justice was that they occurred before the Police and Criminal Evidence Act and before the tape recording of interviews, with the implication that they could not happen today. Yet the Cardiff Three case not only occurred some years after the implementation of PACE but the interviews, including the manner of the police questioning, were tape recorded—

---

[27] *Silcott, Braithwaite and Raghip* (1991) *The Times* 6 Dec.; in the case of Raghip, the conviction was quashed on the additional ground that psychiatric evidence of his mental condition, not available at the time of the trial, had since come to light.

[28] *Paris, Abdullahi and Miller* (1993) 97 Cr.App.R. 99, at 103.

perhaps suggesting that the officers did not think that their approach was any-thing to be ashamed of.

This simplified sketch of several complex cases suffices to expose some recurrent problems. The most common pre-trial faults lay in the concoction or falsification of evidence by the police officers, in non-disclosure by foren-sic scientists, and more generally in non-disclosure by the prosecution to the defence. In some cases there was oppressive conduct by the police during questioning, with or without actual violence. These faults have implications for the rules on confessions and the controls on police investigations, and for the ethical orientation of the police, prosecution lawyers, and the Forensic Science Service. The most common post-trial faults lay in the slow and cum-bersome procedure for referring cases to the Court of Appeal, and in that Court's reluctance (at least until recently) to overturn jury verdicts, especially if such a decision would imply that the police had not told the truth. These faults called into question the machinery for dealing with alleged miscarriages of justice. Indeed, the term 'miscarriage of justice' should not be restricted to wrong outcomes, as it commonly is. Wherever there is a departure from proper practice, this should be regarded as a miscarriage of justice irrespective of its effect on the outcome of the case. Thus, speaking generally at this early stage, if a person who is factually guilty is convicted as a result of wrongful pre-trial or trial practices, that should count as a miscarriage of justice. On the other hand, the term is also apt to cover cases in which a guilty person is acquitted. Justice can miscarry in either direction.

While the focus hitherto has been on cases that were or ought to have been known to the Royal Commission, it should not be thought that the stream has dried up since then. One case manifesting a catalogue of errors was *Fergus* (1994),[29] in which the Court of Appeal quashed the conviction of a 13-year-old boy who had already served the equivalent of a six-month sentence of detention for attempted robbery. In a powerful and incisive judgment, Steyn LJ found clear errors by several of those involved in the case. The police had refused or declined to interview four alibi witnesses despite half a dozen requests from the Crown Prosecution Service. The defence solicitor prepared the case so badly that files were missing and key witnesses were not called at the trial. Defence counsel also failed to carry out his duties, among other things in failing to make a submission of no case. The trial judge gave an inac-curate summary of the evidence of the lone eye-witness and failed to warn the jury about the difficulties of identification evidence. After conviction the boy's mother sought advice from different solicitors, but was erroneously advised that legal aid would not be available to obtain a transcript, without

---

[29] (1994) 98 Cr.App.R. 313.

which nothing could be done. Only when Mrs Fergus contacted a third firm of solicitors was the correct advice given, and an application for leave to appeal made.

The Fergus case shows again that it is not merely the police whose acts or omissions may give rise to miscarriages of justice, although around the same time the case of the Taylor sisters turned largely on the suppression by the police of a key statement by a principal prosecution witness, which contained a description of the suspects inconsistent with the identification evidence he gave in court.[30] Perhaps the most notorious case of miscarriage of justice uncovered in the last few years is that of the Carl Bridgwater killing, for which four men were convicted, three of them spending many years in prison (the fourth man died in prison in 1982). In July 1997 the Court of Appeal overturned the convictions, stating that the men had not received a fair trial because the process of investigation and of preparation for the trial was unfair. The men had long stated that their confessions were false, and the Court of Appeal found that one of them was tricked into confessing, because the police showed him a confession by a co-defendant (which was forged), and that draft accounts of incriminating statements alleged to have been made spontaneously by the defendants had been found in the case file.[31] This is one of many cases of miscarriage of justice stemming from the activities of the West Midlands Regional Crime Squad in the last twenty years.[32]

Finally, the case of Stephen Lawrence serves as a reminder that the term 'miscarriage of justice' should not be limited to cases of wrongful prosecution or conviction. Stephen Lawrence was attacked and killed at a bus-stop in South London in 1993 by five white youths. The CPS declined to prosecute on the ground that there was insufficient evidence, and a private prosecution brought by the victim's family against five white youths was unsuccessful. A report for the Police Complaints Authority is said to have found that the initial investigation by the police failed to follow up lines of inquiry, ignored vital witnesses and handled identification evidence badly. Weak leadership and poor supervision of investigating officers are also mentioned.[33] The Lawrence case demonstrates once again, although from a different viewpoint, how vital the early stages of a criminal investigation are to the administration of justice.

---

[30] *Taylor and Taylor* (1994) 98 Cr.App.R. 361.   [31] Reported in *The Times*, 31 July 1997, 4.

[32] On 20 January 1998, a man was awarded £200,000 damages for five years' imprisonment for an offence that he had not committed: *The Guardian*, 21 Jan. 1998.

[33] *The Guardian*, 14 Mar. 1998.

4. Dealing with Miscarriages of Justice

The problem of errors in the system, whether caused by conscious or by careless departures from the rules, and whether favourable or unfavourable to the defendant, may be dealt with in two ways. Steps should be taken to prevent miscarriages of justice from occurring but, recognizing human fallibility within any system, there ought to be mechanisms for correcting them after they have occurred. One of the few worthwhile outcomes of the Royal Commission on Criminal Justice was the proposal for a Criminal Cases Review Commission, now constituted under the Criminal Appeal Act 1995. The Commission has many cases under investigation, and is beginning to bring cases to the Court of Appeal for review.

Within the regular court system, the primary method of error correction is the appeal against a decision of the trial court: in England there is a strong tradition that appeals against the decisions of magistrates and judges should be open to the defendant and not to the prosecution, because a prosecution appeal is tantamount to placing the defendant in double jeopardy. Other countries are less willing to allow defendants to take advantage of windfalls provided by erroneous rulings or verdicts. For the defendant, however, there is no need to wait for the appeal process in order to challenge the propriety of the treatment received from police, prosecutors, and others at the pre-trial stage. Where the defendant alleges that there have been departures from the rules at the investigation stage—for example, by improper questioning, unlawful search, or failure to allow access to legal advice—this may be raised in court as an objection to the admissibility of the evidence thereby obtained. The court has a duty to exclude a confession obtained by oppression, and has further powers to exclude oral or real evidence where it is likely to be unreliable or might adversely affect the fairness of the trial.[34] There is also the possibility of police disciplinary proceedings in these cases, but from the defendant's point of view any unfair advantage to the prosecution should be removed by excluding the tainted evidence.

Two further means of challenging procedural irregularities are judicial review and inviting the court to stay proceedings. Judicial review is available *inter alia* where a public body exercises its powers unreasonably or by taking account of irrelevant considerations. In recent years the Divisional Court has accepted that decisions to prosecute or not prosecute, by the police, the Crown Prosecution Service, or a regulatory agency, may be susceptible to judicial review on these grounds.[35] A decision by a magistrates' court at com-

---

[34] PACE, ss. 76, 78, and 82(3).   [35] Several cases are discussed at Ch. 6.7 below.

mittal proceedings, and other decisions of magistrates' courts, may also be challenged by this method. To ask the court to stay proceedings in a case involves invoking the doctrine of abuse of process, and it has been used against the misuse of prosecutorial power (e.g. attempting to circumvent a magistrates' court decision that an either-way case should be tried summarily, by dropping the either-way charge and prosecuting for an indictable-only offence),[36] against unreasonable delay or the unreasonable grant of an extension of custody time-limits,[37] and also in some cases of impropriety at the investigation stage.

The effect of a successful action for judicial review is to nullify the decision taken by the agency or court reviewed. The effect of a stay of proceedings is to terminate the case. The effect of a successful appeal depends on the grounds: where there has been a procedural irregularity the conviction would normally be quashed, but the Court of Appeal does have the power to order a retrial, which it is now beginning to exercise more frequently. The effect of a decision to exclude evidence depends on the centrality of the excluded evidence to the prosecution case: in many instances the prosecution will founder. It should be added that there are other ways in which a court can reflect what it considers to be less fundamental departures from procedure, mitigation of sentence being the most flexible.

This, however, raises questions. For what kinds of departure from procedure should each of the methods of challenge be available? Are there some departures from the PACE Codes of Practice, for example, to which exclusion of evidence would be too severe a response? Are there some forms of unfair or improper conduct in investigation to which mitigation of sentence is an inadequate response? Is the use of the term 'response' sufficiently accurate, or would other terms such as remedy, compensation, or penalty be more appropriate descriptions of the function that the law should perform here? These are among the questions that will be raised periodically throughout the book.

Turning to the preventive approach to errors, brief mention may be made of training, guidelines, and best practice. Legal rules might be regarded as the primary means of preventing errors, but it is because errors (deliberate and accidental) have taken place despite the existence of legal rules and powers that it is necessary to look for wider solutions. Proper training is the basis of prevention. It should help to minimize the number of accidental departures from proper procedure. Training is much sharper if it is possible to rely on fairly detailed guidelines for dealing with cases and taking decisions: the PACE Codes of Practice might be an example of this. In many situations, however, guidelines are laid down by superior authorities as a means of shaping

---

[36]   e.g. *Brooks* [1985] *Crim. LR* 385.
[37]   *Attorney-General's Reference (No. 1 of 1990)* [1992] 1 QB 630.

decision-making. They may not cover the ground fully, or may need to be supplemented by 'best practice'—practices developed on the ground by decision-makers that fit most appropriately with the purposes to be achieved. Training in itself is therefore not of great assistance unless there is something definite with which to train the decision-makers. On the other hand, rules, guidelines, and best practices are invariably open to interpretation and manipulation by those who are out of sympathy with the aims they seek to achieve. Most professions have one or more occupational cultures, which may sometimes breed a defensive and sectional approach to tasks. It will therefore be argued in Chapter 3 below that training must confront these cultures and must seek to inculcate an ethical perspective on decision-making in the criminal process.

5. The Decision-Makers

Victims of crime have a central role as decision-makers, albeit informally. Theirs is usually the initial decision to call the police, and they will often give information to the police that is useful in the investigation. The victim's wishes are stated to be relevant to the decision to caution rather than prosecute, and to the decision to discontinue a prosecution, but those wishes may be overridden by considerations of 'public interest'. The interests of the victim may be taken into account in remand decisions, particularly where there have been threats, but there is no formal procedure for that. It is apparent that victims have no formal role as decision-makers.

The police have considerable power and discretion in relation to suspects and defendants. Decisions about reasonable suspicion, arrest or summons, detention for questioning, and remand in custody before first court appearance are all for the police, although the custody officer is supposed to maintain a certain independence from other officers. The crucial decision whether to prosecute, caution, or take no formal action is also for the police, and this is a decision that can have a profound effect on the course of an individual's life. There are 'national standards' applicable to the cautioning decision, but the working practices of the police may prove to be of greater importance than the letter of the law or the guidelines. The influence of the early decisions taken by the police often endures through later decisions, such as bail, mode of trial, and plea.

Similar power is wielded by the officers of the various regulatory agencies, although they tend to use it for different purposes. Often there are strict liability offences for which they could prosecute, rendering conviction almost certain. But their tendency is to place compliance above punishment, and to use prosecution as a last resort when other methods of bringing about conformity with the legal standards have failed.

The Crown Prosecution Service was created in 1985, and consists of salaried lawyers whose primary tasks are to review cases to decide whether the prosecution commenced by the police should be continued, whether the charges should be changed, and to conduct prosecutions in the magistrates' courts. The CPS briefs counsel for prosecutions in the Crown Court and, except for the few cases conducted by Treasury Counsel, barristers acting for the prosecution will be independent counsel who may sometimes act for the defence. The CPS makes representations to magistrates' courts at remand hearings and (where a plea of not guilty is indicated) on mode of trial, and will normally be consulted if there is plea negotiation before a Crown Court trial.

Defendants have a number of decisions to make throughout the process. They have to decide whether or not to accept the offer of free legal advice at the police station, and also to decide what (if anything) to say to the police, bearing in mind the probability of adverse inferences from silence (under the Criminal Justice and Public Order Act 1994). If a police caution seems to be a possibility, they will be asked whether they admit the offence, and the prospect of a caution may lead them to accept guilt even if they believe they have a possible defence. The same may apply to young offenders who are offered a reprimand or final warning. Defendants who are prosecuted and remanded for trial will have the opportunity personally or through their advocate to make representations on bail. If they are charged with an offence triable either way, they will have the absolute right to elect trial by jury in the Crown Court. In the period before trial they will have to decide on their plea, and they may make a decision to change their plea from not guilty to guilty.

As for defence lawyers, they are entitled to be present at the police station during police questioning of a suspect, and any omission to prevent unfair questioning may be treated as a decision taken by them. The solicitor will advise the client about the possibility of adverse inferences from silence, and should press the police for proper details of the evidence against the client. More remotely but no less significantly, the organization of a solicitors' practice may determine whether a solicitor or an unadmitted member of staff deals with the preparation of the case and the taking of statements from the client.[38] Much may turn on the confidence and experience of the legal adviser, as well as on the ethos of the particular firm. The defence lawyer may make representations to the court at remand proceedings. The defence lawyer, whether solicitor or retained counsel, will play a role if there is to be any plea negotiation prior to trial in cases where the defendant has entered a plea of

---

[38] On this and related issues, see M. McConville *et al.*, *Standing Accused* (1994).

not guilty. Indeed, the way in which the defence lawyer puts the alternatives to the defendant may well have a profound effect on the defendant's decision.

Probation officers and social workers have no formal role in decision-making. However, social workers may participate in youth justice panels and other multi-agency groups for deciding how to deal with young offenders. Probation officers and social workers may also be involved in supplying information to the Crown Prosecution Service as part of bail information schemes and Public Interest Case Assessment schemes. At the sentencing stage, the pre-sentence report has been of increased significance since the Criminal Justice Act 1991.

Magistrates and judges hear the various representations mentioned above and take decisions. Magistrates take decisions on remand (on bail or in custody), and on mode of trial in offences triable either way to which the defendant indicates an intention to plead not guilty. In cases tried in magistrates' courts, they decide on the admissibility of evidence and then on guilt or innocence, passing sentence if there is a conviction. Crown Court judges preside over Plea and Directions hearings. They may also be approached in chambers by counsel seeking indications of sentence with a view to change of plea. At the trial they decide on the admissibility of evidence and they direct the jury, passing sentence if there is a conviction. Crown Court judges sit on appeals against the decisions of magistrates' courts (usually sitting with two lay magistrates), and in the Court of Appeal judges of the High Court sit with Lords Justices of Appeal to hear appeals from the Crown Court, as well as hearing references to the Court from the Criminal Cases Review Commission.

6. Changing the System

A further part of the context of the analysis in the chapters to follow is the series of official reports that have had a bearing on reform of the English criminal process. Some twenty years ago the Criminal Law Revision Committee's report on evidence was published.[39] Its recommendations to remove the 'right of silence' in the police station and to reword the police caution to suspects aroused fierce opposition, and many of the less controversial proposals for reforming the laws of evidence were also lost in the ensuing furore. However, reform of police powers remained a live question in public debate,[40] and in 1977 the Government announced the appointment of a Royal

---

[39] Criminal Law Revision Committee, Eleventh Report, *Evidence (General)*, Cmnd. 4991 (1972).
[40] See Michael Zander, 'The Criminal Process: A Subject Ripe for a Major Inquiry' [1977] *Crim. LR* 249.

Commission on Criminal Procedure. In its 1981 report, the Commission made proposals for the rationalization of police powers and for the introduction of an independent prosecuting agency.[41] The Police and Criminal Evidence Act 1984 amounts to a statutory code of police powers of arrest, search, and questioning, and it is supported by Codes of Practice issued by the Home Office. Some of the provisions extended police powers whereas others curtailed them. The Prosecution of Offences Act 1985 created the Crown Prosecution Service, and gave it statutory authority for the prosecution of almost all cases commenced by the police. The Royal Commission had argued strongly in favour of an independent prosecution service but, in the face of a strong police lobby, it recommended that the police should still retain the initial decision whether to prosecute, caution, or take no formal action. This leaves the English prosecutor in a much less powerful position than the Scottish, or than prosecutors in continental Europe.

In April 1990 the disturbances at Strangeways Prison, Manchester, and at other establishments led to an official inquiry by Lord Justice Woolf and Judge Tumim. Among the many points made in their report in 1991,[42] two are particularly relevant in the present context. The first is that the Inquiry was extremely critical of the conditions in which remand prisoners awaiting trial were held. The Government accepted most of the recommendations on this point,[43] but overcrowding remains a problem for remand prisoners particularly. The second is that the Inquiry emphasized the need for greater co-operation among agencies dealing with criminal justice. Its main recommendation on this point was implemented: there is a national Criminal Justice Consultative Council, supported by a number of area committees at which representatives of various agencies meet and discuss the approach to particular problems. However, the impact of the Council is still not clear, and it seems not to have been consulted on any regular basis by the previous Government before changes of policy were announced.

The Royal Commission of 1981 had declined to follow the 1972 report in relation to the right of silence, deciding that it would not be wise to abandon this right at the stage of police questioning, before the prosecution case was known to the suspect. However, the Government introduced severe curtailments of the right of silence into Northern Irish law, by an Order in Council made in 1988.[44] In 1989 the report of a Government working group was

---

[41] Royal Commission on Criminal Procedure, *Report*, Cmnd. 8092 (1981).

[42] *Prison Disturbances April 1990: Report of an Inquiry by the Rt. Hon. Lord Justice Woolf (Parts I and II) and His Honour Judge Stephen Tumim (Part II)*, Cm. 1456 (1991).

[43] Home Office, *Custody, Care and Justice*, Cmnd. 1647 (1991), ch. 7.

[44] A. Ashworth and P. Creighton, 'The Right of Silence in Northern Ireland', in J. Hayes and P. O'Higgins (eds.), *Lessons from Northern Ireland* (1990); J. D. Jackson, 'Curtailing the Right of Silence: Lessons from Northern Ireland' [1991] *Crim. LR* 404.

published, recommending similar curtailment of the right of silence in England and Wales.[45] Before this could be acted upon the succession of cases of miscarriage of justice, summarized in Section 3 above, began to receive wide publicity. Silence became one of the subjects central to the work of the Royal Commission on Criminal Justice, which was appointed in 1991 and reported in 1993.[46] Among over 300 recommendations in its Report may be found some proposals for greater police powers in dealing with suspects, a review of police disciplinary procedures, disclosure by the prosecution and the defence, abolishing the defendant's right to elect Crown Court trial of an 'either-way' offence, and creating a new review body for alleged miscarriages of justice. The Commission did not recommend the abolition of the right of silence, although neither did it recommend the corroboration of all confessions.

The Government swiftly rejected the Royal Commission's recommendations on the right of silence, and the Criminal Justice and Public Order Act 1994, sections 34 to 37, has introduced provisions on the drawing of adverse inferences from silence at the police station and in court. Several of the 1993 Royal Commission's recommendations were implemented, however. The 1994 Act widened the powers of the police to take intimate and non-intimate samples from suspects. The Criminal Appeal Act 1995 created the Criminal Cases Review Commission and amended the Court of Appeal's powers when dealing with appeals against conviction. The Criminal Procedure and Investigations Act 1996 introduced a new procedure for prosecution disclosure of evidence to the defence, and also, for the first time, a form of defence disclosure. These and many other recent changes are discussed in the chapters that follow.

7. Process and System

Although many who speak and write about criminal justice tend to refer to 'the criminal justice system', it is widely agreed that it is not a 'system' in the sense of a set of co-ordinated decision-makers. Even from the broad survey above it will be apparent that many groups working within criminal justice enjoy considerable discretion, and that they are relatively autonomous. None the less, the inappropriateness of the term 'system' should not be allowed to

---

[45] Home Office Working Group on the Right of Silence, *Report* (1989), reviewed by A. A. S. Zuckerman, 'Trial by Unfair Means' [1989] *Crim. LR* 855.
[46] See above, n. 19.

obscure the practical interdependence of the various agencies.[47] Many depend on other agencies for their case-load or for their information, and decisions taken by one agency can impinge on those taken by others. Thus, to take a few examples, the Crown Prosecution Service depends entirely on the police for its case-load, and largely on the police for information, although some information is now being supplied by the Probation Service. Decisions taken by the Crown Prosecution Service affect the case-load of the courts, and may constrain the powers of magistrates' courts and of defendants to determine mode of trial. Many other examples of interdependence and influence will be found throughout the book, and in the first section of the chapter it was emphasized that decisions should be viewed in this context rather than as discrete and objectively based determinations.

References to systems and interdependence are, however, very much in the managerial mode. The criminal process impinges directly on victims, suspects, and defendants. It impinges on them in the form of one or more contacts and decisions. A defendant who has been questioned by the police, charged, kept in police custody, remanded by the court, perhaps offered a plea bargain, and then tried in court is already likely to feel 'punished' irrespective of whether a guilty verdict and sentence follow. A person who is acquitted after such a sequence of events may well feel 'punished' by the process to which he or she has been subjected, even if relieved at the outcome. Of course this is a misuse of the term punishment, which is properly confined in the present context to sentences imposed by courts after findings of guilt. But it accords with the results of American research by Malcolm Feeley, encapsulated in the title of his book *The Process is the Punishment*.[48] Suspects and defendants often feel that the way in which they are treated is equivalent to punishment, in the sense that it inflicts on them deprivations (of liberty, of reputation) similar to those resulting from a sentence. This is particularly true for defendants who have been remanded in custody, and may flow from a single decision such as the decision to prosecute. Alternatively it may be a consequence, not so much of decisions taken in their case, but rather of what they regard as disrespect for their rights by the officials dealing with them. For present purposes, it is sufficient to make the point that the pre-trial process is a process to which defendants are subjected by officials who have the power of law behind them. It amounts to an exercise of State power—necessary, as part of the political system, but no less real for that. It is therefore appropriate to

---

[47] For further discussion, see H. Pullinger, 'The Criminal Justice System Viewed as a System', and F. Feeney, 'Interdependence as a Working Concept', both in David Moxon (ed.), *Managing Criminal Justice* (1985).

[48] M. Feeley, *The Process is the Punishment* (1979).

consider standards, accountability, and other issues relevant to dealings between the State and individual citizens.

Victims are also individual citizens whose interests should be protected. There is no shortage of empirical research findings that victims have been and are being treated in the criminal process in ways that can be described as 'punishment'. In the language of victimologists, victims who report crimes are often subjected to 'secondary victimization' at the hands of police, prosecutors, and courts.[49] While some steps have been taken to reduce these effects by improving techniques of police questioning and by granting anonymity to victims of certain offences, there is little doubt that some victims still suffer psychologically and socially from their involvement in the criminal process. In absolute terms this may be unavoidable, even though efforts must be made to minimize it, for example through improvements in courtroom facilities and familiarisation, and more particularly by amending procedures for witness protection and restricting the manner of courtroom questioning. It is sufficient here to state that the pre-trial process is a process to which victims of crime, too, are subjected by officials.

If one adds to these processual elements the fact that the one 'temporal' decision—remand before trial—may result in loss of liberty, and the effects that dispositive decisions can have (as a form of sentence without trial), it is evident that there is much at the pre-trial stage that needs to be justified, or changed.

---

[49] See Ch. 2.3(b) below.

2   Towards a Framework for Evaluation

WHAT should we expect of a criminal process? What aims should it pursue and what values ought it to respect? In answering these questions the links between the different parts and aspects of the criminal justice system must be kept in view. The purpose and scope of the criminal law itself have a bearing on pre-trial matters such as powers of arrest and even plea negotiation. The rules of evidence at trial may place some limits on the investigative powers of the police and other enforcement agencies. And the principles of sentencing are strongly related both to the criteria for diversion from the criminal process and to the system of plea negotiation. This chapter will keep those wider relationships in view while focusing on a framework for evaluating pre-trial justice. After reviewing Packer's two models of the criminal process, and then discussing the ubiquitous notion of 'balance' in criminal justice, the chapter will examine the strengths and limitations of the European Convention on Human Rights, considering derogations from the Convention and moving on to explore possible supplements to the rights declared therein. It will then turn to dispositive values. In conclusion, the chapter discusses the role of information in the protection of rights and interests, and sketches an evaluative framework. Chapter 3 will go on to explore the links between this framework and the practical realities of pre-trial justice

1. Herbert Packer's Two Models

The previous chapter demonstrated that a large number of decisions have to be taken in the pre-trial process. Many are concerned with the processing function, some with the dispositive function, and then there is the 'temporizing' remand decision. The possible consequences of these decisions for the suspect or defendant are considerable—from loss of liberty and loss of job, to family tensions, inability to sleep, and illness—and this is why there must be justifications for particular practices. Necessary as it is for the State to take measures to ensure the proper administration of criminal justice, it should take no more power over a person at this stage than is absolutely necessary for the carrying out of the proper functions of law enforcement. There has been no finding of guilt yet, and even if there has been an admission of guilt it is for a court to determine whether any measures (and, if so, what) should be taken against the defendant. Nothing done during the pre-trial process should have a punitive element to it, except where a defendant consents to submit to an obligation as a means of diverting the case from the process (the dispositive function).

Would it be relevant to argue that such concern for defendants is misplaced, since victims also have to undergo pain and hardship that is not their choice? Surely not. In order to maintain that a person who has been charged with an offence (though not yet convicted) should be treated no better than he or she is alleged to have treated the victim, one would need to argue not only for a form of talionic justice in sentencing but also that this approach to the infliction of punishment should dominate the period before trial. There are formidable difficulties in arguing that people may be punished before they are tried, as we will see when we come to discuss the presumption of innocence in Section 4 of this chapter: it is a mark of civilized society that punishment may be inflicted only after a finding of guilt by a court (or a satisfactory admission of guilt to an official in cases where some form of fixed penalty is payable.)[1]

Nevertheless, decisions in criminal justice often involve acute conflicts and awkward choices, particularly if the full range of interests is considered. How ought these choices to be made? What rights and interests should be recognized? Are some rights stronger (or more fundamental) than others? It will be argued in Section 3 of this chapter that mere references to balancing, without careful analysis of these issues, are unhelpful. How, then, should we proceed? The best-known framework for evaluating the criminal process is that of Herbert Packer, developed in the 1960s.[2] It has been subjected to considerable criticism and modification in subsequent years, and will not be adopted as a starting-point here, but it remains worthwhile to consider. Packer suggested that tendencies in criminal justice might be evaluated by means of two models, the Crime Control model and the Due Process model. 'The value system that underlies the Crime Control model is based on the proposition that the repression of criminal conduct is by far the most important function to be performed by the criminal process.'[3] This calls for 'a high rate of apprehension and conviction', placing a 'premium on speed and finality', and therefore pre-

---

[1] This refers to the widespread use of fixed penalties for road traffic offences and fare evasion on transport systems, and also extends to the practices of the Customs and Excise and Inland Revenue. For the principle that access to a court must be possible if the defendant contests liability, see Ch. 5.2.

[2] H. Packer, *The Limits of the Criminal Sanction* (1968).　　　　　　　　　　[3] *Ibid.* 158.

ferring informal to formal procedures, with minimal opportunity for challenge. To work efficiently, the Crime Control model should ensure that weak cases are discarded at the earliest opportunity and that strong cases are taken forward to conviction and sentence as expeditiously as possible. The police are in the best position to judge guilt, and, if they form the view after their investigation that a person is guilty, the subsequent stages of the process should be as truncated as possible.

Packer contrasts with this the Due Process model, which takes cognizance of the stigma and loss of liberty that might fall on the individual defendant as a result of the criminal process, and which insists on fairness criteria and other protections for the suspect or defendant. Thus the emphasis should be on formal and open adjudication of the facts in court, with the possibility of appeal, in order to give maximum protection to the innocent. Some proponents of the Due Process model would claim that it is a more accurate method of discovering the truth than the Crime Control model, but others would emphasize its recognition that errors do occur and its attempt to erect safeguards against mistaken judgments.

These models are, of course, artificial constructs which list the features of a 'pure' or extreme form of a particular approach. They are designed as interpretive tools, to enable us to tell (for example) how far in a particular direction a given criminal justice system tends, and they do not of themselves suggest that one approach is preferable to the other. But even as models they have met with a number of objections, of which five may be mentioned briefly here.

- First, Packer failed to give a clear explanation of the relationship between his models. He recognized that 'the polarity of the two models is not absolute',[4] and stated that the ideology of Due Process 'is not the converse of that underlying the Crime Control model', since 'it does not rest on the idea that it is not socially desirable to repress crime'.[5] His models might be reconstructed so as to suggest that Crime Control is the underlying purpose of the system, but that pursuit of this purpose should be qualified out of respect to Due Process. That, however, would need to be supported by careful arguments.
- Secondly, Packer assumed that the system of pre-trial justice is capable of affecting the crime rate, since he used the term Crime Control. It is true that Packer included powers of arrest and detection rates in his discussion of pre-trial justice, but evidence is needed of a significant relationship between the extent of police powers and the crime rate. Variations in the crime rate may be influenced more greatly by

---

[4] H. Packer, *The Limits of Criminal Sanction* (1968), 154.   [5] *Ibid.* 163.

social and economic factors, and it is fairly well established that different styles of policing have a minimal effect on the rate of convictions,[6] even though they may enhance control of the streets or control of certain types of people. The notion that different methods of processing defendants before trial might affect crime rates is not only unproven but also question-begging at a more fundamental level: surely Packer's models would be more realistic if he posited, as the primary State interest in pre-trial processes, convicting the guilty rather than controlling crime.

- Thirdly, and related to this, Packer underestimated the importance of resource management as an element in the criminal process. However, this may have assumed greater significance in the years since Packer wrote, as governments have come under much greater financial pressure, and have brought this pressure to bear on criminal justice agencies.[7]
- Fourthly, Packer's models make no allowance for victim-related matters. Again, this may be because there was far less consciousness of victims' interests and rights in the 1960s, but it is a significant drawback in using Packer's models today. Indeed, the models could hardly be expected to accommodate this perspective: a new model would need to be added.
- Fifthly, it is possible to mount various internal critiques of the two models. One example is the premium on speed, which Packer describes as an element in the Crime Control model. However, delays are also a source of considerable anxiety and inconvenience, and occasionally prolonged loss of liberty, to defendants. A properly developed notion of Due Process would surely insist that there be no unreasonable delay.[8]

Consideration of Packer's models begins to demonstrate the complexity of the criminal process and the problems of devising a satisfactory theoretical framework. The models may help us to identify elements of two important strands, but they neglect other, conflicting tendencies. Rather than pursuing the search for further possible models,[9] however, the time has come to reflect on the purpose of discussing values in the criminal process.

---

[6] See e.g. M. Hough, 'Thinking about Effectiveness' (1987) 27 *BJ Crim.* 70.

[7] Cf. however the criticisms of A. E. Bottoms and J. D. McClean, *Defendants in the Criminal Process* (1976), ch. 9, writing only 8 years after Packer.

[8] See the discussion of the European Convention on Human Rights, Art. 6(1), below in Section 4.

[9] On which see M. King, *The Framework of Criminal Justice* (1981).

2. Theory and the Pre-Trial Criminal Process

Packer's two models are certainly no longer satisfactory for the task of inter-preting the tendencies of criminal justice systems, since one might also wish to know about the victim's perspective and the extent of bureaucratic or fiscal tendencies. But they are also unsatisfactory in their failure to propose any nor-mative or evaluative criteria. What kind of theoretical framework should then be sought? The answer depends, of course, on the enterprise in which one is engaged. The purpose here is to locate a set or number of principles which have the authority or the persuasiveness to serve as goals for the criminal process or criteria by which to judge it. In this chapter, then, it is hoped to make progress towards a theoretical framework which is essentially *normative rather than descriptive*: in other words, the purpose is not to devise a theory which is apt to rationalize the practices that actually take place in the name of criminal justice in England and Wales, but rather to construct principles by which one can assess whether or not the rules and practices are justifiable. Any normative framework is bound to have a certain fragility, being incapable of dealing satisfactorily with all aspects of a complex group of practices such as the pre-trial criminal process, but that should not be taken as a conclusive objection to the search for broad principles of aspiration. In response to this fragility, however, the theoretical framework should be *reflexive* as well as nor-mative: in other words, it should respond, so far as possible, to the practical problems of operating a criminal justice system in this society at this time. This requires, for example, a refusal to accept official rhetoric or official descriptions of the system, and instead using independent empirical research as a foundation for discovering and assessing problems such as differential power and social disadvantage in relation to the formal pre-trial process. The normative structure should be *neutral* as between styles of criminal proce-dure, not assuming either an adversarial or an inquisitorial system to be preferable but providing (so far as possible) general criteria that can apply or be adapted to either approach or to a mixed system. And the normative struc-ture sought here is *not comprehensive*: it is not expected that the principles outlined below will supply answers, or even permit the deduction of answers, to all the issues that arise in the pre-trial process. There may be points at which other principles or standards need to be invoked, for specific purposes. It is hoped to work towards a normative structure that covers sufficient issues to have general usefulness as a set of standards by which pre-trial processes and procedures can be judged.

3. The Pervasive Notion of Balance

Much discussion of criminal justice by official bodies gives a central role to the notion of balance. The clearest examples of this in recent times are to be found in the report of the Royal Commission on Criminal Justice in 1993, and the same theme runs through many government documents. This is a rhetorical device of which one must be extremely wary. At worst, it is a substitute for argument: 'achieving a balance' is put forward as if it were self-evidently a worthy and respectable goal. Of course the criminal process is often the scene of conflicting aims and interests. Of course one would want the criminal process to be well balanced. But the difficulty is that many of those who employ this terminology fail to stipulate exactly what is being balanced, what factors and interests are to be included or excluded, what weight is being assigned to particular values and interests, and so on. Where this occurs—and it is evident throughout the report of the Runciman Royal Commission in 1993—it amounts to either self-delusion or intellectual dishonesty. How can one invoke the notion of balance without having prepared the ground con-scientiously? In this connection the most glaring omission from the Runciman report is the failure even to mention, let alone to consider and to draw upon, the rights enshrined in the European Convention on Human Rights. To support recommendations on the criminal justice system by means of the notion of balance, without taking any account of human rights, weak-ens much of the report and exposes its inadequacy on matters of principle. The centrality of human rights, and the contents of the European Convention, will be explored in Section 4 of this chapter.

At best, on the other hand, the rhetorical device of 'balancing' imports a kind of realism and pragmatism into arguments that might otherwise be blighted by an unworldly absolutism. Thus, some of those who advocate a 'rights' approach decline to recognize that rights should ever be qualified or limited in practice, arguing as if rights must be upheld even if the consequence is death, social catastrophe, or whatever. Now this leads into an area of con-siderable controversy, which cannot be explored here. If rights are to be rec-ognized at all, they must be in the form of anti-consequentialist claims—claims to protection from treatment of certain kinds, despite the fact that this goes against the majority wishes or the overall benefit of the community.[10] But it does not follow from this that rights are always absolute, and may never yield to even the most powerful consequentialist arguments: it can be main-tained that, in certain limited circumstances, there may be justifications for

---

[10] See R.M. Dworkin, *Taking Rights Seriously* (1977).

this. Likewise, it can be argued that pure utilitarian calculations are practically unacceptable, in a twentieth century that has seen major wars and oppressive regimes, without assigning some special weight to certain individual rights. Both rights theorists and consequentialists sometimes write as if the inevitable conflicts must be resolved by favouring their own perspective. The balancing approach may provide a kind of mechanism and rhetoric for avoiding extreme positions and recognizing practical realities,[11] although, as argued below, it must treat as given the absolute and strong rights enshrined in the European Convention on Human Rights.

Those arguments in favour of 'balancing', however, must be taken in their context. They do not excuse, let alone justify, the cavalier use of the term by the Runciman Commission and some others. They refer to the use of the metaphor as the inevitable conclusion of a lengthy and careful process, whereby rights and interests are identified; arguments for including some and excluding others are set out; appropriate weights or priorities are assigned to particular rights and interests, either generally or in specific contexts; and so forth. Above all, this must be a properly researched, reasoned, and principled course of argument, not simply the pronouncement of a conclusion.

The first step is to consider what interests ought to be recognized at the pre-trial stage of criminal justice. This is certainly a question which is easier to avoid than to answer. It is a relatively simple matter to criticize the rhetoric of a particular system, or set of reforms, as unduly individualistic, or as neglecting rights issues, or as favouring the strong at the expense of the weak. It is far more difficult to move towards a constructive formulation of interests and goals, let alone to rank them in order of priority. But a start has to be made somewhere, and the main purpose of this chapter is to take steps in that direction. The European Convention on Human Rights (below, Section 4) is to be the centrepiece but, in anticipation of some of its shortcomings, it is proposed to develop here some wider and less constrained notions of the interests that need recognition.

Many discussions of criminal justice state or assume that there is a pervasive conflict between the State and the individual, and that exploration of this relationship holds the key to satisfactory theorizing about the criminal process. But this neglects the interests of victims of crime, which ought to be examined in this context. It also assigns no place to the interests of the community, as distinct from those of the State. Each individual is a member of a community, or of communities, and that interaction gives rise to mutual interests and (on some views) obligations. If one goes further and regards the

---

[11] Cf. the debate between G. Maher, 'Balancing Rights and Interests in the Criminal Process', and J. Cottingham, 'The Balancing Act: Weighing Rights and Interests in the Criminal Process', in A. Duff and N. Simmonds (eds.), *Philosophy and the Criminal Law* (1984).

family either as part of the community or as a community, the point gains in importance. Turning to defendants' rights, those undoubtedly need to be examined and taken into account. But defendants' rights may conflict not only with State interests but also with the interests of victims of crime, a conflict that cannot be taken into account by a simple 'individual versus State' approach. It might also be asked if defendants' rights should be the same whether the defendant is an individual or a corporate body: there are those who argue that different issues here require different approaches, and this debate needs to be drawn into the analysis. One reason for urging a different approach to corporate defendants arises from their (usually) greater power, and this serves as a reminder that the dimension of power should not be neglected. To consider only rights and interests, without reference to practical power, would be to embrace a fragile conception of criminal justice, somewhat detached from reality. Thus we might begin with brief discussion of five standpoints, in terms of interests and power: the State, the victim, the community, individual defendants, and corporate defendants.

(a) The State

The proper place of the State in matters of criminal justice has come under increasing scrutiny in recent years. It is no longer sufficient to assert that criminal offences are offences against the State, and that the State takes power over suspects and offenders in order to preserve and to vindicate the Queen's Peace or—more prosaically—to safeguard the security of citizens. Challenges to that notion have been mounted from several angles. Is not the primary offence against the victim?[12] Even if in theory the primary offence is against the State, does this theory have much practical meaning when the wishes of the victim are so strongly determinative in the institution and successful conclusion of prosecutions?[13] Alternatively, why should we assume that the State in all its remoteness, rather than the community in which the offence was committed, has the primary interest in safeguarding the security of citizens? Perhaps the role of the State should be residual and facilitative, with each community taking the lead.

These approaches will be developed further in the paragraphs that follow. But they serve to raise questions, at this early point, about the true role of the State. Is it right that the State should be the authority that organizes and controls the police, the courts, the prisons and correctional services, and so forth? It is possible to give an affirmative answer without denying a central role to the victim

---

[12] N. Christie, 'Conflicts as Property' (1977) 17 *BJ Crim.* 1.

[13] A. Cretney, G. Davis, C. Clarkson, and J. Shepherd, 'Criminalising Assault: the Failure of the "Offence against Society" Model' (1994) 34 *BJ Crim.* 15.

in matters of criminal justice. The argument against that is the separate one that it is a primary function of the State to provide a system of law enforcement that is distinct from private justice, and which assures to suspects and offenders an impartial and relatively constant standard of justice rather than one that may vary according to the preferences of the victim. On this view, the State stands against private vengeance and vigilantism. Does the same view suggest that there is a weakness in arguing that communities, rather than the State, should have the primary role in criminal justice? At one level it might appear to do so, in the sense that community justice might vary considerably from community to community. There would be no consistency: justice by geography would be not a criticism but part of the design. On the other hand, community justice might be bounded by insisting on respect for rights and interests in the same way as State justice. There is no universal formula for translating, for example, human rights into criminal justice systems. There are considerable variations, not only between the many European countries but within some of them (e.g. Scotland, Northern Ireland, England and Wales), and thus we already have a form of justice by geography. Further diversity, in order to empower local communities, would not breach any principle, so long as it could be defended satisfactorily at the level of political and constitutional theory.

If, however, there were concerns about the theoretical justification or the practical consequences of community criminal justice (a matter to be explored at point (c) below), that would bring the argument back to State responsibility for the criminal justice system. Like defence of the realm, it is a task that the State takes over from individual citizens. In the case of criminal justice, there are strong reasons for the State to do so: it avoids the excesses that might result from leaving justice in the hands of individuals, and provides the mechanism for guaranteeing whatever rights and interests should be respected. It is, in effect, a part of the 'rule of law' or *Rechtsstaat* that such matters should be decided by impartial tribunals on the basis of criteria announced beforehand. An individual convicted of a crime does not forfeit all claims to be treated proportionately, fairly, and humanely. Neither does a person suspected or accused of a crime.

(b) Victims

Until recent years there had been a relative neglect of victims' needs for support, respect, and compensation. Now, urged on by the United Nations,[14] by the Council of Europe,[15] and by the US President's Task Force on Victims of

[14] United Nations, *Basic Principles of Justice for Victims of Crime and Abuse of Power* (1985).
[15] Council of Europe, *The Position of the Victim in the Framework of Criminal Law and Procedure* (1985).

Crime,[16] there is increasing recognition that the victims of crime have rights to respectful and sympathetic treatment from law enforcement agents; to support and help in the aftermath of the offence; to proper information about the progress of their case; to facilities at courtrooms that separate them from other members of the public; and to compensation for the crime, either from the offender or (if that is not possible) from the State, at least for crimes of violence.[17]

These rights to services should be regarded as an important element in social provision for the disadvantaged, and it should be the concern of people working in the criminal justice system to ensure that they are recognized and fulfilled. But completely different justifications are needed if it is claimed that victims have procedural rights in the criminal process. Should the victim have the right to be consulted on the decision whether or not to prosecute, on the bail/custody decision, on the acceptance of a plea to a lesser offence or to fewer offences, or on sentence? The answer to these questions depends on the proper purposes of the criminal process. On what has become the 'conventional' punishment paradigm, the emphasis is on the crime as an offence which the State, through the courts, should visit with censure if appropriate. This is not to dispute or to overlook the victim's right to receive compensation from the offender, which may properly be regarded as part of the criminal process for pragmatic reasons of speed and efficiency. However, the State has the primary interest in prosecution and sentence, so as to ensure both that vigilantism and private vengeance are supplanted and that fairness and constancy in a process that may involve restrictions on, or even deprivation of, the liberty of accused citizens. It follows from this that punishment is a transaction between the State and the offender, on which the victim's personal view should be no more significant than the judge's personal view or those of any other individual. The court, not any individual, has the right to order punishment. The form and intensity of the sentence should embody a judgement, according to the law, of the relative heinousness of the offence, and should comport fairly with the sentences imposed on others who have committed similar crimes. Admittedly all the key concepts here (e.g. seriousness of offence, severity of sentence, proportionality) are essentially contestable, but it is possible to develop criteria that can be debated in their social context.[18] What a particular victim would like to see as the punishment is not a relevant consideration: the victim might be vindictive or forgiving, demanding or

---

[16] Which gave rise, e.g., to the federal Victim and Witness Protection Act of 1982.

[17] See generally D. Miers, 'The Responsibilities and the Rights of Victims of Crime' (1992) 55 *MLR* 482.

[18] For further discussion, see A. von Hirsch, *Censure and Sanctions* (1993); for discussion and relevant readings, see A. von Hirsch and A. Ashworth (eds), *Principled Sentencing* (2nd edn., 1998), esp. chs. 4 and 7.

afraid of the offender, well informed or unable to grasp the differences between types of sentence, and it would be unfair and wrong that punishments should vary according to these factors.

A similar analysis can be applied to decisions taken at earlier stages, since the pre-trial process should also be a matter chiefly between the State and the offender. The decision to prosecute should be taken in the public interest, not according to the desires of the victim. However, most systems have one or more 'complainant offences', typically assault, for which no prosecution will be brought unless there is an official complaint from the aggrieved party.[19] The justifications for regarding these offences as different in principle seem unconvincing: they are personal offences, and in practice a prosecution cannot succeed unless the victim is willing to testify. However, these considerations apply to several crimes, as a matter of practice, and this has been used as a pragmatic argument against the idea that offences are crimes against anyone other than the victim.[20] The practical position does not alter the principle, one might reply, and in bringing prosecutions for 'domestic violence' despite the wishes expressed by the victim some police forces are attempting to demonstrate this. Moreover, English law provides a further complication, because an enforceable order for the offender to pay compensation to the victim can only be made if a prosecution is brought. But the general principle is unaffected by these two points. Similarly, the decision between bail and custody should be taken in the public interest, but that decision should be informed by any fears the victim may have about harassment or retaliation if the alleged offender is granted bail. As for decisions on acceptance of plea, these are entirely parallel to sentencing decisions. If consultation with the victim on any of these issues suggests that the victim should be able to influence the outcome, it should be resisted. However, there may be good arguments for allowing victims to have an input into proceedings on questions of fact—for example, to submit a victim impact statement that details the precise harm resulting, for purposes of compensation—but even then it should be ensured that the contents of such statements are subjected to proper evidential requirements. Just as a defendant should not be allowed to make unsupported allegations about the victim's role in an offence, so equally the victim should not be permitted to make unsubstantiated claims about things done or harm or loss inflicted by the defendant.[21]

In some jurisdictions the victim is given a significant role within a conventional punishment system. Where victim impact statements are permitted, as

[19] See P. J. P. Tak, *The Legal Scope of Non-prosecution in Europe* (1986), 53.

[20] See Cretney *et al.*, above, n. 13, taking issue with the view propounded here and in other writings.

[21] For further discussion and references, see A. Ashworth, 'Victim Impact Statements and Sentencing' [1993] *Crim. LR* 498.

in some Australian states and many states of the USA, they may contain information relevant not merely to compensation but also to sentence (e.g. detailing the after-effects of the crime). Some jurisdictions also provide for consultation with victims before such decisions as prosecuting or not and accepting a 'plea bargain' or not. Some American states go further and allow the victim impact statement to include a recommendation on sentence, or indeed grant to victims a right of allocution that allows the victim to address the court before sentence.[22] On the view taken here, such a development should be opposed on the grounds that either it infiltrates irrelevant considerations (personal views) into the sentencing process, or it raises victims' expectations unfairly, or both. The interests of the victim ought to be recognized as forming part of the public interest, so that prosecutors should take account of victim-oriented matters in their judgements at various stages of the criminal process. This is why threats against the victim constitute a strong reason for opposing bail, for example.

In contrast to the punishment paradigm stand various forms of restorative approach to criminal justice. On one such approach, the overall purpose might be described as 'the restoration into safe communities of victims and offenders who have resolved their conflicts'.[23] This places a form of mediation between victim and offender at the centre of criminal procedure, with compensation from offender to victim as a significant element. Clearly victims' procedural rights would be extensive in such a system, although many versions of restorative justice also recognize the importance of restoring the damage to the community, and decisions on this must surely be the function of a court.[24] In some jurisdictions there are 'Family Group Conferences', chiefly to deal with offences by young people. The conference includes not only members of the families of the victim and the offender but also representatives of the wider community. The task is to decide on the response to the offence; in cases where the victim is unwilling to participate or the conference cannot reach agreement, the case goes before a court. Although new systems of this kind have not yet been used on a large scale, and are mostly confined to young offenders or to non-serious offenders,[25] they are being developed and evaluated, especially in the context of the system for young offenders introduced by

---

[22] See further Ashworth, 'Victim Impact Statements and Sentencing'.

[23] The words of Daniel van Ness, 'New Wine and Old Wineskins: Four Challenges of Restorative Justice' (1993) 4 *Criminal Law Forum* 251.

[24] See van Ness, above n. 23, who recognizes this as a matter for the court; cf. the critical observations of A. Ashworth, 'Some Doubts about Restorative Justice' (1993) 4 *Criminal Law Forum* 277.

[25] These are generalizations: in this country the Leeds Mediation and Reparation Project deals with some non-minor cases, and the Northamptonshire Adult Reparation Scheme deals with adults: see the ch. by J. Dignan in A. Duff, S. Marshall, R.E. Dobash, and R.P. Dobash (eds.), *Penal Theory and Practice* (1994).

the Crime and Disorder Bill 1998. Such approaches assign a more central role to the victim and to the victim's wishes, but most of them recognize that the offence is also committed against the community or the State and therefore do not necessarily allow free rein to the victim's preference of outcome.[26]

(c) Community

In discussing the interests of the State and of victims in the criminal process, references have already been made to the community. Analyses of social and political institutions which place emphasis on the rights of the individual are often criticized for regarding the individual as abstracted from the wider community—as failing to take due notice of the fact that we are social beings and that each of us has 'a number of community attachments, articulated in terms of factors such as race, ethnicity, class, gender, age, sexuality, occupation'.[27] Thus, in this connection, community is not merely a geographical concept but also indicates other forms of, as it were, horizontal social groupings. What implications does that have for criminal justice? The implications can be discerned on at least two different levels. On one level there would be increased consciousness of collective values: conflicts should not simply be presented as the individual versus the State, and we should be explicit about the interest of all citizens in the environment, public amenities, public safety, and so forth. On the level of systems, it was argued above that the pre-trial process, trials, and sentencing should be recognized as functions of the State, and two reasons were advanced—that this ought to displace vigilantism and private vengeance, and that it ought to ensure some measure of consistency in a task which may involve the exercise of great power over citizens. But the State is often a remote entity, whereas it can be said that many citizens have some daily interactions with their communities. If one of the purposes of the criminal process is the general prevention of crime, then it could be argued that one way of achieving this is to reintegrate offenders in their communities. This form of reintegration underlies some of the developments in restorative justice and family group conferencing.[28] However, even apart from restorative justice, there is good reason to consider whether the monolithic State is the most appropriate dispenser of criminal justice. It could be argued that those who are most touched by crimes should have some role in the criminal

---

[26] For further discussion, see M. Cavadino and J. Dignan, *The Penal System: an Introduction* (2nd edn., 1997), and A. von Hirsch and A. Ashworth (eds.), *Principled Sentencing* (2nd edn., 1998), ch. 7.

[27] N. Lacey, 'Community in Legal Theory: Idea, Ideal or Ideology' (1996) 15 *Studies in Law, Politics and Society* 105, at 121.

[28] See, e.g., J. Braithwaite, *Crime, Shame and Reintegration* (1989); H. Blagg, 'A Just Measure of Shame? Aboriginal Youth and Conferencing in Australia' (1997) 37 *BJ Crim.* 481; and J. Braithwaite, 'Conferencing and Plurality: Reply to Blagg' (1997) 37 *BJ Crim.* 502.

process, trials, and sentencing. At present, it could be argued that the lay magistracy and the jury system in England and Wales constitute gestures in that direction; it could also be argued that, in the absence of a national police force, there is room for and evidence of local sensitivity in the approach of police forces to their tasks. Indeed, local experimental schemes, through the magistracy, the police, and the probation service, have produced several worthwhile innovations in criminal justice.

There are, however, obvious difficulties in giving power over the criminal process to communities, whether constituted by local area or by other shared characteristics. One is the fairness argument based on like treatment of like cases: granted the heavy burdens that the criminal justice system can impose on individuals, there might be a legitimate argument that it is unfair if one is treated very differently in two comparable communities. To an extent we already tolerate significant differences among the several jurisdictions in the United Kingdom: would the argument be different if, say, England and Wales were to be divided into forty-three or 143 or more communities? The second difficulty is that of limits: at worst, community justice might tend towards mob justice, and all manner of repressive sentences might be imposed on people who, at a particular stage of history in a particular community, are viewed as thoroughly evil. It would be possible to forestall this problem if the State were to prescribe limits or minima, setting out minimum standards for the pre-trial process and limits on sentencing. But that would concede to the State various powers which some communitarians might not wish to concede. These are issues on which the search for a 'genuinely persuasive and [socially] inclusive' solution must go on.[29]

(d) Individual Defendants

In the rhetoric of the criminal process, at least, there has long been recognition that individual suspects and defendants who are caught up in the criminal process have rights that ought to be protected. In Sections 4 and 5 of this chapter we will consider what those rights may be. For the present, mention may be made of two reasons why individual rights ought to be recognized in this sphere. The first is that the criminal process, even at the pre-trial stage, may involve the imposition of all manner of restrictions and deprivations on the defendant (including, for example, detention for questioning and remand in custody), and many of the decisions taken at this stage have significant implications for the course of any subsequent trial and for sentence. The interest of the citizen in minimal restrictions on liberty and in fair procedures

---

[29] Lacey, above, n. 27, at 135.

is surely a strong one. A second argument is that pre-trial decisions may be made, and powers exercised, by officials whose position of authority and resources place them at a distinct advantage over individual citizens. The recognition and enforcement of rights form part of the means for ensuring that the imbalance of power is not too great, and that power is exercised responsibly without taking advantage of the relatively weak position of suspects. These, however, are rather general arguments. The subject will be taken up in detail in Section 4 below.

(e) Corporate Defendants

Are the arguments in favour of recognizing rights equally strong when the suspect or defendant is a body corporate? In legal theory a company is a legal person, just as an individual is. However, in recent times it has come to be accepted that a different legal framework is desirable for dealing with criminal offences by companies. So far as criminal liability is concerned, it may be difficult to hold companies liable for offences: even to the extent that corporate criminal liability exists, based on the conduct of a 'controlling officer' of the company, it may be difficult to trace which company officer was responsible and to establish knowledge or lack of knowledge. The Law Commission has recently proposed that, for the offence of manslaughter by a company, the usual approach should be abandoned in favour of asking whether the company ought to have been aware of the risk of death and ought to have taken precautionary measures.[30] So far as sentencing is concerned, it has been argued that there is a need for different sanctions and, possibly, a wholly different response to corporate criminality;[31] but little has changed in that sphere. Should the approach to corporate suspects be different at the pre-trial stage? Many of the arguments about power differentials between the law enforcement agencies and individual suspects might be inapplicable, especially with large or multi-national companies. Indeed, it could be the officials who are at a disadvantage in terms of resources and practical power. Strong as the arguments may be for requiring companies to demonstrate the absence of fault when they are found to have caused a certain harm, it is not clear that they should apply at the investigation stage when there has not yet been proof or acceptance that the company is the cause of the harm. If a company denies this, should it have the same protections as an individual defendant? After all, the company must operate through individuals, and any questioning will have to be of individuals. On the other hand, one reason why the Law Commission has proposed a change in the basis of liability for manslaughter is the difficulty

[30] For discussion, see A. Ashworth, *Principles of Criminal Law* (2nd edn., 1995), 111–18.
[31] B. Fisse and J. Braithwaite, *Corporations, Crime and Accountability* (1993).

of identifying who are the key individuals in certain (large) companies, and that is likely to be no less of a problem at the investigatory stage. We should therefore keep an open mind on whether there is a need for different pre-trial procedures for companies, and the extent to which human rights protections are and should be applicable to them.

Having sketched five sets of interests that might have a claim to be taken into account in pre-trial criminal justice, we now move on to consider the justifications for, and extent of, individual rights in much greater detail. The range of other possible interests, neglected by much rights-talk, should be borne in mind throughout.

4. Rights and the European Convention

So far as this country's international obligations go, there are two major international declarations of human rights to which we are subject. One is the International Covenant on Civil and Political Rights, drawn up by the United Nations and monitored by the ICCPR Human Rights Committee. The extent and formulation of rights in the ICCPR differ in some respects from those in the European Convention on Human Rights, which is considered in detail below. The ICPPR remains a document of some importance,[32] not least because reference may be made to it (in view of its wider international status) when interpreting the European Convention.

At present, the obvious starting point for an authoritative statement of rights to be upheld in the criminal process is the European Convention on Human Rights and Fundamental Freedoms. The ECHR was signed in 1950, ratified by the United Kingdom in 1951, and came into force in 1953. It has been ratified by all member states of the Council of Europe. In recent years many countries from the eastern part of the continent have been granted or have applied for membership of the Council of Europe, and ratifications of the ECHR are therefore increasing year by year. The Convention contains a range of rights, covering different aspects of individual liberty, and various protocols have been added to it. The discussion below will be limited to those rights relevant to the criminal process.[33]

---

[32] See the essays in D. Harris and S. Joseph (eds.), *The International Covenant on Civil and Political Rights and United Kingdom Law* (1995).

[33] For fuller discussion, see, e.g., D.J. Harris, M. O'Boyle, and C. Warbrick, *The Law of the European Convention on Human Rights* (1995); for a briefer survey, see C.A. Gearty, 'The United Kingdom', in C.A. Gearty (ed.), *European Civil Liberties and the European Convention on Human Rights* (1997).

Since 1966 the United Kingdom has allowed individual petition to Strasbourg. The system has been that an individual may make an application to the European Commission, which adjudicates on whether or not it is admissible (i.e. whether the applicant appears to have suffered from a breach of a Convention right). Admissible cases are then heard by the European Court of Human Rights. If the Court rules against the member state, the State will usually alter the law so as to comply with the judgment, but there is no absolute obligation to do so. The Committee of Ministers monitors state responses to findings of the Commission and the Court. The system of petition to Strasbourg is to change towards the end of 1998, in the hope of reducing delay: the European Commission on Human Rights is to be abolished, under the Eleventh Protocol to the ECHR, and all decisions will be taken by a single, though expanded, Court.

The United Kingdom has been the subject of many successful applications to Strasbourg, and has been found by the Court to be in breach of the Convention in some forty cases. For at least thirty years it has been argued that the United Kingdom ought to do as most other member states have done, and incorporate the ECHR into its domestic law.[34] The arguments have been manifold, but one recurrent theme is that it is frustrating, embarrassing, and unnecessary that individuals should have to go outside the UK to secure the enforcement of rights to which the British Government committed itself long ago. The incoming Labour Government accepted the case for incorporation, and at the time of writing the Human Rights Bill 1998 is making its way through Parliament. The essence of the new law is that British courts and public authorities will have a duty to take account of the European Convention in all their decisions and policies. Thus courts are required to take account of the rights enshrined in the ECHR and of decisions, declarations, and opinions given by the Court, the Commission, and the Committee of Ministers. This does not require courts always to follow decisions of the European Court in interpreting the ECHR, although one would expect little significant divergence. If a British court finds that the ECHR and its own precedents are in conflict, the judges will have a duty to depart from its own precedents. However, the ECHR will not necessarily have priority over legislation. If a court finds that a UK statute cannot be interpreted so as to be compatible with the Convention, the court may make a 'declaration of incompatibility'; there is then provision for a fast-track procedure to amend legislation which falls foul of the Convention.

---

[34] See, e.g., A. Lester, 'Fundamental Rights: the U.K. Isolated?' [1984] *Public Law* 46; M. Zander, *A Bill of Rights?* (3rd edn., 1985); Sir Thomas Bingham, 'The European Convention on Human Rights: Time to Incorporate' (1993) 109 *LQR* 390.

The Human Rights Bill does not apply only to the courts. It is unlawful for a 'public authority' to act in a way that is incompatible with one or more of the Convention rights. This is intended to allow challenges to the decisions of 'central government (including executive agencies); local government; the police; immigration officers; prison; courts and tribunals themselves; and, to the extent that they are exercising public functions, companies responsible for areas of activity which were previously in the public sector'.[35] Proceedings against a public authority may be brought only by a person who is or would be the victim of an unlawful act. It remains unclear to what extent legal aid will be available for such actions.

The Human Rights Bill has not received an unqualified welcome. Much depends not only on the Government's continuing commitment to the spirit of the ECHR, by amending swiftly any legislation found to be incompatible with the Convention, but also on the approach taken by the judiciary. Many senior judges argued strongly in favour of incorporation and, even though the judiciary does not have such strong powers as its brethren in the United States and Canada, judges do have general powers to interpret and apply the Convention and to make declarations of incompatibility in respect of legislation. Some fear that this will place too much power in the hands of unelected and unaccountable people. Some, on the other hand, fear that the powers will be used too sparingly, and that many judges will continue to adopt the view that the ECHR really encapsulates the common law in most respects.[36] How willing the courts will be to follow decisions of the European Court of Human Rights will be a significant test of the reach of the spirit of the Convention. In this connection, it is important to keep in mind the distinctive approach of the European Court to its functions. It has operated as a court of review, rather than as an appellate court. What it reviews is whether the outcome of a particular case has been affected by practices that involved a breach of the ECHR—not whether, in the abstract, a particular law is compatible with the Convention. The Court has also recognised that member states have a 'margin of appreciation' when interpreting certain Articles of the ECHR, and so it has tended to find a breach only where there is a clear and significant departure from the declared rights.

It should also be added that there is a growing European Union dimension to criminal law and criminal justice, particularly after the Maastricht Treaty. Treaty Articles, Regulations, and Directives have priority over UK law, which should in any event be interpreted so as to accord with EC law.[37] In cases that have been referred to the European Court of Justice, the Court has tended to

---

[35] Home Office, *Rights Brought Home: the Human Rights Bill* (1997), para. 2.2.
[36] For an example of this judicial conservatism, see Gearty, above n. 33, 82–3.
[37] J. Dine, 'European Community Criminal Law' [1993] *Crim. LR* 246.

insist on procedural protections and notions of fair trial analogous to those declared by the ECHR.[38] Although there will be no separate discussion of the ECJ authorities below, its part in the growing Europeanisation of criminal justice should be kept in mind.

In the first edition of this book, a central place was given to the ECHR on the basis that it ought to be regarded as an authoritative statement of fundamental rights, operating as a kind of external constitution for this country. The Human Rights Bill 1998 will establish the credentials of the ECHR to be regarded as a fundamental constitutional document, even if it differs in various ways from the US Constitution or the Canadian Charter of Rights. In this edition the presentation of the ECHR will be somewhat different, since it is now necessary to have both a working knowledge of the text of the Convention and an appreciation of its actual and potential application to the English criminal process. References to the ECHR and to decisions of the European Court of Human Rights in the remainder of the book will therefore be more frequent than in the first edition, and the emphasis at this stage will be upon the text of the relevant Articles of the Convention and a sketch of their range of application to the criminal process. The full text of the ECHR and Protocol 1 is printed in the Appendix below. The focus here is upon Articles 2, 3, 5, 6, 8, 14, and 15.

> Article 2   1. Everyone's right to life shall be protected by law. No one shall be deprived of his life intentionally save in the execution of a sentence of a court following his conviction of a crime for which this penalty is provided by law.
>
> 2. Deprivation of life shall not be regarded as inflicted in contravention of this Article when it results from the use of force which is no more than absolutely necessary:
>
> (a)   in defence of any person from unlawful violence;
> (b)   in order to effect a lawful arrest or to prevent the escape of a person lawfully detained;
> (c)   in action lawfully taken for the purpose of quelling a riot or insurrection.

This Article's relevance resides in paragraph 2(b) and its impact on the use of force in arrest or the prevention of escape. The Commission and the Court have dealt with a succession of cases with Northern Irish connections,[39] of which the most important now is *McCann* v. *United Kingdom*.[40] An undercover team of specially trained soldiers were keeping three IRA members under surveillance in Gibraltar, in the belief that the latter were about to carry out a bombing. When they moved in to arrest the three people, they shot and

---

[38]   For fuller discussion, see E. Baker, 'Taking European Criminal Law Seriously' [1998] *Crim. LR* 361 (forthcoming).

[39]   See Harris, O'Boyle, and Warbrick, above n. 33, 44–54.   [40]   (1996) 21 EHRR 97.

killed them. The European Court of Human Rights found that the planning of the operation was so defective that it made the killings foreseeable, although avoidable, and that this breached the victims' right to life under Article 2.1 rather than falling within the 'absolute necessity' exception in Article 2.2(b).

> Article 3   No one shall be subjected to torture or to inhuman or degrading treatment or punishment.

Perhaps the best-known case on this Article is *Ireland* v. *United Kingdom*,[41] in which the Court ruled that the notorious 'five techniques'[42] used in the interrogation of suspected terrorists by the authorities in Northern Ireland did not amount to 'torture', but did amount to 'inhuman and degrading treatment'. Subsequent cases have raised questions about the application of the terms 'inhuman and degrading' to the conditions of detention and questioning by police forces. However, this Article is also relevant to the conditions in which people are detained on remand pending court proceedings. In one case the Commission referred to 'deplorable overcrowding' in prison, but still took the view that there was no inhuman treatment.[43] Typically, the Strasbourg organs have allowed States a considerable 'margin of appreciation' in their decisions on Article 3. However, the Council of Europe has promulgated the European Prison Rules, designed to set minimum standards for custodial institutions in member states. It has also established the European Committee on the Prevention of Torture and Inhuman and Degrading Treatment, with authority to inspect the prisons and police stations of all member states. This proactive approach constitutes some recognition that individual detainees are not always in a good position to pursue breaches of their rights, and that the Strasbourg system's delays make this even more impractical.

> Article 5   1. Everyone has the right to liberty and security of person.
>   No one shall be deprived of his liberty save in the following cases and in accordance with a procedure prescribed by law . . .
>> c) the lawful arrest or detention of a person effected for the purpose of bringing him before the competent legal authority on reasonable suspicion of having committed an offence, or when it is reasonably considered necessary to prevent his committing an offence or fleeing after having done so . . .
>   2. Everyone who is arrested shall be informed promptly, in a language which he understands, of the reasons for his arrest and of any charge against him.

---

[41] (1978) A.25.

[42] Wall standing, hooding, subjection to noise, deprivation of sleep, and deprivation of food and drink.

[43] *B* v. *UK* [1981] Com. Rep. 26, concerning conditions at Broadmoor special hospital.

3. Everyone arrested or detained in accordance with the provisions of paragraph 1(c) of this Article shall be brought promptly before a judge or other officer authorised by law to exercise judicial power and shall be entitled to trial within a reasonable time or to release pending trial. Release may be conditioned by guarantee to appear for trial.

4. Everyone who is deprived of his liberty by arrest or detention shall be entitled to take proceedings by which the lawfulness of his detention shall be decided speedily by a court and his release ordered if the detention is not lawful.

5. Everyone who has been the victim of arrest or detention in contravention of the provisions of this Article shall have an enforceable right to compensation.

This is a rather ill-structured Article, but the European Court has generally taken a constructive view of the various paragraphs. A group of decisions tightened the criteria for detaining people as mental patients in hospital, and reasserted their right to challenge the legality of their detention,[44] leading to changes in patients' rights which were incorporated into the Mental Health Act 1983. It will be evident that Article 5 also contains general provisions on the grounds for arrest, and on remands in custody pending trial, which may have some impact on English law.[45] However, the provisions of the Prevention of Terrorism Acts, allowing the detention of suspected terrorists for up to seven days without access to a court, were found contrary to Article 5.3 in *Brogan* v. *United Kingdom*:[46] the government did not alter the legislation, and instead entered a derogation from Article 5.3 in respect of the Prevention of Terrorism Acts.

Article 6   1. In the determination of his civil rights and obligations or of any criminal charge against him, everyone is entitled to a fair and public hearing within a reasonable time by an independent and impartial tribunal established by law...

2. Everyone charged with a criminal offence shall be presumed innocent until proved guilty according to law.

3. Everyone charged with a criminal offence has the following minimum rights:

   (a) to be informed promptly, in a language which he understands and in detail, of the nature and cause of the accusation against him;
   (b) to have adequate time and facilities for the preparation of his defence;
   (c) to defend himself in person or through legal assistance of his own choosing or, if he has not sufficient means to pay for legal assistance, to be given it free when the interests of justice so require;

[44] e.g. *Winterwerp* v. *Netherlands* (1979) A.33; *X* v. *UK* (1981) A.46.
[45] See below, p. 216, n. 38, on the incompatibility of s. 25 CJPO Act 1994.
[46] (1988) A.145–B; see also *Brannigan and McBride* v. *UK* (1993) A.258–B.

(d) to examine or have examined witnesses against him and to obtain the attendance and examination of witnesses on his behalf under the same conditions as witnesses against him;

(e) to have the free assistance of an interpreter if he cannot understand or speak the language use in court.

This Article has many different implications, but its central aim is to guarantee the right to a fair trial.[47] The minimum rights in Article 6.3 can be seen as non-exhaustive elaborations of that basic right. The European Court has not held back from developing the right to a fair trial in other directions not set out in Article 6.3, as (for example) through the doctrine of 'equality of arms' in terms of equal access for the defence to information and expert assistance before and at trials.[48] Many of the specific rights in Article 6 will be discussed at the appropriate places in later chapters. Thus the presumption of innocence (Article 6.2) has implications for the burden of proof, and for curtailments of the 'right to silence' in recent legislation.[49] The boundaries of the right to free legal aid (Article 6.3(c)) have not yet been fully established, but it should certainly be provided when a person is in danger of being committed to prison.[50] Article 6.3(d) has a bearing not only on changes to the hearsay rule but also the use of anonymous witnesses and of statements from witnesses unable to attend court. The requirements of Article 6 cannot be avoided by deeming the proceedings to be civil or regulatory: the European Court has shown a willingness to examine the substance of the proceedings, particularly in respect of their possible consequences, and to treat them as criminal nonetheless.[51]

Article 8   1. Everyone has the right to respect for his private and family life, his home and his correspondence.

2. There shall be no interference by a public authority with the exercise of this right except such as is in accordance with the law and is necessary in a democratic society in the interests of national security, public safety or the economic well-being of the country, for the prevention of disorder or crime, for the protection of health or morals, or for the protection of the rights and freedoms of others.

This Article sets out the right to privacy, and then goes on to circumscribe it in various ways. Despite the breathtaking width of some of the exceptions in Article 8.2, the European Court has shown a willingness to scrutinize claims of necessity, and it has asserted that tolerance and broad-mindedness are characteristics of a democratic society. Its insistence that telephone tapping

---

[47] For a wide-ranging study, see S. Stavros, *The Guarantees for Accused Persons under Article 6 of the European Convention on Human Rights* (1994).

[48] See, e.g. *Edwards* v. *UK* (1992) 15 EHRR 417, on disclosure, below pp. 134–5.

[49] See pp. 105–8 below.

[50] *Benham* v. *UK* (1996) 22 EHRR 293, on non-payment of poll tax.   [51] *Ibid.*

and other forms of intrusive surveillance should be 'in accordance with law' has slowly led to the passing of relevant legislation in this country,[52] although there is still no general statutory framework. The Court has also distilled from Article 8.2 (and from the second paragraphs of Articles 9, 10, and 11, which are not considered here) various general principles of interpreting the exceptions to declared rights. Not only must the exception be prescribed by law, but account must also be taken of the principles of proportionality (significant intrusions into privacy only for serious offences), subsidiarity (intrusive techniques must be the last resort), accountability (prior independent authorization for intrusions on the declared right, supported by record-keeping and monitoring), and finality (information obtained by exceptional means should be used only for the purpose for which it was obtained). These principles lend considerable concreteness to the exceptions to the declared right.

> Article 14   The enjoyment of the rights and freedoms set forth in this Convention shall be secured without discrimination on any ground such as sex, race, colour, language, religion, political or other opinion, national or social origin, association with a national minority, property, birth or other status.

This is a much clearer statement of the principle of non-discrimination than the rather weak and circuitous provision in English law, in section 95 of the Criminal Justice Act 1991. It has been invoked in a case of alleged racial bias in jury selection,[53] and it will be argued in Chapter 9 that it has implications for the guilty plea discount in English law. However, it must be noted that Article 14 does not amount to a general rule of non-discrimination: its terms are restricted to discrimination in relation to Convention rights, and therefore it can only be used in a situation where one of the other rights under the ECHR is applicable.

> Article 15   1. In time of war or other public emergency threatening the life of the nation any High Contracting Party may take measures derogating from its obligations under this Convention to the extent strictly required by the exigencies of the situation, provided that such measures are not inconsistent with its other obligations under international law.
> 2. No derogation from Article 2, except in relation to deaths resulting from lawful acts of war, or from Article 3, 4 (paragraph 1) and 7 shall be made under this provision . . .

This allows derogations from several of the Articles considered above, although not from the principal parts of Article 2 or from Article 3 at all.

---

[52] *Malone* v. *UK* (1985) 7 EHRR 14, resulting in the Interceptions of Communications Act 1985. Subsequent legislation, most recently the Police Act 1997, has been piecemeal and fails to cover all the forms of intrusive surveillance currently in use. See pp. 114–17 below.
[53] *Gregory* v. *UK* [1997] HRCD 338.

There is only one set of peacetime circumstances in which derogation is allowed—where there is a 'public emergency threatening the life of the nation'—and even then the derogation must be kept to a minimum. In *Ireland* v. *United Kingdom*[54] the Court accepted the UK government's judgement that the situation in Northern Ireland at that time fulfilled the requirements of Article 15.1, and therefore a derogation was valid in respect of breaches of Article 5, although there could be no valid derogation from Article 3, of which breaches were found. In *Brannigan and McBride* v. *United Kingdom*[55] the European Court again upheld the UK government's derogation from Article 5, this time in respect of the Prevention of Terrorism Acts, on the basis that the situation in Northern Ireland was still an 'emergency threatening the life of the nation' and that the derogations were no greater than was strictly necessary.

This discussion of Article 15 brings us to the question of the weighting or priority of the rights declared in the ECHR. It is evident from Article 15, and indeed from the formulation of other Articles, that the various rights have different weight. Thus Articles 2 and 3 are absolute, subject only to the circumscribed exceptions which Article 2 itself contains. All the other Articles are strong rights, but it is possible for a member state to derogate from them in the limited circumstances specified in Article 15. And Article 8 may be termed a *prima facie* right, in that it incorporates its own exceptions, expressed in rather broad terms in Article 8.2 but interpreted more restrictively by the European Court. In crude terms, one might therefore express the effect of the ECHR, in relation to the criminal process, as follows:

> ABSOLUTE RIGHTS: right to life, right not to be subjected to torture or inhuman or degrading conduct.
> STRONG RIGHTS: right not to be arrested without reasonable suspicion, right to be brought before court promptly, right not to be remanded in custody beyond a reasonable time, right to a fair trial, right to be presumed innocent, right to legal assistance if the interests of justice so require, right of confrontation of witnesses, right not to be discriminated against in relation to a declared right, and various other rights.
> PRIMA FACIE RIGHTS: right to privacy.

Of course there are other rights in the ECHR that are not set out above, but this weighting is an important step in arguments about pre-trial justice. It quickly reveals the inadequacy of loose talk about balancing, as we saw in Section 3 of this chapter. In the first place, the ECHR is not optional, and does

---

[54] (1978) A.25, at 78.   [55] (1993) A.258–B.

not create rights that can simply be 'balanced' against any broader public interest one wishes to assert. But, more importantly, there are different weights assigned to the various rights, and different restrictions on the types of argument that may be used to uphold an exception to, or (*in extremis*) to derogate from, the declared rights.[56]

5. Reconstruction and Supplementation

The European Convention has high authority as positive law, which is why its provisions are so central to the analysis here. But should it be the last word? In particular, are there rights which it excludes and which might arguably rank alongside some of those enumerated above? Let us first discuss these questions at the level of the Council of Europe. In 1985 the Council of Europe approved recommendations on *The Position of the Victim in the Framework of Criminal Law and Procedure*, and the United Nations approved a *Declaration of Basic Principles of Justice for the Victims of Crime and Abuse of Power*. No amendment was made, however, and no protocol added to the ECHR. Does that mean that victims' rights ought to be placed in some fourth, lower category of rights, beneath those enumerated above? Surely not. A more likely explanation, in terms of practical politics, is that no-one dared to begin the process of amending the ECHR for fear that it would prove counter-productive, or even so controversial as to undermine the consensus that exists around the existing rights. It can therefore be argued that certain victims' rights should be ranked alongside the individual rights declared by the ECHR, provided that sufficient authority or persuasive argument can be given for doing so. The same would apply to the United Nations Convention on the Rights of the Child (1990), which includes a wide-ranging list of rights including those in Article 40 on 'the administration of juvenile justice'. There is no specific coverage of such rights in the ECHR, although the European Court of Human Rights has drawn on the UN Convention when interpreting ECHR rights in cases of young offenders.[57]

　It can also be argued, more widely and more fundamentally, that the European Convention was not drafted specifically with criminal proceedings in mind and that it ought to be reconsidered in the light of increasing aware-ness of the effects of criminal cases on individuals and emerging standards of

---

[56] Cf. A. Sanders, 'From Suspect to Trial', in M. Maguire, R. Morgan, and R. Reiner (eds.), *Oxford Handbook of Criminology* (2nd edn., 1998), at 1053, and A. Hunt and R. Young, 'Criminal Justice and Academics: Publish and Be Ignored?' (1995) 17 *Holdsworth LR* 193.

[57] See its judgment in *Hussain and Singh* v. *UK* (1996) 22 EHRR 1.

fairness. Of course documents of this fundamental nature tend to be rather minimalist, and to be broadly phrased in places. They are not declarations of aspiration. But the more telling argument is that this Convention, drafted and approved in the aftermath of the Second World War, is not necessarily apt for the first part of the twenty-first century; and particularly not in the sphere of criminal justice.[58] Since it is unlikely that arguments for the reform and re-drafting of the ECHR would meet with success in the foreseeable future, and yet since the ECHR fails to deal with some important issues, the discussion that follows will place its reliance on arguments of principle only. The ECHR must be supplemented and, to an extent, reconstructed if a satisfactory normative framework is to be produced. Acceptance of the arguments will depend on their persuasiveness.

1. *Right not to be wrongly convicted*: the structure of ECHR rights places the presumption of innocence at the level of strong rights. This means, for example, that a member state may justifiably derogate from the presumption of innocence in times of national emergency, under Article 15. The question may be raised whether this is the appropriate ranking. That, in turn, depends on what is understood by the 'presumption of innocence', as it is declared in Article 6.2. Its customary field of application is to the burden of proof and the privilege against self-incrimination, as we shall see in Chapter 4 below. This suggests that its direct concern is not the right of an innocent person not to be convicted, and that we are therefore justified in considering whether the claims of this right are more powerful.

One fundamental purpose of the criminal process is to ensure accuracy of outcomes, or what Bentham termed 'rectitude'. In practical terms, this requires recognition of the weaknesses of certain types of evidence, and the taking of steps to avoid or minimize the risks of mistaken assessments of evidence (particularly but not exclusively by lay tribunals), leading to wrongful acquittals or convictions.[59] The right not to be wrongly convicted is a strong expression of principle which relates closely to one aspect of rectitude. Ronald Dworkin has argued that the right of an innocent person not to be convicted should be regarded as fundamental.[60] In his terms it is not a mere harm but a moral harm. For one thing there is a misapplication of blame and public censure, which is a deep injustice. But there are also the consequential wrongs, which may include deprivation of liberty, or at least restrictions on liberty,

---

[58] For proposals, see A. Ashworth, 'The European Convention on Human Rights and English Criminal Justice: Ships passing in the Night?', SPTL paper, 1997.

[59] For discussion, see W.L. Twining, *Theories of Evidence: Bentham and Wigmore* (1987), and the review article by D.J. Galligan, 'More Scepticism about Scepticism' (1988) 8 *OJLS* 249.

[60] R. M. Dworkin, 'Principle, Policy and Procedure', in C. Tapper (ed.), *Crime, Proof and Punishment* (1981).

which may severely curtail social functioning. The argument here is that this right ought to be regarded as a fundamental right in civil society.

However, to place it alongside the right not to be subjected to torture, or inhuman or degrading treatment or punishment, and the right to life, might be thought to raise difficulties. The essence of those rights is that governments and public authorities should avoid certain forms of behaviour towards citizens—life-threatening conduct, torture, and inhuman or degrading conduct. The right of the innocent not to be convicted, on the other hand, does not proscribe distinct forms of behaviour: it insists on a criminal process and justice system that is designed to avoid inaccurate outcomes (miscarriages of justice), and notably those that result in the conviction of the innocent. Moreover, it is evident that there are degrees of protection against inaccurate outcomes. Does recognition of this right mean that unlimited resources must be devoted to the elimination of risks of inaccuracy? It would be socially and politically unrealistic to suggest that we devote no funds to other social goals until all known risks of convicting the innocent had been removed. Matters such as education, health, social security, transport systems and even expenditure on other aspects of criminal justice would be curtailed in order to make way for elaborate schemes (or extensive experiments) aimed at eliminating these risks. A second pragmatic argument is that some of the measures taken to remove the risk of convicting the innocent would also reduce the probability of convicting the guilty. If there were fewer prosecutions and fewer convictions, this might well lead to a severe loss of confidence in the criminal justice system, with considerable implications for public order (e.g. vigilantism) and social stability.

Recognition of these counter-arguments should not, however, deliver us back to a shadowy world of balancing. These conflicts can and should be resolved in a principled way. Dworkin argues for two other rights at this point. The first is a right to procedures that place a proper valuation on moral harms such as those arising from breach of the right not to be convicted if innocent. This can be taken to indicate proper respect for the various human rights set out above—the right to a fair trial, the right to confrontation, the presumption of innocence, and so forth—insofar as they presage a criminal procedure of a certain kind: that is, a system in which the risk of wrongful conviction is acceptably low. Dworkin's second supporting right is the right to consistent treatment within declared policies. This may be developed as an argument in favour of consistent weighting of the importance of avoiding moral harm throughout the system, not giving advantages to any particular group of citizens. The wrongful conviction of an individual is surely a greater wrong than an unjustified acquittal, which wrongs no individual even though it reflects badly on the system and may reduce the community's confidence in the legal system. More generally, it may be argued that the low risk of wrongful conviction should be spread evenly, and that everyone in society should be likely to benefit from the savings achieved by not pursuing maximum accuracy through myriad expensive procedures.

These theoretical arguments point to certain policy objectives. One is that there should be more and thorough research into the sources of miscarriages of justice: even some well-known causes, such as the handling of identification evidence from its reception by the police through to its use in court, have not been thoroughly investigated. Others have simply not been examined in much detail at all. One might conjecture, charitably, that the speed with which the Royal Commission on Criminal Justice was expected to report made it difficult to commission research of the necessary breadth and depth. What is needed is research that examines the realities, pressures, and sources of error at each stage of the criminal process. A second step would then be to devise systems or safeguards for ensuring a significant reduction of the risks discovered. At this stage, too, it would be important to examine the extent to which any such safeguards might reduce the probability of convicting guilty people, and/or reduce the probability that the rights of victims are properly respected. Too often it is assumed that there is a hydraulic effect, whereby if wrongful convictions are to be reduced a reduction in unmerited acquittals will automatically follow. It would be foolish to deny that conflicts will arise here, and equally foolish to deny that ultimately such conflicts will need to be resolved by means of some compromise or balancing. What is distinctive about the approach advocated here is that the process of resolving the conflicts should be securely based on facts established by research, and firmly grounded in a proper appreciation of the rights and interests of all relevant parties.

2. *The integrity principle*: this principle, strongly stated in some quarters, is that the integrity of the administration of criminal justice requires that law enforcement officers should not use methods of investigation which breach the law, and that courts should not act upon evidence obtained by those means. The criminal justice system is intended to respond authoritatively to cases of law-breaking by citizens: it would be a deplorable contradiction if the system itself were to take advantage of law-breaking by its officials. If the system is to retain its legitimacy and moral authority, it must ensure that its agents do not themselves break the law.

Some of the arguments for the integrity principle are instrumental. Thus Justices Holmes and Brandeis, in their famous dissenting speech in *Olmstead* v. *United States*, argued that:

> Our government is the potent, omnipresent teacher. For good or for ill, it teaches . . . by its example. If the government becomes a law breaker, it breeds

contempt for law; it invites every man to become a law unto himself; it invites anarchy.[61]

A similar approach is adopted by some modern writers on evidence and procedure. Thus Andrew Choo maintains that 'what the public interest demands is that offenders are brought to conviction in a civilized and publicly acceptable manner'.[62] The difficulty with a justification that rests on probable public reactions, whether in terms of anarchy or public acceptance, is that it is contingent and possibly self-defeating. Is it not possible, especially in view of the strong influence of the mass media, that there would be expressions of public support for an approach that did countenance some breaking of the rules by law enforcement officials in order to catch suspected offenders, at least of certain types? To ground the arguments for integrity on probable public reactions is unprincipled and inadequate. A slightly different instrumentalist approach would be to argue that criminal justice systems depend for their authority on public acceptance of their legitimacy. Thus a criminal justice system must always strive to retain legitimacy, and one way of doing this is to ensure that its operations conform to publicly stated rules.[63] There is strong evidence that individuals are more likely to accept decisions if they believe that they are the outcome of fair procedures:[64] the argument now is that a criminal justice system is more likely to be regarded as legitimate if it declines to act on the results of unlawful activities by law enforcement agencies. Whether this is in fact true is a different question, for we might find that a majority of citizens do not object to a little illegality if apparently major criminals are brought to book. It can therefore be argued that the integrity principle must be supported because it is right, rather than because the consequences of following it are thought likely to be acceptable to some version of public opinion.

A preferable approach is that adopted by the House of Lords in *R. v. Horseferry Road Magistrates' Court, ex parte Bennett*,[65] a case in which the doctrine of abuse of process was invoked to stay the prosecution of a man whom the police had brought to the UK by means that deliberately flouted the rules on extradition. The House of Lords held that English courts should not 'countenance behaviour that threatens either basic human rights or the rule of law', and should not 'turn a blind eye to executive lawlessness beyond the frontiers of its own jurisdiction'. This is an important restatement of the integrity principle, for two reasons. First, it accepts the point that unlawful behaviour at one stage in the criminal process can reflect upon the integrity

---

[61] (1928) 277 US 438, at 484–5.
[62] A. Choo, *Abuse of Process and Judicial Stays of Criminal Proceedings* (1993), 13.
[63] This borrows from the work of D. Beetham, *Legitimacy and Power* (1991).
[64] T. Tyler, *Why People Obey the Law* (1990).　　　[65] [1994] 1 AC 42.

of the whole. Secondly, it links the integrity principle to both basic human rights (for which the ECHR may be said to stand) and 'the rule of law', a principle with possibly wider applications than the European Convention. Of course the link is still by way of the principle of non-contradiction. At one level that would seem to be a sound principle: it would be a nonsense for a legal system to have contradictory rules, for example, because that would give conflicting signals to citizens and/or adjudicators, and that in turn would flout one of the basic elements of the idea of law as a method for guiding conduct. Contradictory norms fail to fulfil one of the basic requirements of law. But we are not concerned here with contradictory norms, with laws which say both 'do not do X' and 'you may do X'. If the *Bennett* case had been decided the other way, that outcome could have been supported by arguing that the laws of extradition are quite different from the rules of criminal procedure, and that the solution is to punish the police officer for acting illegally in bringing the man back to the UK, and yet to allow the trial to go ahead because that is a separate matter. This separation argument has been made many times in relation to the question whether evidence obtained by unlawful means should be admissible or inadmissible. In effect, it denies that subsequent proceedings are in any way tainted by the manner in which the evidence was obtained: if that was wrong, action should be taken against the culprit, but it does not necessarily reflect on the integrity of the trial of the accused. What this argument denies is the unity of the criminal justice system, and the notion that what is done by officials at one stage can be said to have any symbolic or other connection with what is done at a later stage.

It is noteworthy that, in a case decided by the House of Lords more recently than *Bennett*, the House did not follow its previous decision but equally did not deny that notions of the integrity of the process are relevant. In *Latif and Shahzad*[66] certain drugs had been imported unlawfully by an under-cover officer, who then lured the defendant to this country by means of a trick. In this case the House of Lords held that the unlawful act and deceptive practices of the customs officer were not such an affront to the public conscience that the proceedings should be stayed for abuse of process. Lord Steyn held that:

> the judge must weigh in the balance the public interest in ensuring that those that are charged with grave crimes should be tried, and the competing public interest in not conveying the impression that the court will adopt the approach that the end justifies any means.[67]

The two conflicting approaches are phrased in terms of 'the public interest' here. Certainly it can be questioned whether the integrity principle is related to any rights of the defendant (although it is possible that some rights could

---

[66] [1996] 1 WLR 104.   [67] *Ibid.* at 113.

be supported by the protective principle, discussed elsewhere).[68] But the main point is that Lord Steyn does not rule out the integrity principle. His argument is that there are circumstances in which it might have to yield to other considerations. Reflection quickly reveals that broad references to 'the integrity principle' do not confront the question whether absolutely every departure from procedure should be held to have the strong chilling effect of rendering the court unable to act on any evidence thereby obtained, or unable to try the particular defendant. There are at least two ways in which the integrity principle could operate: that of staying the proceedings for abuse of process is more appropriate where it is the defendant, rather than the evidence, that has been produced by some unlawful behaviour; and that of excluding evidence obtained unlawfully, which leaves open the possibility of proving guilt by other means. Should every irregularity, however venial, be held to compromise the integrity of the whole process? Certainly not: but that argument should only be used to rule out fairly small and inconsequential deviations from the proper procedure. It should not be used to argue, as did the US Supreme Court, that 'while courts must ever be concerned with preserving the integrity of the judicial process, this concern has limited force as a justification for the exclusion of highly probative evidence'.[69] This undermines the whole rationale. Nor should it be used to argue as Lord Steyn did in *Latif and Shahzad*, when he remarked that 'any criminal behaviour of the customs officer was venial compared to that of Shahzad'. Once comparisons of the wrongdoing of the law enforcement officer and the wrongdoing of the defendant are brought into debate, false trails are bound to follow. This argument is pursued at point 4 below.

3. *Right not to be tricked*: we saw earlier that one of the absolute rights guaranteed by the ECHR is the right not to be subjected to torture, inhuman or degrading treatment. One reason for recognition of this right would be that such treatment may lead to false confessions, and therefore to wrongful convictions. An independent reason is that underlying the human rights and fundamental freedoms declared in the ECHR is the idea of respect for the dignity of individuals. This is not simply a right to be free from the use of force by officials, or the right to liberty and security of person (declared separately in Article 5). It is a right not to be treated in certain ways: thus, the absolute ban on degrading treatment is surely designed to secure minimal respect for the dignity of an individual in the hands of public officials. In this country we have built upon that minimum in the Police and Criminal Evidence Act 1984, which (with its Codes of Practice) aims to secure somewhat greater protections for the dignity of an individual who is under investigation.

---

[68] See Ch. 4.3, below.   [69] *Stone* v. *Powell* (1976) 428 US 465, at 485.

It is for debate whether the ECHR ought to be supplemented by the recognition of other rights of persons under investigation. Does it make sense to regard as absolute the rights not to be subjected to inhuman and degrading treatment, and yet not to recognize (even at the level of *prima facie* rights) the right not to be required to give an intimate sample, the right not to be subjected to an intimate body search, and others? This argument can evidently be developed in several directions, but the focus here will be upon the right not to be tricked by public authorities. This potential right has been chosen for discussion precisely because it is *not* covered either by PACE or by the Code of Practice issued under PACE. At this stage in the argument, beyond the ECHR, it is not positive law but the strength of argument that matters. The argument, in brief, is that, just as respect for the dignity of the individual justifies the right not to be subjected to degrading treatment, so the same principle supports a right not to be tricked, at least in respect of criminal process rights. Thus, for a public official to lie in court is absolutely wrong, as are 'tricks about rights' at earlier stages of the criminal process, such as tricking a suspect about the right to consult a lawyer. Also objectionable are tricks during police interviews—for example, where a suspect is told, untruthfully, that a co-suspect has confessed or that there is forensic evidence linking the suspect to the scene. These arguments are relatively under-developed in the literature, and cannot be set out in full here.[70] To some extent, they draw strength from the integrity principle, discussed above. But the essence of the right not to be tricked resides in the propositions that telling lies is generally wrong and that for law enforcement officers to tell lies, to suspects being questioned or investigated, is even more wrong. It therefore deserves recognition in the present context.

4. *The public interest in convicting serious offenders:* a powerful and recurrent consideration in modern times is the desirability of ensuring that as many serious offenders as possible are prosecuted and convicted. Not only has it been used in judicial decisions, such as *Latif and Shazad*, as a justification for overlooking misconduct which might otherwise have been held to compromise the integrity of the criminal process. It has also been used frequently by legislatures to justify taking extra powers against certain types of suspect and offender, sometimes without much respect for human rights. Thus the Prevention of Terrorism Acts authorize detention for up to seven days without access to a court where a person is suspected of involvement in terrorism: this runs against Article 5 and, as we noted earlier, the UK government has derogated from Article 5 in this respect. The Criminal Justice Act 1987 granted far-reaching investigative powers to the Serious Fraud

---

[70] For fuller discussion, see A. Ashworth, 'Should the Police be Allowed to Use Deceptive Practices?' (1998) 114 *LQR* 108.

Office, without much reference to Article 6.2 of the ECHR.[71] Extended investigative powers have been proposed for other areas such as organized crime and child abuse.

Can this be the proper approach? Surely it is flawed, in that any public interest in the greater pursuit of serious crime must be set against the rights of innocent individuals not to be wrongly convicted, which ought also to be protected more vigorously if the crime alleged is a serious one. If rights are to have value, they must operate to protect individuals against the demands of the collectivity. And, as was argued at point 1 above, the right of an innocent person not to be convicted surely ranks as a fundamental right. There may, however, be a subtle distinction to be taken into account here. The right of an innocent person not to be convicted has its most powerful application to measures attended by a risk of miscarriage of justice (e.g. in the use of identification or confession evidence). Insofar as any wider powers granted or proposed carry this risk, the greater seriousness of the offence ought surely to be outweighed by the right not to be wrongly convicted. However, if the aim of the wider powers is to secure real evidence, and insofar as that carries no significant risk of wrongful conviction, the argument might be different. This might apply to some of the powers under section 2 of the Criminal Justice Act 1987, authorizing the seizure of documents in serious fraud investigations. Equally it might apply to the various statutes authorizing the use of electronic surveillance or telephone tapping. Here the concern is not so much wrongful conviction of the factually innocent as the breach of basic human rights. Thus the powers in respect of serious fraud must be shown to be compatible with the presumption of innocence set out in Article 6.2 of the ECHR, a provision containing no exceptions. On the other hand the powers taken in respect of surveillance must be shown to be compatible with Article 8 on privacy— termed a '*prima facie* right' above, because it is subject to exceptions including the 'prevention of disorder and crime', which has been held to be confined to 'serious crime'.[72] Without developing the point fully here, it can be seen that vague references to 'the seriousness of the offence' fail to supply a convincing justification for any extension in investigative powers. Instead, an argument must be made which avoids the fallacy of overlooking the defendant's right not to be wrongly convicted, on the basis of evidence with a significant risk of inaccuracy, or which enables the gathering of real evidence without infringing any rights. Two examples of such rights in the ECHR have been given here. The right not to be tricked might, as argued above, be added to the list.

Brief consideration should also be given to the kindred argument that derogations from individual rights may be justified where offences of a certain

---

[71] Cf. *Saunders* v. *UK* (1997) 23 EHRR 313.   [72] *Malone* v. *UK* (1985) 7 EHRR 14.

kind are especially difficult to investigate. This argument is heard most persistently in relation to so-called 'victimless crimes', particularly drug trafficking. To the extent that the reasoning draws on the seriousness of the offences involved, it is merely a variation of the argument considered in the previous paragraph. If the difficulty of investigation is advanced as an independent argument, two problems stand in the way of acceptance. The more formidable is the point of principle: is it really being suggested that, for example, the presumption of innocence declared in Article 6.2 should vary in strength according to the difficulties of proving guilt of certain crimes? Similarly, is the suggestion that the use of deceptive practices in investigation, against which strong arguments were raised above, is more justifiable where offences might otherwise be difficult to prove? The other problem is that any concessions towards the 'difficulty of proof' argument ought surely to be dependent on, and limited by, the principle of subsidiarity (as applied to adjudications under Article 8.2, for example). Thus it must be established that no other method of investigation, which intrudes less upon individual rights, is feasible in the circumstances. That, however, is a consequential point. In principle, the case for derogating from declared rights on this ground is weak.

5. *The principle of non-discrimination:* this principle ought to be restated here at a general level. We have already seen (in Section 4 above) that Article 14 of the ECHR declares the right not to be discriminated against in relation to other Convention rights. That is a limited principle, which is strictly speaking inapplicable (for example) to victims' rights of the kind discussed in paragraph 7 below. It is therefore important—and surely does not call for separate justification here—that the general principle of non-discrimination in matters of criminal justice be reasserted. This is particularly so, in view of the circuitous provision in section 95 of the Criminal Justice Act 1991. The principle should be applied both to direct and to indirect discrimination. For example, the discount for pleading guilty (discussed in Chapter 9 below) may be said to constitute indirect discrimination on grounds of race, since it can be demonstrated that it results in longer prison terms for significant numbers of people from an Afro-Caribbean background who wish to exercise their right to be tried. Similarly, one might argue that remands in custody may be significantly more onerous for women, because they often result in them being imprisoned a long distance from their homes. These points will be developed below.

6. *Protection of the vulnerable:* a related argument, not confronted by Article 14 of the ECHR, is that certain groups of people who become involved in the criminal process deserve special protection, perhaps in the form of extra support and advice, perhaps in the form of special procedural provisions. Two such groups are the young and the mentally disordered. When young or mentally disordered people are victims or witnesses, there is an especially strong

case for support and careful treatment. Victims of crime are considered below, but it is worth noting here that there are now provisions for the reception of children's evidence in courts by means of live video link, thereby sparing them the ordeal of testifying in open court. Although the system may not be perfect,[73] the decision to introduce it demonstrates support for the principle of protection of vulnerable people in the criminal process.

The principle does not appear in the European Convention on Human Rights, but that omission surely does not weaken it. If authority is needed, the United Nations Convention on the Rights of the Child (mentioned above) can be invoked. Thus suspects and defendants under a certain age (18 in England and Wales) require special protection during the criminal process for the same general reason as victims. They need support when being questioned by the police, because they may be impressionable and vulnerable. The Police and Criminal Evidence Act 1984 introduced a provision for an 'appropriate adult' (usually a parent or relative, sometimes a social worker) to be present during police questioning. This is clear recognition of the principle of protecting the vulnerable, although it is now widely recognised that the system does not operate as intended and stands in need of revision.[74] There is also a provision for young suspects, like adult suspects, to have a lawyer present during questioning. However, as we shall see in Chapter 5 below, the most frequent means of disposal of young people in the criminal process has been the formal police caution, and there is no requirement of access to legal advice before deciding whether or not to accept a caution (or, under the new system, a reprimand or final warning). In view of the serious consequences which such recorded disposals may have, this is one respect in which the principle of protecting the vulnerable is not being upheld.

The case for support and advice for the mentally disordered is no less compelling. These are people who may be at an intellectual or other disadvantage in their dealings with agents of law enforcement. It is quite unfair that they should suffer as a result of such a disadvantage, particularly in the light of the strong policy in favour of the diversion of the mentally disordered.[75] Code of Practice C under the Police and Criminal Evidence Act 1984 introduced special protections for mentally disordered or mentally handicapped persons who are interviewed by the police. Once again it is important to be satisfied that these protections are being granted to those who need them: one survey found that as many as one in five suspects was 'mentally incapable of understanding the significance of questions put to him or his replies', the words of Code C, compared with a mere 4 per cent whom the police identified as

---

[73] For discussion, see J.R. Spencer and R. Flin, *The Evidence of Children* (2nd edn., 1993).
[74] For further detail and references, see Ch. 4.2.10 below.
[75] Home Office Circular 66/1990, *Provision for Mentally Disordered Offenders*.

such.[76] Proper identification of the mentally disordered or handicapped is important because they are also entitled to support and protection during police questioning. This shows further recognition of the principle of special protection for the vulnerable, even though the 'appropriate adult' system stands in need of improvement.[77]

7. *The rights of victims, complainants, and witnesses:* the rights and interests of victims of crime were discussed briefly in Section 3(2) above. The purpose of this paragraph is to emphasize the importance of ensuring that at the pre-trial stage proper respect is paid to the legitimate interests of all those involved in the criminal process who are not suspects or defendants. These include victims, complainants, and witnesses. Unfortunately the European Convention on Human Rights fails to deal with victims of crime, let alone witnesses. However, the Council of Europe has a recommendation on *The Position of the Victim in Criminal Justice*, which follows a similar path to the United Nations declaration of 1985 in declaring certain rights of victims of crime in the criminal justice system. It declares various rights to respect and information at the pre-trial stage, many of which have found their way into the British Government's *Victim's Charter*. It is to the credit of the European Court of Human Rights that it has begun to recognize the rights of victims and witnesses as a relevant factor when considering the fairness of trial procedures. Thus in two cases on the anonymity of witnesses, brought under Article 6.3(d), the Court developed its jurisprudence so as to hold that the interests of victims and their families also deserve protection in the criminal process.[78] Although the issues are complex, it is important to build upon this small beginning.

8. *Equality of arms:* this, as we have seen, is a principle that has been developed out of the 'fair trial guarantees' in Article 6 of the ECHR by the European Court of Human Rights. But there are reasons for stating it more widely. It is evident from many of the cases of miscarriage of justice set out in Chapter 1 that injustice may arise if information possessed by the police or prosecution is not shared with the defence, and if the defence do not have equal access to facilities such as expert opinion. But there is also the point, outlined in Section 2(5) of this chapter, that some corporate defendants may have considerable resources and power. We will see in Chapter 4, below, that the principle of equality of arms has profound implications for the restrictions on

---

[76] G. Gudjonsson, I. Clare, S. Rutter, and J. Pearse, *Persons at Risk during Interviews in Police Custody: The Identification of Vulnerabilities,* RCCJ Research Study 12 (1993).

[77] See generally the essay by P. Fennell, 'Mentally Disordered Suspects in the Criminal Justice System', in S. Field and P. Thomas (eds.), *Justice and Efficiency* (1994).

[78] *Doorson* v. *Netherlands* (1996) 22 EHRR 330, and *Van Mechelen* v. *The Netherlands* [1997] HRCD 431.

defence access to prosecution evidence, on equal access to expert forensic science services, and on the duty of defence disclosure.

6. Dispositive Values

We now turn away from the framework within which process values operate, and consider some values relevant to the 'dispositive' aspects of pre-trial decisions.[79] The focus here is on police cautioning, final warnings, discontinuance of cases, and other forms of diversion from the formal process. To a large extent the values relevant here reflect the purposes at the stage of sentencing, which is the best-known and most widely publicized dispositive decision, but there should also be a philosophical connection with the principles discussed above in relation to process values. In particular, the right of an innocent person not to be punished is relevant to both types of decision.

1. *Prevention of crime*: the prevention of crime is among the reasons for having a criminal justice system, with police, courts, and sentences. It is also an underlying reason for diversion, but this is not to say that it should be determinative in individual cases. These two points should be kept separate. It is one thing to argue that the system of diversion should operate in such a way that it contributes to the overall prevention of crime, at least by dealing with offenders in ways that do not increase the chances of further law-breaking by them or by others. It is another thing to maintain that the prospect of a particular person not reoffending should be a necessary or sufficient reason for diverting that offender from the formal criminal process: that might conflict with the principle of proportionality in (4) below. The point here is that, since dispositive decisions without trial may be regarded as part of or analogous to the sentencing system, they should not increase the probability of people committing offences.

2. *Freedom and fairness*: this principle has a direct connection with process values. The system should ensure that, as far as possible, a person's decision whether or not to accept diversion is a free and informed one, and that there is a right of access to a court if guilt is disputed. The idea of a completely free decision may be regarded as unattainable, in the sense that the alternative of going to court will often be perceived as more stressful, but there are ways of maximizing this freedom. For example, legal advice should be available so as to help a suspect with this decision, not least because cautions and final warnings are recorded and may be cited in subsequent proceedings. In cases where

---

[79] See Ch. 5 for elaboration.

the prosecutor or police offer diversion and the defendant wishes to contest guilt, there should be a rule that the court could impose no more severe a penalty than was offered for diversion.[80] The right of access to court has been insisted upon by the European Court of Human Rights,[81] and is essential so as to ensure that methods of diversion do not become methods of subversion, as far as fairness and the protection of the innocent are concerned.

3. *Victim compensation*: any arrangement for diversion should ensure that the victim does not thereby lose a right to compensation. The system should remain committed to certain victims' rights, for the reasons elaborated above. This does not necessarily mean that offenders should be required to pay full compensation to their victims as an element in diversion: as argued in Sections 2(2) and 5(7) of this chapter, the victim's right to compensation is a fundamental right but not an absolute one. But it does mean that arrangements for diversion should not be made in a way that precludes an enforceable agreement for compensation, unless there is a strong argument for overriding the right in this situation.

4. *Proportionality of imposition*: there should be a sense of proportion between the seriousness of the offence and that which the offender is asked to agree to as the condition of diversion. This is not merely a means of ensuring that consent is as voluntary as it can be. It is also a basic element of desert: a person who has committed an offence deserves to be punished, but only to an extent that may be described as appropriate to the seriousness of the offence committed (seriousness being composed of harm and culpability). The idea of deserved punishment is grounded in the belief that those who commit crimes are rightly liable to punishment: they deserve censure, to appeal to people's sense of the wrongfulness of the conduct, combined with some kind of prudential reason for future compliance.[82] The impositions on those who are 'diverted' must be proportionate to one another, in the sense that more serious cases should involve more onerous sanctions and less serious cases should involve less onerous sanctions. The impositions should also be of modest severity overall, so that they can appropriately be ranked below court-imposed penalties.

It will be evident that, although the parameters of desert are fairly clear at a conceptual level, their application in practice leaves room for variations according to the cultural and political context. What is regarded as a sufficiently minor offence for diversion or too severe a sanction for diversion may to a large extent be culturally determined. The principle of proportionality

---

[80] Unless considerations of public expenditure are deemed relevant to such decisions: see the discussion of plea bargaining in Ch. 9.

[81] See the decisions cited in Ch. 5 n. 29.

[82] For discussion, see von Hirsch, *Censure and Sanctions* (1993).

should, however, be regarded as a fundamental one—not absolute, since questions of priority will necessarily arise, but fundamental. If 'legality' values are to be respected, the questions of priority should be decided on principle and not *ad hoc*. A great deal has been written about these issues in the context of sentencing,[83] but a few general points should suffice here. One serious question is whether (young) repeat offenders ought to receive multiple cautions or other forms of diversion from prosecution, and whether previous criminal record should affect other dispositive decisions such as plea bargaining. As we will see in Chapter 5 below, there have been distinct changes of policy in recent years towards a 'cumulative' approach of escalating severity of response for repeat offenders. Desert theorists would be cautious about such moves: although they accept that responses to the first and second offences should be muted (which allows for an element of cumulation), they insist on the importance of focusing on the seriousness of each offence, and would oppose the escalation of responses simply because of repetition.

The rehabilitation of offenders rightly remains an objective of many of those working in the criminal justice system, but a difficulty arises if rehabilitative schemes involve greater restrictions on liberty than is compatible with the modest demands of diversion. We will see in Chapter 5 that some forms of diversion do involve participation in schemes that have rehabilitation as an aim. The point to be made here is that such participation must be voluntary— at least in the sense that acceptance of any diversion (rather than going to court) is voluntary—and that any restrictions on liberty should be proportionate to the demands of other diversionary measures.

7. Rights, Decisions, and Information

The principle that information ought to be assured to those who have to take decisions about the exercise of rights or about the progress of cases might seem to be so self-evident as not to be worth stating. Yet research has shown that many of those who have rights do not exercise them because they are ignorant that the right exists, or that its exercise carries no penalty, and so forth; that some defendants do not learn about information possessed by the police and not used by the prosecution; and that some officials who have to take decisions about cases receive information predominantly in favour of one party and hardly ever in favour of the other. Referring to the case of the

---

[83] e.g. A. Ashworth, *Sentencing and Criminal Justice* (2nd edn., 1995), ch. 3; M. Cavadino and J. Dignan, *The Penal System: An Introduction* (2nd edn., 1997), ch. 2.

Maguire Seven,[84] where non-disclosure by the Forensic Science Service was a reason for quashing the convictions but one defendant had died in prison, Patrick O'Connor writes: 'perhaps there is no more moving reminder of the power that goes with the control of information. It can be a matter of life and death.'[85] Recent changes in the rules on disclosure will be discussed in Chapter 4 below.

If it is decided that a suspect, defendant, or victim should have a certain right, one can assume that a significant value is thereby respected. Yet if there is no machinery for informing the right-holders of their rights, and if it is shown that many, or even, some of them are ignorant, this practical deficiency undermines the very value that the right was intended to respect. For example, victims of violent crime have access to the Criminal Injuries Compensation Board for compensation (within the regulations): an early study showed that only 39 per cent of victims of violence got to know about the Board's existence,[86] and efforts to improve information by imposing a duty on the police have not met with complete success, largely because of incomplete understanding by police officers of the scheme and its relationship to court compensation.[87] According to the *Victim's Charter* victims have a right to receive information about the progress of 'their' case, but the struggle to ensure that this occurs in practice has been long and still continues.[88]

Another example is provided by the suspect's right to legal advice in the police station: attempts were made in the revised Codes of Practice (under the Police and Criminal Evidence Act 1984) to ensure that suspects are fully informed of the right and its extent. Research following the introduction of the revised Codes in 1991 showed that some three-quarters of suspects were now informed of the right, and that legal advice is free; just over a half were told that the legal advice is independent, but very few were told that the consultation is in private.[89] Moreover, information may still be received in a fashion that discourages the full exercise of rights: greater attention should be devoted to techniques of communication: being told is not the same as being caused to understand.[90] Other examples could be given, but the point of principle should now be clear. If it is known that people who should have the

---

[84] See Ch. 1.3.

[85] P. O'Connor, 'Prosecution Disclosure: Principle, Practice and Justice' [1992] *Crim. LR* 464, at 467.

[86] J. Shapland, J. Willmore, and P. Duff, *Victims in the Criminal Justice System* (1985), 124.

[87] T. Newburn and S. Merry, *Keeping in Touch: Police–Victim Communication in Two Areas*, HORS 116 (1990), ch. 5.

[88] See H. Fenwick, 'Rights of Victims in the Criminal Justice System: Rhetoric or Reality?' [1995] *Crim. LR* 843.

[89] Brown, Ellis, and Larcombe, *Changing the Code*, Home Office Research Study 129 (1993).

[90] I. Clare and G. Gudjonsson, *Devising and Piloting an Experimental Version of the 'Notice to Detained Persons'*, RCCJ Research Study 7 (1993).

opportunity to exercise certain rights fail to realize their existence or to grasp their extent, this undermines the value that the rights are supposed to respect.

A slightly different point about information relates to the input into various decisions. Magistrates' decisions on bail have tended to follow the prosecutor's representations, and one reason for this may be that most of the information comes from the prosecutor. The information necessary to decide in favour of the accused (e.g. information on address, employment, family ties, etc.) is not routinely available to the Crown Prosecution Service or to the courts. Bail information schemes have been developed with a view to filling this gap, particularly in cases where a defendant who is otherwise likely to be remanded in custody might be found a place in a bail hostel.[91] There have also been a few 'Public Information Case Assessment' schemes, designed to provide the Crown Prosecution Service with personal information about a defendant that might lead to discontinuance of the case: without such information, a favourable decision is unlikely. The point of principle is that, where a decision-maker is expected to take account of conflicting considerations, fairness is unlikely to be achieved if the available information relates predominantly to one set of considerations.

8. Conclusions

In this chapter we have considered some elements in a framework for evaluating the criminal process. Central to the discussion is the European Convention on Human Rights, but it has been argued that this fails to deal with all the issues that one would expect a fundamental document on criminal justice to deal with. Arguments for the recognition of other principles and interests have therefore been presented. But there remains one fundamental question that has not been answered: what is the chief purpose of the criminal process?

It may be thought unlikely that a single purpose could be identified. After all, the decisions discussed in this book vary in their function: some are processual, others dispositive, and the remand decision has been termed 'temporizing'. But if, for a moment, we suspend consideration of the last two functions, is it possible to identify a fundamental purpose of the processual decisions? Why do we process cases through the system towards a court appearance? Surely the answer to this question cannot be found in respect for human rights, whether in the form of the ECHR or any other declaration. We

[91] C. Lloyd, *Bail Information Schemes: Practice and Effect*, Home Office Research and Planning Unit Paper 69 (1992).

do not have a criminal process in order to show respect for human rights. We have a criminal process in order to assist in the conviction of the guilty and the acquittal of the innocent, in a way that respects the human rights of all individuals affected. The protection of human rights therefore needs to form part of the fundamental justification but it cannot be the sole or even the primary justification. It should be an inseparable part of any statement of purpose relating to processual goals—processing suspected offenders through the system to court appearance, whilst diverting from the process as early as possible those against whom the evidence in weak or whose cases are sufficiently non-serious to be diverted.

3 Ethics, Conflicts and Conduct

In this chapter we move on from examining the interests which ought to be respected in the criminal process, and explore the problems of putting principles into practice. Much of the chapter concerns the ethical principles that ought to shape the way in which those exercising power within the criminal process should conduct themselves towards citizens. One reason for framing the discussion in terms of ethical principles is to draw attention to the rival influences on the conduct of actors in the criminal justice system—not just the police and state officials, but also lawyers in private practice. Particular interest is taken in the occupational cultures that currently dominate the practices of some actors in the system—the 'Spanish customs', the judgements of moral character,[1] and even the conceptions of 'public interest' and of 'justice'. The chapter opens with a brief discussion of the idea of ethical conduct. Next it outlines some unethical practices, and then attempts to examine and reconstruct some possible justifications for such practices. Consideration is then given to the problems of displacing the occupational cultures and other influences which may lead to resistance against change. Formal accountability systems are also discussed, and the chapter concludes with a consideration of the prospects for bringing about changes in the conduct of practitioners within the system.

1. Rules, Roles and Ethics

Is there any need to discuss ethics when there are so many legal rules, codes, and guidelines impinging on the work of law enforcement agents? Is there really any room for moral disputation when we have such documents as the Police and Criminal Evidence Act 1984 and its Codes of Practice, the Code for Crown Prosecutors, the Victim's Charter, and countless recent statutes on

[1] On judgements of moral character, see e.g. K. Hawkins, *Environment and Enforcement* (1984), on pollution inspectors and H. Parker, M. Sumner, and G. Jarvis, *Unmasking the Magistrates* (1989), on magistrates. This use of 'moral' is a good reason for adopting the term 'ethical' in this chapter.

criminal justice? Three good reasons may be offered for pressing ahead with ethical inquiries.

First, ethical principles should apply to those who lay down rules and guidelines as well as to those who are subject to them. Thus there should be no suggestion that ethical issues affect only the lower ranks: the decisions of members of the legislature, the Home Secretary, the Director of Public Prosecutions, and the Lord Chief Justice should be equally subject to appraisal on ethical grounds. However, there should be no confusion between legal rules and moral or ethical principles. It is good that legal rules should be based on ethical principles, rather than (say) on short-term pragmatism, but the function of ethical principles is to supply strong reasons for adopting a particular rule. In so far as incorporation of the European Convention on Human Rights into English law imports a kind of higher law, which even legislators should respect, this formalizes the notion of ethical principles for policy-makers. But, as we saw in Chapter 2, the European Convention does not contain all the rights and principles one might wish to see upheld.

Secondly, there is no warrant for the view that the criminal justice system is entirely covered by rules and clear-cut guidance. Recent years have seen greater efforts to introduce various forms of guidance and accountability, but there are still vast tracts of discretion, some of it left deliberately so as to enable flexibility, some eked out by practitioners in order to allow them to follow their preferred practices. Wherever there is discretion, and even where there are rules, there may be choices between following ethical principles and following other policies or preferences.

Thirdly, it is well known that there are strong occupational cultures among the various professional groups in the criminal justice system. The point is clearest in relation to the police. For example, a study of detectives for the Royal Commission on Criminal Justice concluded that a necessary step towards improving the situation would be 'raising CID officers' awareness of the faults in the traditional "detective culture" ("macho" and "elitist" attitudes, belief that "rules are there to be bent", excessive secrecy and suspicion of outsiders, and so on) and the ease with which young officers are sucked into it, almost without realising it'.[2] In its report, the Royal Commission referred to 'the culture and approach of the Criminal Bar' as a possible obstacle to the success of some of its proposals for streamlining pre-trial procedure.[3] Research into the conduct of criminal defence lawyers has also shown how the culture of many solicitors' firms operates so as to adapt the law and the role,

---

[2] M. Maguire and C. Norris, *The Conduct and Supervision of Criminal Investigations*, RCCJ Research Study 5 (1992).

[3] Royal Commission on Criminal Justice, *Report*, Cmnd. 2263 (1993), para. 7.36, on preparatory hearings.

in ways that differ from the formal rhetoric and procedures, and which result in less than full protection for suspect-defendants.[4] There is also an argument that judges sitting in the Court of Appeal are received into an occupational culture which has, over the years, resulted in a particular approach to the exercise of the Court's statutory powers.[5] In the face of such well-entrenched cultures, what are the prospects for rules, let alone guidelines or unfettered discretion? In practical terms these cultures seem to be direct competitors with ethical principles, partly because they often put sectional interests first, but partly also because they sometimes challenge the values of those who argue for the recognition of rights. Exploration of these occupational cultures will be one of the principal tasks in this chapter.

What kind of principle may be described as ethical? It should be a principle that is impartial as between persons, and for which one can give reasons which show a respect for the rights and interests that the system is supposed to uphold. Impartiality in this context requires that no preference should be shown towards persons (whether suspects, victims, defendants, or whatever) on extraneous grounds such as wealth, connection, sex, race, and so forth. It also forbids conduct based on the self-interest of the official or criminal justice practitioner, who ought to behave according to the assigned role (e.g. investigating officer, defence lawyer) rather than according to personal convenience, profit, or other extraneous motivation. As for the rights and interests that the system is supposed to uphold, this refers not merely to the interests discussed in Chapter 2 above, but also to the fundamental orientation of the criminal process towards either an inquisitorial or an adversarial approach. Although some of the procedures in English criminal justice blur the line between the two, there is little doubt that the overall orientation is towards an adversarial model. This, in turn, invests various actors with certain role responsibilities. Thus the role of the defence lawyer is to promote fearlessly and by all lawful and proper means the lay client's interests.[6] It is perfectly proper for the defence lawyer to take advantage of any legal point in favour of the defendant, however 'technical', and to advise the defendant on the best tactical means of pursuing the line of defence on which instructions have been given. The defence lawyer's role is essentially partisan, whereas the prosecutor's role is not that of an advocate appearing for a party.[7] The prosecutor in an adversarial system is supposed to act impartially, not seeking convictions

---

[4] M. McConville, J. Hodgson, L. Bridges, and A. Pavlovic, *Standing Accused* (1994); M. Travers, *The Reality of Law* (1997).

[5] D. Schiff and R. Nobles, 'Criminal Appeal Act 1995: the Semantics of Jurisdiction' (1996) 59 MLR 573, at 577.   [6] Per Lord Reid in *Rondel* v. *Worsley* [1969] 1 AC 191, at 227–8.

[7] General Council of the Bar, *Code of Conduct for Barristers* (1990, with 1997 Amendment), Annexe H, para. 11.1, cited by M. Blake and A. Ashworth, 'Some Ethical Issues in Prosecuting and Defending Criminal Cases' [1998] *Crim. LR* 16.

as such but taking on the role of a 'minister of justice'. The prosecutor's goal should be to conduct the case dispassionately, seeking justice according to the law (not relying, for example, on inadmissible evidence) and disclosing to the defence all evidence that should be disclosed. We saw in Chapter 1 that the failure of prosecuting lawyers to disclose evidence to the defence lay at the root of some of the notorious cases of miscarriage of justice. In the present context, the point about disclosure illustrates the way in which roles and ethics are subject to alteration by statute, the Criminal Procedure and Investigations Act 1996 having introduced an altered system of pre-trial disclosure. The differing roles and responsibilities of defending and prosecuting lawyers will become relevant at several points in this and the following chapters.

2. Identifying 'Unethical' Practices

In order to provide a factual basis for the discussion in the rest of the chapter, it is now proposed to identify fairly briefly some eight presumptively unethical practices. Many of them are discussed in greater detail later in the book, but it is important at this early stage to illustrate the context in which ethical arguments take place. Whether the practices can properly be termed 'unethical' will not be determined until we have discussed the explanations for them, but they are discussed here because they appear unethical. There is no suggestion that all the practices are widespread, but it is believed that they occur on some occasions, and references are given to support this belief.

1. *'Helping the police with their inquiries'*: one of the purposes of introducing new rules on detention in police stations under the Police and Criminal Evidence Act 1984 was to ensure that persons brought to police stations under arrest are only detained if it is necessary to do so, and if there is sufficient evidence for a charge.[8] Research by McKenzie, Morgan, and Reiner showed that custody officers routinely authorized detention without an examination of the sufficiency of evidence, and did so by reference to the need 'to secure or preserve evidence or to obtain evidence by questioning'.[9] This practice is unethical because it deprives suspects of protection against being detained unless that is absolutely necessary, a protection that Parliament intended to give them.[10]

---

[8] PACE, s. 37.

[9] I. McKenzie, R. Morgan, and R. Reiner, 'Helping the Police with their Inquiries: The Necessity Principle and Voluntary Attendance at the Police station' [1990] *Crim. LR* 22; see, to the same effect, M. McConville, A. Sanders, and R. Leng, *The Case for the Prosecution* (1991), ch. 3.

[10] The Home Secretary at the time stated the principle that detention must be necessary, 'not desirable, convenient or a good idea but necessary': cited by McKenzie, Morgan, and Reiner, above n. 9, 23.

2. *Rights of suspects:* the 1984 Act and its Codes of Practice were also designed to lay down standards of fair treatment and to restate the courts' discretion to exclude evidence obtained in contravention of the standards. The reason behind these protections is to spare defendants intimidation, and to enhance the reliability of any evidence that is obtained. Yet the years since 1986 have seen a steady stream of cases in which police officers have been found to have departed from the Code of Practice on Questioning and on Identification.[11]

3. *Failure to inform suspects of rights:* another purpose of the 1984 Act was to require the police to inform each suspect/defendant of certain rights—the right to make a telephone call from the police station, the right to have someone informed of the detention, and the right to have legal advice that is free, independent, and given in a private consultation. After the implementation of the new law in 1986 it was found that not all suspects were being informed of these rights.[12] The relevant Code of Practice was altered in 1991, and subsequent Home Office research showed that the rate of informing suspects had increased but was still less than complete; almost all suspects were told of the right to legal advice, but only 73 per cent were told that it is free, 56 per cent were told that it is independent, and hardly any were told that the consultation would be private.[13] No less significantly, in over a quarter of cases where information was given, it was spoken in an unclear or unduly rapid fashion. There was also evidence that some police officers emphasized the possible problems (such as delay) in summoning legal advice, presumably in order to encourage a suspect to waive the right. All three practices discussed above are probably unethical, and seem to stem from the police's belief that the law inhibits them from adopting the most effective approach to investigation. The law is regarded as an impediment to be circumvented.

4. *Failure to disclose relevant evidence:* similar motivation may have underlain the failure by the police to disclose to the prosecution or the defence certain evidence in favour of the defence, which was a reason for quashing the convictions in the cases of the Maguire Seven,[14] the Birmingham Six,[15] and Judith Ward.[16] The Attorney-General's Guidelines on disclosure were not in

[11] For a few examples from recent years, see *Conway* [1994] Crim.LR 838, *Allen* [1995] *Crim. LR* 643, and *Khan* [1997] *Crim. LR* 584.

[12] See e.g. A. Sanders and L. Bridges, 'Access to Legal Advice and Police Malpractice' [1990] *Crim. LR* 494.

[13] D. Brown, T. Ellis, and K. Larcombe, *Changing the Code: Police Detention under the Revised PACE Codes of Practice* (1993); to similar effect see M. Zander and P. Henderson, *Crown Court Study* (1993), 8–10. Rather surprisingly, no up-to-date evidence on these points was provided by T. Bucke and D. Brown, *In Police Custody* (1997).

[14] *Maguire et al.* (1992) 94 Cr.App.R. 133.   [15] *McIlkenny et al.* (1991) 93 Cr.App.R. 287.

[16] *Ward* (1993) 96 Cr.App.R. 1; cf. the Court of Appeal's change of direction in *Johnson et al.* [1993] Crim. LR 689, and the recommendations in RCCJ Report, paras. 6.50–6.53.

force at the time of the original trials in these cases, but the principle of disclosure did exist. Similarly, in the case of the Maguire Seven the results of certain tests carried out by the Forensic Science Service, with results favourable to the defendants, were not notified to the defence. Non-disclosure of forensic evidence also occurred in the cases of the Birmingham Six and Judith Ward. These omissions can be regarded as unethical. Breaches of the disclosure rules were not confined to the 1970s, as the case of *Fergus* amply demonstrates.[17] The rules on disclosure have now been changed by the Criminal Procedure and Investigations Act 1996: knowing failure to follow the Act's requirements conscientiously is unethical, whether it is the police, the prosecution, or the defence that is at fault.

6. *Failure to protect a client at interview:* one of the reasons for allowing suspects the right to consult a lawyer at a police station is to ensure that the conduct of the police towards the suspect is scrupulously fair. However, in some cases legal advisers are reluctant to intervene to protect their client, allowing hostile and hectoring modes of questioning to pass without comment.[18] In clear cases this is unethical conduct by the legal adviser, particularly where the lawyer's motivation for failing to intervene is not related to advancing the interests of the lay client.

6. *Failure to follow pre-trial procedures:* the Royal Commission also chided defence barristers for failing to abide by the regulations for pre-trial hearings introduced at certain Crown Court centres under the authority of a Practice Direction. Even though the Commission made recommendations for improving the situation, it recognized the need to provide sanctions for non-compliance, for otherwise 'the defence lawyers called upon to make it work will in practice ensure that it fails'.[19] Such conduct could be regarded as unethical, since defence lawyers are supposed only to use 'lawful and proper' means of defending their clients. The extent to which such conduct has continued in the context of Plea and Directions Hearings since 1995 is not known.

7. *Failure to discontinue a weak case:* a primary reason for introducing the Crown Prosecution Service was to bring professional prosecutorial review into the system, to prevent weak or inappropriate cases from going to court,[20] and for this they were given a power of discontinuance.[21] Despite a discontinuance rate of around 13 per cent, there are still cases in which the CPS fail

---

[17] (1994) 98 Cr.App.R. 313, discussed at Ch. 1.3 above.

[18] J. Baldwin, *The Role of Legal Representatives at Police Stations*, RCCJ Research Study 3 (1992); M. McConville and J. Hodgson, *Custodial Legal Advice and the Right to Silence*, RCCJ Research Study 16 (1993). At that time most 'legal advisers' attending to give advice at police stations were not qualified solicitors: the position is now changing (see below, pp. 124–5).

[19] RCCJ, para. 7.36.

[20] Royal Commission on Criminal Procedure, *Report*, Cmnd. 8092 (1981), para. 7.6.

[21] Prosecution of Offences Act 1985, s. 23.

to discontinue a case where they know that there is insufficient evidence, perhaps in order to retain good relations with the police or out of a pro-prosecution motivation inconsistent with the 'minister of justice' role that prosecutors are meant to fulfil.[22]

8. *Avoidance of 'presumptive' mode of trial:* under the existing system for determining mode of trial, various cases have arisen in which the prosecution has preferred an either-way charge, the defendant has elected Crown Court trial, and the prosecution has thereupon dropped the either-way charge and brought a charge that is triable summarily only, in a magistrates' court. Defendants have challenged these tactics by means of judicial review, and the Divisional Court has held that in general the choice of charge lies within the discretion of the prosecutor so long as the substituted charge is not inappro-priate and there is no bad faith, oppression, or prejudice.[23] The CPS Code now instructs prosecutors not to do this, save in exceptional circumstances, but it remains possible to alter the charges before the mode of trial proceed-ings have begun. This raises similar ethical issues: it is one thing to lower the charge to ensure that the case is heard quickly (avoiding the waiting time for the Crown Court) if there are reasons for this, perhaps connected with victims or other witnesses; it is quite another thing to do this in the hope of taking advantage of the higher conviction rate in magistrates' courts. This ethical argument is complex, as we shall see in Chapter 8, but such conduct by the prosecution is presumptively unethical.

3. Understanding 'Unethical' Behaviour

The preceding section has set out some examples of behaviour that might be described as 'unethical', in the sense that it fails to show proper respect for cit-izens and often removes, circumvents, or weakens certain rights of the suspect or defendant. There may be other sources of miscarriages of justice, but the focus here is on conduct that may be said to involve some conscious circum-vention of the rules. Suspending final judgement on whether these practices are to be termed unethical, we must first inquire into the reasons for them.

There is often a tendency to regard practices of this kind as the product of individuals, exercising a discretion unconstrained by context or by colleagues.

---

[22] J. Baldwin, 'Understanding Judge Ordered and Directed Acquittals in the Crown Court' [1997] *Crim. LR* 536, esp. at 550–2.

[23] *R. v. Liverpool Stipendiary Magistrate, ex p. Ellison* [1989] *Crim. LR* 369; however, where the magistrates have decided that a charge should be tried summarily, it would be an abuse of process for the prosecutor to drop that charge and prefer one that is triable only on indictment: *Brooks* [1985] *Crim. LR* 385.

This is the 'rotten apple' theory, assuming that a small number of 'rogue' individuals decide to defy the rules. This ignores the fact that these individuals work in a professional context in which several influences such as organizational rules and occupational pressures operate, sometimes fuelled by the unrealistic expectations of the public and others.[24] Thus research into the police has often concluded that much police behaviour is influenced by a 'cop culture' that is spread widely through the organization. There is no need here to enter into an extensive analysis of the findings of the various researchers. It is sufficient to mention four elements that seem to be at the core of 'cop culture'—(1) support for colleagues' decisions and the inappropriateness of close supervision; (2) what is termed 'the macho image', which includes heavy drinking and physical presence, and may extend to sexist and racist attitudes; (3) the idea that rules are there to be used and bent; and (4) the sense of mission in police work.[25] The suggestion is that these and similar attitudes are widespread, not that they are universal. There may be differences from division to division, particularly between rural and urban areas. There may be individuals or groups, particularly women and some younger police officers, who accept few or no aspects of the culture. Senior officers may argue that changes are taking place, but the stronghold of the culture has always been in the lower ranks. The phenomenon of police culture has been observed so frequently that its existence in some quarters cannot be doubted, even if it must be accepted that its form and intensity are variable.

In an attempt to unravel the reasons which underlie the culture, we may begin by considering (1), support for colleagues' decisions and the inappropriateness of close supervision. In order to set aside the claim that this part of the culture has changed, it is worth recalling that two recent research studies for the Royal Commission on Criminal Justice found that the supervision of junior officers in the conduct of inquiries and in questioning was not the norm and was often regarded as a breach of the trust that should be shown in every officer's skills.[26] This is linked to the idea of police solidarity and the duty to support a fellow officer, although it may have a darker side, as the Royal Commission recognized in its reference to officers and civilian staff being 'deterred by the prevailing culture from complaining openly about malpractice'.[27] To some extent the isolated position of the police in society may

---

[24] K. Hawkins, 'The Use of Legal Discretion: Perspectives from Law and Social Science', in K. Hawkins (ed.), *The Uses of Discretion* (1992), at 22.

[25] For detailed discussion, see J. Skolnick, *Justice without Trial* (1966); P. Manning, *Police Work* (1977); S. Holdaway, *Inside the British Police* (1983); D. J. Smith and J. Gray, *Police and People in London: The Police in Action*, PSI study, vol. iv (1983); and R. Reiner, *The Politics of the Police* (2nd edn., 1992), ch. 3.

[26] J. Baldwin, *Supervision of Police Investigations in Serious Criminal Cases*, RCCJ Research Study 4 (1992); Maguire and Norris, above n. 2.

[27] RCCJ Report, para. 2.65.

breed a form of solidarity and defensiveness. To some extent the culture may reflect the differing perspectives of police officers 'at the sharp end' and those officers who are managers, with the lower ranks covering for one another and trying to shield from senior officers various deviations from the rules.[28]

Perhaps the strongest evidence for the existence in the British police of (2), what is termed the 'macho image', came from the PSI study of policing in London.[29] Other researchers refer to the physical dangers of the job, to 'the alcoholic and sexual indulgences' of male police officers, and to the struggle of women police officers to gain acceptance.[30] In respect of racism, however, Robert Reiner suggests that some allegations fail to take proper account of the nature of police work in a society that places ethnic minorities at a disadvantage in many respects.[31] Indeed, Reiner argues more generally that, just as it is unrealistic to regard police malpractices as stemming from isolated individuals without reference to the wider police culture, it is equally unrealistic to focus on the culture without reference to the social structures that contribute to and sustain it. He argues that it is not solely (or even mainly) a result of the type of person attracted into the police force but also a product of 'the role the police are assigned in the social order: moral street-sweeping . . . Police prejudices are more a product than a cause of the differential use of police powers, which is a result of the socially structured nature of the police mandate.'[32]

Central to the cop culture is (3), the idea that rules are there to be used and bent. There are two strands to this. The first emphasizes the use of the criminal law as a resource for legitimating or reinforcing police handling of a situation: the police officer has available a range of offences with which to support his or her authority, and may decide whether or not to invoke one of them as a reason for arrest and charge.[33] Of course this is hardly applicable to crimes such as murder, rape, and armed robbery, but it can be applied to the range of public order offences, obstruction and assault on police officers, and a number of other charges. The primary objective of the police may be to keep the peace and to manage situations; in this they use and exert authority; anyone who resists that authority may be arrested and even charged. The second strand concerns the various procedural rules about questioning, notably the Codes of Practice under the Police and Criminal Evidence Act. The reason these rules are broken from time to time is that they are seen as unwise impediments to proper police work, standing in the way of vigorous questioning

---

[28] See further Reiner, above, n. 25, 115–17.
[29] Smith and Gray, above n. 25.
[30] Reiner, above n. 25, 124–5.
[31] *Ibid.* 156 f.
[32] R. Reiner, 'Policing and the Police', in M. Maguire, R. Morgan, and R. Reiner (eds.), *Oxford Handbook of Criminology* (2nd edn., 1997), at 1024.
[33] For a classic study that highlights this, see E. Bittner, 'The Police on Skid Row: A Study in Peacekeeping' (1967), 32 *American Sociological Review* 699.

which will get at the truth, or (sometimes) will produce the results which senior police officers or the media seem to want. Thus, on the one hand there is pressure arising from the high expectations of others; on the other hand there is a belief that those expectations cannot be met when lawmakers fail to understand the realities of police work. This led Smith and Gray to comment that deviations from proper procedures can be expected to continue 'as long as many police officers believe that the job cannot be done effectively within the rules'.[34]

These two strands coalesce to suggest that there is a police motivation that lies beyond and above the formal rules of the criminal justice system. It flourishes partly because of the discretion actually left to the police by the system, and partly because of their continued ability to circumvent what they regard as fetters unjustifiably imposed on them. This leads us to inquire about (4), the sense of mission in police work. It is an essentially conservative outlook, in social terms, which celebrates the position of the police as a 'thin blue line' standing between order and chaos. It is worth re-emphasizing that the mission, like the culture, is certainly not monolithic. Indeed, the conflict in police ideologies between advocates of 'zero tolerance' and advocates of the 'problem-solving' approach demonstrates one clear difference. The research evidence regards the mission as strengthened by seeing the police as being on the side of the right, serving society and ranged against offenders and other miscreants who are in the wrong. Reiner describes the subtle interplay of three themes—'of mission, hedonistic love of action, and pessimistic cynicism'—that constitute the core of the police outlook.[35] Many officers join the police with a sense of mission, in terms of defending society and its institutions against attack and disorder, and then develop a kind of cynicism about social trends that seem to threaten existing ways of doing things. The Royal Commission appeared to accept some such view:

> We recognize that police malpractice, where it occurs, may often be motivated by an over-zealous determination to secure the conviction of suspects believed to be guilty in the face of rules and procedures which seem to those charged with the investigation to be weighted in favour of the defence.[36]

To be sceptical about the moral quality of this police mission would be easy: it certainly contains its contradictions, in that it purports to emphasize established moral values when there is evidence that some officers rejoice in various sexual exploits, and in that it adopts a puritanical attitude towards drug-users when police alcoholism is a long-standing problem.[37] Yet, these contradictions apart, there is a true sense in which the police are performing

---

[34] Smith and Gray, above n. 25, 230; see also Reiner, *Politics of the Police*, 81–5.
[35] Reiner, above n. 25, 114.   [36] RCCJ Report, para. 1.24.
[37] Reiner, *The Politics of the Police* (2nd edn., 1992), 124.

an essential and central social function. To this extent both the term 'police force' and its modern successor, 'police service', contain elements of realism. There is nothing unhealthy in having a sense of mission about that, any more than it is unhealthy for doctors, nurses, or even lawyers to have a sense of mission. Just as people are right to expect medical care when ill or injured, so citizens are entitled to expect official action when they fall victim to a crime or in the face of threats to good order. Often, this does amount to the protection of the weak against the predatory. But while the vital nature of this social function cannot be disputed, its definition can be. The police culture evidently defines it differently from Parliament, for example, since police officers often express contempt for 'legal restrictions'. There is no question that the maintenance of good order counts, but there is room for debate about what counts as the maintenance of good order.

Rather less is known about the occupational cultures of other groups within the criminal justice system. The police culture has been discussed extensively because it is so well documented. But it should not be thought that other groups do not have occupational cultures which pull against the ethical discharge of their role responsibilities, and a few words can be said here about defence solicitors and crown prosecutors. In the detailed study of a number of criminal defence practices in England and Wales by McConville, Hodgson, Bridges, and Pavlovic, several unethical practices were discovered at various stages. Once again, the researchers do not claim that all criminal defence practices operate, or operated, in this way: indeed, they point out that some practices are well run and properly orientated. But they draw attention to some defence lawyers' failure to protect clients in police stations from improper questioning,[38] encouraging or even engineering a plea of guilty in spite of the client's inclinations,[39] 'selling out' clients in court by using a particular phraseology that makes it clear to magistrates that the lawyer believes that the client's instructions are unworthy of belief.[40] Why might defence lawyers and their staff indulge in these and other kinds of unethical behaviour? The research leads to various suggestions. One of these is that some of the practices are driven by financial considerations, arising from the structure of the legal aid system. There was also evidence that some defence lawyers subscribe to what, in police language, may be termed 'toe-rag theory': that particular clients (or clients of a particular kind, or from a certain family or housing estate) are guilty anyway, are always committing crimes, and therefore it is pointless to go through the motions of a 'full and fearless defence'.[41] This

---

[38] McConville *et al.*, above n. 4, 61–2, 112–15, and 124.
[39] *Ibid.* 70 and 194ff.; also Travers, above n. 4, chs. 5 & 6.
[40] *Ibid.* 180–1; see also A. Hucklesby, 'Remand Decision Makers' (1997) *Crim. LR* 269, at 278–9.
[41] On this, see also A. Mulcahy, 'The Justifications of "Justice" ' (1994) 34 *BJ Crim.* 411.

approach may be underpinned by a desire to keep 'on the right side' of the police and the courts where possible, rather than losing credibility by mounting a vigorous defence of a presumptively guilty villain. This leads the authors to suggest that one of the defects may be in the training of solicitors, in that it fails to emphasize individual rights (now, human rights) and their centrality to the defence lawyer's role responsibilities. In other words, the adversarial system of criminal justice cannot work properly if and to the extent that lawyers fail to provide 'full and fearless' defence of their clients, let alone if they share some of the police views about certain types of client. Even if they happen to be right about certain clients, it is not their function to allow their own judgement to detract from their proper role responsibility.[42]

Lastly, what about unethical behaviour by crown prosecutors? In this sphere there is considerably less research to draw upon, but there is some evidence that crown prosecutors sometimes resolve the conflicting pressures upon them by indulging in unethical conduct. One example already given is that prosecutors may fail to discontinue a weak case, even though aware of the weakness, for reasons which can only be described as unethical—for example, a desire to keep 'on the right side' of the police, or fear of an adverse reaction from the police, or even agreement with the police view that the defendant deserves to be put through a trial.[43] A closely-related example might be where a key exhibit or a vital witness goes missing at the eleventh hour: the ethical approach might be to discontinue, or at least to draw the predicament to the attention of the defence, whereas continuing with the case in the hope that the loss will not come to light is surely unethical. If it is accepted that the role of the prosecutor, even in an adversarial system, is to act as a minister of justice, these and related practices should be condemned as unethical.

4. Justifying 'Unethical' Behaviour by Challenging the Ethics

In the foregoing paragraphs we have discussed possible reasons for the occupational cultures of various criminal justice agencies and for resulting conduct which appears unethical. One element running through these explorations is that some, even many, of those who act in the ways described might argue that their behaviour is ultimately ethical. In other words, they might claim the moral high ground, and argue that the concept of the ethical being relied upon here is flawed, limited, and inappropriate.

[42] See Blake and Ashworth, above n. 7, for further discussion.
[43] Baldwin, above, n. 22.

In order to establish the context for any such redefining of the ethical, we might consider three standpoints that appear to ooze practicality and good sense, particularly among those who work in particular parts of the criminal justice system. The first, already mentioned in one context, is the argument that certain rules should be circumvented because the rulemakers do not understand the practical problems. The second is that it is wrong to expect police, prosecutors, etc. to operate with 'their hands tied behind their backs'. And the third is that, when the Crown Prosecution Service drops a case, or when a court gives a lenient sentence, or even when the Court of Appeal quashes a conviction, this is bad for morale. All these standpoints are connected, but they deserve brief discussion individually.

Is it right to circumvent rules on the ground that the rulemakers do not understand the day-to-day on-the-ground problems of the criminal process? The claim is heard in various quarters. It is heard among some police officers in relation to the Police and Criminal Evidence Act and its Codes of Practice: these are restrictions imposed by people who expect 'results' and yet do not understand the difficulties the police have to encounter. A similar claim might be heard among barristers who resent the procedural imperatives and preparation times associated with Plea and Directions Hearings.[44] There are three problems with a claim of this kind. First, there is the constitutional argument: any official or public organization that substitutes its own judgement for one reached through the appropriate democratic channels is behaving unconstitutionally. Secondly, there is the values argument: that this claim assumes that crime control, in a fairly absolute form, is the only worthwhile value. It gives no weight to the protection of the rights of suspects. And thirdly, there is the evidential argument: is it really true that 'the job' cannot be done if the restrictions are observed? In fact this is less likely to be a matter of evidence than a question of values again, since the claim that the job cannot be done suppresses the unarticulated clause, 'within the prevailing culture'. If a different culture prevailed, perhaps the job could be done. One can only plausibly assert that it cannot be done if one assumes no change in the culture. These three arguments expose the weaknesses of the claim that rules made by out-of-touch rule-makers may be circumvented. They apply no less to the view said to obtain among some magistrates' clerks some years ago, that High Court rulings were there to be circumvented because 'the judges did not understand the practicalities, e.g. of dealing with truculent, often regular, customers, or a busy court schedule'.[45] This, again, seems to have been based

---

[44] RCCJ, para. 7.36, written before the 1996 changes came about. No empirical evidence of compliance since 1996 has appeared.

[45] The words of a magistrates' clerk, quoted by A. Rutherford, *Criminal Justice and the Pursuit of Decency* (1993), 62.

on the assumption that the conviction of the guilty is important above all else.

The second claim is similar in some respects. It is that society expects the police to combat crime with their hands tied behind their backs, or that society expects prosecutors to obtain convictions with one hand tied behind their backs. The precise formulation varies, but the target is always the 'restrictions' imposed, usually by the legislature but sometimes by the higher judiciary. The claim could be countered by means of the three arguments deployed above— the constitutional point, the values argument, and the question of evidence. However, another argument is worth raising here: the assumption that respecting the rights of suspects significantly diminishes the number of convictions and therefore the protection of the public and of victims. This is a complicated argument, requiring considerable space to develop and to rebut. Suffice it to say here that pre-1994 research suggested that the number of extra convictions likely to result from, say, abrogating the right to remain silent during police questioning, without adverse inferences being permitted, was relatively small; it is arguable that the pre-1994 law had a greater impact on police and prosecutors' perceptions than upon the outcome of cases.[46] This brings the discussion to the question of morale.

The third claim is that it is bad for police morale when the Crown Prosecution Service decides to drop a prosecution commenced by the police. Parallel claims are sometimes heard when a court gives a low sentence on conviction, and there is also the suggestion that one reason why station sergeants tend not to refuse charges from officers who bring in arrestees is that it might affect morale. Now as an empirical proposition this claim may well be correct. Such events may reduce police morale, as may new restrictions on their questioning of suspects, changes in their pay and conditions, and several other matters. The problem here is whether one should defer to the conservatism that underlies the morale of many professions, including the police, a conservatism no doubt linked with a sturdy defence of the police mission. The police mission is therefore a crucial element in any attempt to redefine the ethical approach. What kind of ethics, it might be asked, could call into question the vigorous pursuit of the fundamental social functions of crime prevention and conviction of the guilty?

To answer this question, we might begin by constructing a model version of the mission. Some of the main elements have been described above, but there is a need for a rounded version that could fit the words and opinions of police officers. The key element is crime control: this is surely the point of the criminal justice system. It means that law observance should be maintained.

---

[46] See R. Leng, *The Right to Silence in Police Interrogation*, RCCJ Research Study 10 (1993); McConville and Hodgson, *Custodial Legal Advice*, RCCJ Research Study No 16 (1993).

In this the police are inevitably in the front line, having peace-keeping functions that (in terms of time spent) outstrip the processing of suspected offenders. A second element is that, where the interests of the defendant conflict with those of the victim or society, priority should be given to the latter. A third and connected element, following from the first two, is that the police should pursue this society-centred approach so far as is possible, exploiting any discretion left by the criminal justice system in order to further the conviction of those whom they believe to be guilty. Taken together, these elements of crime control and the protection of society may be treated as establishing a powerful case in favour of the police mission. If we are not to descend into anarchy, someone has to do it. Better that it be done in a committed way than without any sense of its social importance.

Assuming that there is some truth in this account, is it defensible? Almost every step suffers from confusion which, when examined, mixes overstatement with understatement and neglects important features of social life. It would be easy to claim that this is because this version of the police mission has been formulated in a way favourable to the thesis being advanced: but the counter-arguments below can be ranged against any other version of the police mission that keeps faith with what has been found by recent on-the-ground research.[47] The counter-arguments are these.

The first element refers to crime control as if it were to be pursued without regard to any other values. Is it plausible to advance such an uncomplicated notion? To take an extreme but telling example, does it suggest that the police should be free to use repressive measures wherever they regard them as appropriate, or that torture should be available for use on those suspected of serious crimes? If the answers are negative, then we need to adopt a more sophisticated and sensitive notion than 'crime control'. Many people might accept at first blush that crime control is the ultimate aim of the criminal justice system, but on reflection they would surely recognize that it ought not to be pursued without qualification. That would lead to a police state.

The second element is that priority should be given to the victim or society over the interests of the suspect/defendant. In the vernacular this might be called 'toe-rag theory', since its essence is that the interests of the innocent and good should be preferred over those of the suspect or defendant. As one constable stated some years ago, 'Speaking from a policeman's point of view it doesn't give a damn if we oppress law-breakers, because they're oppressors in their own right.'[48] This seems to suggest that accused persons should have no rights, or few rights, or at least rights that can be overridden when that is

---

[47] e.g. the research of Maguire and Norris (1993, n. 2 above), for the Royal Commission on Criminal Justice.
[48] Reiner, above n. 25, 111.

necessary in the public interest (as interpreted by the police). This is to turn the idea of rights on its head. The whole idea of rights is that they respect the individual's autonomy and ensure that the individual is protected from certain kinds of inappropriate behaviour and is furnished with certain assistance when he or she is in the hands of public officials. Rights have been termed anti-utilitarian claims, in the sense that they represent claims that the individual be not treated in certain ways even if that might be thought to enhance the general good. However, the idea of priority for 'the interests of society' seems to accord the individual suspect or defendant no particular rights, and to deny the whole legitimacy of human rights such as those incorporated in the European Convention and discussed in Chapter 2 above.[49] Moreover, it does so at a stage before the suspect or defendant has been convicted, thereby affirming a strong presumption of guilt arising from the investigating officer's belief. Is it really acceptable to place so much emphasis on the judgement of one or more police officers, especially when one element in the cop culture is a mutual support and respect for the skills of others which frowns on routine supervision?

These arguments also show the weakness of the third element, always seeking to promote the interests of society against those of the suspect. This is flawed for various reasons. Suspects are members of society. Even members of society who are unlikely to be suspected of crime might accept that those who are suspected should be accorded some rights. Few would agree that it should be for the police to decide which suspects should be accorded rights and which not. The notorious cases of miscarriage of justice leave us well aware that police officers' judgements of someone's guilt or innocence should not be determinative. Surely the ethical approach for the police is to ensure that evidence is collected fairly and then presented to the court for its adjudication. If the right to a fair trial is to be upheld, then it surely requires fairness in the gathering of evidence and construction of the case.

The conclusion is therefore irresistible that the 'police mission' described above cannot claim the moral high ground. It overstates the notion of crime control by assuming that this should be pursued either without qualification or with only such qualifications as the police deem appropriate. It assumes that respect for the rights of suspects is bound to detract from crime control, and does so for insufficient reason. In this it understates the importance of respect for human rights even when accused of a crime. We saw in Chapter 2 that not all human rights are absolute, and that there are various points at

[49] This is not to overlook the importance of victims' rights, which may on occasion conflict with those of suspects or defendants. However, this argument should not be taken as far as those who readily convert 'the interests of society' to 'the interests of victims' would wish to take it. One must first decide what the rights of victims should be: see Ch. 2.3.

which 'public interest' arguments of certain kinds might prevail. If an ethical approach is to be adopted, it is important to adhere to the framework of the European Convention on Human Rights and kindred declarations, rather than to allow 'public interest' reasoning to overpower human rights as and when thought necessary.

Any challenge by prosecutors to the ethical approach might take a similar form: the essence would be that certain rules and procedures stand in the way of what is right in terms of crime control. For example, John Baldwin found that some crown prosecutors would run a relatively weak case where the charge was a serious one: he quotes one as saying that 'the more serious the case and the more finely balanced it is, the more you stretch the point'. He concludes that 'some CPS lawyers share a common value system with the police, a core element of which is that serious cases ought to be prosecuted, almost irrespective of considerations as to evidential strength'.[50] The supporting argument would be, therefore, that this is necessary to ensure that wrong-doers are brought to book, and that the 'stretching' of the rules is justified by that end. The counter-arguments are (a) that this is not the prosecutor's function in an adversarial system, since the prosecutor should act as a minister of justice who is not concerned to maximize the number of convictions but to ensure that the due process of the law is carried through; and (b) that the purported justification that 'there is a lot more at stake in letting a potential rapist, murderer or child abuser off the hook'[51] overlooks what is at stake for the individual defendant, which is why the Royal Commission of 1981 insisted that 'a realistic prospect of conviction', not simply a *prima facie* case, should be required before a defendant is put through a trial.[52]

Might the ethical approach to determining criminal appeals also be challenged? The Court of Appeal (and before it, the Court of Criminal Appeal) has long had statutory powers to quash a conviction if it concludes that a miscarriage of justice has taken place. One might think that the ethical approach is to quash any conviction where the Court takes the view that a miscarriage of justice has occurred. Instead, as both Pattenden and Nobles and Schiff have argued, the Court has always tended to take a narrow view of its proper role.[53] Throughout this century it has exercised its powers in cases where there has been a judicial misdirection or other irregularity, but it has rarely done so where the accuracy of the verdict itself has been challenged. Predominant among the reasons for this has been respect for the institution of the jury—

---

[50] Baldwin, above n. 22, 551.   [51] A senior crown prosecutor, quoted by Baldwin, *ibid.*
[52] For further discussion, see Ch. 6.2.
[53] R. Pattenden, *English Criminal Appeals, 1844-1994* (1995), ch. 4, and the review by R. Nobles and D. Schiff, 'The Never Ending Story: Disguising Tragic Choices in Criminal Justice' (1997) 60 *MLR* 293.

the notion that to go behind the verdicts of juries would be to undermine a cornerstone of English criminal justice. This suggests the existence of an appellate culture which takes a certain view of the proper exercise of the statutory power, even to the extent that the wording of the legislation is rarely considered explicitly by the Court.[54] The suggestion is not that the Court has been subverting the letter of the law, but rather that it has been reluctant to exercise its power for fear of exposing the fallibility of the jury system (a fear that may also underlie the provision in the Contempt of Court Act prohibiting the recording of juries' deliberations). To the extent that this analysis is true, it suggests once again that some wider notion of the public good is being deployed to deny defendants the right to have the fairness of their trials reviewed. Whether the provisions of the Criminal Appeal Act 1995 will succeed in altering the appellate culture remains to be seen.

5. Accountability

It will be evident from the foregoing paragraphs that many of the decisions to be taken by criminal justice agencies are characterized by discretion rather than by binding rules. We have seen, however, that even where rules and procedures have been laid down, they may not be followed faithfully by those to whom they apply. How can it be ensured that the various authorities fulfil their functions and exercise their powers as they ought to? One way of approaching this is through systems of accountability.[55] We have already seen how values such as the protection of declared rights (of victims and suspects or offenders) and the prevention of abuse of power by officials might be threatened if the policies or the practices of a law enforcement agency diverge from the purposes of the system. Methods of accountability should include proper scrutiny of general policies, rules, and/or guidelines for decision-making, active supervision of practice, avenues for challenging decisions, and openness rather than secrecy at key stages.

In a democratic form of society, issues of public policy should be decided by the legislature. However, in matters of law enforcement the tendency has been for Parliament to avoid such issues and to leave them to each agency itself, usually without any check other than the formal requirement to submit annual reports to the House of Commons. Thus agencies such as the Inland Revenue, Customs and Excise, and the Health and Safety Executive are relatively free to determine their own policies—'semi-autonomous', as Dennis

---

[54] K. Malleson, *Review of the Appeal Process* (1993).   [55] *Borgers* v. *Belgium* (1991) A. 214.

Galligan puts it[56]—although some of their procedures will be authorized by statute. The Crown Prosecution Service has been similarly unregulated: statute requires the Service to formulate a code and to report annually to Parliament, but there is no legislative guidance on substance. The police are also relatively free in this regard, although the Home Office sends guidance by circular to chief constables which is then used as a basis for appraisal by Her Majesty's Chief Inspector of Constabulary. The police are still subject to local control through police authorities, but one effect of the Police Act 1996 is to increase the power of central government over these bodies. It is, of course, possible for the Government to put pressure on agencies to modify their policies, by relating financial provision to the fulfilment of performance targets, but that hardly qualifies as a form of accountability. Law enforcement bodies are also open to scrutiny from various government and parliamentary sources. The Select Committee procedure applies, and thus the Home Affairs Committee has examined the performance of such organizations as the police, the Crown Prosecution Service, the Forensic Science Service, and the Prison Service. Within Government, there is also the role of the Audit Commission in assessing the performance of agencies. The existence of these bodies adds to accountability, even though their direct powers are limited. However, there are too few official inspectorates in the criminal justice system. The police, the Probation Service, and the Prison Service have long been overseen by Her Majesty's Inspectors. But neither the CPS nor any of the other prosecuting authorities, including the regulatory agencies and the Inland Revenue, for example, is subject to any form of inspectorate. And there is certainly no such body to oversee the work of defence lawyers who receive criminal legal aid money, let alone the work of the judiciary.

Are law enforcement agencies accountable to the courts? There is a number of public law doctrines available, but the tendency has been to confine judicial review to the outer limits of unreasonableness (by applying the *Wednesbury* principle).[57] In recent years there have been some moves towards the scrutiny of certain policies for and against prosecution,[58] but the prevailing attitude remains one of reluctance. It is possible that judicial scrutiny will become greater when the Human Rights Bill 1998 comes into force: the legislation will require 'public authorities' to respect the rights in the European Convention on Human Rights, and this is likely to lead to challenges from individuals in respect of policies or decisions which are alleged to have breached the Convention to their detriment.

Claims for greater openness, as a step towards public accountability, are always likely to be unwelcome in a sphere that has long known secrecy.

---

[56] (1978) A. 25, at 78.   [57] (1989) 11 EHRR 117.   [58] (1993) *The Times* 27 May.

Following the Scarman Report,[59] the Metropolitan Police developed local consultative committees, neighbourhood watch schemes, and other links with the community.[60] There are schemes for lay visitors in police stations,[61] and 'appropriate adults' must be summoned to interviews of young people and of mentally handicapped people at police stations. Proposals for greater openness in plea bargaining might have similar benefits, in so far as they lead the participants in decision-making to take greater care to follow the rules, but the judiciary has opposed them.

Accountability is an important feature of a criminal justice system. It encourages transparency, it may enhance the protection of the rights of individuals, and it helps to ensure that the power entrusted to law enforcement authorities is not abused. However, it would be wrong to rely on *post hoc* accountability methods to secure these desirable goals. There is plenty of evidence, discussed in detail in Section 2 above, that rules and guidelines may be limited in their practical effect if their purpose and spirit are not accepted by those who are supposed to operate them. It will therefore be argued that there is a key role for training and for ethical orientation.

6. Criminal Justice Reform through Ethics

Law enforcement agencies and the administration of criminal justice are governed by masses of legislative rules, and yet it is well established that (i) even rules can be adapted, (ii) there are wide areas of discretion, and (iii) there must continue to be some areas of discretion. One step, to respect the principle of legality declared in Article 7 of the ECHR and 'rule of law' ideals,[62] is to attempt to structure discretion by the use of guidance and guidelines. Other common features of reform proposals are better training of criminal justice personnel and better lines of accountability. Measures of this kind, espoused in various forms by such politically disparate groups as the 1993 Royal Commission on Criminal Justice after their review of criminal justice processes and by Michael McConville, Andrew Sanders, and Roger Leng at the end of their sharply critical research report on police and prosecution services,[63] are now recognized to be far more promising than mere changes in legal rules.

---

[59] Cf. von Hirsch and Ashworth, *Principled Sentencing* (2nd edn., 1998), 55–6 and ch. 2 generally.
[60] *Report 82* (1984), para. 81.
[61] Y. Kamisar, 'Comparative Reprehensibility and the Fourth Amendment Exclusionary Rule' (1987) 86 *Michigan LR* 1, discussed in Ch. 4.
[62] For discussion, see P. H. Robinson, 'Legality and Discretion in the Distribution of Criminal Sanctions' (1988) 25 *Harvard Journal on Legislation* 393.
[63] M. McConville, A. Sanders, and R. Leng, *The Case for the Prosecution* (1991), ch. 10.

The reason for this is the strength of occupational cultures within such key agencies as the police, the Prosecution Service, the various regulatory inspectorates, defence solicitors, the criminal Bar, the Forensic Science Service, and so on. More has been said here about the occupational culture of the police, to some extent justifiably since they form the principal filter into the criminal justice system, but we have also reviewed evidence on occupational cultures within the Crown Prosecution Service, among defence lawyers, and even among appellate judges. What is noticeable about at least some of the occupational cultures in criminal justice is that their concern is not simply to preserve established working practices or to defend traditional territories of influence, but also to see that 'justice' is done. This is the sense of mission. Everything turns, of course, on what one takes to be 'justice' in this context. We must refuse to accept references to 'the interests of justice', 'the public interest', and even (more emotively) 'the interests of victims'—unless it is carefully spelt out how exactly these rather sweeping claims have been arrived at. We need to identify the values that underlie such statements, and then consider what values should be recognized in criminal justice. This is where the ethical approach should be reasserted.

In order to expect those working in the criminal justice to adopt an ethical approach, it is necessary to have some kind of code of ethics. To expect rules alone to change behaviour may be naïve, but without some rules or guidance it is unlikely that behaviour will be changed at all. So the priority must be to formulate and to develop codes of ethics that not only set out the proper spirit and orientation of those performing certain functions, but also give examples of points at which an ethical approach might differ from an unethical approach. In this respect, both the General Council of the Bar's *Code of Conduct for Barristers* and the Law Society's *Code for Advocacy* stand in need of some reconsideration. Both have been revised in recent years, of course, but the use of examples could improve them significantly. Although the Bar's *Code of Conduct* includes some ethical principles for prosecutors, these should be reconsidered and an ethical code for Crown Prosecutors developed in parallel. It is, to say the least, unfortunate that the CPS's *Statement of Values and Purpose* does not include a proper set of ethical principles.

In order to formulate such principles, reflection on the proper roles of the various groups and agencies within the criminal justice system would be needed. The literature of English criminal procedure is replete with statements about the proper role of the prosecutor. In the nineteenth century it was said that the motivation of a prosecutor should be that of a Minister of Justice,[64] and this was elaborated by Sir Herbert Stephen when he wrote that

---

[64] Crompton J in *Puddick* (1865) 1 F. & F. 497.

the object of the prosecutor should be 'not to get a conviction, without qualification, but to get a conviction only if justice requires it'.[65] Christmas
Humphreys, writing as Senior Crown Counsel, stated that 'the Crown is interested in justice; the defence in obtaining an acquittal within the limits of lawful procedure'.[66] The rhetoric of this position recognizes that crime control
should not be regarded as the sole or dominant aim of the prosecutor, and
that the concept of justice also includes recognition of certain rights of defendants and of victims.[67] The CPS *Statement of Purpose and Values* refers to the
importance of treating victims with 'sensitivity and understanding' and com-
mits the Service to 'treat all defendants fairly'. There is a little elaboration of
the latter point,[68] but this particular document stops short of giving guidelines or even examples of practices this would favour or disfavour. Among the
issues that need to be discussed are cases where the prosecutor realizes that the
court has made an error in favour of the prosecution, where the prosecutor
realizes that certain evidence may have been obtained unfairly, where the
prosecutor enters into plea negotiations despite doubts that the charge(s) can
be sustained in court, and where the prosecutor makes representations at
remand proceedings even though it is unclear that the statutory requirements
for a custodial remand are fulfilled.[69]

In respect of defence lawyers the reasons for spelling out the ethical
approach are no less pressing. It is insufficient to state, in a broad way, that the
lawyer should seek to protect the client while not misleading the court. There
must be a sharper statement of the defence lawyer's primary function: if it is
'to promote fearlessly and by all lawful and proper means the lay client's interests',[70] then it is essential to spell out what this entails in a range of common
situations. Among those would be the problems of defending a person
believed to be guilty, particularly where the lawyer believes that perjury has
been or will be committed; where the defence lawyer knows of an error of law
in the proceedings which favours the defence; where the defence lawyer knows
of an error of fact in favour of the defence; where advice has to be offered to a
client who wishes to plead not guilty; where the client wishes the lawyer to
make an application for bail against the lawyer's professional judgement; and
so on.[71]

[65] H. Stephen, *The Conduct of an English Criminal Trial* (1926), 11.
[66] C. Humphreys, 'The Duties of Prosecuting Counsel' (1955) *Crim. LR* 739, at 741.
[67] Cf. C. M. Nissman and E. Hagen, *The Prosecution Function* (1982), 2: 'In pursuing his goal to
seek justice, the prosecutor must punch through the tiresome criminal defender, whose goals are
necessarily in conflict with the search for truth and justice.'
[68] CPS, *Statement of Purpose and Values*, 8, 10; cf. also CPS, *Statement on the Treatment of Victims
and Witnesses by the Crown Prosecution Service* (1993).
[69] For elaboration, see Blake and Ashworth, above n. 7.
[70] For references, see *ibid.* 17–18.
[71] See *ibid.* and, more generally, D. A. Ipp, 'Lawyers' Duties to the Court' (1998) 114 *LQR* 63.

The reason for emphasizing the importance of giving examples is to try to give the ethical principles the greatest chance of practical success. While many lawyers are dismissive of rules of this kind, on the basis that 'each case depends on its own facts', this is most likely when the principles are highly abstract. The purpose here, as elaborated in the earlier parts of this chapter, would be to confront those elements of occupational culture that are known to run counter to an ethical approach. Defining the role responsibility of a defence lawyer, prosecutor, or appellate judge is the first step. But no less essential is the further step of putting together examples of situations where there may be a divergence between the ethical and other approaches.

Once this has been done, the next step would be to inculcate the principles through training and other means. The main task would be to convey the reasons why these principles are worth adhering to, whether by abstract instruction or by means of role-play exercises, debates, etc. This approach must be integrated into a programme for retraining personnel at all levels, from senior management down to new recruits. Otherwise, a statement of ethical principles would be a poor match for a well-entrenched occupational culture. The key questions must be addressed convincingly: why must I show respect towards someone who admits to a dreadful crime? If I feel that I can solve a difficult case by deviating from the rules, is it not in the interests of society that I should do so? Both the democratic argument and ethical principles should be elaborated in reply.

These broad prescriptions should be no less applicable to other groups such as judges, court clerks, the forensic science service, the so-called 'regulatory' agencies and so on. No doubt some will be sceptical of the claims of the ethical approach, particularly when pitted against entrenched occupational cultures in certain spheres. Certainly no claim is being made here that, even if successfully defined and then inculcated, it would solve the problems of the pre-trial process. Rather the argument is that it ought to be recognized as a worthwhile part of altering the orientation of the system towards the ideals and values set out in Chapter 2 above. Simply declaring those principles, or other legal rules, is unlikely to work, for reasons that have been explained. The ethical approach may be viewed as preventive, in the sense that it seeks to foster ethical conduct that will lead to fewer 'system errors' and fewer miscarriages of justice. But of course it would need to be supported by a full system of accountability, which is why the importance of inspectorates was urged in Section 5 of this chapter. Other remedies, including independent and workable complaints mechanisms, should also be developed. More will be said on these issues as we proceed through the next six chapters, in which the interactions of the various criminal justice agencies among themselves, and with suspect-defendants and victim-complainants, will be examined.

Part II

Particular Decisions

4   Investigating Crime

THE process of investigating crime, before a suspected offender is charged or summoned, is the subject of this chapter. The process varies between simple and complex cases, between police and non-police agencies. What remains fairly constant, however, is the high significance of judgements made at this early stage. As the case against a particular person begins to take shape, so (in most cases) does the investigator's belief that that person is guilty. Much as the system may provide for review of investigators' judgements—see, for example, Chapter 6 on prosecutorial review—the original file put together by the police will have a considerable hold. Prosecutors do not review two files, one for the prosecution and one for the defence. They are merely provided with the police file, and that may well have been constructed in a way that is selective in what it includes and excludes, that interprets certain phenomena in accordance with the investigating officer's beliefs, and that tends to present the 'evidence' so as to support a particular conclusion. These are familiar aspects of arguing a case, whether in business, in a debate, in court, in the family, etc. Attention has been drawn to this tendency of the police by various committees and commissions,[1] and some officers would say that the police now guard against it. But police culture may be more resilient than that, and there have certainly been cases in the 1990s where a blinkered approach to investigation has come to public attention in a high-profile case.[2]

The legislative framework of pre-trial investigation has altered quite significantly in the past two decades. In the 1980s the trend was to increase the amount of formal regulation, largely through the Police and Criminal Evidence Act 1984 and its Codes of Practice. This body of rules is not simply designed to improve the reliability of investigative practices, with a view to minimizing the number of mistakes and maximizing the pursuit of the truth. Some of the rules uphold certain rights of suspects and defendants, such as the right to legal advice. Others are mainly aimed at increasing accountability, although that can be linked ultimately to the protection of individuals

---

[1] For example, the Fisher report into the *Confait* case (1977), the Royal Commission on Criminal Procedure (1981) and the Royal Commission on Criminal Justice (1993).

[2] e.g. *Fergus* (1994) 98 Cr.App.R. 313, discussed in Ch. 1.3 above.

from the wrongful or excessive use of official power. Rules of these kinds create a tension if it is assumed that the primary purpose of the police is to prevent and detect crime, since it is then a short step to regarding as obstructive those rules designed to uphold rights or to enhance accountability. The tension may sometimes be resolved, as we saw in Chapter 3, by indulging in unethical behaviour. Wide-ranging as the regulations flowing from the Police and Criminal Evidence Act are, they leave some unregulated discretion and, and more tellingly, leave room for the police to 'cover their backs'[3] by appearing to have complied with the formalities when they have not.

The trend in the 1990s has been somewhat different. The tape recording of questioning in police stations has become the norm, with a special Code of Practice to regulate the conditions and requirements. Thus, as the police have found that the questioning of suspects has become more fully regulated, and (which the police would emphasize) as more crimes have become difficult to investigate by traditional methods, they have tended to turn more towards proactive or 'intelligence-led' policing.[4] Thus the 1990s have seen a shift away from the centrality of the interviewing of suspects towards the targeting of people believed to be involved in crime currently, bringing to bear on them a whole range of techniques from informants to sophisticated listening devices or cameras. Among the more publicized steps in this direction have been the development of NCIS, the National Criminal Intelligence Service, and the Audit Commission's 1993 call on the police to 'target the criminal, not just the crime'.[5] At the same time the police have begun to alter their interviewing techniques, leading one of England's foremost Chief Constables to state that:

> The result is that training within the service today encourages a far less confrontational style of interviewing, and this is underpinned by psychological research which has demonstrated conclusively that aggressive questioning of victims or witnesses is rarely the most effective way to learn the truth.[6]

The terms of this remark are confined to the interviewing of victims and witnesses, but there are more general claims about the effect of 'ethical interviewing' styles on the police approach.[7] Indeed, even in 1993 these claims

---

[3] A major practical concern, as identified by R. Reiner, *The Politics of the Police* (2nd edn., 1992), ch. 3.

[4] For a valuable review, see M. Maguire and T. John, 'Covert and Deceptive Policing in England and Wales: Issues in Regulation and Practice' (1996) 4 *European Journal of Crime, Criminal Law and Criminal Justice* 316.

[5] Audit Commission, *Tackling Crime Effectively* (1993), 54.

[6] C. Pollard, 'Public Safety, Accountability and the Courts' [1996] *Crim. LR* 152, at 154, citing G. Kohnkren, 'The Evaluation of Statement Credibility: Social Judgment and Expert Diagnostic Approaches', in J. R. Spencer *et al.* (eds.), *Children's Evidence in Legal Proceedings* (1989).

[7] T. Williamson, 'Reflections on Current Police Practice', in D. Morgan and G. Stephenson (eds.), *Suspicion and Silence* (1994).

were sufficient to persuade the Royal Commission that there was no need for further regulation in this sphere.[8] To what extent the new interviewing style is 'ethical' depends very much on one's definition of the term: it has been argued that the new style is 'ethical' largely in its endeavour to avoid tactics which have led courts to exclude the resulting evidence, rather than out of any deeper commitment to respecting the rights of suspects.[9]

The 1990s have in fact seen a shift in power that few would have predicted in the opening years of the decade. We saw in Chapter 1 that the major miscarriages of justice uncovered at that time led to the appointment of the Royal Commission, partly to restore confidence in English criminal justice. Yet the police were promoting the argument that the miscarriages case arose from (a) the misconduct of individuals and (b) mistakes in the past which could not be repeated in the modern, post PACE era, and that the real need was to move on and to give the police greater powers to deal with new, threatening, and insidious forms of crime. The strongest police lobby was for the abolition of the suspect's right of silence. The Royal Commission, as discussed in detail below, rejected this argument and recommended the retention of the existing protections for suspects (although much wider police powers to take samples from suspects were recommended). But the political climate was so different when the Royal Commission reported from the climate at the time it was appointed that the police continued to press. In Michael Howard as Home Secretary they found a receptive politician, and a police 'shopping list' emerged that was bold enough to go against one of the Royal Commission's principal recommendations. That 'shopping list' had a least three major items on it: abolition of the right of silence, radical overhaul of the system of pre-trial disclosure, and statutory authorisation for electronic surveillance of suspects. The middle years of the decade saw the enactment of legislation to bring about all three changes—partly a testimony to the continuing power of the police in British politics, partly a result of the resonance of their demands with the interests of a government desperately hoping that tough 'law and order' policies would bring electoral success, and perhaps partly as a way of dealing with the seemingly insoluble conflicts in policing. These conflicts stem from the facts, on the one hand, that the police themselves solve relatively little crime (victims, witnesses, and even defendants take the major role in most detections) and that there is substantial evidence that increasing the number of police officers makes little impact on detection rates,[10] and on the

---

[8] *Report*, ch. 4.

[9] T. Newton, 'The Place of Ethics in Investigative Interviewing by Police Officers' (1998) 37 *Howard JCJ* 52.

[10] See, e.g., M. Hough, 'Thinking about Effectiveness' (1987) 27 *BJ Crim.* 70, and R. Reiner, 'Policing and the Police', in M. Maguire, R. Morgan, and R. Reiner (eds.), *The Oxford Handbook of Criminology* (2nd edn., 1997), 1036–9.

other hand the continuous pressure from governments for greater effectiveness and higher performance in controlling crime. It is hardly surprising that these pressures lead the police to call for greater investigative powers. What is unfortunate is that the rhetoric of senior police officers is so dismissive of individual rights: thus Charles Pollard wrote, *in 1996*, that 'exclusive promotion of the defendant's legal rights [*sic*] has helped insulate the trial from the need to prevent offending behaviour and the broader issue of public safety', [11] and an influential document from the Association of Chief Police Officers made occasional vague references to the rights of suspects and defendants without any clear statement of what they are and with the clear implication that they should be kept to the minimum.[12] These points will be taken up again at the end of the chapter.

This chapter will consider a wide range of techniques and stages in investigation. It will refer frequently to the police, as the major law enforcement agency, but it should be borne in mind that HM Customs and Excise and some other agencies operate in similar ways and are often (but not always) subject to similar limitations. The second and third items on the police 'shopping list' for reform (pre-trial disclosure of evidence, authorization of intrusive surveillance) will be discussed in Section 2 below, with over a dozen other issues. But we begin with a detailed discussion of the 'right of silence' debate. This has been, and will probably continue to be, the major battlefield of the 1990s; the Royal Commission's preference for retention, the curtailments introduced by the 1994 Act, the operation of that Act in practice, and the impending challenge under the European Convention on Human Rights (particularly in view of the Human Rights Bill).

1. Silence and the Presumption of Innocence

One of the fundamental principles discussed in Chapter 2 was the presumption of innocence. The link between the presumption and the right to remain silent during police questioning has been recognized many times, notably by the Royal Commission on Criminal Procedure in 1981[13] and by the European Court of Human Rights in 1993.[14] If there is to be a presumption that a person is innocent until proved guilty by the prosecution, there appears to be some inconsistency in holding that the defendant can through his or her silence supply an element in that case. On the other hand there is the power-

---

[11] C. Pollard, 'Public Safety, Accountability and the Courts' [1996] *Crim. LR* 152, at 153.
[12] ACPO, *In Search of Criminal Justice* (1995).   [13] RCCP Report, paras. 4.51–4.52.
[14] *Funke, Cremieux and Miailhe* v. *France* (1993) A. 256.

ful rational appeal of the argument that, if a person is presented with a set of apparently incriminating facts, it is reasonable to expect a reply and silence may be evidence of guilt. But the rationality of this approach is weakened when it is recalled that there may be other reasons for silence, apart from guilt. In dealing with the issues, the Royal Commissions of both 1981 and 1993 took the 'middle line' that adverse inferences from silence would be permissible once the defendant had received full notice of the prosecution case and had declined to comment on it.[15] But both Royal Commissions argued that it would be inappropriate to permit adverse inferences to be drawn from silence in the face of police questioning, since the defendant is unlikely to know what evidence the police have and police stations are known to be perceived by many suspects as intimidating. This approach signals the importance of keeping separate the arguments for allowing adverse inferences from silence during the trial and the arguments for allowing adverse inferences from silence at the interviewing stage. Although much of the discussion below will be in general terms, we will return periodically to this vital distinction.

The discussion below is in four parts. First, the case in favour of retaining a right of silence is outlined. Secondly, the changes introduced by the 1994 Act are examined. Thirdly, recent evidence on the operation of the 1994 Act in practice is discussed. And fourthly, the prospects of challenging the 1994 Act as an encroachment on the right to a fair trial, guaranteed by Article 6 of the European Convention on Human Rights, will be explored.

1. *The right of silence debate*: from among the many arguments in this debate,[16] we may select for brief discussion three theoretical and three practical reasons which appear to have played their part. The first theoretical argument stems from the presumption of innocence: that a defendant should be presumed innocent until and unless proved guilty by the prosecution, and to cast any burden on the defendant breaches this principle. This argument is at its strongest in the police station: if a suspect's refusal to answer questions from the police may be treated as supplying evidence for the prosecution, then the rule that permits such inferences weakens the presumption of innocence. Part of the strength of this argument stems from a second principle, described sometimes as the privilege against self-incrimination. There is no constitutional or statutory declaration of the privilege against self-incrimination in English law, but it has been recognized judicially in the House of Lords: 'The underlying rationale . . . is, in my view, now to be found in the maxim *nemo*

[15] For a thoughtful review of the debate until 1990, see S. Greer, 'The Right to Silence: A Review of the Curent Debate' (1990) 53 *MLR* 709.

[16] See S. Easton, *The Right to Silence* (1991); R. Leng, *The Right to Silence in Police Interrogation: A Study of Some Issues underlying the Debate*, RCCJ Research Study No. 10 (1993); and I. Dennis, 'Instrumental Protection, Human Right or Functional Necessity? Reassessing the Privilege against Self-Incrimination' (1995) 54 *Camb. LJ* 342.

debet prodere se ipsum, no one can be required to be his own betrayer or in its popular English mistranslation "the right to silence".'[17] Although spoken in a different context, these words recognize the place of the privilege against self-incrimination in the English criminal process. It can be justified by arguing that the State should not indulge in the unfairness of forcing on defendants a choice between speaking and convicting themselves out of their own mouths, or not speaking and being convicted by default. This does not suggest that it is wrong for investigators to question suspects at all, but it does yield a strong argument of principle against drawing adverse inferences from an unwilling-ness to answer. The argument may, however, be less strong if the prosecution has already made out a case to answer at trial.

A third argument, based on privacy, has been developed by Dennis Galligan and receives support from Article 8 of the European Convention: 'everyone has the right to respect for his private and family life, his home and his corre-spondence.' Galligan argues that the right not to be compelled to vouchsafe one's secrets is particularly important when the aim of questioning is to obtain evidence for use against the person. If the right of privacy is to have any meaning, then these are surely the cases in which it should be asserted. We should no more approve of the imposition of a requirement to answer ques-tions, on pain of adverse inferences, than of the compulsory use of machines that can extract information directly from the human memory.[18] This rationale can claim to be more fundamental than the privilege against self-incrimination and the presumption of innocence, since it is directly con-nected with the concepts of personhood and respect for individual autonomy. However, Galligan recognizes that privacy cannot be regarded as an absolute right, and we have seen that Article 8.2 of the ECHR sets out various grounds on which the right to privacy might justifiably be infringed, the investigation of serious crime being one of them. This does not empty Galligan's argument of significance—indeed, it bolsters his view that the propriety of derogating from it cannot be left to the judgement of police officers and ought to be set-tled at the level of general policy—but it warns of the need for careful and principled decisions on the justifications for derogating from the right.

Turning now to the pragmatic reasons, these are often thought to work in favour of abolition of the right of silence. Thus it is argued that the right has enabled defendants to 'ambush' the prosecution by withholding the nature of their defence until the trial is underway, thereby reducing the prosecution's opportunity to assess and/or rebut it. This point was recognized by statute in 1967, when the Criminal Justice Act introduced a requirement on the defence to give notice of an alibi defence, so as to afford the police adequate time to

[17] *R. v. Sang* (1979) 69 Cr.App.R. 282, at 290, per Lord Diplock.
[18] Galligan, 'Right to Silence Reconsidered', [1988] *CLP* 80, 88–90.

check it; it was recognized again in the Police and Criminal Evidence Act 1984 in relation to expert evidence. However, the notion that the prosecution suffers greatly from ambushes has been questioned in research for the 1993 Royal Commission by Roger Leng, who points out that at most 5 per cent of contested trials involved a line of defence that could be described as an ambush, and that in some of these cases the surprise stemmed from a failure by the police to take a suspect's earlier explanation seriously enough to investigate it. Of the cases where the defence was known before the trial, Leng calculated that this advance notice assisted the prosecution in about one-fifth.[19]

Another practical challenge, equally difficult to substantiate, is that the right of silence was used by professional criminals to avoid conviction. The Royal Commission of 1993 concluded that this argument was unproved,[20] but it has a powerful rhetorical effect, especially when images of organized crime and ruthless gangsters can be mobilized in support.

A further pragmatic argument, this time used in support of the right, is that the balance of power in the pre-trial stages of the criminal process is so much in favour of the investigators that the right of silence is needed to protect suspects from being overborne. Among the evidence led in support of this are the findings on the psychological effects of police interrogation;[21] the finding that the police still sometimes fail to inform suspects of their full rights or, when they do give the information, convey it in a manner calculated to persuade them to waive some rights;[22] and the superior access of the police to forensic science laboratories and other expert services.[23] This is challenged by those who want to see the right of silence removed or curtailed. They argue that the spread of legal aid and duty solicitor schemes now puts suspects on a par with the police, and that the provisions for an 'appropriate adult' afford sufficient protection to vulnerable suspects. In favour of this reply are those cases in which a defendant arrives at a police station with his or her own solicitor, with the result that the constable questioning the suspect may feel under greater pressure than the suspect. This was the position described by Lawton LJ in the judgment in *Chandler*.[24] However, it is a relatively unusual situation, as we will see in paragraph 3 below. Whether the wider availability and (possibly) higher quality of legal advice ought to be relevant depends very much on the legal adviser's knowledge of the evidence that the police possess against the suspect, to which problem we return several times below.

---

[19] Leng, *The Right to Silence*, RCCJ Research Study No. 10 (1993).
[20] RCCJ Report, para. 4.17.
[21] e.g. Irving and Hilgendorf, *Police Interrogation*, Royal Commission on Criminal Procedure Research Study No. 1 (1980) and Gudjonsson, *The Psychology of Interrogations* (1992).
[22] See below, s. 2(8).   [23] See below, s. 2(16).   [24] (1976) 63 Cr.App.R. 1.

The 1993 Royal Commission expressed its recommendations in terms of a 'balance' of practical considerations: the risk to innocent persons, especially those who are less experienced and more vulnerable, is such as to outweigh the probable increase in convictions of the guilty. Evidence of breaches of the PACE Codes of Practice by the police shows that they cannot be trusted to honour the compromise struck by the existing law under the Police and Criminal Evidence Act, and this tells against giving them more legal power in relation to suspects.[25] It should be noted, however, that this is merely a contingent argument, as was that advanced by the Royal Commission of 1981. Since it is not expressed as resting on any fundamental principles, it is an argument that could be rebutted if certain practices were altered. The conclusions of the majority of the 1981 Royal Commission are worth stating at length:

> Quite apart from the psychological pressures that such a change [sc. abolishing the right of silence] would place upon some suspects it would . . . amount to requiring a person during investigation to answer questions based upon possibly unsubstantiated and unspecific allegations or suspicion, even though he is not required to do that at the trial. Such a change could be regarded as acceptable only if, at a minimum, the suspect were to be provided at all stages of the investigation with full knowledge of his rights, complete information about the evidence available to the police at the time, and an exact understanding of the consequences of silence.[26]

This shows recognition of the pressure on suspects in police custody. It also recognizes the dangers of allowing answers or non-answers to questions put by the police at that time to constitute evidence: much depends on the basis for and the form of the questions put, a point developed powerfully by Michael McConville and Jacqueline Hodgson in their research report for the 1993 Royal Commission.[27] But it still seems to suggest that there might be a regime under which silence at the stage of police questioning might fairly be regarded as providing evidence against a defendant; and, by implication, it does not militate against drawing adverse inferences from silence in court.

2. *The 1994 legislation*: it was the pragmatic arguments, pushed forward by the alliance of the police and the Home Secretary, that led to the extraordinary spectacle of the Government rejecting one of the Royal Commission's most carefully reasoned recommendations. The Royal Commission had recommended changes in other respects which would assist the police—notably, by proposing reforms of the disclosure rules which would, for the first time, require disclosure by the defence that might be expected to reduce the inci-

---

[25] RCCJ Report, para. 4.23.   [26] RCCP Report, para. 4.52.
[27] McConville and Hodgson, *Custodial Legal Advice*, RCCJ Research Study No. 16 (1993).

dence of 'ambush' defences—but this did not divert the Home Secretary from striking what he presented as a significant blow for 'law and order'. Arguments that the Royal Commission had considered and rejected were repeated without qualification—particularly the 'professional criminals' claim—and the legislative proposals passed into law without major difficulty. It is not appropriate in the present context to analyse sections 34 to 37 of the Criminal Justice and Public Order Act 1994 in detail:[28] the paragraphs below outline the main provisions and refer to their interpretation by the courts.

It is convenient to begin with section 35, which concerns silence at trial. The essence of this section is that a jury or magistrates 'may draw such inferences as appear proper from the failure of the accused to give evidence or his refusal, without good cause, to answer any question'. The first point about section 35 is that it assumes that the prosecution have already adduced sufficient evidence to raise a 'case to answer':[29] no adverse inferences can be drawn from the defendant's silence unless and until the prosecution has cleared that hurdle. It is not yet known what factors might amount to 'good cause' for declining to answer certain questions. However, section 35 also makes it impermissible for the court to draw an adverse inference if 'the phsyical or mental condition' of the accused makes it 'undesirable for him to give evidence'. The defence attempted to invoke this proviso in *Friend*,[30] where a 15-year-old (described by the clinical psychologist as 'mentally handicapped', with a mental age of around 9 to 10) declined to give evidence. The judge considered the matter fully and decided that the jury should be allowed to draw inferences from the boy's failure to testify, and the Court of Appeal held that this ruling was not manifestly 'unreasonable'—a rather harsh and restrictive decision. Where the grounds for drawing an adverse inference are present, it does not follow that the court has to infer guilt. Counsel may be able to suggest plausible reasons for drawing other inferences, but 'if the jury conclude the silence can only sensibly be attributed to the defendant's having no answer or none that would stand up in cross-examination, they may draw an adverse inference'.[31]

The central provision in the 1994 Act is section 34, which allows a jury or magistrates to draw inferences from an accused's failure to mention, when questioned under caution or on being charged with an offence, any fact on which he subsequently relies in his defence, so long as the fact is one which in the circumstances he could reasonably be expected to mention. The first point is that this only applies to silence after having been cautioned, and the new

---

[28] For a thorough examination, see P. Mirfield, *Silence, Confessions and Improperly Obained Evidence* (1997), ch. 9.

[29] See s. 38(3) and also *Cowan* [1996] QB 373.   [30] [1997] 2 Cr.App.R. 231.

[31] Per Lord Taylor CJ in *Cowan* [1996] QB, at 381.

form of caution draws attention to the possibility that silence 'might harm your defence'. The silence itself, i.e. the failure to mention a matter, may occur at any time after caution, and this may include questioning outside the police station which is not tape recorded. Most of the appellate rulings on section 34 relate to the question of when an accused might reasonably be expected to have mentioned a fact. The court must have regard to 'the circumstances existing at the time', and this was held in *Argent*[32] to include the accused's mental and physical condition. In *Condron and Condron*[33] the accused were drug addicts suffering from withdrawal symptoms. The police surgeon certified them as fit to be interviewed, whereas their solicitor took a different view. The Court of Appeal's decision focuses on the legal advice (to remain silent) then given to the defendants, rather than on the sufficiency of the original condition as a 'circumstance' that might make it unreasonable to expect a response in interview. This takes us to what has emerged as the key issue: whether a lawyer's advice to remain silent constitutes, of itself, a reasonable excuse for silence. The Law Society's guidance to solicitors made it clear that one reason for advising a client to remain silent is where the police have failed to give a full and clear summary to the lawyer of the evidence then in their possession. This is the issue which was regarded by the two Royal Commissions as crucial: that a suspect's silence should not be used by the prosecution if he does not know what case he has to meet. However, the Court of Appeal seems to have been impressed with the argument that, once 'lawyer's advice' were treated as a reasonable excuse, that would render section 34 wholly nugatory. This was a primary reason for the finding in *Condron and Condron* that there was no reasonable excuse for the silence. In *Argent*[34] the defendant's solicitor did not believe that the police had given him sufficient information about the case against his client and so he advised silence. The accused appealed against his conviction, citing his solicitor's advice as reasonable grounds for remaining silent. The Court of Appeal would go no further than to suggest that the advice given and the reasons for it were matters to be considered by the tribunal of fact when deciding whether to draw an adverse inference from the silence. Although the Court was right to say that the compliance of the solicitor with Law Society guidance was not conclusive of reasonableness, it was once again conscious that any general concession to legal advice as reasonable grounds would emasculate section 34. The fine line drawn by the courts was evident again in *Roble*,[35] where Rose LJ accepted that if 'the interviewing officer had disclosed little or nothing of the nature of the case against the defendant' this may amount to good reason for a solicitor to advise silence and a defendant to remain silent. But the matter remained one

---

[32] [1997] 2 Cr.App.R. 27.   [33] [1997] 1 Cr.App.R. 185.   [34] [1997] 2 Cr.App.R. 27.
[35] [1977] *Crim. LR* 449.

to be considered by the jury or magistrates, along with any other circumstances.

There is also the question of what inferences from a defendant's failure to mention a fact are 'proper'. In some circumstances a court is highly likely to draw the inference of guilt, unless the defence can suggest another plausible explanation for silence. Various other explanations are possible: it seems that a court should consider the possibility that the accused remained silent because that was the legal advice received, or even (going to 'second-order' reasons) because that legal advice was based on his lawyer's view of his mental or physical condition at the time or because the advice was based on the police's failure to declare what evidence they had against the accused. The authorities cited in the previous paragraph show that none of these situations necessarily defeats the reasonable expectation that the accused would reply to police questions, but it remains possible that they might suggest to the jury other inferences they could properly draw from silence. Probably, however, the most powerful explanation for silence is where it appears that the defendant was trying to shield another: this has long been recognized as a reason why an accused might tell lies to the police,[36] and there may be cases in which it can be advanced as the proper inference to draw from failure to mention key facts at an early stage.

Sections 36 and 37 of the 1994 Act create the possibility of adverse inferences in two further situations. Section 36 allows an adverse inference from the failure to give an explanation for objects, substances, or marks on him or in his possession or at the place where he was arrested. The section is peremptory: there is no question of whether or not it would be reasonable to respond, or whether the defendant subsequently relies on the matter in his defence. Failure to give an explanation may become part of the prosecution case, subject to the drawing of proper inferences from the accused's silence when it was put to him. Section 37 allows an adverse inference from the accused's failure to account for his presence at a place or about the time when the alleged offence was committed: again, the section is peremptory in its operation. Before either a section 36 or a section 37 inference may be drawn, it must be established that the police officer gave a 'special warning' to the accused about the possibility of adverse inferences being drawn from a failure to offer an explanation.

3. *The 1994 Act in practice*: in what ways have the provisions on adverse inferences from silence altered practices in the criminal process? No figures have yet been produced on the effect of section 35, and the proportion of defendants declining to give evidence or declining to answer some questions

---

[36] See, e.g., *Lucas* [1981] QB 720, *Goodway* (1993) 98 Cr.App.R. 11.

in court is not known. A Home Office study by Bucke and Brown, based on cases at some twenty-five police stations, shows that 'special warnings' under section 36 or 37 were given to 7 per cent of all suspects interviewed.[37] It seems that these were all interviewees who exercised their right of silence generally, since it is reported that the 7 per cent constituted 39 per cent of 'suspects exercising silence'. In this study some three-quarters of those given 'special warnings' under sections 36 and 37 offered no explanation for the incriminating evidence or for their presence at the scene, and a further 10 per cent gave what the police regarded as an unsatisfactory explanation. Thus in only around 15 per cent of cases was a plausible explanation given. Since this study did not follow cases to court, it is not clear what impact the suspect's silence in these respects had upon the course of the prosecution.

What effect did section 34 have upon the course of interviews? The study by Bucke and Brown confirms that the number of police detainees requesting legal advice continues to grow: it was around 25 per cent in 1989, went up to some 32 per cent in 1992, and reached 40 per cent by 1996.[38] Of those interviewed by the police in Bucke and Brown's study, some 52 per cent had received no legal advice, 9 per cent had received only pre-interview advice, whereas some 39 per cent had a legal adviser present during the interview. Legal advisers would presumably inform their clients of the possibility of adverse inferences from silence, as well as tendering whatever other advice they think fit in the case.[39] Bucke and Brown found that the rate of confessions was 'broadly similar' (slightly higher) after the 1994 Act compared with earlier (58 per cent of interviewees, compared with a pre-Act study yielding 55 per cent). On the crucial issue of silence at interview, much depends on the way in which the figures are calculated. Bucke and Brown show that more suspects were invoking their right of silence in the early 1990s than in previous years, and speculate that this may be linked to the higher proportion of suspects taking advantage of legal advice. They then compare the figures from the post-Act study (in late 1995 and early 1996) with another Home Office study prior to the 1994 Act, and produce the following table:

	Refused all questions	Refused some questions	Answered all
Phillips and Brown (pre-1994 Act)	10%	13%	77%
Bucke and Brown (post-1994 Act)	6%	10%	84%

[37] T. Bucke and D. Brown, *In Police Custody: Police Powers and Suspects' Rights under the Revised PACE Codes of Practice*, Home Office Research Study 174 (1997), ch. 4.
[38] *Ibid.*, 19.   [39] All figures in this paragraph are taken from *ibid.* ch. 4.

In so far as these figures are robust,[40] they suggest a significant but only partial shift in practice. Refusals to answer questions were more common where the offence charged was serious and, independently, refusals were higher for men than for women and for suspects from an Afro-Caribbean background compared with suspects who were white or from an Asian background.

The study also yields interesting data on the types of questions suspects refused to answer. An analysis of some 314 cases in which suspects answered some questions and refused to answer others shows that 48 per cent of questions refused concerned the suspect's involvement in the offence, but 46 per cent concerned only the involvement of others in the offence, and 6 per cent were questions unrelated to the offence. This is important for two reasons. First, it would rarely be proper to draw an adverse inference under the 1994 Act from failure to answer a question relating to another person's involvement—certainly no inference can be drawn against that other person. And secondly, it seems plausible that a proportion of the interviews in which the suspect refused to answer all questions could be explained by the desire to shield someone else: this was the argument made at point 2 above, although it would not be easy for the defence to establish this in a way that persuaded a court not to draw an adverse inference from the silence.

The study by Bucke and Brown does not link these investigative practices to the outcome of cases, and so we lack post-1994 data on the conviction rate and its relationship to exercises of the right of silence. In their study for the Royal Commission, Zander and Henderson found that about one-half of defendants who remained silent in the police station went on to plead guilty, and that, of those who remained silent and pleaded not guilty, a higher proportion were convicted than acquitted.[41] Post-1994 data are awaited.

4. *Challenging the 1994 Act*: it was argued at point 1 above that Parliament was wrong to alter the law in 1994. However, it did not 'abolish the right of silence' as such, for various reasons. For one thing, it is still lawful for a defendant to remain silent when interviewed: there is no compulsion to speak, and the statistics above show that a small proportion of suspects exercise their right and take their chance on the consequences. What the 1994 Act has done is to extend significantly the possibility of courts drawing adverse inferences from failure to answer some or all questions, in the police station or at court. For another thing, there was no general 'right of silence' before 1994: Parliament had introduced some forms of compulsion in certain types of

---

[40] They come from the same 8 police stations. However, (a) data elsewhere in Bucke and Brown's report show considerable variations in practice among police stations across the country, and (b) the authors promise a further report with more detailed evidence in due course.

[41] M. Zander and P. Henderson, *Crown Court Study*, Royal Commission on Criminal Justice Research Study No. 19 (1993), para. 1.2.2.

case,[42] and even at common law there were situations in which adverse inferences might lawfully be drawn. However, the 1994 Act did introduce momentous changes, and the fact that Parliament had previously curtailed the 'right of silence' in particular spheres does not establish that it was right to do so. The question to be considered here is whether these various legislative incursions on the right are vulnerable to challenge under the European Convention on Human Rights.

We saw in Chapter 2.4 that Article 6 of the ECHR declares a right to a fair trial, followed by several specific guarantees for criminal cases in 6.2 and 6.3. The provisions most likely to be invoked in a challenge to sections 34–37 of the 1994 Act are the right to a fair hearing (Article 6.1) and the presumption of innocence (Article 6.2). The starting point must be the proposition that 'the right to remain silent under police questioning and the privilege against self-incrimination are generally recognised international standards which lie at the heart of the notion of fair procedure under Article 6'. This was laid down by the European Court of Human Rights in *Murray* v. *UK*,[43] and it explains why in the subsequent decision in *Saunders* v. *UK* the Court found that the use of statements obtained from Saunders under the compulsory powers in section 434 of the Companies Act 1985 was oppressive and deprived him of a fair hearing. The Companies Act gives inspectors the power to question individuals, with a penalty of up to two years' imprisonment for failure to answer, and such a provision squarely interferes with the right to silence in a way that a power to draw adverse inferences may not do. So the first point to be made is that the various statutory powers in English law which compel people to answer questions on pain of imprisonment will have to be repealed when the Human Rights Bill comes into force, unless a decision is taken by the Government to defy the ECHR on this point. It should be noted, however, that the Court in *Saunders* drew a rather unexpected distinction between admissions and statements by the accused and real evidence obtained as a result of compulsory procedures. Referring to material 'which has an existence independent of the will of the suspect', it held that provisions for the seizure of documents obtained pursuant to a warrant, for the taking of samples of breath, blood or urine, and for taking bodily tissue for DNA purposes do not necessarily conflict with the right to a fair procedure. This was an unexpected statement, because in the earlier case of *Funke, Cremieux and Miailhe* v. *France*,[44] the court held that by prosecuting Funke in order to compel him to provide documentary evidence of offences that the customs authorities thought he had committed, the French

---

[42] See J. D. Jackson, 'The Right of Silence' (1994) 57 *MLR* 270.

[43] (1996) 22 EHRR 29, at 60; reiterated by the Court in *Saunders* v. *UK* (1997) 23 EHRR 313, at 317.

[44] (1993) 16 EHRR 297.

customs infringed 'the right of anyone "charged with a criminal offence" . . . to remain silent and not to contribute to incriminating himself'. This ruling applied to documents seized under compulsory powers. However, the result of this part of *Saunders* seems to be to confine the privilege against self-incrimination to compelled oral statements. That may mean, in turn, that there is no room for an argument that various compulsory powers to take intimate samples contravene the privilege. This conforms to the view taken by the United States courts, following Wigmore,[45] but it is far less persuasive in theory than it is as a matter of practical policy.[46]

Against that general background, what specific grounds exist for challenging the 'right of silence' provisions in the 1994 Act? The leading case is *Murray* v. *UK*, based on the Northern Ireland evidence ordinance (in similar terms to the 1994 Act) as applied in a trial by judge alone. The trial judge stated that he drew adverse inferences from Murray's failure to account for his presence at the scene (equivalent to section 37 of the 1994 Act) and from his failure to give evidence at his trial (equivalent to section 35). The European Court of Human Rights held that the trial did not involve a breach of either Article 6.1 (fair hearing) or 6.2 (presumption of innocence). However, in interpreting *Murray* it is essential to keep in mind the precise reasons given by the Court, and the fact that the appeal did not concern silence in the face of police questioning. The first point about the Court's judgment is its endorsement of the privilege against self-incrimination and right of silence in general. Then, it is important to recall that the question is whether Murray's trial itself was fair. The Court held that it was, chiefly because the other evidence against him was strong. The Court took the view that it would be 'incompatible' with the right of silence and privilege against self-incrimination 'to base a conviction solely or mainly on the accused's silence or refusal to answer questions or give evidence himself'. In this case the adverse inference was fairly obvious in view of all the other evidence. Thus the *Murray* decision does not in any way give ECHR approval to sections 34 to 37 of the 1994 Act.[47] On the contrary, it is clear from the judgment that in a case where the evidence is much less convincing than it was in *Murray*, any drawing of adverse inferences might well violate the right to a fair hearing and the presumption of innocence. One such case is to come before the Court soon.[48] The 1994 Act itself does state that an

---

[45] Cf. S. Easton, 'Bodily Samples and the Privilege against Self-Incrimination' [1991] *Crim. LR* 18 with Dennis (above, n. 16) at 373–5.

[46] Art. 6 declares what was termed (in Ch. 2, above) a 'strong right', rather than a *prima facie* right that leaves room for exceptions based on certain clearly defined criteria.

[47] See generally R. Munday, 'Inferences from Silence and European Human Rights Law' [1996] *Crim. LR* 370.

[48] Another Northern Ireland case, *Quinn* v. *UK* (1996) 23 EHRR CD 41, has been found admissible by the Commission.

inference drawn under one of the four sections may not be the sole reason for committing a case for trial, for holding that there is a case to answer, or for convicting an accused. But the *Murray* judgment suggests that a higher threshold may be necessary to show compliance with the ECHR. The point is reinforced by the European Court's insistence that the accused should have been cautioned (which is required by all four sections of the 1994 Act) and its reference to the importance of legal advice. Legal advice was not crucial in the decision on the facts in *Murray*, but one would have thought that it is essential if inferences drawn under section 34, 36, or 37 are to be held not to fall foul of the ECHR. This is because of the emphasis placed in *Saunders* on the right of silence as a right not to be coerced into speaking, and also because of the rather restrictive interpretation given by the English courts to the notion of a reasonable excuse for remaining silent. There is a strong hint in the European Court's decisions that, if the police have not informed the suspect and his lawyer about the case against the suspect, a subsequent failure to answer questions (following advice to this effect from the lawyer) should not lay the defendant open to adverse inferences in court. The emphasis in *Murray* on the strength of the other evidence against the defendant gives considerable support to this interpretation.

The submission here, then, is that section 34 of the 1994 Act probably does breach Article 6.1 and 6.2 of the ECHR, and that in a case such as *Argent*,[49] where the police had failed to give the legal adviser sufficient information on the case against the accused, an English court (applying the ECHR, once the Human Rights Bill is in force) ought not to permit adverse inferences and ought to hold that section 34 is incompatible with the ECHR. The point may be thought to be strengthened by the fact that in *Murray* v. *UK* the European Court relied on the professionalism of the judge-only tribunal in that case. In an ordinary trial by jury, the tribunal's deliberations cannot be discovered; even if the judge's summing up is fair, one cannot be sure about the inferences actually drawn by the jury. The difficulties are no less acute in a magistrates' court.

2. Issues in Investigation

None of the eighteen issues will be discussed in full here.[50] In respect of each one, the law and/or regulations will be described, research on practice will be

---

[49] [1997] 2 Cr.App.R. 27, above, p. 102; of course the court would need to be satisfied, as a matter of fact (and judgment), that the police had failed to furnish sufficient details of the case against the accused.

[50] For fuller discussion of the relevant rules of evidence and court decisions, see P. Mirfield, *Silence, Confession and Unfairly Obtained Evidence* (1997) and S. Sharpe, *Judicial Discretion and Criminal Investigation* (1997); for fuller discussion of relevant research and policy, see A. Sanders and R. Young, *Criminal Justice* (1994).

noted, any sanctions for non-compliance will be mentioned, and there will be brief discussion of any relevant proposals from the 1993 Royal Commission on Criminal Justice and any recent legislative or judicial developments. The concern is more with the general ethos and general problems of investigation than with a comprehensive or critical survey of the law and practice. However, one general point should be made about the PACE Codes of Practice and the legal significance of any breach. The Court of Appeal has emphasized on several occasions that proof of breach of a Code of Practice does not lead automatically to exclusion of the evidence thereby obtained.[51] Much will depend on such matters of judgement as whether the breach is substantial, whether it had a significant effect on the defendant's conduct, whether it was deliberate or in good faith, and so forth. These judgements will be made in applying two provisions in the Police and Criminal Evidence Act 1984. The first is section 76 (2):

> If, in any proceedings where the prosecution proposes to give in evidence a confession made by an accused person, it is represented to the court that the confession was or may have been obtained—
> (a) by oppression of the person who made it; or
> (b) in consequence of anything said or done which was likely, in the circumstances existing at the time, to render unreliable any confession which might be made by him in consequence thereof,
> the court shall not allow the confession to be given in evidence against him except in so far as the prosecution proves to the court beyond reasonable doubt that the confession (notwithstanding that it may be true) was not obtained as aforesaid.

It will be seen that, if 'oppression' is proved, the court must exclude the resulting confession.[52] In other cases, the test is whether the circumstances and what was said or done were likely to render unreliable 'any confession which might be made by him', a hypothetical question that leaves room for evaluative judgments in the courts. However, confessions in general and breaches of the Codes of Practice in particular may also be brought within section 78 (1), which states:

> In any proceedings the court may refuse to allow evidence on which the prosecution proposes to rely to be given if it appears to the court that, having regard to all the circumstances, including the circumstances in which the evidence was obtained, the admission of the evidence would have such an adverse effect on the fairness of the proceedings that the court ought not to admit it.

Although this section refers expressly to the circumstances in which the evidence was obtained, it also leaves the court with an evaluative judgment to

---

[51] e.g. Delaney (1988) 88 Cr.App.R. 388, Keenan (1989) 90 Cr.App.R. 1.
[52] See *Fulling* [1987] 2 All ER 65.

make. It will be seen below that not all breaches of a Code of Practice have resulted in exclusion.

There is, however, a further factor to be taken into account when considering the exercise of the court's discretion under section 78. This is the ECHR, assuming that the Human Rights Bill becomes law. Where one or more of a defendant's rights under the Convention have been breached, should not the court be obliged to exclude the evidence resulting from that breach? At present there is no case law on this, since the ECHR has not been treated as binding on English courts. However, the matter was considered by the House of Lords in *Sultan Khan*,[53] although unfortunately the speeches contained rather more in terms of general rhetoric than detailed analysis of Article 8 and the European Court's jurisprudence. The conclusion was that, even if there had been a breach of Article 8, a judge would not be required to exclude the resulting evidence. That statement should be read against the background of the ECHR in the distance. When the Human Rights Bill propels it into the foreground, English courts ought surely to hold that breach of a Convention right is a strong, if not conclusive, reason in favour of exclusion. In so far as a breach of Article 6 is established, that must surely follow. In respect of Article 8 the approach is more complex, since a breach of the right of privacy guaranteed by Article 8.1 can be justified if the conditions set out in Article 8.2 are fulfilled. If those conditions are found not to have been fulfilled, exclusion under section 78 ought surely to follow. There will be further references to the ECHR as we review the various decisions at the investigative stage.

1. Entrapment: the vast majority of offences coming to the notice of the police are reported by members of the public. Indeed, in a majority of cases the public also gives information which leads the police to the suspect.[54] However, there are some forms of crime (notably drug dealing) of which the police cannot obtain much evidence without engaging in undercover operations. Police officers may themselves infiltrate groups as part of under-cover operations, and the police may make use of informers—themselves often small-time criminals—in order to obtain information about offences and offenders. It has already been argued that recent years have seen a trend towards proactive policing, of which the use of informers and of undercover police officers are examples. There is, however, the important issue of safeguards: if the operations of the police or their informers instigate the commission of offences that would not otherwise have been committed, is this not unfair on the entrapped person? Is it right that the police should be able to tempt people into committing offences?

---

[53] [1996] 3 WLR 162, below, para. 14.

[54] e.g. M. McConville, A. Sanders, and R. Leng, *The Case for the Prosecution* (1991), 19, who found that 70% of arrests stemmed from information from the public.

In focusing on entrapment, our attention here is confined to the activities of police and informers *before the commission of an offence*. Methods of detection after an offence has been committed are discussed in several other paragraphs below. When activities bordering on entrapment came to the attention of the courts in a number of cases in the late 1960s, the issue was mainly one of ensuring that courts were told where one of the parties was an informer, particularly in cases where this might have a bearing on the legal elements in the offence.[55] The Home Office issued guidelines on this matter, stating without qualification that no police officer should counsel, incite, or procure the commission of a crime.[56] Subsequently, however, defence counsel pressed the issue of the impact of entrapment on the culpability of the defendant, and the question came before the House of Lords in *Sang* (1980).[57] The House upheld previous decisions to the effect that entrapment cannot be a defence to criminal liability in English law, and then argued that it would be inconsistent to approve a discretion to exclude evidence obtained by entrapment, since this would often have the same practical effect as allowing a defence. So far as the court was concerned, mitigation of sentence and the disciplining of errant police officers were the most appropriate responses to clear instances of instigation. There is no shortage of examples of sentences being mitigated to reflect the possibility that the offence might not have taken place if there had been no entrapment,[58] although the courts have been unwilling to mitigate the sentence if it appears that the offence was substantially planned before or without the involvement of the informer.[59]

There is a strong argument of principle that mitigation of sentence is not a sufficient safeguard for people who are approached by undercover police officers and tempted into crime:[60] it fudges the question whether this was really an example of the police creating a crime and a criminal, in which case there is a strong argument for a defence to liability, or was in fact a routine criminal transaction by the defendant which on this occasion happened to involve an informer or police officer. In many practical situations the line between encouraging the commission of an offence and 'stringing along' a person in order to obtain evidence may be gossamer thin, but it is highly significant in point of principle. Moreover, there is a powerful argument that law enforcement officers

---

[55] The leading case was *Birtles* (1969) 53 Cr.App.R. 469; cf. also *Macro* [1969] *Crim. LR* 205.

[56] Home Office Consolidated Circular to the Police on Crime and Kindred Matters (1969).

[57] [1980] AC 402; see J. D. Heydon, 'Entrapment and Unfairly Obtained Evidence in the House of Lords'. [1980] *Crim. LR* 129.

[58] e.g. *Underhill* (1979) 1 Cr.App.R(S) 270; *Beaumont* (1987) 9 Cr.App.R(S) 342; *Chapman and Denton* (1989) 11 Cr.App.R(S) 222; *Perrin* (1992) 13 Cr.App.R(S) 518.

[59] *Kelly and Holcroft* (1989) 11 Cr.App.R(S) 127.

[60] A. Choo, *Abuse of Process and Judicial Stays of Criminal Proceedings* (1993), ch. 6; A. J. Ashworth, 'Entrapment' [1978] *Crim. LR* 137.

whose duty is to prevent crime should not be allowed to engage in the creation of crime and that, when they do so, it is inadequate simply to exclude evidence or to mitigate sentence. The courts should insist on the integrity of the criminal process by granting a judicial stay of the proceedings where the entrapper's activities have crossed the boundary of permissibility.[61]

In the last decade the courts have shown a greater willingness to address the problems of entrapment through the law of evidence and criminal procedure. The enactment of section 78 of the Police and Criminal Evidence Act 1984 provided courts with a new statutory discretion to exclude evidence and a new opportunity to elaborate some guidance. In *Gill and Ranuana* (1989)[62] the Court of Appeal held that *Sang* does not preclude the exercise of the section 78 discretion in entrapment cases, although the speeches in *Sang* must be kept in mind. The Court of Appeal then gave rounded consideration to the issues in *Smurthwaite* and *Gill* (1994),[63] two separate cases in which the defendants had sought the murder of a spouse by soliciting a person who turned out to be an undercover police officer. The court accepted that entrapment could be relevant to the exercise of the section 78 discretion, and it set out six considerations to be taken into account. These will now be examined critically:

(i)   '*Was the officer acting as an* agent provocateur *in the sense that he was enticing the defendant to commit an offence he would not otherwise have committed?*' This factor may be said to roll together two separate issues. The first is whether the undercover officer's conduct amounted to 'enticing' or inducing the defendant to commit the offence. There are questions of degree here: merely expressing a willingness to respond to a request to perform a task may be one thing, whereas positively offering to do that (e.g. by killing another or asking for a certain quantity of drugs) goes significantly further. But there is also the key question of the defendant's disposition. By what means can we tell whether this is an offence 'he would not otherwise have committed'? In the United States, where entrapment may afford a defence to a criminal charge, the central issue is whether or not the defendant had a 'predisposition' towards the offence. The House of Lords endorsed the relevance of this factor in *Latif and Shahzad*,[64] where there was some evidence that the defendant had previous involvement in drugs. A previous criminal record may be thought strong evidence of 'predisposition', but this

---

[61]   Choo, above n. 60; see now *R. v. Horseferry Road Magistrates' Court, ex p. Bennett* [1993] 3 WLR 90, where the House of Lords went beyond *Sang* in holding that a prosecution may be stayed 'if it offends the court's sense of justice and propriety to be asked to try the accused in the circumstances of a particular case'.

[62]   [1989] *Crim. LR* 358.   [63]   [1994] *Crim. LR* 53.   [64]   [1996] 1 WLR 104.

draws the inquiry into the controversial area of targeting known criminals (with the danger of 'rounding up the usual suspects') or of targeting people whom the police *believe* to be involved in a certain illegal activity. These dangers make it imperative that, at the least, there is strong accountability for the actions of undercover officers and informers engaged in this type of work.

(ii) *'What was the nature of the entrapment?'* This should really be the first question, a pure question of fact.

(iii) *'Does the evidence consist of admissions to a completed offence, or does it consist of the actual commission of an offence?'* This alerts the court to the distinction between entrapment proper (involvement in the commission of the offence) and other forms of proactive policing in order to detect crimes already committed, which are sometimes loosely termed 'entrapment' but are dealt with separately in the following paragraphs.

(iv) *'How active or passive was the officer's role in obtaining the evidence?'* This is an important issue in determining the answer to question (i) above, but its formulation here gives no clue to where exactly the line is to be drawn between permissible and impermissible encouragement by the officer. For clarity and for the protection of police officers there is a need for some guidance on how to deal with standard types of situation, even if complete guidance is unattainable.

(v) *'Is there an unassailable record of what occurred, or is it strongly corroborated?'* This is a question of evidence, although it carries a clear implication that good practice should lead to the tape recording of these kinds of encounters with suspects. The question raises no issues of principle.

(vi) *'A further consideration for the judge in deciding whether to admit an undercover officer's evidence is whether he has abused his role to ask questions which ought properly to have been asked as a police officer and in accordance with the Codes.'* This relates, not so much to cases of entrapment proper, but more widely to cases where the undercover officers are seeking to obtain evidence of offences already committed. The point is discussed in some detail below.[65]

These guidelines range fairly widely, but they do not cover the whole field. They should be read as a senior judge's attempt to bring some order to an otherwise uncertain part of the law, i.e. the exercise of the section 78 discretion in this type of case. They are no substitute for a more comprehensive set of guidelines, drawn up in response to the different types of proactive policing

---

[65] See para. 2 below.

and aimed at law enforcement officers in the first instance. Exclusion under section 78 is retrospective and therefore not always helpful in conveying the boundaries of permissibility to police officers, particularly since such a small proportion of cases result in a trial in which the section is invoked.

Why should such guidance be drawn up? The main reason is that people should not be at risk of having their virtue tested by the operations of the police or other agencies, unless there are (at least) reasonable grounds to suspect the person's involvement in unlawful activities. As emphasized earlier, there are dangers in allowing the police to mount these operations, particularly against people with previous convictions. What should be the purpose of the guidance? Its purpose should be to form part of a system of accountability in which this type of proactive policing, whether by undercover officers themselves or by officers briefing informers, is subjected to prior authorization, careful recording, and proper supervision. There is evidence that at present the use of informers, in particular, is little regulated in some police areas;[66] given the power over individuals involved in these activities, accountability is essential. What form should the guidance take? Guidance cannot be comprehensive. What it should do is to articulate certain principles, and then apply them to a range of situations. Among the principles should be subsidiarity (entrapment-type methods should not be used if less intrusive or less compromising approaches are possible) and proportionality (any use of these methods should be proportionate to the seriousness of the crime). Among the situations to be covered should be the areas described as 'entrapment' above: how far may officers go in arranging a meeting on request from others, initiating such a meeting; telling other conspirators that the officer has contacts of a certain kind, pressing people to supply items (typically drugs) by making repeated requests, etc. (The current Home Office circular states merely that the role of the participating informer should be 'passive and minor', but greater detail should be given through selected examples. And what inducement may the police properly offer to an informer?) The guidance should also extend to other forms of proactive policing such as 'sting' operations and 'manna from heaven' operations (which are difficult to justify, since they are indiscriminate and amount to widespread virtue-testing). The guidance should ideally be published as a Code of Practice.

Of great practical relevance is how the defence is to discover whether an informer or under-cover officer was involved in the case. The general issue of disclosure is examined in paragraph 18 below, but it should be stated here that the judge ought always to be told when an informer or undercover officer has played a part in the offence. This would be a minimum requirement. In prin-

---

[66] See C. Dunnighan and C. Norris, 'A Risky Business: Exchange, Bargaining and Risk in Recruitment and Running of Informers by English Police Officers' (1995) unpublished.

ciple, the defence ought to be told because of the possibilities of abuse and overstepping of proper boundaries by the informant or officer; but the police would protest that this might reveal the identity of the informant or officer, with consequent risks to that person's safety. One answer to that would be for English criminal procedure to introduce procedures to allow witnesses to remain anonymous without detracting from the rights of defendants to examine witnesses.[67]

There remains the question of sanctions. No doubt it is right that a police or customs officer who breaches the Code of Practice should be subjected to internal disciplinary procedures. The more fundamental issue is what effect such a breach should have upon proceedings against the defendant. In principle, there is a strong argument for introducing a defence of entrapment into English law, at least to deal with those cases where a person who has no proven predisposition to commit this type of offence (a highly contestable concept) is induced to commit an offence.[68] Similarly effective, however, would be reliance on the power to stay proceedings, as in Canada where there is a well-developed set of criteria to determine whether the conduct of the police or informer has exceeded the proper boundaries.[69] It is now established that the doctrine of abuse of process might be invoked in England in an entrapment case, even though in *Latif and Shahzad*[70] the application failed. The section 78 discretion should be used in cases where the police methods involve a significant breach of the Code of Practice to the detriment of the defendant's rights, without constituting entrapment as such. This would be, as it were, a second line of defence. Mitigation of sentence is simply not an adequate response to cases of entrapment or rank flouting of the rules. This is not the place, however, to develop detailed guidance and criteria. The main purpose is to establish the principles.

2. Electronic surveillance: we move now from proactive policing before the commission of a crime to proactive policing after the commission of the crime and in order to detect the offender. That may, of course, involve the use of informants and under-cover officers. Although there will be no further specific discussion of that here, all that was written in the previous paragraphs about the need for accountability and record-keeping remains equally relevant. Although we are not now dealing with entrapment in the strict sense, there is still the possibility of deceptive practices and other techniques that might involve either abuse of power or infringement of suspects' rights. (Some of these issues are taken further at point 14 below.)

---

[67] Cf. *Doorson* v. *Netherlands* (1996) 22 EHRR 330 with *Van Mechelen* v. *Netherlands* [1997] HRCD 431.

[68] See further A. Ashworth, *Principles of Criminal Law* (2nd edn., 1995), 237–9.

[69] *Mack* (1988) 44 CCC (3d) 513; for discussion, see G. Robertson, 'Entrapment Evidence: Manna from Heaven or Fruit of the Poisoned Tree?' [1994] *Crim. LR* 805.

[70] [1996] 1 WLR 104 (HL).

The focus of this point is upon electronic surveillance. It is widely acknowledged that the use of surveillance devices has increased considerably in recent years, particularly (but by no means exclusively) in the detection of drugs offences. This raises a range of issues, particularly in relation to the right of privacy under Article 8 of the ECHR, and more generally about the propriety of surveillance cameras in many public places. Some of the issues concern the use of the devices at all, others concern the use to which the resulting recordings are put. The brief discussion here will be confined to the electronic surveillance of individuals' private communications, by whatever method (telephone tapping, electronic eavesdropping, secret filming, accessing e-mail, and so on).

At first sight it may appear that this subject has been well taken in hand by the legislature, and that concerns about the protection of privacy and controls on the use of power by investigative agencies are being met. It is certainly true that there has been considerable legislative activity: the Interception of Communications Act 1985, the Intelligence Services Act 1994, the Security Services Act 1995, and the Police Act 1997. The 1985 Act established a regime for the approval, recording, and monitoring of the interception of telephonic communications: a senior judge is appointed as Security Commissioner, and issues annual reports. There was much public debate when it was originally proposed, in the Police Bill 1997, that police entry on to private property to plant surveillance devices should be authorized by a senior police officer. The principle of prior judicial authorization was resisted on the basis that decisions needed to be taken rapidly and that police authorization was therefore the only practicable approach, despite the fact that judicial authorization is the norm in many other Commonwealth and European countries. In the end the Police Act 1997 provides for initial authorization by a police officer of at least Assistant Chief Constable rank, with review by a Commissioner, who will also investigate complaints of abuse brought by citizens. Although the police maintain that their own internal procedures provide more effective scrutiny than a judicial procedure, that remains to be established by objective evidence (particularly in respect of Canada, where independent security-cleared counsel may appear at judicial authorization proceedings). In principle, judicial authorization is the right approach where the right of privacy is in question.

There are also other difficulties with the English approach, among them the definition of 'serious crime' and the attitude to the ECHR. On the former point, all the statutes rightly provide (following the *Malone* ruling[71]) that

---

[71] *Malone* v. *U.K.* (1984) A.82, a decision of the European Court of Human Rights that the absence of a statutory procedure for the approval of telephone-tapping breached Art. 8 of the ECHR, since it could not be said that the invasion of privacy was 'in accordance with the law'. This ruling led to the 1985 Act.

intrusive surveillance is permissible only where the crime is serious. However, the definitions in the Interception of Communications Act and subsequent statutes approach this awkward issue (for there is no simple dividing line) by reference to the probability that a first offender would receive a sentence of at least three years for the offence, or where the offence 'involves the use of violence, results in substantial financial gain or is conduct by a large number of persons in pursuit of a common purpose'. The last three categories are extremely loose: does any violence, however minor, suffice? Would a planned protest demonstration fulfil the last requirement? Moving to the compliance of English law with the ECHR, the difficulty is that the legislature has dealt only with specific situations and specific types of surveillance device. The legislation is piecemeal and casuistical, and provides no general procedure for all kinds of surveillance which might intrude on privacy. Thus in *Halford* v. *UK*[72] the European Court of Human Rights found that English law breaches Article 8 because the 1985 Act fails to extend to internal telephone systems within the police or within a company, which it ought to do. Similarly, there is no legislative regime to deal with several other forms of intrusive surveillance, such as accessing a person's e-mail. If the spirit of the Human Rights Bill is to be followed, the government should make haste to introduce a unified procedure which provides, preferably, for prior judicial authorization of all forms of surveillance which involve an infringement of the right of privacy protected by Article 8. Similarly, the legislation should ensure that the restrictive principles in Article 8.2 are honoured when providing for exceptions to the right. Prominent among those should be the principle of subsidiarity (that a breach of Article 8 should only be contemplated when no other method of investigation is likely to be effective) and the principle of proportionality (that the invasion of privacy should be in proportion to the crime under investigation). This is an area where, in the past, arguments about the public interest in investigating serious crime have been allowed to trample over human rights arguments without much pause.

3. *Interviewing victims*: in relation to the majority of crimes, which are reported to the police by members of the public, one of the first tasks is to obtain a statement from the victim. Where the alleged offence is a particularly sensitive one, such as a sexual assault or violent attack, the need to show due respect for the victim's feelings is obvious. About three-quarters of the victims of violent or sexual crimes participating in the survey by Shapland, Willmore, and Duff expressed satisfaction with the approach of the police, whereas some 6 per cent were not satisfied.[73] At that time, in the early 1980s, much publicity

---

[72] [1997] HRCD 555; cf. also the effect of *Effik and Mitchell* (1994) 99 Cr.App.R. 312 (cordless phones outside 1985 Act).

[73] J. Shapland, J. Willmore, and P. Duff, *Victims in the Criminal Justice System* (1985), 34–5.

had been given to the overbearing and disrespectful manner of some police officers when dealing with women who alleged they had been raped. In 1985 the Women's National Commission produced a report recommending changes of approach in the questioning of victims of rape and domestic violence,[74] including awareness training about the effects of victimization. It is often said that police practices now show greater respect for victims, following a circular of 1990,[75] but research on child victims by Morgan and Zedner casts doubt on this.[76] In over a third of their cases—mostly involving sexual abuse or assault, physical assault, or theft—dissatisfaction was expressed by children or parents about the police response to the complaint. This was a reaction to the whole investigation, but many were distinctly dissatisfied with the manner of police questioning. The majority of child victims of violence or sexual offences said they felt that the police did not believe their account,[77] although some police forces have set up specialist units for sexual abuse cases and the response of victims and their families was much more favourable here.[78] The Royal Commission noted the difficulties of interviewing victims and witnesses who may be in a distressed or vulnerable state, recommending improved police training and the adoption of the guidelines for rape and domestic violence cases in other cases too.[79] In so far as the police fail to measure up to these standards, it seems that the causes lie partly in ignorance about the psychological state of the victims and the effect of their questioning, and partly in a desire to determine whether the victim would be a credible witness in court.[80] The latter point raises an awkward conflict between respect for the victim's feelings and the importance (for victims as well as defendants) of not proceeding to trial if the case lacks reasonable prospects of conviction.[81] The Victim's Charter does not deal with the treatment of victims by the police during questioning, but it does indicate how to complain about police practices or procedures.[82]

4. *Stop and search*: sections 1–3 of the Police and Criminal Evidence Act 1984 permit the police to stop and search a person when they have reasonable grounds for suspicion that articles unlawfully obtained or possessed are being carried. Code of Practice A sets out the procedure to be followed when exercising this statutory power. Official statistics show that the number of stop-

---

[74] For discussion of the report and its reception, see L. Smith, *Concerns about Rape*, HORS 106 (1989), 6–9; see also I. Blair, *Investigating Rape: A New Approach for the Police* (1985).

[75] Home Office Circular 60/1990 sets standards for the police approach to cases of domestic violence. See also House of Commons Home Affairs Committee, Third Report, Session 1992–3, *Domestic Violence* (1993), recommendations 3–10.

[76] J. Morgan and L. Zedner, *Child Victims* (1992), 96–105.   [77] *Ibid.* 101–2.

[78] *Ibid.* 80–1.   [79] RCCJ Report, Cmnd. 2263 (1993), para. 2.16.

[80] Morgan and Zedner, above n. 76, 102–4 and 122.

[81] See Ch. 6 on prosecutorial review.

[82] Home Office, *The Victim's Charter* (2nd edn., 1996), 13.

searches declined from some two million per year before PACE, and stood at some 110,000 in 1986, but McConville, Sanders, and Leng argue that the post-PACE figures give a false impression. They found that in practice the police tend to ask people's consent to search them. If they consent, the statutory power is not invoked and no formal record is necessary. If they refuse consent, the refusal is treated as grounds for reasonable suspicion, and the statutory power is then invoked.[83] Since 1986 there has been a considerable upturn in recorded stop-searches: the figure for 1996 was 814,500, some seven times as many as in 1986 and 18 per cent more than in 1995. About one-third of the searches were to look for stolen property, and another third were to look for drugs. However, as the numbers of stop-searches have risen, the proportion resulting in arrests has fallen. 'During 1996, 11 per cent of stop/searches led to an arrest, the lowest proportion recorded since 1986', when the figure was 17 per cent.[84] This seems to be evidence of a tendency to over-use these powers, under the cover of the broad phrase 'reasonable grounds for suspicion'. [85]

The 1981 Royal Commission, when recommending the new powers, argued that 'there must be safeguards to protect members of the public from random, arbitrary and discriminatory searches',[86] but the statistics (not to mention the likelihood of many unrecorded cases of people who 'consent' to being searched when stopped) suggest that the various safeguards incorporated in Code of Practice A are applicable only in a minority of cases. One particular cause for concern is racial prejudice in stop-searches, where the evidence shows higher rates of stop for those of Afro-Caribbean origin than for whites, and higher rates for whites than for those of Asian origin.[87] Robert Reiner draws a careful distinction between discrimination and differentiation, arguing that some account must be taken of the different rate of involvement of certain groups in some forms of activity, and that discrimination occurs less frequently than would appear from the bald statistics.[88] None the less, there is a strong argument for reviewing police practice and the law so as to make a renewed attempt to implement the proposals of the 1981 Royal Commission.

5. *Arrest, charge, or summons:* section 24 of the Police and Criminal Evidence Act 1984 provides that a police officer may arrest any person whom

---

[83] McConville, Sanders, and Leng, above n. 54, 95.

[84] This quotation and all the statistics in this para. come from Home Office Statistical Bulletin 27/97, *Operation of Certain Police Powers under PACE, England and Wales, 1996.*

[85] This leaves out of account searches conducted under other provisions: e.g., s. 60 of the Criminal Justice and Public Order Act 1994 gave the police a power to search people and vehicles when they suspected future violence. Nearly 8,000 such searches were conducted in 1996, with an arrest rate below 10% (see *ibid.*).

[86] RCCP, *Report*, Cmnd. 8092 (1981), para. 3.24.

[87] M. Fitzgerald, *Ethnic Minorities and the Criminal Justice System,* RCCJ Research Study 20 (1993), 14–16.

[88] Reiner, above n. 3, 156–70.

he or she has reasonable grounds to suspect of having committed, committing, or being about to commit an arrestable offence. Section 25 extends the power to non-arrestable offences where certain conditions, the 'general arrest conditions', are met. Arrest is not the only way of beginning an investigation into the involvement of a suspect, but it is the most coercive. The Royal Commission on Criminal Procedure, reporting in 1981, found that 'arrest represents a major disruption to a suspect's life', and that 'police officers are so involved with the process of arrest and detention that they fail at times to understand the sense of alarm and dismay felt by some of those who suffer such treatment'.[89] They recommended that the police should make greater use of the summons, and that arrest and the consequent detention should be confined to cases of necessity, for which they articulated five criteria.[90] The 1984 Act failed to insist on this restrictive approach, and indeed widened police powers through the 'general arrest conditions'. Moreover, research has found evidence of two police practices following arrest that further neutralize the intended reform. One is that detention following arrest seems to be authorized as a matter of routine and that there is no fresh application of the 'necessity principle' by the custody officer at the police station, as the 1981 Royal Commission had hoped. The other practice, less widespread but little less effective, is not to make an arrest but to rely on the 'voluntary' attendance of the suspect at a police station, circumscribed by various disincentives to leave.[91]

The Royal Commission of 1993 failed to deal with these issues, leaving the police to continue their adaptive behaviour towards the provisions of the 1984 Act. It was probably naïve to think that the custody officer, a colleague of the arresting officers and receiving information only from arresting officers, could act as an independent arbiter on the necessity for detention. The result is that the custody record is meaningless on this issue, and that what Reiner describes as 'a central tenet of the highly practical culture of policing—that "you can't play it by the book" '[92] has once again asserted itself. It is quite wrong that the police should have been able to succeed in preventing 'mere' legislation from obstructing their established practices, and the Royal Commission should have made a fresh attempt to engineer change. Arrest remains a significant incursion on liberty. Article 5 of the ECHR, which also uses the language of 'reasonable suspicion', is unhelpful in controlling the exercise of this intrusive discretionary power. The need is for greater supervision within, and accountability of, police forces. The possibility of suing for

[89] RCCP Report, para. 3.75.   [90] *Ibid.* para. 3.76.
[91] See generally I. McKenzie, R. Morgan, and R. Reiner, 'Helping the Police with their Inquiries' [1990] *Crim. LR* 22.
[92] Reiner, above n. 3, 107.

damages for wrongful arrest,[93] which results in the payment of considerable sums by police forces every year, or the possibility of the exclusion of evidence obtained as a result of an unlawful arrest,[94] hardly amount to sufficient safeguards for the suspect or disincentives for individual police officers.

6. *Interviews outside the police station:* it will be seen below that one of the great changes in police interrogation in the last ten years has been the advent of tape recording. However, the move towards tape recording has not been accompanied by restrictions on the use by the police, and in court, of unrecorded statements attributed to the defendant. Does this mean that the well-known practice of 'verballing' suspects, when the police attribute to them statements that they did not make, continues to flourish unchecked? The 1993 Royal Commission relied upon research that found questioning to have taken place outside the police station in 10 per cent of cases in one study[95] and in 8 per cent in another study.[96] Unfortunately this is an insecure basis for analysing the issues, partly because there are some informal exchanges taking place in the police station, but more particularly because these studies relied largely on self-reports by police officers which seem likely to produce under-estimates.[97] The 1993 Royal Commission was attracted by the idea of tape recording remarks by suspects outside police stations, whilst trying to ensure that any actual questioning is left until arrival at the police station. It expressed an interest in an experiment in which police officers carry tape recorders for use when remarks are likely to be made by suspects, and it recommended that a suspect should be invited to comment on any alleged confession when a recorded interview subsequently takes place at a police station.[98] What it failed to recommend, however, was that unrecorded remarks should be inadmissible in court. This leaves open the possibility of abuse, recognized even by the Royal Commission itself: 'it is difficult, if not impossible, to devise rules that ensure that those who are determined to evade those rules are prevented from doing so'.[99] In view of this, the proper course would have been to emphasize that there are safeguards for questioning (such as legal advice), that these apply only at the police station, that questioning should therefore take place only in a police station, and that remarks made spontaneously by a suspect outside the police station should be admissible only if recorded.

---

[93] See generally R. Clayton and H. Tomlinson, *Civil Actions against the Police* (1987).

[94] A rare example of this was the Crown Court case of *Fennelley* [1989] *Crim. LR* 142.

[95] D. Brown, T. Ellis, and K. Larcombe, *Changing the Code: Police Detention under the Revised PACE Codes of Practice*, HORS 129 (1993).

[96] S. Moston and G. Stephenson, *The Questioning and Interviewing of Suspects outside the Police Station*, RCCJ Research Study 22 (1993).

[97] R. Leng, 'A Recipe for Miscarriage: the RCCJ and Informal Interviews', in M. McConville and L. Bridges (eds.), *Criminal Justice in Crisis* (1994).

[98] RCCJ Report, paras. 3.11–3.15.

[99] *Ibid.* para. 3.5.

The courts are not able to make elaborate rules of this kind, but they formerly tended to give a broad interpretation to the term 'interview'. In *Absolam* (1989)[100] the word was said to encompass all questioning 'with a view to obtaining admissions on which proceedings can be founded', and in *Cox* (1993)[101] the Court of Appeal cast doubt on a previous decision that had purported to distinguish questioning designed to give the suspect an opportunity to offer an innocent explanation as falling outside the definition of an interview.[102] Behind these decisions lay an appreciation of the importance of ensuring that the protections in Code C are available in most cases where questions are asked, other than questions merely to establish identity.[103] In cases involving an element of entrapment, where the police have put questions without revealing that they are police officers investigating offences, the Court of Appeal drew a distinction between cases where this has been done in order to maintain the officers' cover (evidence not excluded)[104] and cases where the officers were really trying to question the suspect outside the requirements of the 1984 Act (evidence excluded).[105] The 1995 version of Code C places a general duty on the police not to interview a suspect outside the police station, once they have decided to arrest him, but it also restricts the meaning of 'interview' to questioning in cases where the duty to administer a caution has arisen and the questions relate to the suspect's involvement in the offence. The Court of Appeal has emphasised that non-compliance may lead to the exclusion of evidence.[106] Parliament should avoid the need for discretionary exclusion by declaring the principle that unrecorded statements attributed to a defendant are inadmissible.

7. *Search of premises:* the Police and Criminal Evidence Act 1984 contains various powers for the search of premises, apart from search under a warrant. Section 8 contains the principal powers for the grant of a search warrant by a magistrate. In other cases, section 18 empowers an officer to enter premises occupied or controlled by a person arrested for an arrestable offence, to search for evidence relating to that offence or a similar offence. Section 19 contains the companion power to seize evidence found on such premises. Section 32 (2) empowers an officer to enter premises where the arrestee was when or immediately before he was arrested, to search for evidence relating to the

---

[100] (1989) 88 Cr.App.R. 332; see also *Keenan* (1989) 90 Cr.App.R. 1 and *Matthews, Dennison and Voss* (1990) 91 Cr.App.R. 43.

[101] [1993] *Crim. LR* 382.

[102] *Maguire* (1989) 90 Cr.App.R. 115; this decision was also distinguished in *Weekes* [1993] *Crim. LR* 211, where the evidence was excluded.

[103] As the Court noted in *Cox*, n. 11A to Code C is most unclear in its terms. RCCJ Report, para. 3.10, calls for the note to be redrafted.

[104] *Christou and Wright* (1992) 95 Cr.App.R. 264.　　　　[105] *Bryce* (1992) 95 Cr.App.R. 320.

[106] *Miller* [1998] *Crim. LR* 209, analysing paragraph C.11 of the 1995 Code.

offence for which he was arrested. Code of Practice B regulates the conduct of such searches, but the provisions for accountability are no better than for wrongful arrests (see paragraph 5 above). In *Beckford* (1992)[107] the Court of Appeal held that the power under section 32(2) should only be used in good faith, and not in order to search premises for other reasons. If the court finds that the search was unlawful it may decide to exercise its power to exclude any evidence thereby obtained under section 78 of the 1984 Act, although there are many decisions in which this step has not been taken and the unlawfulness of the search has been held to be a separate matter from the admissibility of the evidence.[108]

8. *Reading the suspect's rights:* paragraph 3.1 of Code C provides that persons arriving at a police station under arrest or voluntarily must be informed clearly of three rights—the right to have someone informed of their arrest, the right to obtain independent legal advice privately from a solicitor free of charge, and the right to consult the Codes of Practice. Research findings in the mid-1990s appeared to agree on two things. First, custody officers were then performing their duty to inform suspects more frequently and more fully than before 1991, although about one-quarter of suspects were still not told everything that they should be told.[109] And secondly, in a significant minority of cases the words were spoken in an unclear or unduly hurried fashion, and/or the police emphasized the possible problems of insisting on a solicitor (such as delay before one arrives).[110] Some of these failures might stem from forgetfulness in the heat of the moment, but others suggest that the police officers resent the 'rights' and think that lawyers would impede the smooth progress of the investigation. Courts have excluded evidence in cases where suspects have not been notified of their rights or have been misinformed, and the Court of Appeal has upheld this approach.[111] The Royal Commission paid little attention to the important ethical issues raised by attempts to persuade suspects not to exercise their rights, but recommended further testing of a new notice of rights, intended to create a fuller understanding of what is being said.[112] No post-1995 studies of these issues have been published.

9. *Legal advice at the police station:* section 58 of the Police and Criminal Evidence Act 1984 provides that 'a person arrested and held in custody . . .

---

[107] (1992) 94 Cr.App.R. 43.   [108] *Ibid.* at 50.

[109] Brown, Ellis, and Larcombe, above n. 95; M. Zander and P. Henderson, *Crown Court Study* RCCJ Research Study 19 (1993), 9.

[110] Brown, Ellis, and Larcombe, above n. 95, about a quarter of cases; see also A. Sanders and L. Bridges, 'Access to Legal Advice and Police Malpractice' [1990] *Crim. LR* 494 at 498, some 41% of cases; McConville, Sanders, and Leng, above n. 54, 47. Code C, para. 6.4, states: 'No attempt should be made to dissuade the suspect from obtaining legal advice'.

[111] e.g. *Absolam* (1989) 88 Cr.App.R. 332, *Beycan* [1990] *Crim. LR* 185.

[112] RCCJ Report, para. 3.40, following I. Clare and G. Gudjonsson, *Devising and Piloting an Experimental Version of the 'Notice to Detained Persons'*, RCCJ Research Study 7 (1993).

shall be entitled, if he so requests, to consult a solicitor privately at any time'. Paragraph 6 of Code C contains detailed guidance on the presence and rights of legal advisers. The percentage of suspects requesting legal advice has increased from 24 after the 1984 Act to 32 following the introduction of the revised Code in 1991, and then to 40 after the 1995 revision of the Code.[113] This still leaves over a half of suspects refusing 'the offer of a free gift',[114] in some cases because they see no reason to have it, in others because there would be a delay.[115] Not surprisingly, the proportion requesting legal advice is much higher in serious cases; less understandably, there seem to be considerable local variations in the rate of requesting legal advice, as well as in the delivery of that advice.[116]

Research has called into question whether those who do request legal advice receive advice and support of the appropriate quality. Two studies in the early 1990s found that a majority of legal advisers attending police stations are not admitted solicitors, but clerks or other staff.[117] Michael McConville and Jacqueline Hodgson found that when legal advisers arrive at the police station they have difficulty in ascertaining details of the allegations, and usually have nothing more than a hurried interview with their clients.[118] Whether from inexperience or from lack of familiarity with the case or both, the advice given to suspects was variable in quality and the protection given to suspects during interviews was sometimes non-existent. McConville and Hodgson state that some advisers 'fail to protect clients from improper, inappropriate and irrelevant—but potentially damaging—questions';[119] John Baldwin argues that some legal advisers are, by their passivity during interviews, failing to safeguard their client's interests in the face of hostile or repetitive questioning.[120] Following the Royal Commission report, the Law Society began an 'accreditation scheme' in an effort to ensure that, when non-solicitor legal advisers attend police stations, they have some relevant training in their powers and duties. Although we have no assessment of the effectiveness of this scheme,[121] a recent study reveals that in early 1996 some six out of ten lawyers consulted were the suspect's own legal adviser and the other four were duty solicitors. Before the scheme at least 25 per cent of legal advisers attending police stations were 'unaccredited'. The proportions found by Bucke and

---

[113] Bucke and Brown, above, n. 37, ch. 2.

[114] *Ibid.* 32–3.   [115] *Ibid.* 22.   [116] *Ibid.* 25.

[117] Baldwin, *The Role of Legal Representatives at Police Stations* (1992); McConville and Hodgson, *Custodial Legal Advice and the Right to Silence* (1993).

[118] McColville and Hodgson (above, n. 117), ch. 4.

[119] *Ibid.*

[120] Baldwin (above, n. 117), 35.

[121] L. Bridges and J. Hodgson, 'Improving Custodial Legal Advice' [1995] *Crim. LR* 101, who review the scheme at its inception.

Brown were 84 per cent solicitors, 10 per cent accredited representatives, and 6 per cent unaccredited.[122]

There are provisions in the 1984 Act for a senior officer to authorize delaying a detainee's exercise of the right to legal advice, where a serious arrestable offence is concerned and interference with the course of justice is thought likely.[123] The Court of Appeal took a strong view on this, requiring the police to give persuasive evidence of the existence of justifying circumstances, and the quashing of the conviction in *Samuel* (1988)[124] was a notable symbolic blow in favour of the right to legal advice. In over 12,000 cases Bucke and Brown found no recorded example of legal advice being formally delayed.[125] What is urgently needed now is a qualitative appraisal of the operation of the system for providing legal advice in police stations, including such matters as the efficacy of telephone advice (which accounted for 9 per cent of cases in Bucke and Brown's study) and the protection afforded by legal advisers during interviews. It should be added that this is an issue on which the ECHR is silent, and that in some European countries access to a lawyer in the police station is still restricted.[126]

10. *An appropriate adult:* Code of Practice C provides that, if it is proposed to question a juvenile, mentally disordered, or mentally handicapped person, the police must inform an appropriate adult (e.g. parent, social worker) and ask him or her to come to the police station to see the person.[127] The appropriate adult is allowed to consult privately with the person and to be present during any interview, and these rights are additional to the normal right to legal advice. Research by Bucke and Brown in 1995–6 found that nine out of ten juveniles but only two-thirds of mentally disordered suspects were interviewed in the presence of an appropriate adult.[128] Earlier evidence for the 1993 Royal Commission had revealed that there were some interviews in which juveniles are 'harangued, belittled or indirectly threatened that they will not be left alone until either the police obtain irrefutable evidence or the suspect confesses', and where the parent, social worker, or legal adviser remains silent none the less.[129]

There is overwhelming evidence that the system is not fulfilling its purpose. Research by Clare Palmer demonstrates the practical difficulties in getting the police to recognize mentally disordered or handicapped suspects who require

---

[122] Bucke and Brown, above n. 37, 26.   [123] PACE 1984, ss. 56 and 58.

[124] (1988) 87 Cr.App.R. 232; cf. *Alladice* (1988) 87 Cr.App.R. 380, where the Court advanced the same principle but upheld the conviction.

[125] Bucke and Brown, above n. 37, 23.

[126] For the position in France, see H. Trouille, 'A Look at French Criminal Procedure' [1994] *Crim. LR* 735, at 740 and 743.

[127] Code C, paras. 1 and 3.   [128] Bucke and Brown, above, n. 37, ch.2.

[129] R. Evans, *The Conduct of Police Interviews with Juveniles*, RCCJ Research Study 8 (1993).

an appropriate adult, leading to considerable under-protection of the vulnerable.[130] Bucke and Brown show that many appropriate adults are unclear about their proper function, and that (in the case of family members who attend interviews with juveniles) considerable numbers of them either tend to support the police view or are too distressed or angry to support the interviewee.[131] Jacqueline Hodgson reviews the evidence to show that appropriate adults are not giving the protection to vulnerable suspects for which they were introduced. There needs to be clearer instruction on their functions, and ideally a group of specially-trained personnel (possibly social workers) to act in this capacity, rather than relying on the relatives of juveniles, who are likely to have mixed emotions.[132] She also demonstrates that the courts have not been consistent in their approach to interviews of vulnerable suspects conducted without an appropriate adult, with the recent decision in *Lewis*[133] showing that the Court of Appeal fails to appreciate the separate functions of legal adviser and appropriate adult. An official committee was said to be reviewing this area of law and practice in the mid-1990s, but there has been no published outcome. The evidence shows that there is an urgent need for both review and reform.

11. *Recording of interviews:* there is no statutory basis for the audio or video recording of interviews, but Code of Practice E now sets out guidance for recording. Little difficulty seems to be caused by audio recording itself: the problems are rather that the police choose to ask some questions outside the police station, as we saw in (6) above, and that there is a tendency to rely on police summaries (which are often defective) rather than to listen to the tapes themselves.[134] There have been several experiments with the video recording of police interviews, and two particular problems have emerged. One is that jurors and magistrates may attribute too much importance to the facial expressions of the interviewee, failing to understand the stresses and perhaps strangeness of the conditions.[135] The other is that the videotapes might appear to cover the whole interview, whereas there are documented examples of the police conducting other, off-the-record interviews in order to change the suspect's mind about certain things.[136] The Royal Commission recommended further experimentation and research on audio taping, and in order to reduce malpractice put faith in its proposal that there should be a perma-

---

[130] C. Palmer, 'Still Vulnerable after all these years', [1996] *Crim. LR* 633

[131] Bucke and Brown, *In Police Custody*, pp. 10–11.

[132] J. Hodgson, 'Vulnerable Suspects and the Appropriate Adult', [1997] *Crim. LR* 785

[133] [1996] *Crim.LR* 261.

[134] J. Baldwin, *Preparing the Record of Taped Interviews*, RCCJ Research Study 2 (1992).

[135] See RCCJ Report, paras. 3.71–3.72.

[136] For details, see M. McConville, 'Videotaping Interrogations: Police Behaviour on and off Camera' [1992] *Crim. LR* 532.

nent camera in the custody suites of police stations.[137] Beyond that, there remains the difficulty that unrecorded statements are still admissible in evidence (see paragraph 6 above).

12. *The conduct of interviews:* Code of Practice C contains not only guidance on the detention of persons in police stations and the rights to be accorded to them, but also guidance on when a suspect should be cautioned about his or her rights (altered in consequence of the possibility of adverse inferences from silence[138]) and on the conditions in which interviews should be held. Those conditions include heating, periods of rest, breaks for refreshment, and so on. The origins of the guidance lie in the Report of the 1981 Royal Commission: that Commission received considerable evidence on the psychological tactics and psychological effects of police interrogation,[139] but made no specific recommendations on the style of questioning.[140] In a similar vein, the 1993 Royal Commission emphasizes the benefits of better police training, 'instilling in officers a recognition that oppressive interviews are liable to be inaccurate. Fatigue is an important factor in increasing the suggestibility and the inaccuracy of a suspect's performance.'[141] The courts have frequently expressed disapproval of departures from Code C, but have rarely held that such departures justify the exclusion of the resulting evidence, taking the view that only serious misconduct is likely to have an adverse effect on the fairness of the proceedings (section 78 of the 1984 Act) or likely to render any subsequent confession unreliable (section 76 of the 1984 Act).[142]

The 1993 Royal Commission received much evidence, from its own research programme, of 'undue pressure amounting to bullying or harassment' by the police during interrogations.[143] One particular example that has become notorious is the tape-recorded interrogation of the so-called Cardiff Three, involving repeated questions and assertions on the same point and described by the Lord Chief Justice as a 'travesty'.[144] Even when such extreme tactics were not used, there was evidence of a range of techniques from the vigorous to the beguiling, not least in the case of young interviewees.[145] The Royal Commission's response was to endorse a recent Home Office circular

---

[137] RCCJ Report, paras. 3.72.   [138] For full discussion, see Section1 of this ch.

[139] Notably B. Irving and L. Hilgendorf, *Police Interrogation: The Psychological Approach*, RCCP Research Study 1 (1980).

[140] RCCP Report, para. 4.113.

[141] RCCJ Report, para. 2.24; this para. also contains a recommendation that Code C be revised.

[142] e.g. *Samuel* [1988] QB 615; *Alladice* (1988) 87 Cr.App.R. 380. For a detailed discussion see P. Mirfield, *Silence, Confessions and Improperly Obtained Evidence* (1997), ch. 6.

[143] RCCJ Report, para. 2.18; see Baldwin, *Role of Legal Representatives*; Evans, *Conduct of Police Interviews*; McConville and Hodgson, *Custodial Legal Advice*.

[144] *Paris, Abdullahi and Miller* (1993) 97 Cr.App.R. 99, discussed in Ch. 1.3.

[145] See McConville and Hodgson, *Custodial Legal Advice*, RCCJ Research Study No. 16 (1993); and Evans, *The Conduct of Police Interviews with Juveniles*, RCCJ Research Study No. 8 (1993).

and new guide to interviewing, and to emphasize the need for better police training and supervision.[146] However, there is also a need to articulate clearly those approaches to questioning that are not acceptable: the Royal Commission accepts too readily the notion that there is 'no simple rule that applies to all police interviews',[147] when its own research demonstrated the need to be clearer about the boundaries of unacceptable conduct. The Court of Appeal has shown a willingness to apply the concept of oppression to repetitive, hectoring questioning, thereby excluding the confession under section 76(2)(a).[148] Lesser departures from the proper approach to questioning may justify exclusion under section 76(2)(b) or section 78.[149] However, the prospect of the ultimate exclusion of evidence may not be effective to protect suspects from unfair treatment in the first place. Nor, it appears, is the presence of a legal adviser a guarantee against abuse. There is much discussion of the spread of 'ethical interviewing' methods among the police;[150] and, of course, a significant change must have resulted from the 1994 Act and the possibility of adverse inferences from silence (discussed in Section 1 of this chapter). Until we have empirical evidence of genuine changes of tone and style, from independent research, history suggests that concern about safeguards ought to remain high.

13. *Confessions:* it has often been said that the police see the primary purpose of questioning as the obtaining of a confession, and this is perfectly natural. There are secondary purposes, such as the obtaining of criminal intelligence, but confessions and admissions are the goal. To what extent this has altered with the advent of 'ethical interviewing' remains unknown, for the reasons given in the previous paragraph. In so far as they are still deployed, some of the techniques of interviewing referred to in the previous paragraph may lead some suspects to confess when they have not committed the crime, simply as a reaction to the pressure placed upon them. The Royal Commission recognized this as a possibility,[151] but recommended little by way of legal safeguards. In fact, as we saw in Section 1 of this chapter, the Royal Commission supported the retention of the right of silence, whereas the Government soon amended the law (in 1994) to allow adverse inferences from silence. This change must have had an effect on the conduct of interviews, notably by strengthening the position of the police or other investigator. Although there is little qualitative evidence of the styles of police

---

[146] RCCJ Report, para. 2.22.   [147] *Ibid.* para. 2.17.
[148] See the case of the 'Cardiff Three', above, n. 144.
[149] e.g. *Canale* (1990) 91 Cr.App.R. 1; *Weekes* [1993] *Crim. LR* 211.
[150] e.g. T. Williamson, 'Police Practice', in Morgan and Stephenson (eds.), above n. 16.
[151] RCCJ Report, para. 5.32, citing G. Gudjonsson, *The Psychology of Interrogations, Confessions and Testimony* (1992).

questioning since 1994, research by Bucke and Brown shows a slight rise in the rate of confessions from 55 per cent of interviewees before 1994 to 58 per cent in 1995–96.[152] This relatively small rise seems comparable to the small decrease in the percentage of suspects who give 'no comment' answers throughout all or part of their interview.[153]

Accepting the 1994 changes as a fact, there remains the concern about false confessions. The Royal Commission rejected (by a majority) a rule requiring supporting evidence before a confession is admitted into evidence, preferring instead a judicial warning of the great care needed before convicting on the evidence of a confession alone.[154] However, sections 32 and 33 of the Criminal Justice and Public Order Act 1994 abolished corroboration requirements in English law, leaving judges to draw attention to the dangers of acting on unsupported evidence in cases where they think this appropriate.[155] Since there is no tradition of regarding confessions as being in need of supporting evidence, this change in the law is likely to weaken rather than strengthen the position of the innocent person who confesses falsely. It is regrettable that the Royal Commission was not more insistent on the need for supporting evidence where the prosecution case rests on a confession,[156] although it seems unlikely that this would have prevented the Government from following the Law Commission's recommendations and returning the whole issue to one of judicial discretion. However, where there is evidence that the confession may have been obtained in circumstances falling within section 76 of PACE, the exclusion of evidence is a distinct possibility. The courts have shown some willingness to exclude confessions, not only applying the mandatory rule of section 76(2)(a) when conduct amounting to 'oppression' has been found, but also using their discretion in cases where there have been serious and intentional breaches of the Codes of Practice.[157] But they have continued to maintain that not every breach of the Codes justifies exclusion, and have favoured the disciplinary approach (was the police officer in bad faith?) rather than the protective approach (was the defendant prejudiced by the breach?).

14. *Deceptive investigative practices:* it has already been argued that the investigative practices of the police and other law enforcement agencies are moving towards greater reliance on proactive or intelligence-led methods.

---

[152] Bucke and Brown, above n. 37, 33–4; different criteria may be used in determining what amounts to a 'confession', and this study counts suspects who admit to only some of the offences being investigated.

[153] See the discussion in Section 1 above, text at n. 40.

[154] RCCJ Report, paras. 5.85–5.87 and 5.77.   [155] See *Makanjuola* [1995] 2 Cr.App.R. 469.

[156] See R. Pattenden, 'Should Confessions be Corroborated?' (1991) 107 *LQR* 319.

[157] e.g. *Doolan* [1988] *Crim. LR* 747; *Everett* [1988] *Crim. LR* 826.

One aspect of this has been called 'the trend from coercion to deception',[158] and points to the increased use of deceptive strategies. These are many and varied, and only a few can be discussed here. Essentially, they run from bogus businesses, through lying to suspects about their rights or about the evidence against them, to covertly recording their conversations in the police station. Perhaps it is the relatively recent upsurge in these developments that accounts for the absence of guidance in the Codes of Practice, let alone in primary legislation.[159] Thus it is only the courts, in the exercise of their exclusionary discretion, that have had to deal with the issues of principle.

If the police tell lies in order to mislead a suspect into confessing, the courts may well exclude the resulting confession. This was done in *Mason* (1987),[160] where the police told the suspect and his solicitor that his fingerprints had been found on incriminating evidence, when this was quite untrue. The Court of Appeal excluded the resulting confession under section 78 of the 1984 Act, stating that a deceit practised both on a suspect and on his solicitor would have an adverse effect on the fairness of the proceedings. However, this does not mean that the practising of any deceit during an investigation ought to lead to the exclusion of any resulting evidence. We have seen that in *Christou and Wright* (1992)[161] there was an element of deceit, in that the under-cover police officers were running a jewellery shop in the hope that criminals would offer them stolen goods, but there was no particular lie or inducement. The Court of Appeal has also held that the covert recording of conversations between two defendants placed in the same police cell is a passive deceit rather than an active lie,[162] but there are more doubtful cases in which the court has declined to overrule a trial judge's decision to admit evidence obtained by subterfuge.[163] If the deception goes to the root of the proceedings, it may be argued that the prosecution should be stayed for abuse of process. This argument was rejected on the facts in *Latif and Shahzad*,[164] where drugs had been brought into this country (unlawfully) by a customs officer, who then lured the defendant into England by a trick. The House of Lords held that the unlawful act and trick perpetrated by the customs officer were not such an affront to the public conscience that the proceedings should be stayed. Lord Steyn was conscious of the dangers of giving the impression that the end justified any means, but his main reason for not invoking the

---

[158] J. Skolnick and R. Leo, 'The Ethics of Deceptive Interrogation' (1992) 11 *Criminal Justice Ethics* 3.

[159] With the exception of surveillance devices covered by the statutes considered at pt. 2 above.

[160] (1988) 86 Cr.App.R. 349.   [161] [1992] *Crim. LR* 792, above, para. (1).

[162] *Bailey and Smith* [1993] *Crim. LR* 681.

[163] Especially close to the borderline is *Maclean and Kosten* [1993] *Crim. LR* 687.

[164] [1996] 1 WLR. 104.

abuse of process doctrine was 'the public interest in ensuring that those charged with grave crimes should be tried'.[165]

These decisions show a typical common law, case-by-case approach. It is submitted that there is a need to consider the issues on principle, and to deal with them both in legislation and in Codes of Practice. In principle,[166] for law enforcement officers to lie in court is absolutely wrong. At any earlier stage of the criminal process a 'trick about rights' is equally wrong. However, there are distinctly fewer moral objections to covert tape recording or surveillance in police stations and (within certain boundaries) in other public places.

15. *Samples from the suspect-defendant:* sections 61–5 of the Police and Criminal Evidence Act 1984 provide for the taking of fingerprints and bodily samples. In brief, non-intimate samples may be taken without the suspect's consent so long as a police officer of at least superintendent rank believes that the suspect is involved in a serious arrestable offence; intimate samples may only be taken if a police superintendent has such a belief and the suspect consents. Following the report of the Royal Commission of 1993, the relevant section of which reads (in the words of Robert Reiner) 'like the straightforward endorsement of a police shopping list', [167] these powers were broadened by the Criminal Justice and Public Order Act 1994. In particular, saliva and mouth swabs were reclassified as non-intimate samples, allowing them to be taken without consent, and the range of offences for which samples might be taken was expanded from serious arrestable offences to 'recordable offences'. A post-1994 study shows that non-intimate samples are taken from some 7 per cent of suspects detained by the police: about three-quarters were mouth or body swabs, and only 18 per cent were taken in order to ascertain the suspect's involvement in the offence.[168] The remainder were taken for the DNA database. Intimate samples, usually of blood, were taken in 0.4 per cent of cases. (It may be added that intimate body searches were even rarer.)

Typically, the Royal Commission made these recommendations without any reference to human rights law. For one thing, refusal of consent entitles the court to draw whatever inferences are proper.[169] There are some who argue that these provisions violate the right to silence or privilege against self-incrimination, but that depends on the strength of analogies between

---

[165] *Ibid.*, at 113, distinguishing the House's earlier decision in *Ex parte Bennett*, discussed in Ch. 2 at pp. 53–5.

[166] What follows is a short summary of the conclusions in A. Ashworth, 'Should the Police be Allowed to Use Deceptive Practices?' (1998) 114 *LQR* 108.

[167] R. Reiner, 'Investigative Powers and Safeguards for Suspects' [1993] *Crim. LR* 808, at 813, commenting on the RCCJ report, paras. 2.28 to 2.38.

[168] From Bucke and Brown, above n. 37, ch. 5.

[169] s. 62(10) of the 1984 Act so provides.

compelled speech and compelled yielding of samples.[170] As Wigmore pointed out, if a defendant refused to come to court on the basis that he did not wish to show his face to witnesses and jurors, we would surely waste little time in concluding that he should be compelled.[171] The argument is that compelling him or her to yield bodily samples, or at least threatening adverse inferences from refusal, may be displeasing for the defendant but cannot be connected with any right other than, perhaps, the right to privacy. There is also an argument based on the right of privacy under Article 8: essentially, it must be clear that the provisions in PACE, as amended by the 1994 Act, fall within all the requirements in Article 8.2 for an exception to be made. This calls for careful discussion, not least because the 1994 amendments go beyond 'serious arrestable offences' and extend to all 'recordable offences'. Whether such a broad power would be upheld in respect of non-serious offences is open to doubt.[172]

16. *Forensic science evidence:* it seems that there is some kind of scientific evidence in about one-third of contested Crown Court cases. About one-half of such cases involve medical evidence of the victim's condition, and one-quarter relate to the analysis of drugs. Only the remaining quarter come within the field usually described as 'forensic', relating to fingerprints, blood samples, etc.[173] In some of these cases the Forensic Science Service carries out a number of tests. In the cases of the Maguire Seven, the Birmingham Six, and Judith Ward, the results of certain tests favourable to the defendants were not disclosed to the prosecution, let alone to the defence.[174] The Royal Commission took the view that the Forensic Science Service has become better regulated and more impartial since the 1970s when those cases were decided,[175] but one of its research studies found continuing evidence of an adversarial approach among some forensic scientists, excluding certain items from their reports and arguing that it is for the defence to expose the limitations of their findings.[176] The Commission's principal recommendation was for a free market in forensic science services, with a Forensic Science Advisory Council to monitor performance and to formulate codes of practice for forensic scientists.[177] Among its other recommendations were greater defence rights in relation to scientific evidence possessed by the prosecution, and pre-trial

---

[170] S. Easton, 'Bodily Samples and the Privilege against Self-Incrimination' [1991] *Crim. LR* 18.

[171] H. Wigmore, *Evidence* (McNaughten edn.), para. 2265, cited by Easton, above n. 170.

[172] In *Malone* v. *UK* (above n. 71) the European Court confined the Art. 8.2 exception to 'serious crimes'. Cf. now the unexpected dictum in *Saunders*, discussed at pp. 106–7 above.

[173] All statistics from Zander and Henderson, above n. 109, 84–5.   [174] See Ch. 1.3.

[175] RCCJ Report, paras. 9.27 and 9.47.

[176] P. Roberts and C. Willmore, *The Role of Forensic Science Evidence in Criminal Proceedings*, RCCJ Research Study 11 (1993).

[177] RCCJ Report, paras. 9.33–9.35.

conferences between prosecution and defence expert witnesses when both are to be called in a case.[178] Important as these recommendations are, they lack a certain sharpness. Stronger words should have been written about the adversarial tendency revealed by the research carried out for the Commission, and proper attention given to the notion of the Forensic Science Service as a trustee of samples and of findings of analysis. A major reorientation of ethics and attitudes seems to be required, and it is far from clear that either this or proper regulation would occur if a free market were to be established.[179]

17. *Identification evidence:* cases of mistaken identification have been well documented over the years. The fragility of identification is widely recognized.[180] The Devlin Committee drew together various cases in which mistaken identification had occurred,[181] but the only official reaction to its report was a decision of the Court of Appeal requiring a special form of warning to be given in cases resting on evidence of identification.[182] Appeals based on the failure of summings-up to incorporate proper warnings about the dangers of identification evidence continue to come before the courts.[183] Code of Practice D deals with 'The Identification of Persons by Police Officers'. It establishes that the four alternative methods of identification should be considered in order of priority in each case—(a) identification parade; (b) group identification; (c) video film; (d) confrontation. Failure to give proper consideration to each may result in unfairness to the suspect, and is therefore a ground for excluding the evidence under section 78 of the 1984 Act.[184] Code D also sets out rules for the conduct of identification parades and other procedures. There are several cases in which evidence has been excluded because of departures from the Code,[185] particularly where the breach was deliberate,[186] but the Court of Appeal has maintained that the fact of a breach is not sufficient. There appears to be a need for proof of unfairness, and, where the breach was minor or where it is established that the breach did not prejudice the suspect, the Court has been willing to admit the evidence.[187] What the decisions provide is considerable evidence of deviations from Code D, some

---

[178] *Ibid.*, paras. 9.52 and 9.63.

[179] For full discussion, see P. Roberts, 'What Price a Free Market in Forensic Science Services? The Organization and Regulation of Science in the Criminal Process' (1996) 36 *BJ Crim.* 37.

[180] See e.g. E. Loftus, *Eyewitness Testimony* (1979), and S. Lloyd-Bostock and B. Clifford (eds.), *Evaluating Witness Evidence* (1983).

[181] Home Office, *Evidence of Identification in Criminal Cases* (1976).

[182] *Turnbull* [1977] QB 224; see J. D. Jackson, 'The Insufficiency of Identification Evidence Based on Personal Impression' [1986] *Crim. LR* 203.

[183] See, e.g., *Slater* [1995] 1 Cr.App.R. 584; *Spencer* [1995] *Crim. LR* 235.

[184] e.g. *Gaynor* [1988] *Crim. LR* 242.

[185] e.g. *Gall* [1989] *Crim. LR* 745; *Finley* [1993] *Crim. LR* 50.

[186] *Nagah* [1991] *Crim. LR* 55.

[187] *Jones* [1992] *Crim. LR* 365 (breach minor); *Ryan* [1992] *Crim. LR* 187 (no prejudice apparent).

deliberate, some apparently stemming from ignorance. Since it appears that identification evidence is of some importance in about one-quarter of contested cases,[188] not to mention those cases that end in a guilty plea for one reason or another, police practice in this area requires scrutiny. Courts operating months after the event are hardly the appropriate body, even though they may be able to detect a miscarriage of justice arising from misapplication of procedures relating to identity (as in *Fergus*).[189] There is a need for better training and for greater accountability at the time, probably through the involvement of defence solicitors and of officers at a higher level of seniority.

18. *Duties of disclosure:* it was evident from the major miscarriage of justice cases, discussed in Chapter 1.3, that the prosecution's failure to disclose all relevant evidence to the defence lay at the root of several wrongful convictions. Nonetheless, the Royal Commission on Criminal Justice recommended a reformed system of disclosure, in which disclosure by the defence would take its place for the first time. This recommendation should, of course, be seen in the context of the Commission's support for the retention of the right of silence: it therefore saw defence disclosure as a convenient way of preventing 'ambush defences'.[190] In the event, the government both rejected the Commission's recommendations on the right of silence and also somewhat widened its proposals on disclosure. The provisions of the Criminal Procedure and Investigations Act 1996 are of considerable practical and theoretical importance.[191]

The scheme of the Act consists of three steps. First, the police have a duty to disclose to the defence any prosecution material which 'in the prosecutor's opinion might undermine the case for the prosecution against the accused', and which is not to be relied upon by the prosecution. This is known as primary disclosure. The system is objectionable on the grounds that, not only do the police decide what evidence is disclosable, but also the test is the subjective one of what they believe might undermine their case. The upshot is that primary disclosure is less than full disclosure (indeed, no complete list of evidence need be made available to the defence), and this may be held to breach the requirement of a fair trial in Article 6.1 of the ECHR. The European Court has insisted on the doctrine of 'equality of arms', in terms of giving the defence access to evidence held by the prosecution, and the new procedure falls significantly short of that.[192] (In France the defence lawyer has access, albeit

---

[188] Zander and Henderson, above n. 109, 92.

[189] See the discussion of this case in Ch. 1.3, text at n. 19.

[190] It should be noted that Prof. Michael Zander dissented strongly from the proposals on defence disclosure : RCCJ, *Report*, 221–3.

[191] For full discussion, see R. Leng and R. Taylor, *The Criminal Procedure and Investigations Act 1996*; for a brief outline, see J. Sprack, 'The Duty of Disclosure' [1997] *Crim. LR* 308.

[192] Cf. *Edwards* v. *UK* (1992) 15 EHRR 417; see also *Foucher* v. *France* [1997] HRCD 392, emphasising that the same doctrine applies in the lower (Magistrates') courts.

limited in time, to the full dossier).[193] The second step is defence disclosure, which requires a statement of the nature of the accused's defence, and of the reasons why the accused takes issue with certain elements of the prosecution case. The objection to this is that it may infringe the presumption of innocence, guaranteed by Article 6.2 of the ECHR, in that (taken together with the inadequacy of primary disclosure) it requires the defence to make disclosures which may assist, or even be used by, the prosecution. The third step is secondary prosecution disclosure, at which stage the prosecutor must respond to defence disclosure by disclosing any prosecution material 'which might be reasonably expected to assist the accused's defence'. The objection here is that this material ought to have been liable to disclosure in the first place. It remains possible to refrain from disclosing evidence covered by public interest immunity, and this is an issue that can be tested in court.[194]

The provision for defence disclosure is reinforced by section 11 of the 1996 Act, which allows adverse inferences to be drawn where the defence fails to disclose a line of defence or depart from its disclosed defence at the trial. When combined with the possibility of adverse inferences from silence, discussed in Section 1 of this chapter, this demonstrates the extent to which the balance of power has shifted in favour of the prosecution and against the defence. Although there is no empirical or qualitative evidence about the operation of the disclosure provisions, and their effect on trials, it is abundantly clear that this element of the 'police shopping list' has been adopted with some vigour. The police's difficulties with the previous regime were that the disclosure requirements took considerable time, that they might require disclosure of the involvement of informants or under-cover officers, and the police were sometimes forced to drop a prosecution rather than risk exposing the identity of an officer or informer.[195] Unfortunately, in attempting to meet these practical difficulties, the government changed the system in a way that both ignores the history of miscarriages of justice (by entrusting the police with the task of primary disclosure) and risks incompatibility with the European Convention on Human Rights. In both these respects, the language and tone of the previous Government's paper, *Disclosure: A Consultation Document*,[196] stand as a monument to the kind of pro-prosecution complacency and disrespect for rights that generated the miscarriage of justice cases.

---

[193] Trouille, above n. 126, at 741–2.

[194] The principles developed at common law in *Ward* (1993) 96 Cr.App.R. 1 continue to govern this.

[195] See, e.g., C. Pollard, 'A Case for Disclosure?' [1994] *Crim. LR* 42; the compatibility of the Public Interest Immunity system with the ECHR is under challenge in *Rowe and Davis* v. *UK* [1998] EHRLR 92.

[196] Cmnd. 2864 of 1995, discussed by R. Leng, 'Losing Sight of the Defendant' [1995] *Crim. LR* 704.

3. Investigations, Rights, and Power

In this chapter we have reviewed the stark changes in the significance of silence in interviews, and many other developments in the eighteen areas of pre-trial justice selected for brief comment. In political terms there is little doubt that the police have gained considerably from recent changes: what was described earlier as their 'shopping list' of reforms has been delivered, whilst other needed reforms to protect suspects (such as improvements in the system of 'appropriate adults' for vulnerable suspects) have been accorded little or no priority. Yet, if the new government is to be taken at its word, the passing of the Human Rights Bill will usher in a new era of rights-consciousness, in which the legislature and all public authorities will be required and expected to respect the rights declared in the ECHR. This could have major implications for the law in several of the areas discussed above. At least four aspects of the current English system will require re-appraisal. Are the provisions of the Criminal Justice and Public Order Act 1994 which allow adverse inferences from silence, particularly section 34 (failure to mention facts to the police), compatible with the right to a fair trial and the presumption of innocence declared in Article 6? Are the provisions of the Criminal Procedure and Investigations Act 1996, particularly the limited nature of primary prosecution disclosure, compatible with the right to a fair trial and the doctrine of 'equality of arms' under Article 6.1? Are forms of intrusive surveillance which fall outside discrete English statutes compatible with the right to privacy in Article 8, especially since they cannot be regarded as 'in accordance with the law' when there is no law which sets out a procedure for these other forms of surveillance? Do the powers to take intimate and non-intimate samples from suspects, as enlarged by the Criminal Justice and Public Order Act 1994, infringe the right of privacy declared by Article 8, especially now that there is no restriction to 'serious crimes' as required for compliance with Article 8.2?

Quite apart from these momentous issues, it is plain that law and policy have failed to keep pace with developments in policing. The Police and Criminal Evidence Act 1984 and its accompanying Codes of Practice amount to important steps to protect and clarify rights, but they neglect the recent trend towards proactive and intelligence-led policing. They simply fail to cover many police activities which carry dangers to individual liberty. Thus there is no authoritative guidance on the deployment of informers or undercover police officers, whether prior to the commission of offences or in the detection of crimes already committed, and there is no guidance on the various deceptive practices that have come to be used increasingly. The lack of guidance is in one sense disadvantageous to law enforcement agencies, since it does not state what is permissible and lays them open to the possibility that evidence thus obtained will be excluded in court. But the main difficulty with the lack of guidance is that individuals are left with little protection from temptation, incitement, and trickery. Of course there is a whole range of normative issues to be debated before it is decided what ought and ought not to be permitted. However, to leave the area virtually unregulated, as it is now, is quite wrong.

There is the further question of how individuals should be protected and the conduct of law enforcement agencies regulated. At present the rules are distributed between primary legislation and the PACE Codes of Practice drawn up by the Home Office in consultation with other bodies. The distribution of topics between primary legislation and Codes of Practice ought to be reviewed: the main principles and policies should be declared in the legislation, with the Codes refining and developing the practical details in accordance with those principles and policies. This is not the case with the Police and Criminal Evidence Act and its Codes, and there is a danger that topics appearing only in the Codes (e.g. tape recording) may be regarded as less important than those in primary legislation.

Once the rules are set out, the main task is to ensure that the police and other investigative agencies are properly trained. This requires the absorption and acceptance of an ethical approach, as outlined in Chapter 3, which recognizes the purpose and importance of individual rights in the field of law enforcement, and which recognizes the constitutional dimension of the compromise which legislation and Codes of Practice represent. No police force, nor any other profession, can guarantee absolute observance of any set of rules. Certainly the police must do much more by way of supervision of junior officers, and the report of the 1993 Royal Commission contained a few recommendations along these lines.[197]

What ought to happen when a breach of the rules relating to the treatment of suspects is substantiated? There are three lines of answer to this question. The first is that there should be internal disciplinary procedures against the officer(s) concerned. An efficient mechanism for dealing with complaints against the police is needed in the first place. The Police Complaints Authority is an independent body, but it is still limited to supervising police inquiries rather than undertaking its own investigations, and it therefore fails to satisfy the test of independence from the police. Then there should be a disciplinary procedure within the police that deals credibly with misconduct: the Royal Commission had some worthwhile recommendations on this point.[198]

[197] RCCJ Report, paras. 2.59 and 2.61.
[198] *Ibid.* para. 3.103; for comment, see Reiner, 'Investigative Powers and the Police' [1993] *Crim. LR* 808, at 816.

The second approach considers the damage to the suspect or defendant. A person who has been wrongfully arrested or detained may (unusually) bring an action for habeas corpus to secure release, or may (less infrequently) pursue a civil action for damages against the police.[199] This is much more likely in the case of someone who has been released without charge or who has been acquitted at trial, although it is in theory no less possible if the defendant is convicted of the offence concerned.

Where there is a prosecution the third approach comes into view—whether to stay the prosecution, or to exclude the evidence tainted by police misconduct, or to mitigate sentence, or to regard the irregularity as irrelevant. As a basic proposition, the court should exclude the resulting evidence if the proper procedures were not followed. The main justification for this is that it is a method of ensuring that the defendant is not disadvantaged by the infringement of his or her rights. The evidence is tainted—the 'fruit of the poisoned tree'—and a court should not admit it. However, there may be a strong temptation for the court not to take this course when the evidence resulting from the breach appears cogent and central to the case. The English courts remain ambivalent in their attitudes and decisions. Not only has the Court of Appeal excluded evidence under section 78 for deliberate failure to accord rights or deliberate deception of the defendant and his solicitor, but there have been strong declarations of the power to stay proceedings for abuse of process. It will be recalled that in R. v. *Horseferry Road Magistrates' Court, ex parte Bennett*[200] the House of Lords declared that English courts should not 'countenance behaviour that threatens either basic human rights or the rule of law'. Likewise in *Winston Brown*,[201] Steyn LJ in the Court of Appeal stated that:

> the right of every accused to a fair trial is a basic or fundamental right . . . In our adversarial system, in which the police and prosecution control the investigatory process, an accused's right to fair disclosure is an inseparable part of his right to a fair trial.

However, that resounding statement was followed by a judgment that accommodated the prosecution rather than the defence. There are, as we have seen in the course of this chapter, many other appellate decisions in which the conviction has been upheld despite some pre-trial irregularity by a law enforcement agency. This is not only inconsistent with the 'integrity principle', discussed in Chapter 2, but also affords no protection to defendants since it allows the prosecution to reap the advantage of unlawful or unfair tactics. With the advent of Plea and Directions Hearings in the Crown Court, it is

---

[199] Clayton and Tomlinson, *Civil Actions against the Police* (1987).
[200] [1994] 1 AC 42, n. 195 above.   [201] [1995] 1 Cr.App.R. 191.

possible that some disputes about unfairly obtained evidence or other pre-trial irregularities could be resolved prior to the trial. It is worth adding that in France the defence may apply to the *chambre d'accusation* to have any evidence obtained in contravention of the criminal procedure code declared a *nullité*, well before the case would come to trial.[202] There are strong reasons for resolving these matters in advance of trial—the reduction of anxiety and stress for defendants and witnesses, and also reductions in cost for the Government.

[202] Trouille, above n. 126, at 74.

5   Gatekeeping Decisions

THE concern of this chapter is with those decisions that determine whether or not a case enters the criminal justice system and, if so, what course it is set upon.

Out of all the criminal offences committed in any one year, only a very low proportion result in formal proceedings being taken against a suspect/defendant. The process of attrition, as it has come to be known, is gradual and substantial. Figures derived from the British Crime Survey, dealing with eight of the most frequently committed types of indictable offences, suggest that no more than 2 per cent result in a conviction.[1] Starting with those offences actually committed, around half of them are never reported to the police. Members of the public may choose not to report an offence because they think the police unable to help, because they regard the offence as too minor to report, because the offence is regarded as a private or domestic matter, because of fear of reprisals, or for other reasons. Of the 47 per cent that are reported to the police, a significant proportion are not recorded as crimes. A variety of reasons may come into play here: the offence may be attributed to a child below the age of criminal responsibility, or the police may not accept the victim's account, or the incident may have been resolved quickly and informally.[2] This reduces the number of offences remaining in the system to 27 per cent. The next difficulty is that only a proportion of recorded offences are 'cleared up', in the sense of being detected or otherwise resolved. In relation to the eight types of crime studied in the British Crime Survey, about one-fifth are cleared up and this reduces the percentage remaining in the system from 27 to 5 per cent. Some of the offences that are cleared up result in nothing more than an informal warning or no further action at all, particularly when they are traced to young offenders. Thus only 3 per cent of the offences result in a formal caution or in prosecution. One-third of those are cautions, which

---

[1] G. C. Barclay (ed.), *Digest 3: Information on the Criminal Justice System in England and Wales* (1995), 25. The offences are criminal damage; thefts of a motor vehicle; theft from a motor vehicle (including attempts); bicycle theft; burglary; wounding; robbery; and theft from the person.

[2] For an outline of police recording practices, see P. Mayhew, D. Elliott, and L. Dowds, *The 1988 British Crime Survey*, HORS 111 (1989), 11.

are widely used for younger offenders, leaving some 2 per cent to be sentenced by the courts.

This startling rate of attrition does not apply equally to all crimes. Among those studied in the British Crime Survey, offences of wounding resulted in a much higher rate of court appearance. A higher proportion of recorded offences were cleared up and were then dealt with formally, so that 10 per cent of offenders were sentenced by the courts. (For homicide the percentage would be much higher still.) In a sample of ninety-three assault victims treated at a hospital casualty unit in 1991, the attrition rate was lower but still marked. Thus Clarkson, Cretney, Davis, and Shepherd found that, of the ninety-three cases, nineteen victims failed to inform the police, and a further twenty made no formal 'complaint' (often cases described as 'domestic'). Sixteen further cases did not proceed for lack of evidence. Of the thirty-eight cases then remaining, some twenty-two resulted in a conviction. A major finding was that the objective seriousness of the assault was not related to the probability of the offender being brought to court and convicted.[3]

What are the implications of the rate of attrition? One is that it demonstrates the naïveté of expecting the sentences passed by the courts to act as a significant control on crime. Those sentences deal with a small proportion of offenders—although, for the most part, they will be the most serious offenders—and, even making allowances for the probability that the symbolic effect of those (few) sentences will be greater than their proportionate size, this suggests that a strategy for the prevention of crime should not place great emphasis on sentencing. This is not to deny that sometimes sentences may exert a specific and/or general deterrent effect, but it is to counsel caution against overestimating those effects in the context of low rates of reporting, detection, and so on. A second implication is that decisions taken by law enforcement agents have a considerable influence on the selection of cases that go forward into the criminal process. Their decisions have a qualitative as well as a quantitative effect: the offenders who find themselves convicted in court are not a random group of the totality of offenders, nor necessarily are they the most serious group. They are chosen, when others are not, for a variety of reasons that ought to be explored.

The focus of this chapter will be upon the decisions taken by the gatekeepers of the criminal process. The discussion of different types of gatekeeper will be less detailed than the extensive literature would permit, in order to facilitate the analysis of general issues. There will be some discussion of the police, of some regulatory bodies, and of the Serious Fraud Office as agencies that select for official action certain types of person or situation, a selection that

---

[3] C. Clarkson, A. Cretney, G. Davis and J. Shepherd, 'Assaults: the Relationship between Seriousness, Criminalisation and Punishment' [1994] *Crim. LR* 4.

may lead either to prosecution and trial or to a form of diversion. The first section looks at practices of reporting and enforcing. The second section considers the range of formal responses to those who are believed to be offenders. The third section looks in greater detail at the approach of some regulatory agencies and of the Serious Fraud Office. The fourth section focuses on police cautioning and related practices. The fifth section analyses the values behind some of the differing policies, and the sixth considers accountability.

1. Reporting and Enforcing

There is a real sense in which society is self-policing. The vast majority of offences are brought to the attention of the police by members of the public, and so the police operate in a reactive role. The decision to report probably means that the victim or witness expects something to be done about the offence. However, as we saw earlier, about one-half of the eight common types of offence studied in the British Crime Survey are not reported, and prominent among the reasons are a belief that the crime was insufficiently serious to report, and a belief that the police would not be able to do anything about it. The latter reason may betray a pessimism about police effectiveness rather than a genuine judgement that no formal response is necessary. In practice, however, many of these cases will also involve the first reason—that the formal invocation of law enforcement machinery is not really necessary. To that extent, then, members of the public may be said to filter out of the system, at the earliest stage, many non-serious offences. This might be regarded as a primitive example of proportionality at work: the idea that, in order to justify reporting an offence to the police or other relevant authority, it has to achieve a certain level of seriousness.

However, the notion of society as self-policing cannot be pressed too far. The police are not simply the agents of the public, reacting whenever requested and not otherwise. There are at least four respects in which the police or other agencies exert a powerful influence. First, we have seen that the police do not record as crimes all incidents that are reported to them as crimes. As many as two-fifths of all incidents reported as thefts, robberies, woundings, etc. are not recorded by the police as such.[4] Some of these incidents may be dealt with by invoking minor public order charges, such as breach of the peace, which are not recorded crimes. But many of them will not be recorded or will be 'no-crimed'. The result is that, although the police are

---

[4] *The 1988 British Crime Survey*, HORS 111 (1989), 70.

largely dependent on the public to report offences, they do not always record what is reported. The police operate as a significant filter on public reports, and even though members of the public may want official action (and, implicitly, official recording of the offence), this may not be what occurs.

Secondly, the idea of society as self-policing does not account for the many offences, perhaps one-quarter of indictable crimes, that are discovered by the police themselves. Here the argument becomes complicated. Sometimes, when the police have a 'crack-down' on certain forms of offences, such as homosexual importuning or drug-dealing in a particular locality, this is a response to complaints from the public. Such cases may be regarded, partly at least, as examples of social self-policing. On the other hand there may be many cases in which the police themselves decide to have a 'campaign' against a particular form of offending: drug-dealing would be more likely to fall into this category, as would drink-driving. The police are operating proactively here, to some extent because the crimes are victimless and therefore there is no victim to make a complaint. In this context the patterns of law enforcement may largely reflect the availability of police officers and the preferences of those in operational control: the police can only mount 'proactive' campaigns if they are not overwhelmed by the 'reactive' demands of crimes reported to them, and when they do adopt a proactive strategy there may be a choice of what type of offence to target.[5] No doubt those preferences will be connected to the concerns of the media and of influential members of the public, as well as to the views of police officers. The same might be said of the regulatory agencies concerned with trading standards, environment, health and safety at work, pollution, and so on. What they hear about the concerns of the media and influential people may have some effect on their enforcement policies, but they may also have their own priorities in the light of the need to allocate their limited resources. It would certainly be wrong to suggest that regulatory agencies tend simply to react to information supplied by members of the public.

A third difficulty with the idea of society as self-policing is that this overlooks, or at least over-simplifies, the nature of the police function. Thus far we have referred to police work as if its focus is enforcing the law by catching criminals, whether as a result of prompting by a member of the public or as a result of a police campaign. Research shows that these kinds of activity do not dominate everyday policing. Much of what the police do is to perform a kind of service function, attending to a wide range of incidents that require something to be done about them—from road accidents and rowdy parties to stray

---

[5] Some police forces have special squads to target certain kinds of crime such as drugs and pornography that are thought to require proactive methods: see the research by M. Maguire and C. Norris, *The Conduct and Supervision of Criminal Investigations*, RCCJ Research Study 5 (1992).

cattle and barking dogs. Into all these situations the police officer brings authority and the ability to draw upon coercive powers if needed. These powers become even more prominent when there is thought to be a risk of public disorder—for example, at a demonstration or march, at a football match, and during other local disturbances. These are the occasions on which the function of the police as maintainers of order comes to the fore. Whether the police use their coercive powers depends on a number of contingencies. If there is a genuine threat to good order they may intervene to make one or more arrests. Studies of police behaviour have long maintained that a police officer is more likely to arrest and charge someone who threatens the officer's authority by means of insults or failure to comply with the officer's commands or requests.[6] This forms part of the working culture of the police, discussed in Chapter 3.[7] Significant as that proposition is in explaining why certain types of person come to be arrested and charged, it should not be allowed to overshadow the probability that some people clearly threaten to cause public disorder and should therefore be prevented from going further.[8] In other words, the use of arrest and criminal charges by the police in incidents thought to threaten good order is likely to be an amalgam of some clearly justifiable cases and others that turn more on the disposition, pride, or self-image of particular officers. Any description that ignores one or the other lacks realism. Both types of case show the criminal law as a resource for the police, however. The notion that Parliament makes the laws and the police then enforce them finds no echo here. The police manage situations so as to maintain order, using the offences in the Police Act 1996 and the Public Order Act 1986 as resources to draw upon, to be invoked against those who threaten the police conception of what constitutes good order and how it should be achieved.

It might be added that this aspect of police work has its parallels in the work of some regulatory agencies. Their primary concern, too, can be described as prevention and the maintenance of a conception of good order. This may indicate a form of negotiated compliance: not immediate compliance with the letter of the law, but evidence of efforts by the offending company or individual to move towards compliance to an extent that the inspector regards as reasonable. Coercive powers are available in reserve and, since these often take the form of strict liability offences (albeit with various defences often available),[9] they may be invoked readily if this is decided to be appropriate.

---

[6] The classic study is that by E. Bittner, 'The Police on Skid Row: A Study in Peacekeeping' (1967) 32 *American Sociological Review* 699.

[7] See Ch. 3.3 above.   [8] See R. Reiner, *The Politics of the Police* (2nd edn., 1992), 212.

[9] Cf. L. H. Leigh, *Strict and Vicarious Liability* (1982).

This leads on to the fourth difficulty with the idea of society as self-policing: that some regulatory agencies operate in fields that lie remote from popular consciousness. Much of the work done by the inspectorates of pollution and health and safety at work is of this nature: of course the public makes occasional demands in relation to notorious incidents, but much of their work lies outside popular notions of crime prevention. The Serious Fraud Office has a higher profile, not merely because it has brought a few well-publicized prosecutions of prominent businessmen, but also because the present minimum of frauds it will investigate is £5 million.[10] It may make its own decisions to investigate a company or an individual, or may accept a reference from the Department of Trade and Industry, the police, or another agency. A good example of lower profile law enforcement, away from popular consciousness, would be insider dealing on the Stock Market: there are agencies charged with the detection of offences of insider dealing[11] and, apart from the debate about their effectiveness, it is apparent that they operate in a sphere with which most people are unfamiliar. Indeed, it seems likely that popular conceptions of crime and criminality are somewhat traditional in nature, and that the media either reflect or cause this by showing little interest in 'modern' forms of criminality.[12] Thus the legislature is ahead of public opinion in enacting a fairly wide range of offences covering activities that lie well outside conventional ideas of crime. This argument must be interpreted carefully. It is not being maintained that the law or its enforcers deal even-handedly with conduct of equivalent social gravity. The point is that there is some law enforcement, mostly by regulatory agencies, that appears to be largely independent of the concerns of many members of the public.

This general survey suggests that society or the community is self-policing only to an extent. Most decisions not to report an offence to the police mean that the offence never comes to light and there is no prospect of the offender being charged and prosecuted to conviction. To that considerable extent, society does police itself. However, we have noted also the influence of the agencies of law enforcement and their own policies, which may be shaped to some extent but not entirely by public expectations and concerns. Later in this chapter we shall look further into the factors that determine the approaches of the police and of other law enforcement agencies. For the present, two final points may be made. First, it is evident that the criminal law in action does not correspond with the criminal law on the statute books. The body of criminal legislation cannot be placed over social behaviour like a template, in the expectation that there will be a 'fit' with the actuality of law enforcement.

[10] Serious Fraud Office, *Annual Report*, 1992–3, 8–9.
[11] Department of Trade and Industry, in conjunction with the Securities Investment Board.
[12] Cf. S. Box, *Power, Crime and Mystification* (1983).

Secondly, the considerable element of discretion in the decision to invoke the criminal law makes it important to scrutinize the reasons why the police and the regulatory agencies decide to proceed against some people and not against others.

2. The Range of Formal Responses

The criminal law provides the framework for formal responses to alleged law-breaking, and yet we have already seen that it sometimes functions merely as a resource to be invoked in situations where this is thought necessary so as to maintain order. Discretion appears to be a key element in what actually happens. Two methods of proceeding have long been available to the police—arrest and summons. The 1981 Royal Commission found that the police used arrest more than was necessary for effective law enforcement, and failed to take account of the fact that 'arrest represents a major disruption of the suspect's life'.[13] Following the Commission proposals, the Police and Criminal Evidence Act 1984 includes not only the requirement that persons only be arrested on reasonable suspicion, but also introduces a category of 'arrestable offences' and provides that an arrested person should not be detained at a police station unless that is necessary for various reasons. However, the 'necessity' principle appears to have been emptied of practical significance by the routine approval of detention by custody officers at police stations[14]—another example of the strength of police culture, in neutralizing inconvenient rules and supporting rather than reviewing the judgement of other (though often junior) officers.

Whether the police choose to proceed by arrest or by summons, the crucial question is what may happen next. In many European systems of law there is a doctrinal contrast between the principle of compulsory prosecution (sometimes called the principle of legality) and the principle of expediency (sometimes called the opportunity principle). Many systems, such as the German and the Austrian, have placed great emphasis on the principle of compulsory prosecution. This may be said to promote the principles of legality and equal treatment, to prevent political interference with the process of justice, and also to heighten general deterrence.[15] In theory all those who commit offences

---

[13] Royal Commission on Criminal Procedure, *Report*, Cmnd. 8092 (1981), para. 3.75.

[14] I. McKenzie, R. Morgan, and R. Reiner, 'Helping the Police with their Inquiries: The Necessity Principle and Voluntary Attendance at the Police Station' [1990] *Crim. LR* 22.

[15] See e.g. J. Herrmann, 'The Rule of Compulsory Prosecution and the Scope of Prosecutorial Discretion in Germany' (1974) 41 *U Chi. LR* 468, at 470; P. J. P. Tak, *The Legal Scope of Non-prosecution in Europe* (1986), 27.

are brought before the courts for an open determination of guilt and (if convicted) for sentencing, and there is no broad discretionary power to avoid prosecution—which might lead to local variations, allegations of political motivation, or the undermining of law by expediency. If the administration of the criminal law produces unjust results, it is for the legislature to amend it and not for prosecutors to make their own policies. Thus section 152 of the German Code of Criminal Procedure requires the public prosecutor to bring a prosecution in respect of all punishable conduct, to the extent that there is sufficient evidence. In practice, of course, there are various exceptions to this, including section 153a, which allows conditional termination of proceedings.[16] There are financial pressures towards the streamlining of criminal justice systems, as well as an increasing realization that prosecution and sentence in court are stressful for the participants and are not necessarily more effective (in terms of reconviction rates) than forms of diversion. Another well-established system of prosecutorial waiver is that whereby Dutch prosecutors may ask defendants to pay a *transactie* in return for a promise of non-prosecution.[17] The Council of Europe has developed this theme in its recommendations for the simplification of criminal justice.[18]

The number of exceptions to the principle of compulsory prosecution might be thought to support an argument that systems such as the German are really little different from the English. The one proclaims a principle of compulsory prosecution and then derogates from it in several ways, whereas the other recognizes from the outset that prosecution policy must be a question of expediency.[19] However, there is good reason to retain some respect for the principle of compulsory prosecution because of the values (the principles of legality and equal treatment) it upholds, even though in Germany the prosecutor enjoys wide discretion in practice. In the heavily pragmatic English system the values and principles have little recognition, even as starting-points. In England and Wales the police have at least five alternative forms of formal response to a case in which there is sufficient evidence that a person has committed an offence.

    A. *No further action:* the police may decide to take no further action. This course should be taken where there is insufficient evidence, but our discussion here is limited to cases where there is sufficient evidence that the defendant has committed a crime. Even in some such

[16] Herrmann, above, n. 15; J. Langbein, 'Controlling Prosecutorial Discretion in Germany' (1974) 41 *U. Chi. LR* 439; J. Herrmann, 'Bargaining Justice: a Bargain for German Criminal Justice?' (1992) 53 *U. Pittsburgh LR* 755.

[17] C. Brants and S. Field, 'Discretion and Accountability in Prosecution', in C. Harding *et al.*, *Criminal Justice in Europe* (1995), esp. 134–6.

[18] Council of Europe, *The Simplification of Criminal Justice*, Recommendation R (87) 18 (1987).

[19] Cf. H. Jung, 'Criminal Justice: A European Perspective' [1993] *Crim. LR* 237, at 241.

cases the police may decide to take no further action because, for example, the defendant has already been sentenced to custody, or indicates a willingness to have it 'taken into consideration' in sentencing for another offence, or the offender is very young, or the offence is non-serious.

B. *Informal warning:* a second alternative is an informal warning or caution, given by a police officer in circumstances where a formal caution is considered unnecessary or inappropriate. Motorists have often benefited from informal warnings of this kind, but there has been a distinct increase in their use for other crimes in the last ten years, with between eleven and eighteen of the forty-three police forces using them regularly.[20] Thus informal warnings, which may not be cited in court, are used widely in some areas and not at all in others.

C. *Formal police cautions:* a third alternative is the formal police caution. The police should only offer to caution an offender when there is sufficient evidence to prosecute: this is a caution for an offence, and should be distinguished from informal cautions or warnings administered by individual officers. 'A caution comprises a lecture from a police officer, usually an inspector' which, in respect of young offenders, is delivered in the presence of a parent or other appropriate adult.[21] There is no legislative basis for the practice of cautioning, but cautions should be recorded by the police and disclosed to the court in an antecedents statement when relevant.[22] Recent years have seen the development of 'caution plus' schemes in certain parts of the country. As noted below, the Crime and Disorder Bill 1998 will introduce a statutory scheme of reprimands and final warnings, which will replace cautioning for young offenders.

D. *Reparation or mediation scheme:* a fourth alternative is to refer the case to a reparation or mediation scheme. These are only available in certain parts of the country, and then only in certain circumstances. A well-established scheme in Northamptonshire aims to reach agreement with offender and victim on a package of reparative measures in each individual case (usually youth cases), whereas a Leeds scheme aims to bring together offender and victim with a view to apology and reparation from the offender.[23]

---

[20] Audit Commission, *Misspent Youth: Young People and Crimes* (1996), para. 30, found 11 forces using informal cautions for young offenders; R. Evans and R. Ellis, *Police Cautioning in the 1990s* (1997), 3, found 18 forces using such warnings.
[21] Audit Commission, above n. 20, para. 31.   [22] Home Office Circular 59/1990, annex B.
[23] See further J. Dignan, 'Reintegration through Reparation: A Way Forward for Restorative Justice', in A. Duff, S. Marshall, R.R. Dobash, and R.P. Dobash (eds.), *Penal Theory and Practice* (1994).

E. *Prosecution:* the fifth course is to prosecute, and it is this alternative alone that results in the defendant being processed through one or more of the decision-making stages discussed in this book. While decisions to take no further action or to give a formal caution have the effect of diverting the offender from the criminal process, the decision to prosecute is the first step on what may become a long road.

The various regulatory agencies have somewhat different powers from the police. They may take no further action. Many of them have the power to issue a warning notice, requiring the addressee to rectify the defects that have led to the commission of the offence. Some agencies, notably the Inland Revenue, have the power to require compounded penalties as an alternative to prosecution. This means that a person may be required to pay, say, twice the underpaid tax under threat of being prosecuted otherwise. This approach is open to relatively few agencies, however. The bringing of a criminal prosecution remains the ultimate sanction. As we shall see, the tendency is for regulatory agencies to regard this as a last resort, whilst the police have tended to use it more widely and more routinely.

Many systems of law include some schemes whereby the police or the prosecution can ask for the payment of money instead of prosecution. For example, in the Netherlands there is an extensive system of 'alternative sanctions' for young offenders, including the well-known HALT programmes for young vandals,[24] and for both young and adult offenders there is the possibility of a 'transaction', whereby the police may nominate a sum of money for a non-serious offence and if the offender pays it the right to prosecute is extinguished.[25] In Germany the prosecutor may offer to terminate proceedings for a misdemeanour on condition that the accused agrees to pay a sum of money to a charity or to the State.[26] Prosecutor fines have also been introduced in Scotland.[27] There is no equivalent of these schemes in England, although there is the fixed penalty notice that, for a large number of traffic offences, may be issued to an offender.[28] Payment of a fixed penalty is the equivalent of a sentence, and a conviction is recorded. In this respect it differs from the Dutch, German, and Scottish schemes, but in one important respect it is the same. All of them allow the defendant the alternative of contesting guilt in

---

[24] Commended in the report of the Audit Commission (1996), para. 74.

[25] See the discussion by Gelsthorpe *et al.* in C. Harding, P. Fennell, N. Jorg, and B. Swart (eds.), *Criminal Justice in Europe* (1995), ch.10, which also explains the HALT scheme (above, n. 6).

[26] Herrmann, above n. 16, at 757–60.

[27] P. Duff and K. Meechan, 'The Prosecutor Fine' [1992] *Crim. LR* 22; P. Duff, 'The Prosecutor Fine and Social Control' (1993) 33 *BJ Crim.* 481.

[28] For discussion, see A. J. Turner, 'The New Fixed Penalty System' [1986] *Crim. LR* 782.

court, by declining to accept the official offer and leaving the authorities to prosecute. This is in accordance with the European Convention on Human Rights, Article 6(1) of which has been interpreted so as to require the possibility of recourse to a court for a person who contests the decision to impose a penalty.[29]

3. The Selectivity of Regulatory Agencies

The regulatory agencies enjoy a wide discretion in deciding how often and in which cases to prosecute. In their 1980 survey, Lidstone, Hogg, and Sutcliffe found that most non-police agencies regarded criminal prosecution as a last resort, and sought to enforce compliance by other, less formal methods as far as possible.[30] Cranston's research into consumer protection departments found that prosecution is usually regarded as a last resort, after informal settlements and warnings.[31] A similar finding emerges from the study of the Pollution Inspectorate by Richardson, Ogus, and Burrows,[32] from the research by Hawkins into environmental health officers,[33] and from the research by Hutter into the approaches of the Factory Inspectorate, the Industrial Air Pollution Inspectorate, and environmental health officers.[34] The Inland Revenue has long pursued its aim, of the maximization of public revenue, by means of settlements and penalties outside the criminal process, with relatively rare resort to the courts.[35]

The usual way to characterize the approach of the various regulatory agencies is to suggest that they follow a 'compliance strategy' or 'accommodative approach', as distinct from a 'deterrence' or 'sanctioning' strategy.[36] The former, 'prosecution as a last resort' approach is shared by most of these agencies, but the degree of their commitment to it may differ. Indeed, Hutter has argued that there is a considerable difference between those agencies that adopt a 'persuasive' version of the compliance strategy and those that adopt what she terms the 'insistent' version. The Industrial Air Pollution Inspectorate has openly committed itself to the persuasive strategy: 'discus-

---

[29] *Le Compte, Van Leuven and De Meyere* (1981) A. 43, 23; *De Weer* (1980) A. 35, 23.

[30] K. Lidstone, R. Hogg, and F. Sutcliffe, *Prosecutions by Private Individuals and Non-police Agencies*, RCCP Research Study 10 (1980).

[31] R. Cranston, *Regulating Business* (1979), 107 and 168.

[32] G. Richardson, A. Ogus, and P. Burrows, *Policing Pollution* (1982).

[33] K. Hawkins, *Environment and Enforcement* (1984).

[34] B. Hutter, *The Reasonable Arm of the Law?* (1988).

[35] J. Roording, 'The Punishment of Tax Fraud' [1996] *Crim. LR* 240.

[36] See the classic essay by A. Reiss, 'Selecting Strategies of Social Control over Organisational Life', in K. Hawkins and J. Thomas (eds.), *Enforcing Regulation* (1984).

sion, persuasion and co-operation leading to mutually agreed solutions are preferred to coercion.'[37] This approach has as long a history as the inspectorate itself, and has sometimes been likened to education rather than policing. It is worth pointing out, however, that the legislation governing air pollution requires companies to adopt the 'best practicable means', a statutory framework that almost encourages negotiated standards. By way of contrast, the Factory Inspectorate has long been characterized by some ambivalence towards prosecution, with significant groups advocating greater use of this approach. As a whole the inspectorate favours compliance over the use of formal sanctions, but there is a much readier resort to oral and written advice and even to improvement notices. Hutter found that inspectors tend to speak of prosecution more frequently, even though they resort to it fairly rarely. In her research among environmental health officers there were also divergences, with some areas tending to resort to prosecution more frequently than others.[38]

It is therefore as well to bear in mind that, not only may the regulatory agencies differ among themselves in their degree of commitment to a compliance strategy, but different local departments may take somewhat different approaches. This may depend on the organizational structure: typically, environmental health officers could not prosecute unless this was approved by a committee of the local council. The resources available to the agency may also influence their enforcement style; this may independently have effects on enforcement policy, inasmuch as there is likely to be more negotiation if inspectors visit company officials more frequently and therefore get to know them more fully. Most agencies, however, respond firmly to incidents that attract considerable publicity, such as an accident at work that causes several deaths or injuries, or an outbreak of food poisoning.[39] Another factor that can lead to prosecution, even under the 'last resort' approach, would be the failure to respond to warnings, advice, or improvement notices.[40]

These variations are of much less significance than the considerable difference in approach between most regulatory agencies and the police. The breadth of discretion under the law is equally great, but there are divergent traditions. It would be too simple to suggest that the police resort to prosecution more frequently because they deal with more serious offences: a more sophisticated analysis would show that some of the offences with which the regulatory agencies deal can be regarded as more serious than many of the small thefts and handlings that the police routinely prosecute. The almost

[37] Quoted by B. Hutter, 'Variations in Regulatory Enforcement Styles' (1989) 11 *Law and Policy* 153, at 161, from the 1981 Annual Report of the Inspectorate.
[38] Hutter, above n. 37, 158–9. [39] *Ibid.* 165–6.
[40] G. Richardson, 'Strict Liability for Regulatory Crime' [1987] *Crim. LR* 295, at 301.

educational spirit in which some inspectorates were founded still dominates their approach, with an understanding of the difficulties faced by employers in finding the money for improvements in safety at a time of economic recession. This leads to awkward questions about social justice and, ultimately, about the aims of law enforcement. The contrast is rendered more complex by (a) the policy of the Inland Revenue, which deals with people from a wide range of backgrounds (but perhaps mostly the middle classes), in pursuing settlements for fairly large amounts of underpaid tax and prosecuting in fewer than 100 cases each year,[41] when those who steal lesser sums are routinely prosecuted; and (b) the co-option of the police into an approach to youth crime that has tended to rely on warnings rather than prosecutions. It is to the impact of cautioning, in respect of both juveniles and older offenders, that we now turn.

4. The Selectivity of the Police

Once the police have sufficient evidence against an offender, they have in theory all five alternatives set out in Section 3 above. They may take no further action, give an informal warning, administer a formal caution, or decide on a prosecution. Only the last alternative is open to review, by the Crown Prosecution Service. All the lesser alternatives have the effect of diverting the case from the criminal justice system, except in those rare cases where a private prosecution is brought, and there is no external review of those decisions. The Home Office made several attempts, in circulars in 1983, 1985, and 1990, to persuade the police to increase diversion and to reduce the proportionate use of prosecutions. These have had considerable success, particularly in respect of juveniles. The cautioning rate for males under 17 rose from 55 per cent in 1984 to 76 per cent in 1991, and for females under 17 from 79 to 90 per cent. For adult males the cautioning rate rose from 5 per cent in 1984 to 18 per cent in 1991, and for adult females from 14 to 40 per cent.[42] The circular of 1990 stated 'that the courts should only be used as a last resort, particularly for juveniles and young adults'.[43] However, there was a hardening of policy in the mid-1990s, and a Home Office circular of 1994—promoted by the then Home Secretary with the phrase 'your first chance is your last chance'—aimed to bring about

---

[41] J. Roording, 'The Punishment of Tax Fraud' [1996] *Crim. LR* 240.

[42] *Criminal Statistics, England and Wales* (1986 and 1991), table 5.5. The 1986 figures for adults are for those aged 17 and over, whereas the 1991 figure for adults is for those aged 21 and over; in fact this understates the magnitude of the increase.

[43] Home Office Circular 59/1990, para. 7.

significant reductions in repeat cautioning and in cautioning for indictable-only offences. The result has been a slight fall in the overall cautioning rate, for offenders under 18 and for adults, whilst the rate for young adults (aged 18–21) continues to grow from its previously low base (see Table 5.1).[44]

A survey in 1995 showed that 14 per cent of police cautions were repeat cautions (compared with 20 per cent in 1991): this is hardly a dramatic drop, and may show both the resilience of pre-1994 attitudes and the effects of the still considerable local variations.[45] In respect of young offenders, a survey in 1995–6 showed that the proportion charged had risen and the proportion cautioned had declined by a similar amount.[46] The new government has shown its preference for the more restrictive 1994 policy, and its proposals to change the system of cautioning for youth offenders will be discussed below.

1. *The formal principles*: the principles on which the police should take their gatekeeping decisions are set out as 'National Standards' in Home Office Circular 18/1994. This document has no legal significance; indeed, police cautioning is almost entirely a set of extra-legal practices. The National Standards do not explicitly lay down an order of preference: although it is stated that 'there should be a presumption in favour of not prosecuting certain categories of offender, such as elderly people or those who suffer from some form of mental illness or impairment, or a severe physical illness', it is made clear, on the one hand, that this does not 'afford absolute protection against prosecution', and, on the other hand, that in dealing with any offender the police must first decide that 'cautioning is the correct course'. The introduction to the National Standards adds that 'there is no intention of inhibiting the practice of taking action short of a formal caution by giving an oral warning . . .'. It is unfortunate that there is no clear commitment to the principle of minimum intervention: this could have been achieved, as in respect of identification procedures, by presenting the four alternatives in their preferred order of use.[47]

The National Standards reaffirm that a formal caution should not be offered unless there is sufficient evidence to prosecute, the offender admits the offence, and the offender gives informed consent. In his study of juveniles, Evans found that as many as 22 per cent of those who had been cautioned had uttered either a denial or a statement falling short of a confession,[48] which strengthens the argument for access to free legal advice at this stage. Assuming, however, that those requirements are fulfilled, the key issue is then

---

[44] Taken from *Criminal Statistics, England and Wales 1996*, Table 5.3.

[45] Evans and Ellis, above n. 20, 2.

[46] T. Bucke and D. Brown, *In Police Custody* (1997), 56–9.

[47] Home Office, Police and Criminal Evidence Act 1984, Codes of Practice (3rd edn., 1995), Code D. ch. 2.

[48] R. Evans, *The Conduct of Police Interviews with Juveniles* (1993).

Table 5.1. Offenders cautioned as a percentage of offenders found guilty or cautioned by type of offence, sex and age group

England and Wales · Percentages

Year	All offenders	Males					Females				
		All ages	Aged 10 and under 14	Aged 14 and under 18	Aged 18 and under 21	Aged 21 and over	All ages	Aged 10 and under 14	Aged 14 and under 18	Aged 18 and under 21	Aged 21 and over
Indictable offences											
1986	28	24	81	44	9	10	44	94	70	18	26
1987	30	26	86	49	11	11	45	96	73	22	28
1988	28	26	86	49	12	12	43	95	70	24	29
1989	29	26	88	52	15	13	44	95	72	27	31
1990	33	30	90	58	19	16	49	96	77	34	34
1991	36	32	90	59	23	18	54	97	80	41	40
1992	41	36	91	63	29	23	61	97	84	50	46
1993	41	37	90	63	32	26	60	97	84	52	46
1994	41	37	87	60	34	25	59	97	81	50	44
1995	41	37	86	58	35	26	59	96	79	51	44
1996	40	36	86	54	35	26	56	96	76	50	44

one of 'public interest'. The factors to be taken into account may be divided into five groups:

(a) the nature of the offence;
(b) the likely penalty if convicted in court;
(c) the offender's age and state of health;
(d) the offender's previous criminal history;
(e) the offender's attitude to the offence.

The decision to caution is a dispositive decision, analogous to sentencing in some of its principles and effects. The seriousness of the offence is a major factor, with some offences being regarded as too serious for cautioning even where the offender fulfils conditions (c), (d), (e), or indeed all of them. On the other hand, less serious offences may result in a caution even though the offender cannot be brought within (c), (d), or (e). The reference in (b) to the likely penalty may be found in the Code for Crown Prosecutors and in the 1990 version of the National Standards for Cautioning, but in most police forces it has now been replaced by a list of 'gravity factors', issued by the Association of Chief Police Officers in 1995. This enables the police to identify aggravating and mitigating factors in cases, and then to calculate a score which may help to indicate whether the correct course is to prosecute, to caution, or merely to give an informal warning.[49]

The clearest and best-established reason for cautioning is where the offender is very young, or elderly, or suffering from ill health. Reference has already been made to the increasingly high probability that a juvenile offender will be cautioned rather than prosecuted: at least until 1998 it has been possible to say that the younger the offender, the higher the probability of a caution—and the change to reprimands and final warnings under the Crime and Disorder Bill 1998 is unlikely to alter this significantly. Elderly offenders are also quite likely to receive a caution, often for theft from a shop. Where an offender is suffering from mental disorder or a severe physical illness, this also militates in favour of a caution. The rationale behind this category has never been made clear. The link with culpability is rather uncertain, although it can be maintained that those who are very young or mentally disordered are less to blame than others. The same could be said of some elderly offenders. However, there is considerable support for the rehabilitative argument that the process of prosecution, conviction, and sentence may cause stigma and otherwise be less effective in turning a young offender away from crime than a caution. In the case of young offenders this approach merges into the argument that sentences may have a harsher impact on certain types of offender,

---

[49] Some details are set out by the Audit Commission, above n. 20, 21.

and therefore that a lesser response would be appropriate in order to preserve proportionality. This is perhaps uppermost in cases of elderly offenders. It therefore appears that three rationales—culpability as an element of seriousness, rehabilitation, and equality of impact—may support this ground for cautioning. The National Standards, without explicitly stating a rationale, may draw promiscuously on all three.

The relevance of factor (e) is more debatable. It includes 'the wilfulness with which it was committed', which is clearly related to the question of culpability. Deliberate acts are usually more serious than 'spur of the moment' excesses. It also includes 'a practical demonstration of regret such as apologising to the victim and/or offering to put matters right as far as he is able'.[50] The difficulty here is that wealthy offenders might be able to buy themselves out of prosecution by offering payments to their victims, whereas impecunious offenders cannot. The law of sentencing contains clear declarations of principle against such inequality,[51] but the National Standards for Cautioning contain none. Moreover, the difficulties go further than this. Only a court can order an offender to pay compensation to the victim, and so one effect of a decision to caution is that there can be no legal framework for the payment of compensation to the victim. On the other hand, the 1994 National Standards state not only that it is desirable to establish the victim's view of the offence, but also that:

> if the offender has made some form of reparation or paid compensation, and the victim is satisfied, it may no longer be necessary to prosecute in cases where the possibility of a court's awarding compensation would otherwise have been a major determining factor. Under no circumstances should police officers become involved in negotiating or awarding reparation or compensation.

The guidance here is not absolutely clear, since there has been widespread commendation of 'caution plus' schemes which may involve reparation or compensation to victims. 'Caution plus' is discussed further below.

The 1994 National Standards were intended to alter practice on the granting of cautions to those who had been cautioned previously. Commenting that 'multiple cautioning brings this disposal into disrepute', the guidance went on to state that a second or subsequent caution should only be considered 'where the subsequent offence if trivial or where there has been a sufficient lapse of time since the first caution to suggest that it had some effect'. We have noted that the figures have gone down, although second and subsequent cautions are still given in some numbers to young offenders (perhaps because

---

[50] N. 22 above, note 3F.
[51] See Ashworth, *Sentencing and Criminal Justice* (2nd edn., 1995), ch. 7.

they fulfil the exceptional criteria of triviality or lapse of time). The new system for young offenders, under the Crime and Disorder Bill, aims to formalize a 'stepwise' approach by ensuring that only one reprimand is given, and only one final warning, so that prosecution must be the response to the next offence committed after a final warning.

2. *For and against cautioning*: why has there been such a strong movement towards cautioning in recent years? The National Standards begin by stating three purposes of cautions:

(a) to deal quickly and simply with less serious offenders;
(b) to divert them from the criminal courts;
(c) to reduce the chances of their reoffending.

The first purpose refers to proportionality, implying that quicker and simpler responses are more appropriate for less serious offences. However, the undertones of economics are also evident here, and the words 'and more cheaply' are implicit. The same undertones might be detected beneath the second purpose, although that might also be seen as a gesture towards the principle of minimum intervention.[52] The third purpose makes a bold claim about effectiveness. Statistics show that some 85 per cent of those cautioned in 1985 and 1988 were not convicted of a serious offence within two years of their caution.[53] This reconviction rate of 15 per cent is much lower than that for offenders convicted at court, at least for first offenders, which is 29 per cent for those without any previous convictions.[54] It could be commented that any such comparison is flawed because the court group is likely to have a higher proportion of people with previous cautions, who are more likely to be reconvicted anyway. A small matched study of juveniles by Mott suggests that those cautioned are still less likely to reoffend than those sentenced in court.[55] However, those who adopt the principle of minimum intervention do not need to establish that cautions are more effective, in terms of reconvictions. It is sufficient to argue that they have not been shown to be less effective than conviction and sentence.

What are the disadvantages of cautioning? Four possible disadvantages merit brief discussion—the danger of net-widening, pressure on defendants to admit to offences, unfairness to victims, and failure to discourage repeat

---

[52] Properly speaking, diversion from the criminal courts cannot be a 'purpose' of cautioning. It is simply its effect. A 'purpose' would offer a reason why offenders should be diverted in this way.

[53] Home Office Statistical Bulletin 8/94, *The Criminal Histories of those Cautioned in 1985, 1988 and 1991.*

[54] G. J. O. Phillpotts and L. B. Lancucki, *Previous Convictions, Sentence and Reconviction*, HORS 53 (1979), 16. This study had a longer follow-up period of 6 years, but it is known that most reconvictions occur early in the period.

[55] J. Mott, 'Police Decisions for Dealing with Juvenile Offenders' (1983) 23 *BJ Crim.* 249.

offenders. Net-widening is the process of using a new measure, not (or not only) to encompass the target group of offenders who would otherwise have been prosecuted, but also to drag into the net people who might otherwise have benefited from a lesser response. This danger was pointed out to the police in the 1985 circular, and there is little evidence that the considerable increases in cautioning during the 1980s have been achieved through any significant net-widening.[56] Whilst there may be some cases of this kind, the figures suggest a genuine transfer of offenders away from prosecution towards cautioning. In respect of young offenders, the vast majority of police forces (thirty-nine out of forty-three) use inter-agency youth panels of one kind or another, to which they may refer some cases for advice.[57] These panels tend to include representatives from social services, the police and other relevant agencies. However, the system is such that the police have the last word on the action to be taken in any particular case, and in the recent 'culture of severity' that may have led multi-agency teams to propose more interventionist measures.[58]

The offer of a caution may put pressure on a suspect to admit an offence when it is not clear that he or she committed it. If the suspect denies knowledge of a certain fact, he or she might wish to decline a caution and have the point adjudicated in court; and yet the disincentives to taking that course are so great (delay, risk of not being believed, risk of conviction) that acceptance of the caution is likely. The National Standards state that 'a caution will not be appropriate where a person does not make a clear and reliable admission of the offence',[59] but there is the additional problem that the police may not fully understand the relevant law, such as the mental element required for the crime or the possible defences.[60] In effect, whenever a person knows or believes that there will be a choice between accepting a caution and risking a prosecution, there is bound to be pressure to accept the caution. The disadvantages of this must be minimized by ensuring, as far as possible, that cautions are only offered if the conditions are strictly met. This would require far greater supervision within the police, or the provision of legal advice, or the transfer of the function to the CPS. As will be argued below, the issue of safeguards is particularly important now that cautions are cited in court and relied upon for other purposes.

---

[56] M. McMahon, 'Net-Widening: Vagaries in the Use of a Concept' (1990) 30 *BJ Crim.* 121.

[57] Audit Commission, *Misspent Youth*, para. 27; for a fuller discussion of one such scheme, see S. Uglow *et al.*, 'Cautioning Juveniles: Multi-Agency Impotence' [1992] *Crim. LR* 632.

[58] G. Hughes, A. Pilkington, and R. Leistan, 'Diversion in a Culture of Severity' (1998) 37 *Howard JCJ* 16.

[59] Above n. 22, annex B, note 2B.

[60] A. Sanders, 'The Limits to Diversion from Prosecution' (1988) 28 *BJ Crim.* 513.

Unfairness to victims is an ingrained problem of the trend towards greater cautioning. The statistics show that since 1988 an ever-higher proportion of convicted offenders is being ordered to pay compensation to victims, and yet those statistics must be read in the context of the increased percentage of offenders who are cautioned rather than prosecuted. Thus in 1991 fewer offenders were ordered to pay compensation by criminal courts than in 1981, some 112,800 compared with 129,400.[61] Of course some offenders will have made voluntary payments to their victims, but the National Standards emphasize that 'under no circumstances should police officers become involved in negotiating or awarding reparation or compensation'.[62] The result is that in some cases a police decision to caution, made on the merits of the case, will mean that the victim's chance of receiving compensation is destroyed. Some ambiguity about this in the National Standards was noted earlier,[63] but this is an awkward practical problem for any system with some commitment to victims. Courts are required to reduce a compensation order so as to take account of the means of the offender: the police could not be expected to make inquiries of this kind. However, 'caution plus' schemes have now been developed in some police areas, although the Audit Commission found that few youth offending cases were dealt with in this way. In some areas, 'agencies were either opposed in principle to addressing offending behaviour outside the court system or the co-ordination between them was inadequate'.[64] Only a few such schemes involve reparation or compensation to victims; others involve some form of social work intervention aimed at reducing the risk of reoffending.

A fourth argument, increasingly heard in recent years, is that cautioning (in particular, repeat cautioning) sends the wrong message to some offenders. The present government links this argument with the relative rarity of 'caution plus' schemes, in its analysis of the problems of cautioning young offenders:

> While some areas operate voluntary 'caution plus' schemes, in others there is no backup to try to prevent further crime. Inconsistent, repeated and ineffective cautioning has allowed some children and young people to feel that they can offend with impunity.[65]

This led them to the proposals in the Crime and Disorder Bill 1998, which allow no more than one reprimand, no more than one final warning (which will 'usually be followed by a community intervention programme, involving

---

[61] *Criminal Statistics, England and Wales* (1991), table 7.24.
[62] See n. 22 above, and text thereat.   [63] Above n. 22, para. 9.
[64] Audit Commission, above n. 20, para. 33.
[65] Home Office, *No More Excuses: A New Approach to Tackling Youth Crime in England and Wales* (1997), para. 5.10.

the offender and his or her family to address the causes of the offending and so reduce the risk of further crime'), even where a case is not thought to warrant prosecution. These are, in effect, to be the successors to 'caution plus' schemes for young offenders. The new scheme means that the exceptions which allowed repeat cautions in the 1994 circular, notably the triviality of the second offence, are no longer to have any effect, unless the police simply decline to take any formal action at all. The result is that some young offenders may be brought to court for relatively minor offences which would previously have justified no more than a repeat caution. Some will regard this as a significant step towards legality, in bringing the response to young offenders more into the open forum of the courts. Others will regard this as an unfortunate step away from a proportionality principle in youth justice.

3. *The practical implementation of National Standards*: there has been long-standing concern about the apparent gap between national standards and local practices. One consequence of this is so-called 'justice by geography', which will be discussed below. But there has been a general concern about the processes whereby national guidelines may be translated into on-the-ground action. One argument in favour of a legislative framework for cautioning is that it might be more effective in altering police practices, which have sometimes lagged reluctantly behind Home Office policy. Thus the 1985 Home Office circular did not find its way into force policies in some police areas, and there was often a tendency to leave the matter for local determination. The 1990 circular required police forces to incorporate the new policies into their force orders, but still there were evident local variations. In 1995 the Association of Chief Police Officers issued a document on 'gravity factors' for deciding on cautions, but Evans and Ellis report that only twenty-five out of forty-two forces have adopted it.[66] One of the objectives of the new statutory scheme of reprimands and final warnings for youth offenders is to foster consistency of approach, but the system for adult and young adult offenders remains without statutory foundation.

In the meantime, the allegation of 'justice by geography' continues to be made against cautioning practice, despite the three Home Office circulars and the 1995 ACPO initiative on gravity factors. Evans and Ellis conclude, on the basis of research in late 1995, that 'the circulars have not been successful in achieving greater consistency between forces'.[67] One possible reason for this is that police forces may be dealing with different mixes of cases. Since cautioning is much used for first offenders, the proportion of first offenders coming to police attention is highly likely to affect the cautioning rate. Evans and Wilkinson found that the percentage of first offenders did differ significantly

---

[66] Evans and Ellis, above n. 20, 2.   [67] *Ibid.* 4.

among areas (from 46 to 64 per cent) and that it was related to the juvenile cautioning rate in the ten forces studied. However, they also found that further variation in cautioning was not explained by the different offence-mix: much cautioning is for shoplifting, but it appeared that forces adopted differing policies towards this.[68] One of the conclusions of this study was that cautioning guidelines tend to say little about the most crucial factor in practice—the type and seriousness of the offence. The ACPO guidelines on gravity factors were probably the first general attempt to tackle this issue, in the sense that they list specific gravity factors for a range of offences.[69]

As with all evidence of local variations in criminal justice, there is the argument that it is not so much different policies being pursued but rather police forces responding to local conditions and particular problems. It is certainly true that many worthwhile initiatives in criminal justice have come about through local attempts to address problems; but there is also the probability that some local variations stem from a stubborn and insular unwillingness to absorb new national policies and to change working practices. This is often possible because of the considerable latitude left to the police, particularly in the absence of legislation. The matter then becomes another instance of police discretion being exercised in various ways. Thus McConville, Sanders, and Leng, on the basis of their research in the late 1980s, argued that the cautioning guidelines are so broadly worded that they can easily be used by the police to justify decisions taken on other grounds.[70] These other grounds are likely to reflect the working practices and concerns of the police. They give examples of a case being prosecuted in response to the insistence of a local business, even though it fell within the cautioning guidelines, and of another case resulting in a caution when (as a theft in breach of trust) it fell squarely within the prosecution category. A more recent study by Evans of attempts to introduce new guidance for the cautioning of young adults in two London police divisions shows once again that it is attitudes and working philosophies rather than written rules that tend to determine outcomes.[71] A 'Caution Consideration Chart' was introduced, but it tended to be used in some police stations as a resource, to legitimate decisions taken by the custody officer on other grounds. Sometimes, too, victims' views were similarly manipulated, being ignored when inconvenient and cited when they supported a decision already

---

[68] Above n. 22, 160–3.

[69] The Metropolitan Police incorporated these into a 'Case Disposal Manual', excerpts from which are set out in the judgment of Schiemann LJ in R. v. Metropolitan Police Commissioner, ex parte Thompson [1997] 1 WLR 1519.

[70] M. McConville, A. Sanders, and R. Leng, The Case for the Prosecution (1991), 122 and ch. 6 generally.

[71] R. Evans, 'Evaluating Young Adult Diversion Schemes in the Metropolitan Police District' [1993] Crim. LR 490.

taken. Overall, the probability is that some decisions result from a simple following of the guidelines, whereas others are motivated more by the 'moral character' of the offender or victim or by concerns related to the police mission.[72] It might also be observed that the police will sometimes take a decision that might be justifiable on the limited information available but that might cease to be justifiable when more information comes to light. Some of the 'public interest' criteria for not prosecuting depend on matters extraneous to the offence, of which the police may have no knowledge.[73]

5. Accountability

It is apparent from the discussion of the gatekeeping practices of the police and of regulatory agencies that discretion is the dominant characteristic. There is little law in these areas, and what law there is aims merely to facilitate rather than to direct. Guidelines have been created, but these are so generally phrased and so lightly enforced that their impact is muted. To what extent, if at all, are these decision-makers accountable? The question has to be answered on two different levels: accountability for general policy, and accountability for individual decisions.

It is not clear to what extent the various regulatory agencies are accountable for their policies. We saw that the Factories Inspectorate and the Air Pollution Inspectorate have long had different policies in respect of prosecution, but is there any higher agency that can point to these divergent traditions and ask for justifications? It appears not. The enforcement practices of the Inland Revenue and the Customs and Excise were examined by the Keith Committee in 1983,[74] and their frequent use of compounded penalties was commended as 'swift and economical', but on a continuing basis the only vestige of accountability is the submission to Parliament of an annual report. For almost all regulatory agencies this is the only means of being called to account for policy.

With the police there is a much greater appearance of accountability. Yet the 'National Standards for Cautioning' are supported merely by a Home Office circular, the terms of which were agreed with the Association of Chief Police Officers and the Crown Prosecution Service. No doubt the terms of the circular are used as a basis for inspections by Her Majesty's Inspector of Constabulary. No doubt, also, there are possible financial implications for

---

[72] See above, Ch. 3.3.   [73] See the discussion of PICA schemes below, Ch. 6.3.
[74] Report of the Interdepartmental Committee, The Enforcement of Revenue Legislation (chairman: Lord Keith), Cmnd. 8822 (1983).

refusal to comply. However, as far as the law is concerned the Chief Constable of each area is solely responsible for decisions on law enforcement in that area. Since the Court of Appeal has held that 'No Minister of the Crown can tell him that he must or must not prosecute this man or that one',[75] the National Standards cannot be binding in law. The 1993 Royal Commission recommended:

> that police cautioning should be governed by statute, under which national guidelines, drawn up in consultation with the CPS and the police service among others, should be laid down in regulations. These regulations should also govern the keeping of records of cautions so that information about whether a suspect has been cautioned can easily be transferred between police forces.[76]

To give statutory authority for police cautions would be a worthwhile step, and in effect that step has been taken by the Government in the provisions of the Crime and Disorder Bill 1998 dealing with reprimands and final warnings for young offenders. The recording of cautions is also an important matter, and since 1995 they have been recorded on the National Police Computer, which should greatly improve consistency and reliability of information.

National guidelines, however, we already have. The key question is whether any newly drafted guidelines would be different and, if so, in what way. The Royal Commission gave no hint of whether it considered the existing National Standards and found them wanting in any respect: the discussion above has identified some respects in which improvement is needed, both on the criteria and in the availability of legal advice. Nor did the Royal Commission deal with the problem of accountability: how would the new regulations be enforced? We saw earlier that the research of Evans and Ellis reveals considerable local variation, despite all the efforts to bring about consistency. There is a need for further research to explore the causes of this variation, any justifications for it, and the most effective and sensitive means of eliminating it.

Accountability for individual decisions depends largely on the internal structure of the agency. Within the police, there may be local police traditions or cultures that lead to variation in interpretation, even if there is a clear force policy.[77] It is a well-known characteristic of the police that the amount of supervision of constables is not great, and that they have much *de facto* discretion.[78] Historically this has not been true of cautioning decisions, since

---

[75] *R. v. Metropolitan Police Commissioner, ex p. Blackburn (No. 1)* [1968] 2 QB 118, per Lord Denning, MR.

[76] RCCJ, *Report*, Cmnd. 2263 (1993), para. 5.57.

[77] For a recent example, in relation to the cautioning of young adults, see the comparison between two police divisions by Evans, above n. 71, 490.

[78] e.g. Maguire and Norris, above n. 5; B. Irving and C. Dunnighan, *Human Factors in the Quality Control of CID Investigations*, RCCJ Research Study 21 (1993).

cases for caution have tended to be referred to inspector level for approval. This is not always so, now that cautioning is becoming a more widespread practice, but it remains true that a key stage is when a constable brings into a police station someone who has just been arrested. The station sergeant has to decide whether or not to accept the charge. The constable may press for the person to be charged, making it into an issue of support or non-support for another officer, and the sergeant may not have sufficient information on 'public interest' factors to be able to resist this even if it were thought advisable. Thus any policy of increasing the use of cautions is far more likely to succeed if there is force-wide commitment to its objectives; if there is not, aspects of the occupational culture are likely to overshadow it in practice.

If in a particular case a person is charged, despite falling within one of the categories for cautioning outlined in the National Standards, it seems that judicial review may be possible but that this would be judicial review of the Crown Prosecution Service if they decide to continue the prosecution rather than discontinuing it. This, the Divisional Court held,[79] is because the police are merely the initiators of proceedings, and the 'last and decisive word' on the issue now lies with the Crown Prosecution Service. The CPS would take this decision within the framework of the Code for Crown Prosecutors (to be discussed in the next chapter), which is similar in terms to the National Standards. A decision to continue the prosecution would be reviewable in the case of a juvenile and, although one court held that judicial review is 'unlikely to be available' if the decision concerns an adult, that decision now seems to have been superseded.[80] What of the reverse situation, where the police decide to caution an offender and the victim or another interested person can demonstrate that the case does not fall within the National Standards? Apart from the possibility of a private prosecution, an action for judicial review of the police decision might be brought. This is a matter on which the police have the 'last and decisive word', since such a case would never reach the CPS. If the decision could be shown to be *Wednesbury* unreasonable,[81] judicial review could be expected to succeed, whether the case concerns a juvenile or an adult.[82]

---

[79] In *R. v. Chief Constable of Kent et al., ex p. L.* (1991) 93 Cr.App.R. 416, per Watkins, LJ, at 426. Cf. *R. v. Croydon Justices, ex p. Dean* [1993] *Crim. LR* 759, dealing with an offence which may only be prosecuted with the consent of the Director of Public Prosecutions, where the CPS have the 'last word' on prosecuting.

[80] Compare *Ex p. L.*, at 428, with the judgement of Stuart-Smith LJ in *R. v. Inland Revenue Commissioner, ex p. Mead* [1993] 1 All ER 772, at 780.

[81] The reference is to the test in the leading case of *Associated Provincial Pictures Houses Ltd. v. Wednesbury Corporation* [1948] 1 KB 223.

[82] See *General Council of the Bar, ex p. Percival* [1990] 3 All ER 137, discussed by C. Hilson, 'Discretion to Prosecute and Judicial Review' [1993] *Crim. LR* 639.

The defendant himself may also challenge a caution if the procedure leading up to the decision was unfair. Thus in *R. v. Metropolitan Police Commissioner, ex parte Thompson*[83] the Divisional Court granted an order of certiorari quashing a caution on the ground that the police inspector failed to make it clear that the decision to caution had been made before asking the defendant whether he admitted the offence. Counsel brought the case on the basis that, where the police appear to be offering a caution if the defendant were to admit the offence, this is an unfair inducement which, on an analogy with the exclusion of confessions, should nullify the acceptance of the caution. The Divisional Court agreed with this proposition. The ruling is significant in two ways: first, it emphasizes the need to ensure that cautions are only offered and accepted in appropriate cases; and secondly, it is important when cautions are recorded and may be relied upon subsequently. The ruling also shows why it is desirable to have access to legal advice before accepting a caution.

As for the regulatory agencies, the research often suggests that there are variations in the local culture of different parts of a single agency—one familiar finding is a divergence of approach between rural areas and urban areas. The accountability of the individual inspector may depend on how paperwork is completed and how thoroughly it is supervised. Good training and retraining may be important factors, but on the other hand these have to fight against any local culture, financial pressures, and other countervailing forces. However, an individual decision to prosecute or not to prosecute is unlikely to be reviewed, within most agencies, unless it is a case of particular sensitivity to which the attention of senior officials has been drawn. Judicial review of a decision to prosecute or not to prosecute would be available in theory, since most of these agencies have the 'last and decisive word' within their own sphere of operation, but the reluctance of the Divisional Court in the *Kent* case to introduce judicial review into prosecution decisions may prove not to have been displaced by the greater willingness of the court in *Mead*.[84]

These uncertainties in the formal avenues of accountability assume greater significance when the consequences of the decisions are recalled. If a case is not prosecuted by the police, but is dealt with by caution or no formal action, this is the end of the process—although the recording and citing of cautions should not be forgotten. The only way to revive the case is by means of a private prosecution: those are rare, and the immense investment of time and money needed to mount such a prosecution means that it cannot realistically be termed a method of accountability. If the decision is in favour of prosecution, the case then goes to the Crown Prosecution Service, which has powers

---

[83] [1997] 1 WLR.   [84] See above, nn. 79–80.

of discontinuance: the extent to which they are exercised is discussed in the next chapter.

6. Values and Principles

The stages of decision-making discussed here raise several questions of value that need further discussion. Is equality of treatment ensured? Are the interests of victims properly respected? Are the rights of defendants respected? Is there too great a sacrifice of crime control? How might the difficulties be dealt with?

1. *Equality of treatment*: in the previous section we saw that the due execution of stated policies is not ensured by the law because legal accountability is rather sketchy in this sphere. The practices of cautioning and diversion operate in a world where there is little law, save at the extremes, and considerable discretion. Decisions are taken in private, without hearing views from the interested parties and without reasons needing to be given. Even after the enactment of the Crime and Disorder Bill 1998 in respect of young offenders, there will still be no statutory basis for the cautioning of adults and young adults, and all the difficulties set out in Sections 4 and 5 of this chapter will remain.

The predominance of discretion might be regarded as a contradiction of the principle of equality before the law and equal treatment. In many European countries, the considerable weight given to the principle of compulsory prosecution shows awareness of the values at stake. It is true that most countries do not regard this as an absolute principle, and in recent years have sought to allow scope to the principle of expediency whereby certain cases are diverted from the courts, usually by prosecutors. But these can be regarded as circumscribed exceptions to the principle that criminal justice should be dispensed in open court, after a full consideration of the issues, with reasons given. While these values are usually compromised in some way,[85] there is surely good reason to ensure that they are expressed and are accorded some respect. The decisions in this chapter are decisions that may profoundly affect the course of a suspect/offender's life, since prosecution itself may be highly significant for the defendant in terms of anxiety and stress, damage to reputation, and possible loss of employment. If discretion is to be bestowed on

[85] In many Continental systems the court proceedings amount to little more than confirmation of what is in the dossier, with the real decisions having been taken earlier by the public prosecutor and others. See e.g. H. Lensing and L. Rayar, 'Notes on Criminal Procedure in the Netherlands' [1992] *Crim. LR* 623.

certain authorities, it should be carefully structured so as to achieve desired policies and properly controlled through channels of accountability. The few laconic remarks of the 1993 Royal Commission on this question were most unsatisfactory.[86]

Cautioning practices and diversion generally do seem to accord appropriately favourable treatment to vulnerable groups such as the mentally disturbed. The diversion of mentally disordered offenders is a well-established practice, although it has been argued that the ready referral of mentally disturbed suspects to the mental health services and hospitals may sometimes be a disproportionately severe response, or may deprive them of rights they would have if prosecuted, or both.[87] There is a growing number of court-based psychiatric schemes, one purpose of which is to identify and assess mentally disordered defendants and to see whether a form of diversion (such as immediate hospital admission) is possible and desirable. A preliminary study of an Islington scheme showed that many of the mentally disordered defendants had problems with living accommodation, problems of substance abuse, and that there was an apparent over-representation of black people with psychotic illness.[88]

Apart from particularly vulnerable groups, does the system ensure equality of treatment? One obvious problem is the difference of approach to 'police' matters and to spheres of conduct that are regulated by the various non-police agencies. Companies, wealthy offenders, and middle-class offenders are more often dealt with by regulatory agencies whereas the more disadvantaged members of society are more likely to find their conduct defined as a police matter. The different approaches are then likely to result in more frequent prosecution of the disadvantaged than the advantaged for offences that may be no different in terms of seriousness. Norval Morris and Michael Tonry might adapt their argument on sentencing, to the effect that it is wrong to insist on equality if it means equality of misery.[89] The effect of this would be to allow middle-class or white-collar offenders to benefit from diversion and other alternatives to prosecution, even though lower-class or blue-collar offenders were processed in the 'normal' way, since to assimilate the treatment of the former group to that of the latter would increase the overall suffering. On a principle of parsimony, minimum intervention may thus be given higher priority than equality of treatment. However, the factual basis for this is the assumption that there is no practical way of extending forms of

---

[86] RCCJ Report, para. 5.59.
[87] D. Carson, 'Prosecuting People with Mental Handicaps' [1989] *Crim. LR* 87.
[88] E. Burney and G. Pearson, 'Mentally Disordered Offenders: Finding a Focus for Diversion' (1995) 34 *Howard JCJ* 291.
[89] N. Morris and M. Tonry, *Between Prison and Probation* (1990).

diversion to lower-class offenders who commit 'police' crimes. This is quite unsubstantiated. Thus, even without attacking their order of priorities, it can be argued that there is a need to devise further forms of diversion that can be operated swiftly for large numbers of small-time offenders.

A second problem of equality of treatment concerns racial discrimination. Several studies suggest that there is some discrimination against Afro-Caribbeans in respect of decisions to prosecute or caution. For example, Tony Jefferson and Monica Walker found that Asians were much more likely to be cautioned than any others, but that Afro-Caribbeans were less likely than whites to receive a caution.[90] The Commission for Racial Equality monitored the cautioning of juveniles in seven police forces and found that Afro-Caribbeans were more likely to be referred for prosecution than whites.[91] It seems likely that part of the difference in prosecution rates revealed by these studies would disappear if account were taken of whether the individual was willing to admit the offence: more Afro-Caribbeans decline to admit the allegations against them, which removes their eligibility for a caution.[92] However, this certainly does not eliminate the differences found, and there remains cause for concern about differential responses. The principle of equality of treatment, enshrined in Article 14 of the European Convention on Human Rights, seems to be being compromised.

A third problem is posed by the differential cautioning rates for females, which are much higher than those for men—in 1991, 90 per cent for juvenile girls compared with 76 per cent for juvenile boys, and 40 per cent for women compared with 18 per cent for men. The overall figures for 1996 show cautioning rates of 56 per cent for females and 36 per cent for males. The face-value interpretation would be that females are receiving unduly favourable treatment, but this fails to take account of the probability that offences of different types and different levels of seriousness would be found in the different groups. Relatively little research into the differences has been reported, but data on cautioning show that, whereas a majority of both sexes had no previous criminal history, cautioned males were twice as likely as females to have been previously convicted.[93] Although this might be expected on the basis of the higher offending rate of males, it does raise questions about the criteria for cautioning and prosecution, and leaves open the possibility that women have failed to benefit from repeat cautioning as often as men.

---

[90]   T. Jefferson and M. Walker, 'Ethnic Minorities in the Criminal Justice System' [1992] *Crim. LR* 83, at 88.

[91]   Commission for Racial Equality, *Juvenile Cautioning: Ethnic Monitoring in Practice* (1992).

[92]   M. Fitzgerald, *Ethnic Minorities and the Criminal Justice System*, RCCJ Research Study 20 (1993), 18.

[93]   C. Hedderman and M. Hough, *Does the Criminal Justice System Treat Men and Women Differently?*, Home Office Research Findings No. 10 (1994), 2.

2. *Victims' rights*: are the existing arrangements for diversion, dominated by the police caution, effective in securing the rights of victims? There is a small number of mediation schemes that may assist victims in coming to terms with the offence and in securing compensation from the offender and the arguments in favour of extending them are considered below. The Crime and Disorder Bill 1998 will encourage restorative approaches to young offenders.[94] As for formal police cautions, these appear inadequate for the purpose of ensuring that victims receive compensation. The National Standards refer to the views of the victim as a factor in the decision whether or not to caution, but this procedural involvement is surely far less appropriate and far less important than ensuring the payment of some compensation. In theory there is no reason why the offer of a formal caution, extra-statutory as it is, should not be made conditional on the payment of compensation to the victim. This might well achieve some of the aims of 'caution plus' schemes and, whilst the 1993 Royal Commission recommends further experiments in using the Probation Service to combine cautions with co-operation in treatment programmes, it is unfortunate that it failed to examine the possibility of incorporating victim compensation when proposing the introduction of prosecutor fines.[95] In some of those European countries that have a system of conditional non-prosecution or conditional waiver of prosecution, this is a possibility.[96] However, the introduction of conditional non-prosecution linked to the payment of compensation would raise some practical problems. It is not clear how the amount of the compensation would be settled, nor whether it might be reduced if the offender were impecunious.[97] It would be important to ensure that such a system did not enable wealthy offenders to buy themselves out of prosecution: there would need to be proper guidelines for the use of this alternative to prosecution. The Crown Prosecution Service, as a quasi-judicial body,[98] would be more appropriate than the police for administering such a system, in view of its overall responsibility for prosecution policy.

One question that remains open is whether a form of mediation should be offered to offenders and their victims. It is easier to give a positive response to this question than to determine exactly how the outcome of such mediation should relate to the formal criminal process. Since the participation of victims in such schemes must remain voluntary, it seems wrong that the victim's decision to participate or not should influence the way in which the criminal

---

[94] See above, p. 157.
[95] RCCJ Report, comparing para. 5.60 with para. 5.62. [96] Tak, above n. 15.
[97] Cf. the informal system of conditional waiver of prosecution in the Netherlands, used to secure compensation for victims: C. Brants and S. Field, 'Discretion and Accountability in Prosecution', in C. Harding *et al.*, *Criminal Justice in Europe* (1995).
[98] In many European countries prosecutors are, constitutionally, part of the judicial branch.

justice system responds to the offence. There are signs, however, that such schemes can operate by way of diversion without prejudicing the interests of victims.[99]

3. *Defendants' rights*: one common feature of diversion schemes is that the defendant can decline the offer made by the police or prosecution if guilt is disputed, leaving them to prosecute in court and have the matter decided there. Whilst this is sufficient to comply with the European Convention on Human Rights,[100] it none the less leaves to the defendant a choice that is not without pressure. There is a strong incentive to take an offer that dispenses with prosecution in court, especially if (as with cautioning in England and Wales) no formal conditions can be attached. It was the making of an offer of a caution before the defendant had admitted guilt of the offence that constituted the unfair procedure in the *Thompson* case.[101] The police should first decide what action is appropriate, and only then ask the defendant whether he admits the offence and is prepared to accept a caution. It still remains possible for the defendant to decline, and for the police then either to drop the case or bring a prosecution. On the one hand, there is considerable temptation to accept a caution, even if one is innocent, since it avoids a court appearance. On the other hand, increasing reliance is being placed on cautions for other purposes. Not only may they be cited in court as part of a record of previous offending, but they may also be raised when there is a question whether the defendant is of good character,[102] and a caution for a sex offence is sufficient for the inclusion of a person on the national register maintained under the Sex Offenders Act 1997.[103]

Two possible means of preventing injustices may be mentioned. First, decisions on cautioning could be transferred from the police to the Crown Prosecution Service, with a view to ensuring that a caution is offered only in cases where the evidence really does fulfil the appropriate legal criteria. Secondly, there could be a provision for access to legal advice before deciding whether or not to accept a caution. The second is important if cautioning decisions are to remain in the hands of the police, but it would be desirable to introduce both safeguards. No doubt these would slow down the system, and would therefore be resisted as making it more expensive and more 'inefficient'. But the transfer of power to the Crown Prosecution Service can be supported

---

[99] See Cavadino and Dignan, *The Penal System* (2nd edn., 1999), 217–18, reporting on a Northamptonshire scheme.

[100] See above, n. 29.

[101] *R. v. Metropolitan Police Commissioner, ex parte Thompson* [1997] 1 WLR.

[102] See the difficulties to which Judge May draws attention in R. May, 'The Legal Effect of a Police Caution' [1997] *Crim. LR* 491.

[103] K. Soothill, B. Francis and B. Sanderson, 'A Cautionary Tale: the Sex Offenders Act 1997, the Police and Cautions' [1997] *Crim. LR* 482.

independently, as we shall see, and the provision for legal advice is necessary to deal with that minority of cases in which defendants may be materially disadvantaged by the present arrangements.

4. *Crime control:* one of the objections frequently raised against forms of diversion is that they undermine crime prevention, simply because many offenders do not take them seriously. It is not uncommon to hear anecdotes about offenders, often young, who express themselves as if they have a 'licence to offend' because they know that nothing worse than a caution will result. As we saw earlier, this has led the present government to propose a rigid escalation of response to young offenders—only one reprimand before a final warning, only one final warning before prosecution. Yet this is despite the generally favourable reconviction figures for cautions (although the government suggests that after three offences a prosecution is less likely to be followed by reconviction than a caution.)[104] The argument that extensive diversion may undermine moral restraints against lawbreaking has also led to changes in the Netherlands, where the policy changed in 1990 towards increasing the proportion of cases that resulted in some formal action by the authorities.[105] A further issue is the rights of victims. An offender should be required to do something to make good any loss or damage inflicted: it will rarely be possible for young offenders to do this by paying money (unless the parents are able to pay), but some other form of reparation may be possible. For older offenders, however, the payment of compensation should be a primary feature of diversion, as argued above. Many questions of detail would need to be resolved, but the principle of compensation to victims from offenders should be respected. This is a major failing of the existing English arrangements, which the encouragement of 'caution plus' schemes, without legislative support, is unlikely to remedy. Important experiments in restorative justice are taking place with young offenders in New Zealand[106] and also in some parts of England (notably the Northamptonshire Diversion Unit and the Leeds Diversion Scheme).[107] There is, however, a distinction between attempting to assure compensation to victims and giving victims a voice in disposals.

---

[104] Home Office, above n. 65, para. 5.9, referring to research (of which scant details are given) reported by the Audit Commission, above n. 20, Exhibit 18, 23.

[105] Ministry of Justice, *Law in Motion* (1990), 40–1.

[106] A. Morris, G. Maxwell, and J. Robertson, 'Giving Victims a Voice: a New Zealand Experiment' (1993) 32 *Howard JCJ* 304; cf. S. Jackson, 'Family Group Conferences in Youth Justice? The Issues for Implementation in England and Wales' (1998) 37 *Howard JCJ* 34.

[107] For details of the former, see G. Hughes, A. Pilkington, and R. Leistan, 'Diversion in a Culture of Severity' (1998) 37 *Howard JCJ* 16.

7. Conclusions

There are good arguments in favour of the diversion of non-serious offenders from the criminal courts, but this should be done at the least possible cost to the rights of victims and of defendants. It is quite proper that the prospect of saving time and money should lead policy-makers to expand diversion, not least because prosecuting offenders is not necessarily more effective in terms of reconviction rates. But the attraction of schemes of diversion should not be allowed to obscure the principles of criminal justice outlined in Chapter 2. Quite apart from the strong criticism of the English cautioning system that it fails to respect victims' rights to compensation, decisions on caution, prosecution, or no further action have tended to be left to the police, without meaningful review or accountability, particularly when a caution is offered. There is even less accountability in respect of the practices of the so-called regulatory agencies.

The existing system encourages the police to caution certain offenders, but does not provide them with sources of information on the factors necessary for a caution. The Crown Prosecution Service benefits from information from PICA schemes in some areas, when reassessing the public interest in prosecution.[108] The police service has to assemble the information for themselves, unless the case involves a juvenile and there is multi-agency co-operation. On the other hand, active defence solicitors will often draw the attention of the police or the CPS to factors in a case that might justify cautioning rather than prosecution. The police also lack expertise on legal issues relevant to guilt, although they can consult the CPS for advice. The recommendation of the 1993 Royal Commission in favour of prosecutor fines seemed likely only to confuse the picture, and has not been acted upon. It raised awkward questions about strategies for diversion. First there are several questions about the role of prosecutor fines. Are they to be treated as more severe than cautions, and therefore to be used for more serious cases or for people who have already been cautioned? How can the Commission's extraordinary failure to consider, let alone to give priority to, victim compensation be explained? Would prosecutor fines be used chiefly for 'victimless' crimes such as public order offences? In Scotland, prosecutor fines do not require an admission of guilt and are not recorded, unlike cautions in England: can these differences be justified? A second issue is the division of responsibilities between the police and the CPS. Hitherto the CPS has not been directly involved in diversion: even in the few cases that have been remitted to the police at the stage of prosecutor-

---

[108] See RCCJ Report, para. 5.61, and Ch. 6, below, p. 187.

ial review, this has been in the form of a request to the police to caution the offender. The CPS is not involved itself. If prosecutor fines were introduced, two agencies would be able to divert offenders. Would the police refer cases to the CPS for prosecutor fines? If so, which cases?

These questions revive the proposal of Andrew Sanders that diversion decisions should be placed in the hands of a single agency, and that that agency should be the CPS.[109] The benefits of this might be greater consistency in the exercise of discretion, once the appropriate criteria had been decided upon, and a fuller separation of the investigative function from the prosecutorial and dispositive. The police would be reduced to the role of investigators, with most of the significant decisions on whether and how to proceed transferred to another agency. Against this might be ranged the long-standing experience of the police in decision-making of this kind, combined with their involvement in some schemes for diversion; the CPS is relatively inexperienced in this kind of decision-making, but if this argument is always given weight the CPS will of course remain inexperienced. The question is whether it has the capacity and could be trained. More to the point is whether the CPS would welcome these wider responsibilities and would adapt to them, and whether they could find suitable staff to take on decision-making of this kind. Other more pragmatic considerations would be the cost of transferring these decisions to the CPS (more staff for the CPS, but perhaps more paperwork for the police, thereby minimizing any staff reductions there), and historically the considerable power of the police lobby.

Apart from the future role of the CPS there are the more general issues about social justice, touched on in various places above. If it is accepted that the criminal justice system should respond to alleged offenders in a way that is consistent according to the amount of harm done and their culpability, then this principle should be considered across the boundaries between the many different enforcement agencies. Why should there be differences in response to someone who pollutes a river, someone who defrauds the Inland Revenue, someone who fails to take proper precautions for the safety of employees, someone who steals property from another, someone who sells unsound meat, and so on? One reply is that it is impossible to compare the relative seriousness of these different offences, and hence each of them must be viewed in its separate context. But that is a stalling reply, using the well-known difficulties of settling on criteria of offence-seriousness as an excuse for avoiding the broader questions of social justice that arise when relatively poor and powerless people are prosecuted whereas the better-connected are enabled to pay

---

[109] A. Sanders, 'The Limits of Diversion from Prosecution' (1988) 28 *BJ Crim.* 513.

their way out of trouble without the stigma of a criminal conviction.[110] The Royal Commission did not accept Levi's suggestion that regulatory mechanisms be used quite widely in fraud cases,[111] but it did recommend that some fraud cases and some of those handled by the Securities and Investments Board might receive different treatment:

> Where the offence is of a technical nature, there has been no specific loss or risk to any member of the public (or if there has, where restitution can be made), and the predominant issues relate to the protection of the integrity of the markets rather than to serious dishonesty as such, then it may be that regulatory action is both appropriate and sufficient.[112]

The Commission insisted that the penalties 'must be sufficiently severe that it could not be alleged that so-called "white-collar crime" was being more leniently handled than other equivalent offences'. That recognizes the point of principle,[113] in terms of consistent treatment, but hardly deals with it in a manner that convinces across the spectrum of crimes. Another example comes from HM Customs and Excise, which in 1990 introduced procedures to streamline the seizure, compounding, and restoration of non-drugs goods smuggled in at Manchester airport:

> For all smuggling offences involving revenue charges of up to £100, offenders were offered the choice of court proceedings or payment of a single sum which combined the compounded penalty and the restoration charge. Most offenders accepted. A parallel experiment under which credit cards could be used as a means of payment (even of fines) undoubtedly helped the success of the scheme. The number of offenders opting to appear in court did not increase.[114]

The questions of social justice raised by this are self-evident: those who smuggle modest amounts can avoid prosecution on payment, whereas those elsewhere who commit ordinary thefts and deceptions of similar amounts may be prosecuted (without option) or may receive a caution (without payment). What is necessary is a thorough review of the prosecution policies of the various regulatory agencies. At present there is virtually no accountability, and certainly no overall accountability to a single body that can oversee consistency in matters of prosecution. It is one thing to argue that the different

---

[110] Cf. S. Uglow, 'Defrauding the Public Purse' [1984] *Crim. LR* 128; A. Sanders, 'Class Bias in Prosecutions' (1985) 24 *Howard JCJ* 176.

[111] M. Levi, *The Investigation, Prosecution and Trial of Serious Fraud*, RCCJ Research Study 14 (1993).

[112] RCCJ Report, para. 7.63.

[113] The RCCP Report, para. 7.43, also raised the possibility of dealing with more regulatory and revenue cases outside the criminal process, without canvassing the issues of principle.

[114] 81st Report of the Commissioners of Her Majesty's Customs and Excise, Cmnd. 1223 (1990), para. 7.7.

contexts in which some agencies work make different approaches appropriate. It is quite another thing to argue that there should be no attempt at a common starting-point, and no concern with broader issues of social justice and the apparent unfairness of these differing arrangements.

The best way forward is to take two steps simultaneously. First, there should be experiments with the use of conditional non-prosecution (conditional on the payment of compensation, usually) as an alternative to cautioning. These experiments would require the involvement of the police and the CPS in co-operation. Secondly, there should be an urgent review of the justifications for different responses to different kinds of law-breaking. For too long the assumptions behind the policies of the Inland Revenue, the Customs and Excise, the various regulatory agencies, and the police have remained without thorough re-examination.[115] The principle of legality should be reconsidered: do the volume and variety of diversion decisions tend to undermine the rule of law, and would it not be more appropriate to decriminalize certain conduct or to relegate it to some non-criminal category? The principle of equality of treatment ought also to be taken more seriously, which means that further steps should be taken to combat racial discrimination and to ensure that there is no discrimination according to class or social status in matters as serious as prosecution.

[115] Cf. the Report of the Interdepartmental Committee, *The Enforcement of Revenue Legislation*; A. Ashworth, 'Prosecution, Police and Public: A Guide to Good Gatekeeping?' (1984) 23 *Howard JCJ* 65; Sanders, above n. 110, 176.

6   Prosecutorial Review

ONCE a case against a suspect has been put together by the police or other investigatory agency, and that person has been charged or summoned, the next step should be prosecutorial review—that is, the review of the case by a legally trained prosecutor. This is one of the main functions of the Crown Prosecution Service in England and Wales. As we will see, the CPS has a number of statutory obligations, but it operates largely in a sphere of discretion. It may create its own policies, and its prosecutors exercise considerable discretion in their day-to-day decisions. Its functions concern almost exclusively prosecutions initiated by the police. The other agencies that bring prosecutions, discussed in the previous chapter, tend to prosecute their own cases. We will see that, once again, this raises questions about equality of treatment.

At the time of writing the CPS is undergoing considerable change and external review, which are likely to change its shape significantly in the coming years. The National Audit Office, which reviewed the CPS in 1989, completed a second audit in 1997.[1] The incoming government had promised both a reorganization of the CPS and a fundamental review of its functions. The former was achieved in mid-1997, when the thirteen areas of the CPS were reorganized into forty-two areas that correspond with police force areas, in the hope of facilitating inter-agency working at local level. And the *Review of the Prosecution Service* was set up, under the chairmanship of Sir Iain Glidewell, to look not only at the structure, policies and procedures of the CPS but also to:

—assess whether the CPS has contributed to the falling numbers of convictions for recorded crime;

—consider the manner in which the CPS influences its relationship with the police;

—consider the validity of criticisms that the CPS has led to unjustified 'downgradings' of charges; and

---

[1] National Audit Office, *Crown Prosecution Service* (1997), following the Committee of Public Accounts, *Review of the Crown Prosecution Service* (1989).

—make and cost recommendations, taking account of the need to operate within existing provision.

The Review will report after the printing of this book, but the criticisms of the CPS implicit in its terms of reference will be considered in the course of this chapter. The chapter begins with a brief description of the CPS, considering its practices in relation to evidential sufficiency and the public interest. The approach of the regulatory agencies is then compared. After that, there is consideration of the role of the victim, and of accountability for prosecutorial decisions. The chapter concludes with a discussion of policy-making within the CPS and of the ethics of prosecution.

1. The Crown Prosecution Service

Prosecution arrangements in England and Wales were altered in the mid-1980s. Until then there were three principal prosecuting agencies. The police brought most prosecutions and, whilst many police forces had developed or begun to develop a prosecuting solicitors' department, it was the police who took most of the decisions since the prosecuting solicitors were in their employ. The Director of Public Prosecutions had a small department in London, dealing with all murder prosecutions, and with a spread of other cases concerned with such matters as national security, public figures, and alleged offences by police officers. And then, thirdly, there were the various agencies such as the Inland Revenue, the Post Office, the Health and Safety Executive (including the Factory Inspectorate), the Pollution Inspectorate, local authorities (including, for example, their environmental health officers), and so forth. For convenience these will be referred to as the 'regulatory agencies', although this is certainly not intended to suggest that the offences with which they are concerned are non-serious.

The Royal Commission on Criminal Procedure, reporting in 1981, had relatively little to say about the regulatory agencies, but it did take the view that the police should not be so heavily involved in prosecution policy. It rejected the full separation of investigative and prosecutorial functions that obtains in many other jurisdictions, and decided to leave in the hands of the police the initial decision whether or not to prosecute. It favoured an independent prosecution service to review decisions to prosecute, applying a higher evidential standard than that hitherto adopted by the police. A primary reason for introducing independent legal review was to prevent weak cases from being prosecuted: in earlier years this had been the function of committal proceedings before examining magistrates, but since the requirement of committal proceedings was abolished in 1967, there had been no control on the quality of cases going to the Crown Court except in the small minority in which either the defence or the prosecution opted for a full committal.

The 1981 Royal Commission recommended a prosecution service based on the principles adopted by the Director of Public Prosecutions.[2] After considerable debate,[3] the Prosecution of Offences Act 1985 became law. The Act created a Crown Prosecution Service, headed by the Director of Public Prosecutions and formally accountable to the Attorney-General. The CPS has a duty to take over all prosecutions instituted by the police (except for certain minor offences), and has a power to take over other prosecutions. The CPS has therefore been accorded a status independent of the police. Section 10 of the Prosecution of Offences Act 1985 lays upon it the duty to publish a Code for Crown Prosecutors and to report annually to Parliament on its work and the use of its powers. Notable among these is its power to discontinue prosecutions in the magistrates' courts.[4] However, unlike public prosecutors in many other jurisdictions, it was not given powers to institute proceedings itself, to direct the police to investigate any matter, or to put questions to any person.[5]

English law imposes a requirement of consent to prosecution, mostly from the Director of Public Prosecutions and a few from the Attorney General, for a lengthy and rather ragged list of offences. All consent requirements from the DPP may be exercised by any crown prosecutor, but there are internal CPS procedures to ensure that consents are not dealt with at the lowest level. In 1997 the Law Commission reviewed the consent requirements, asking whether they can be justified when the CPS has the power to take over and discontinue any prosecution that has been started.[6] The Commission suggests three categories of case where a consent requirement might be justified: first, offences affecting freedom of expression, such as crimes under the Theatres Act 1968 and the Race Relations Act 1965; secondly, offences involving national security or the Government's international obligations; and thirdly, offences for which a civil action might be more appropriate, such as some offences against the Copyright, Designs and Patents Act 1988. The justifications for these three categories are contestable. The first and third could surely be handled by the existing power to take over and discontinue prosecutions, especially in view of the Commission's proposal that all private prosecutions

---

[2] RCCP, *Report*, Cmnd. 8092 (1981), ch. 7.

[3] See in particular the Government's White Paper, *An Independent Prosecution Service for England and Wales*, Cmnd. 9074 (1983).

[4] s. 23 of the Prosecution of Offences Act 1985.

[5] See F. Bennion, 'The Crown Prosecution Service' [1986] *Crim. LR* 4.

[6] Law Commission Consultation Paper No. 149, *Criminal Law: Consents to Prosecution* (1997), summarized at [1997] *Crim. LR* 845.

be notified to the CPS, although individuals and organizations bringing those prosecutions might wish to have a ruling before they commit resources to a prosecution. And the second, particularly in respect of the Official Secrets Acts, might be better exercised by an independent commissioner than by a government official (the Attorney-General) or an officer responsible to that official (the DPP). Perhaps the issue that ought to have received greater attention is the criteria that ought to be used either to withhold consent to prosecution or to take over and drop an existing prosecution: little is said in the Consultation Paper on the substance of this crucial discretion.

That leads on to the question of documentation. We have already seen that the CPS has a statutory obligation to publish its *Code for Crown Prosecutors*. This was first published in 1986, with a second edition in 1992 and a third edition in 1994. The revision in 1994 was intended to be phrased in plain English suitable for lay persons to read, as well as making some changes of substance which will be referred to below. Laudable as the move towards plain English is in this kind of document, one of the consequences of rephrasing the Code was that many matters that had been discussed in the previous versions passed out of public view.[7] To the credit of the CPS it did issue, at the same time, an 'Explanatory Memorandum for use in connection with the Code for Crown Prosecutors', which was subsequently up-dated in 1996. But the fact remains that many statements of policy, especially those relating to particular offences, remain concealed from public view and therefore from accountability. The CPS itself has a five-volume *Prosecution Manual*, which is protected by the Official Secrets Acts. It purports to supplement, not to displace, the published Code. As a whole, the *Manual* is intended to be the principal source of comprehensive, up-to-date casework guidance for the CPS. While volume two deals with the decision to prosecute and volume four with evidential considerations, the greatest supplementation of the published Code is probably found in volume three on specific offences. However, there has been a welcome step towards openness here, with the advent of 'Charging Standards'. In the past few years a team of CPS lawyers and police have been working together to establish guidance on choice of charge in certain common areas of prosecution policy, with a view to assisting the police in setting the charge at the right level initially and ensuring that the CPS has a common starting point when reviewing case files. Three sets of Charging Standards have been published in recent years: on offences against the person (now revised), on motoring offences; and on public order offences. They have met with a mixed reaction, especially from those who see the standards as part of a cost-cutting exercise rather than as a mere attempt to foster greater consistency. Perhaps

[7] A. Ashworth and J. Fionda, 'The New Code for Crown Prosecutors: Prosecution, Accountability and the Public Interest' [1994] *Crim. LR* 894.

the most controversial borderline has been that between the summary offence of common assault and the indictable offence of assault occasioning actual bodily harm, with many writers in the *Police Review* and some justices' clerks arguing that the borderline has been set in a way that is legally debatable and is designed to ensure that as many cases as possible remain in the magistrates' courts.[8] More will be said on these issues later. It should be added that the CPS has published various other documents, including a 'Statement of Purpose and Values' (1993), which acts as a mission statement and makes commitments on such matters as openness, non-discrimination, and the fair treatment of victims, witnesses, and defendants.

2. Evidential Sufficiency

It is wrong for a person to be prosecuted if the evidence is insufficient. The essence of the wrongness lies in the protection of the innocent: if this principle is taken seriously, it should mean not merely that innocent people are not convicted, but also that innocent people should not be prosecuted. The reasons for this may be found in the dictum that 'the process is the punishment':[9] being prosecuted is an inconvenience at least, often a source of profound worry, and sometimes a considerable expense, and it may also lead to an element of stigma and loss of social esteem. The homely phrase, 'no smoke without fire' might well be applied. There are therefore sound moral reasons for not prosecuting someone against whom the evidence is insufficient. There are also good economic reasons: it is a waste of police time in compiling a full file on the case, of prosecution time in reviewing the case, and of court time in dealing with the case. It is therefore desirable in general that weak cases should be eliminated as early as possible, and it was for this purpose that the Royal Commission on Criminal Procedure recommended the introduction of a public prosecution service to provide independent review.

There are at least three major issues to be discussed before the principle of evidential sufficiency can be translated into practice. One is the test of sufficiency—what should it be? Closely intertwined with this is the second—should the test vary according to the stage the case has reached? And third, how can prosecutors be expected to assess cases on the basis of a written file? In discussing these issues, it must constantly be borne in mind that evidential

---

[8] See, e.g., the articles by the then editor of *The Justice of the Peace*, F.G. Davies, 'CPS Charging Standards: a Cynic's View' (1995) 159 *JP* 203, and 'Ten Years of the Crown Prosecution Service: the Verdict' (1997) 161 *JP* 207, at 208–9.

[9] M. Feeley, *The Process is the Punishment* (1979), Ch. 1.

sufficiency is only one of the factors relevant in prosecutions. Another is the lawfulness of the prosecution in procedural terms—have the appropriate formalities been completed? Have the time-limits been observed? Has there been a previous prosecution arising out of the incident, so as to raise considerations of double jeopardy?[10] A further factor is the policy of diversion, discussed in the previous chapter in the context of the cautioning of offenders. Thus, even if a case satisfies the test of evidential sufficiency, there may be strong reasons of public policy or, as it is termed in England and Wales, 'public interest' in favour of dealing with the case by means other than prosecution. In practice questions of evidential sufficiency and public interest often interact, but for clarity of exposition this part of the chapter is devoted chiefly to evidential sufficiency, and the issue of 'public interest' is left over until the following part.

(a) Formulating the Test of Evidential Sufficiency

Until the early 1980s the test that the police were said to apply in deciding whether the evidence was strong enough for prosecution was the '*prima facie* test': is there 'evidence on the basis of which, if it were accepted, a reasonable jury or magistrates' court would be justified in convicting'?[11] This often seemed to mean that as long as there was some evidence on the main points that need to be proved the defendant ought to be brought to court to answer the charge. The test made no explicit reference to the strength and credibility of the evidence, nor to probable lines of defence. In his submission to the 1981 Royal Commission on Criminal Procedure, the then Director of Public Prosecutions denounced this test as inadequate: it was wrong, he argued, that a person could be prosecuted when an acquittal was more likely than a conviction, and the minimum standard should require that conviction is more probable than acquittal.[12] The Director's approach was commended by the Royal Commission on the basis that a lower standard would be 'both unfair to the accused and a waste of the restricted resources of the criminal justice system'.[13] The new test was incorporated into the Attorney-General's Criteria for Prosecution, issued to the police in 1983. These guidelines stated that there should be no prosecution unless there were a 'reasonable prospect of conviction'. At the time this was colloquially known as the '51 per cent' test. The wording was subsequently revised, so that the first edition of the Code for Crown Prosecutors in 1986 referred to a 'realistic prospect of conviction', a test that remains unchanged today.

[10] See the discussion below, in the context of accountability.   [11] RCCP, *Report*, para. 8.8.
[12] Reproduced in RCCP, vol. ii: *The Law and the Procedure* (1981), app. 25.
[13] RCCP, *Report*, para. 8.9.

Paragraph 5 of the 1994 *Code for Crown Prosecutors* requires crown prosecutors to take account of 'what the defence case may be and how that is likely to affect the prosecution case', and to consider 'whether the evidence can be used and is reliable'. The admissibility of evidence is a matter of legal judgement: the Explanatory Memorandum states that the CPS should discount evidence obtained as a result of the breach of PACE Codes of Practice if case law shows that exclusion in court would be likely, but that if there is doubt the CPS should obtain a ruling in court.[14] Reliability is said to turn on such matters as 'the defendant's age, intelligence or lack of understanding' (where a confession is relied upon), the background of prosecution witnesses (in terms of dubious motives or relevant previous convictions), and the strength of any identification evidence.

What is the legal basis for the 'realistic prospects' test, and what are its theoretical justifications? It is clearly predictive in nature: it requires the prosecutor to assess whether, on the evidence likely to be given at the trial, a conviction is more probable than an acquittal. This includes matters such as the admissibility of the evidence and the likely defence. Paragraph 5.2 of the Code states that 'a realistic prospect of conviction is an objective test'. There are two different ways in which this might be interpreted. One is a straight predictive approach: the crown prosecutor's task would be to predict how the court in which the case would be tried would react to the evidence. This might require the prosecutor to take account of the different conviction rates of magistrates' courts and the Crown Court, and of any local trends in willingness or unwillingness to convict in certain types of case. An alternative would be an 'intrinsic merits' approach, according to which the task of the prosecutor would be to judge the strength of evidence and to apply the law to it faithfully. On this approach, prosecutors would exercise the function of keeping cases away from the lay tribunal when they judge that the evidence is insufficient, even though they think that the tribunal might well convict, and correspondingly prosecutors would persevere with a case when they believe that the evidence is sufficient, even though they recognize that the local court is unlikely to convict. Thus on the predictive view the disposition of the local courts sets the standard, whereas on the 'intrinsic merits' view it is a legal standard applied by various prosecutors to case files that determines decisions.[15]

---

[14] CPS, *Explanatory Memorandum* (June 1996), para. 4.20.

[15] A third view would be that the test for the prosecutor should be that a prosecution should only go ahead if there is 'no rational expectation of a directed acquittal', tying the prosecutor's prediction to the power of magistrates or a judge to accede to a submission of no case: see G. Mansfield and J. Peay, *The Director of Public Prosecutions* (1985), 54, discussed in the first edition of this work at 166–7.

Those who believe in the supreme importance of lay adjudications would favour the predictive view. Magistrates and juries should be the central figures, and prosecutors should merely attempt to anticipate their decisions rather than to neutralize or even by-pass them. On the other hand, fidelity to law would favour the 'intrinsic merits' approach, since one might doubt whether there could be sufficient reason why a local bench or justices' clerk, or the juries of a particular neighbourhood, should be allowed to distort or disregard the law of the country as a whole. Thus the American Bar Association has stated that: 'In cases which involve a serious threat to the community, the prosecutor should not be deterred from prosecution by the fact that in his jurisdiction juries have tended to acquit persons accused of the particular kind of criminal act in question.'[16] This is also the view now set out in paragraph 5.2 of the Code: a 'realistic prospect of conviction' means that 'a jury or bench of magistrates, properly directed in accordance with the law, is more likely than not to convict the defendant of the charge alleged'. In the Explanatory Memorandum a straight predictive view is rejected explicitly:

> Crown Prosecutors should not take into account any perceived local views of the bench or juries when considering whether there is a realistic prospect of conviction. The reason for this is simple: if local considerations of this nature were allowed to influence the decision to prosecute, the goal of consistent decision-making would be lost.[17]

The Explanatory Memorandum goes on to set out some of the points to be taken into account when making these judgements. It also includes the extraordinary assertion that 'the quality of justice does not vary from courtroom to courtroom or between tiers of court'.[18] There is considerable evidence that it does, and that many Crown Prosecutors believe that it does.[19] In particular that it is widely believed to differ between magistrates' courts and the Crown Court, as we shall see in Chapter 8 below. The acquittal rates are certainly different. The Memorandum would have been on firmer ground in saying that the quality of justice dispensed by the two levels of court ought not to differ.

The CPS is right to opt for the 'intrinsic merits' approach but, as the Explanatory Memorandum recognizes, it places great weight upon the judgement of prosecutors. The sufficiency of evidence must be judged on the basis of a file, without hearing the witnesses in court, and often without knowing exactly what form the defence will take.[20] It must then be an assessment of the

---

[16] ABA, *Standards Relating to the Prosecution Function* (2nd edn., 1980), 3–3.9.

[17] *Explanatory Memorandum*, para. 4.10.   [18] *Ibid.* para. 4.13.

[19] A. Hoyano *et al.*, 'A Study of the Impact of the Revised Code for Crown Prosecutors' [1997] *Crim. LR* 556 at 563.

[20] Cf. RCCJ, *Report*, para. 6.59, discussed in Ch. 4.2, above, recommending a limited form of defence disclosure.

proper reaction of a reasonable jury or bench of magistrates, correctly directed on the law, including the rules on the admissibility of evidence. None of this is straightforward.

(b) Evidential Sufficiency and the Stages of the Criminal Process

The Code for Crown Prosecutors states a single test of evidential sufficiency: whether there is a 'realistic prospect of conviction'. Can this test really be applicable at all stages? In many cases the prosecutor receives a file for the first time just before remand proceedings are due to begin. This may be the morning after the defendant's arrest. The prosecutor will have no time to listen to any interview tapes, and so it is likely that the police summary will dominate. The police may believe that they have (or will have) sufficient evidence to justify the charge, but they may still have witnesses to interview and forensic reports to receive. In strict terms, there may not yet be a realistic prospect of conviction.

Can a remand in custody be justified in these circumstances? Even one week's loss of liberty—often spent in an overcrowded prison, with poor facilities, away from family, friends, and employment (if any), and without unrestricted access to legal advice—is a serious deprivation. As we shall see in Chapter 7, the Bail Act 1976 directs a magistrates' court to have regard to the strength of the evidence; but, again, this is usually taken on trust from the CPS, who in turn take it on trust from the police. No doubt prosecutors will argue that, in practice, the system could hardly be otherwise. However, the starting point should be the right to liberty safeguarded by Article 5 of the European Convention on Human Rights, and the need for strong justifications for taking it away. Insufficient attention has been given to the compromising of principle by current English practice, and there is a need urgently to explore the possibility of proper CPS scrutiny of files before any remand in custody is sought or authorized.

3. The Public Interest

Less attention has been devoted to the evidential criteria used by the various regulatory agencies, although at least one of them (the Post Office) was stated to be using the 'reasonable prospects of conviction' test rather than the 'prima-facie evidence' test even before the Attorney-General's Guidelines on prosecution were issued in 1983.[21] What is most evident about these agencies, as we saw in the previous chapter, is that many of them tend to have a rather different conception of the public interest from that apparently held, at least

[21] See K. W. Lidstone, R. Hogg, and F. Sutcliffe, *Prosecution by Private Individuals and Non-police Agencies*, RCCP Research Study 10 (1981), 49.

formerly, by the police and prosecutors. For many agencies, the primary goal is to secure compliance with the standards laid down by law. This might take time to achieve, and the approach may be termed accommodative or conciliatory—using persuasion, education, and negotiation as the principal methods, and leaving the power to prosecute as a background threat which is rarely invoked.[22]

This is not the fundamental orientation of the Crown Prosecution Service. Indeed, the 1994 edition of the *Code for Crown Prosecutors* brought significant changes in this respect.[23] Whereas previous versions of the Code were phrased so as to suggest that a prosecution should only be brought if 'the public interest requires' it, paragraph 6.2 of the 1994 Code alters the emphasis:

> In cases of any seriousness, a prosecution will usually take place unless there are public interest factors tending against prosecution which clearly outweigh those tending in favour. Although there may be public interest factors against prosecution in a particular case, often the prosecution should go ahead and those factors should be put to the court for consideration when sentence is being passed.

In terms of language, this is a reversal of substance, probably prompted by criticism about the number of cases being discontinued in the early 1990s. To what extent it has altered practice is a different question, but at the level of rhetoric it may be seen as a move away from the 'principle of opportunity' towards the kind of legality principle embodied in the laws of continental European countries. As the Explanatory Memorandum puts it, 'it is important to uphold the law, and . . . there is a public interest in doing so'.[24] A similar shift in rhetoric is seen in respect of young defendants: there can be no mistaking the move away from the previous emphasis on diversion, even though the Explanatory Memorandum includes a rather enlightened quotation from the UN Convention on the Rights of the Child.[25] The changes coincided closely with the then Home Secretary's decision to 'toughen' justice for juveniles by reducing reliance on cautioning, a political decision which the CPS followed without demur.[26]

Whereas previous editions of the Code focused on public interest factors against prosecuting, the 1994 version contains lists of common factors both for and against prosecution. Among the factors in favour of prosecution

---

[22] For general discussions, see A. Reiss, 'Selecting Strategies of Social Control over Organisational Life', in K. Hawkins and J. Thomas (eds.), *Enforcing Regulation* (1984); G. Richardson, 'Strict Liability for Regulatory Crime: The Empirical Research' [1987] *Crim. LR* 295; B. Hutter, 'Variations in Regulatory Enforcement Styles' (1989) 11 *Law and Policy* 153.

[23] Cf. Ashworth and Fionda, above n. 7 [1994] *Crim. LR* 894, with R. Daw, 'A Response' [1994] *Crim. LR* 904.

[24] CPS, *Explanatory Memorandum*, para. 4.23.

[25] *Ibid.* paras. 4.43–4.45, and Code, Para. 6.8.

[26] See further the debate between Ashworth and Fionda and Daw, above n. 23.

(paragraph 6.4) are the fact that the victim was vulnerable, or the offence was motivated by any form of discrimination, or the defendant has relevant previous convictions or cautions, or the defendant was a ringleader or organizer of the offence, and so on. Many of these are well known as factors which militate in aggravation of sentence.[27] Similarly many of the 'common public interest factors against prosecution' listed in paragraph 6.5 are circumstances which might otherwise mitigate sentence. Some of these are factors personal to the offender which make it likely that prosecution and conviction will have a disproportionately severe effect: old age, mental or physical ill health, mental disorder, and cases where there is evidence that the strain of criminal proceedings may lead to a considerable worsening of the accused's mental health. The justification for tipping the scales against prosecution in these cases is presumably some notion of equality of impact, at least to the extent that it would be unfair to continue with a prosecution if that would have an impact on the particular offender far greater than is warranted by the offence.[28]

Several of the factors in paragraph 6.5 seem to be related to the notion of proportionality, since they refer to types of case in which prosecution and sentence might be an inappropriately severe response to the offence committed. Where the offence is so minor that a court is only likely to impose 'a very small or nominal penalty', prosecution might not be 'in the public interest'. This refers to cases where a discharge or low value fine seems likely, a predictive judgement about the courts' sentencing practice.[29] These would be cases in which the harmfulness of the conduct was relatively low. There would also be cases where the offender's culpability was low, including cases of 'genuine mistake or misunderstanding' or minor harm 'caused by a misjudgement', and some cases where the offender is elderly or suffering from mental illness. These, then, are cases lying towards the foot of any scale of offence-seriousness. The argument is that many of them do not warrant the bringing of formal proceedings, and might be dealt with more appropriately by a police caution, an informal warning, or no action at all. The theory of desert or proportionality,[30] combined with the established finding that the process of being prosecuted may itself involve inconvenience, anxiety, or pain,[31] supports the proposition that a line should be drawn beneath which prosecution as a response is disproportionately strong.

---

[27] For elaboration, see A. Ashworth, *Sentencing and Criminal Justice* (2nd edn., 1995), ch. 5.

[28] For discussion of this principle in sentencing, see *ibid.* 134–47 and 179–82.

[29] CPS, *Explanatory Memorandum*, para. 4.37; note the use of a predictive, rather than an 'intrinsic merits', approach in this part of the Code.

[30] For discussion of that theory, see A. von Hirsch, *Censure and Sanctions* (1993) and, more briefly, A. von Hirsch and A. Ashworth, *Principled Sentencing* (2nd edn. 1998), ch. 4.

[31] Feeley, above n. 9; M. McConville and J. Baldwin, *Prosecution, Courts and Conviction* (1981), 48–50, 69–71; RCCP, *Report*, para. 8.7.

In practice, the positioning of the line appears to be influenced by matters such as expenditure constraints and beliefs in effectiveness. In previous editions of the Code there was a statement in paragraph 8 (i) that prosecutors should 'weigh the likely penalty with the likely length and cost of proceedings'. This meant, in effect, that non-serious cases should not be allowed to proceed in the Crown Court, where trial by judge and jury costs a great deal of public money. At present the law allows any person charged with theft to elect to go for trial in the Crown Court, no matter how small the value of the goods allegedly stolen.[32] Thus a person charged with theft of goods worth £10, and who is prosecuted rather than cautioned (perhaps because of the number of previous convictions), may choose Crown Court trial. The prosecutor, applying the Code, will then reassess the decision to prosecute. The 1994 version of the Code contains no explicit reference to cost, but it is not clear that practice on this point has changed,[33] and perhaps the intention was that these cases would be subsumed within the category of cases where a very small or nominal penalty is likely.

One evident difficulty in a system whereby the CPS is expected to review the public interest factors for and against continuing with a prosecution is that it is likely to have more information about many pro-prosecution factors (which tend to arise from the nature of the offence, or the defendant's previous record) than about many anti-prosecution factors (which tend to be personal or social factors). An attempt to remedy this information deficit was made in the Public Interest Case Assessment schemes, introduced in four areas and staffed by probation officers. The aim is to select cases where there might be personal or other circumstances that might justify the discontinuance of a prosecution on 'public interest' grounds, and to seek information that could assist the Crown Prosecution Service in taking its decisions. An evaluation of the scheme by a Home Office Research Unit team showed that it was generally successful in targeting cases where such information might be uncovered, that the CPS felt that the extra information was helpful, and that discontinuance rates for cases where PICA reports were prepared were double those in other cases.[34] However, the research also estimated that savings to the criminal justice system amounted to only about one-fifth of the costs of the scheme, because of the Probation Service resources needed to staff it. The tone of the report is to suggest that this will be the death-knell for PICA schemes,

---

[32] For discussion, see Ch. 8.4, below.

[33] See, e.g., Hoyano *et al.*, above n. 19, at 563; J. Baldwin, 'Understanding Judge Ordered and Directed Acquittals in the Crown Court' [1997] *Crim. LR* 536, at 545–6.

[34] D. Crisp, C. Whittaker, and J. Harris, *Public Interest Case Assessment Schemes*, Home Office Research Study 138 (1995).

even though the research demonstrated clearly that there is an information deficit and, presumably, that when it is not filled, some defendants are taken to court unnecessarily and even unfairly. The conclusion to the report discusses, without much conviction, other ways of ensuring that the CPS receive the relevant information.

4. Evaluating the CPS

In a history of just over twelve years the Crown Prosecution Service has been subjected to a variety of criticisms. Whatever the merits of its policies as set out in its various documents—and some doubts about those policies have been mentioned in Sections 2 and 3 of this chapter—the most pressing problem is the CPS's performance on a day-to-day basis. Does the practice live up to the rhetoric? Are the criticisms of the CPS justified, or are there deeper structural problems for which it is unfair to blame the CPS? Drawing on recent research, it is proposed to evaluate various criticisms of the CPS, beginning with some of the specific questions addressed to the Glidewell Review (of which the terms of reference were set out earlier). In particular, there will be consideration of whether the CPS has contributed to the falling numbers of convictions, whether the discontinuance rate is too high or too low, whether the CPS is involved in too many 'downgradings' of charges, and whether the CPS succeeds in maintaining independence whilst acting co-operatively when necessary. The related issue of CPS accountability will be left for later discussion.

1. *CPS contribution to falling numbers of convictions:* the first specific point into which the Glidewell Review was invited to inquire was 'whether the CPS has contributed to the falling number of convictions for recorded crime'. This was a concern voiced by the new Labour Attorney General, John Morris, soon after his appointment. It is, unfortunately, a concern that seems to imply considerable misunderstanding. There is no doubt that the total number of convictions for indictable offences has fallen in recent years, from some 385,000 in 1986 to 342,000 in 1990, and 302,000 in 1995. However, as explained in Chapter 5 above, these figures represent the end of a lengthy chain of events. To single out one particular link in that chain may be unhelpful, and the use of the word 'contribute' suggests an assumption that there is a significant element of cause and effect. Yet whilst the overall number of offences reported to the police has stabilized in the 1990s, the rate at which the police clear up reported crimes has declined (from 32 per cent in 1990 to 26 per cent in 1995). Thus, on Home Office figures, only 5 per cent of offences committed

in any one year are 'cleared up' by the police.[35] Some 2.7 per cent result in a caution or conviction, 2.0 per cent representing convictions. Since, as we saw in Chapter 5, in the vast majority of cases it is the police who take the initial decision whether to prosecute, caution, or take no further action, it seems fanciful to suggest that even large variations in CPS performance would have a great influence on the overall figures, since such a small proportion of cases come into their hands. A far more powerful influence is the pro-cautioning policy advocated since the mid-1980s: if one adds to the figures for convictions the figures for cautions of indictable offenders in the three relevant years (137,000 for 1986, 166,300 for 1990, and 202,600 for 1995), one finds the following totals for offenders found guilty or cautioned for indictable offences:

1986	533,000
1990	508,300
1995	504,600

The figures still show a decline, but in the context of the declining rate of recorded crime and the declining clear-up rate, this decline is far less significant than the Glidewell terms of reference imply. None of this is to suggest that there is no cause for concern about CPS practices. It is simply to argue that the conviction rate for indictable offences is subject to far more powerful influences than the CPS. As a term of reference for the Glidewell Review, this was either naïve or misleading.

2. *Discontinuance rates*: a better targeted question would be whether the CPS uses the power of discontinuance as it should do, notably whether the policies set out in the Code are appropriate and whether they are carried out properly in practice. This raises a whole host of issues, including the timing and quality of files passed to the CPS by the police, the different approaches required for evidential sufficiency and 'public interest' factors, and reliance on advice from counsel in Crown Court cases.

The starting point should be the quality of files passed on by the police, and particularly the initial decision to charge. If many police decisions to charge were wrong or inaccurate, a high discontinuance rate would be required of a conscientious CPS. As it is, there have been three initiatives in recent years to ensure that initial charging decisions are improved. One of these, already noted, is the publication of Charging Standards for some categories of offence. Whilst their coverage is still relatively small, they hold out the prospect of more accurate charging in the first place. The second initiative has been for prosecutors in some areas to make regular visits to police stations to

---

[35] Barclay, G., *Information on the Criminal Justice System in England and Wales, Digest 3* (1995), 25.

offer advice on appropriate charges and evidence that needs gathering, with a view to lessening wasted effort both by police and by the CPS. As with the PICA project, there seem to be doubts about the cost-effectiveness of the initiative, in terms of time saved and fruitful use of prosecutors' time.[36] Thirdly, most police forces have internal 'support units' to check case files before they go to the CPS. In practice, most deficiencies in charging or evidence-gathering by the police are likely to fall to the CPS to deal with. It remains open to the police to seek CPS advice about files, although one study found wide local variations in the extent to which the police make use of this facility.[37]

We turn, then, to discontinuance. There seem to be conflicting expectations here. The rate at which the CPS discontinues cases passed to it by the police is around 12 to 13 per cent. On the one hand there has been criticism of the CPS for discontinuing too many cases; on the other hand there has been criticism that too many Crown Court cases end in acquittal, suggesting that the CPS is not fulfilling its function of weeding out weak cases. A first step in disentangling the various strands is to consider the reasons for discontinuance. A Home Office survey in the early 1990s found that, of non-motoring cases discontinued, some 58 per cent were dropped on evidential grounds, 34 per cent on public interest grounds, and among the remainder were some cases where the defendant could not be traced.[38] The CPS's own discontinuance survey in 1994 found that in 43 per cent of cases there was insufficient evidence to proceed, in 28 per cent a prosecution was not in the public interest, and in 19 per cent of cases the prosecution was unable to proceed, largely because of the non-attendance of a key witness.[39]

The next step, then, is to focus on discontinuances for evidential reasons. The Home Office survey found that the top three reasons were a lack of supporting evidence (39 per cent), unreliability of witnesses (35 per cent), and evidence lacking on a key element in the offence (19 per cent).[40] In practice, many of these case files will have been discussed with the police, upon whom the CPS reviewer may often have to rely for judgements about reliability. In his research for the CPS, John Baldwin found that many of the difficult cases turned on the evidence of a single witness, and judgement about whether to proceed was finely balanced.[41] It seems that in many of the cases discontinued

---

[36] National Audit Office, *Crown Prosecution Service* (1997), paras. 3.10–3.12.

[37] D. Crisp and D. Moxon, *Case Screening by the Crown Prosecution Service: How and Why Cases are Terminated*, Home Office Research Study 137 (1995), ch. 4. Advice varied between less than 1% to 14% of cases, according to the area.

[38] Crisp and Moxon, *Case Screening by the Crown Prosecution Service*.

[39] National Audit Office, above n. 1, 42.

[40] Crisp and Moxon, above n. 37, 19, referring to non-motoring cases.

[41] J. Baldwin, 'Understanding Judge Ordered and Directed Acquittals in the Crown Court', [1997] *Crim. LR* 536, at 546.

on evidential grounds, the police would have been in agreement about the poor prospect of conviction. On the other hand, Baldwin's research uncovered a distinct tendency among some prosecutors to proceed with a case despite a probable or manifest weakness. At one level, this meant that 'some prosecutors remain stubbornly of the view that the defendant may do the decent thing and plead guilty even though the prospects of conviction might look precarious on paper'.[42] At a deeper level, Baldwin confirmed that:

> some prosecutors share a common value system with the police, a core element of which is that serious cases ought to be prosecuted, almost irrespective of considerations as to evidential strength. Cases have developed a considerable momentum by the time of committal, and expectations build up that cases will proceed to the Crown Court. In such circumstances, it is easy to understand why some prosecutors, particularly when lacking in experience or self-confidence, hesitate in making hard decisions in complex or serious cases.[43]

In offering three reasons why prosecutors may fail to take the proper decisions at case review stage (shared value system with police, inexperience, lack of self-confidence), Baldwin is concerned to examine why too few cases are discontinued. His sample of cases was constructed with a view to casting light on that issue, which will be discussed further in the next paragraph. It suffices to comment here that many of the cases that were discontinued should probably not have proceeded as far as they did, in so far as there was insufficient reliable evidence from the outset. The criticism that the CPS is discontinuing too many cases on evidential grounds is therefore hard to accept. To prosecute when the evidence is insufficient inflicts unjustified anxiety on the defendant and wastes public resources. Paragraph 4.1 of the CPS Code states clearly that 'if the case does not pass the evidential test, it must not go ahead, no matter how important or serious it may be'.

Much depends, of course, on the quality of judgement within the CPS. A recent rise in the numbers of ordered and directed acquittals in the Crown Court raises questions about this, although more in the direction of failures to discontinue than of over-zealous discontinuances. In the years since the CPS was introduced the number of acquittals by judge has increased so that they now outnumber acquittals by jury. In 1980 acquittals by judge accounted for 42 per cent of all Crown Court acquittals; the proportion peaked at 58 per cent in 1990, and has since steadied at 56 per cent in 1995. The CPS takes comfort from this small recent decline in the number and proportion of both ordered acquittals and directed acquittals,[44] but there remains the question whether many of these cases could and should have been terminated earlier.

---

[42] *Ibid.* 548.   [43] *Ibid.* 551.
[44] Crown Prosecution Service, *Annual Report 1996–97*, Charts 8 and 10.

A judge-ordered acquittal occurs where the prosecutor informs the court that the CPS does not wish to proceed, and the judge formally orders the jury to acquit. A directed acquittal occurs during or at the end of the prosecution's case in court, if the judge decides that there is insufficient evidence on one or more elements of the offence. Research by Block, Corbett, and Peay in the early 1990s suggested that dispassionate scrutineers could identify weak cases among those that ended in acquittals by the judge: a minimum of 22 per cent of acquittals were regarded as foreseeably flawed in the opinion of a trained prosecutor,[45] and the researchers' own assessments led them to state that:

> although fewer than half of ordered acquittals were considered definitely or possibly foreseeable, three quarters of directed acquittals were so classified. This supports our view, derived from the study, that directed acquittals result largely from weak cases that should have been discontinued, whereas ordered acquittals result largely from unforeseeable circumstances.[46]

Baldwin conducted a somewhat similar enquiry for the CPS in 1995, with a sample of around 100 cases ending in acquittal by judge and some seventy other cases. He found that the ordered acquittals occurred chiefly where a key witness retracted a statement or failed to arrive at court (48 per cent), the judge took the view at the outset that the case was too weak (16 per cent), or the case was terminated following the convictions of other people (14 per cent). The directed acquittals occurred chiefly because a key witness failed to come up to proof (34 per cent), or there were problems of law or admissibility of evidence (32 per cent), or the judge ruled the evidence insufficient (12 per cent).[47] The important question is how many of these were foreseeable and ought to have led to earlier discontinuance. Baldwin found that around 41 per cent of all cases resulting in acquittal had reservations of a prosecutor entered upon the file at an early stage, and a further 35 per cent of files mentioned reservations but discounted them. His conclusions run along two main lines. One is the acute difficulty of judging witness credibility and reliability, on the basis of either case files or discussions with police officers on the case. Moreover in certain types of case, particularly child abuse, rape, and 'domestic' violence, there is the risk that very few prosecutions would come to court at all if doubts about witnesses coming up to proof were taken seriously. It is almost inevitable, in the current system, that as Jane Morgan and Lucia Zedner found: 'prosecutors rely heavily on the expertise of the specialist police officers who interview children alleging abuse to provide an indication

---

[45] B. Block, C. Corbett, and J. Peay, *Ordered and Directed Acquittals in the Crown Court* (1993).
[46] Block, Corbett, and Peay, above n. 45, 100.
[47] Baldwin, above n. 41, 539.

of the child's credibility as a witness.'[48] There is thus a conflict between being seen to take complaints seriously and risking a fairly high rate of acquittal, many being acquittals by judge.[49] To some extent, the problems here may stem from wider structural issues about English criminal justice, including such matters as the treatment of victims, the admissibility of evidence in court (such as video tapes of the complainant's early interviews with the police), limits on the cross-examination of complainants about their sexual history, and means of ensuring that defendant's rights are upheld at all times, even if procedures are changed. At the time of writing, some of these issues are under review by the Home Office.

Structural problems of this kind should not be neglected, but Baldwin also uncovered attitudes and practices in the CPS which suggest other, avoidable causes of acquittals by judge. As is apparent from the quotation set out above, Baldwin identified inexperience, lack of self-confidence, and the sharing of values with the police as three reasons why some cases were not terminated as early as they should have been. Lack of self-confidence may in some cases stem from the CPS's relationship, or a particular prosecutor's relationship, with the local police: it may take considerable nerve for a relatively young prosecutor to tell a long-serving police officer that a case has to be dropped, and it may be easier to accede to the police desire to 'run it'. Indeed, there are some weak cases that may result in a conviction, either through a defendant's late decision to plead guilty or through a jury verdict, and this may be regarded as a reason for 'running' such a case, especially if the defendant is thought to be an unworthy type. Even more worrying, although not surprising, is the finding that some CPS lawyers 'share a common value system with the police'.[50] This shows that the CPS has not been successful in inculcating an independent, 'Minister of Justice' approach in the minds and conduct of certain crown prosecutors. Of course Baldwin's interview sample was fairly small, but it would be unwise to dismiss his findings on that account. For one thing, the CPS documentation reveals no concerted effort to set out the ethics of prosecuting as a distinct subject, with goals and good practices indicated. This would only be one step, since there is evidently a culture opposed to any such approach, but it is a step that ought to be taken. As for inexperience and lack of self-confidence, these might be related to the crisis of resources in the CPS, where expectations of performance seem to run ahead of funding. Whether the CPS is able to recruit and retain sufficient staff of the right quality is still,

---

[48] J. Morgan and L. Zedner, *Child Victims* (1992), 122.

[49] See further, J. Gregory and S. Lees, 'Attrition in Rape and Sexual Assault Cases' (1996) 36 *BJ Crim.* 1.

[50] Baldwin, above n. 41, 551.

twelve years after its creation, a question for debate. Whilst there is no doubt that CPS management could be improved, the funding of the CPS also needs some review.

A final and related point on discontinuance for evidential reasons concerns the role of counsel in Crown Court cases. Both the research by Block, Corbett, and Peay[51] and the interviews conducted by Baldwin[52] suggest that counsel are not performing the kind of role one might expect. Crown counsel ought to study the brief and advise that the case be dropped if the evidence seems insufficient or inadmissible. Yet there are various reasons why this rarely happens, notably where counsel only takes over the brief at a relatively late stage or where counsel is afraid that to advise dropping the case might jeopardize future prospects of CPS work. To what extent a new system of briefing and monitoring counsel[53] and the advent of Plea and Directions Hearings have succeeded in removing the former reason is not yet known.

This discussion of discontinuance should not omit reference to 'public interest' factors, which account for 28 per cent of all discontinuances in the magistrates' courts. On CPS figures, half of these are cases in which a very small or nominal penalty is thought likely, and a further quarter are cases in which a caution is thought more appropriate.[54] In so far as it is these cases that are the butt of the criticism that the CPS discontinues too many cases, there is one source of comparison that should not be neglected. That is the proportion of sentences in court that are 'very small or nominal'. It is difficult to find a precise figure for this, since there is no record of the number of small fines handed down by the courts; equally, it could be argued that in some circumstances a conditional discharge is neither very small nor nominal. But it is worth pointing out that the proportion of discharges granted for indictable offences has increased considerably since 1986, so that in 1996 some 14 per cent of adult males and 28 per cent of adult females received a discharge (compared with 10 and 24 per cent in 1986). At the very least, this suggests that there is scope for more discontinuances rather than fewer. Once the hands of the police become tied under the Crime and Disorder Bill 1998, introducing the system of reprimands and final warnings for young offenders (discussed in Chapter 5 above), there may be further shifts in practice.

3. *Downgrading:* the suggestion that the CPS 'downgrades' cases, either by reducing the charge to a lower level or by accepting a guilty plea to a lesser offence, now needs to be assessed. One preliminary point is that the CPS has played a major role in the drawing up of Charging Standards for various categories of offence, and so there are many cases in which the police may

[51] Block, Corbett, and Peay, above n. 45, 67–70.
[52] Baldwin, above n. 41, 552–4.   [53] National Audit Office, above n. 1, 70–5.
[54] *Ibid.* 42.

initially set the charge at a lower level than some critics would wish. As pointed out earlier,[55] there has been persistent controversy over the Charging Standards (particularly those for common assault), and the allegation is that the CPS either was instructed or decided to use the whole exercise as a way of saving public expenditure. Thus many more cases are prosecuted as summary-only offences, when they might fit the definition of a 'triable either way' offence, in order to ensure that they remain in the magistrates' courts and do not find their way into the much more expensive Crown Court. These issues are discussed more fully in Chapter 8 below: the policies behind them stem from the system as a whole, rather than from the CPS particularly.

Mode of trial may supply the reason for some 'downgradings' that occur after the CPS has received a case file from the police. It may conclude, on reviewing a file, that the case ought to be tried in the magistrates' court. To achieve this it may drop the higher charge and substitute a lower one, although it is not supposed to do this after a defendant has elected Crown Court trial on an either-way charge.[56] Paragraph 8.2 of the *Code for Crown Prosecutors* states that speed should never be the only reason for trying to keep a case in the magistrates' court, whereas any greater delays and stress on witnesses might be an adequate reason. It remains to be seen whether the new plea before venue system will alter the practices of the CPS in reviewing charges of triable-either-way offences. As for the allegedly high rate of acceptance of guilty pleas by the CPS, it is difficult to find empirical evidence on this. However, as we shall see in Chapter 9 below, the structure of the English criminal justice system is such as to place considerable pressure on defendants to plead guilty, and the acquittal rate in the Crown Court is significant. It may therefore be rational for the CPS to accept a plea to a lower offence, even though paragraph 9.1 of the Code declares that:

> Prosecutors should only accept the defendant's plea if they think the court is able to pass a sentence that matches the seriousness of the offending. Crown Prosecutors must never accept a guilty plea just because it is convenient.

In view of the known hazards of trials and the cost-effectiveness of guilty pleas, there is significant structural pressure on the CPS to take a flexible view of paragraph 9.1. However, there may also be instances of over-charging, usually by the police and not altered by the CPS. This may prove helpful in inducing a plea of guilty or other bargain, for example in cases where a charge under section 18 of the Offences against the Person Act 1861 is brought in the expectation that a plea to section 20 will be the result, and although there was little evidence of the intent required by section 18. Thus any thorough

---

[55] Above n. 8 and accompanying text.   [56] This is explained further in Ch. 8 below, at p. 251.

research on this issue would need to consider both downgrading and, as it were, upgrading.

4. *Independence and co-operation:* among the many strands of interaction between these concepts, two examples may be given here. First, there is the relationship of the CPS with the police. The recent reorganization of the CPS into forty-two areas, corresponding to police areas, is intended to facilitate co-operation and multi-agency initiatives. But, in so far as it brings local police and local CPS into a closer working relationship, it may have the effect of compromising independence of mind in some CPS decisions. The evidence, cited earlier, of shared value systems and of lack of confidence in certain Crown Prosecutors might be enhanced, rather than inhibited, by the realignment of areas. A second example comes from a much higher level. When in 1994 the then Home Secretary announced a new policy on police cautioning, under the banner of 'your first chance is your last chance', he followed it by issuing a new circular to the police requiring them to change their cautioning policies. The 1994 edition of the Code for Crown Prosecutors fell in with the change of emphasis, with a substantial re-writing of the sections on the treatment of young defendants. When challenged about this apparent lack of independence, and subservience to party politics, the CPS responded that this was the world as it found it.[57] There was no option but to follow the Home Secretary, because otherwise the CPS would have been out of step with police practices and chaos might have ensued. But this episode casts doubt on the CPS's claim to be independent and quasi-judicial, and raises questions about the role of the Attorney General, a member of the government and the minister to whom the Director of Public Prosecutions is accountable. The Crime and Disorder Bill 1998 will introduce changes to the cautioning system for young offenders that will inevitably have an impact upon CPS decision-making, but one difference here is that Parliament has passed legislation. In 1994 Mr Howard did not bring the matter before Parliament, but simply issued a circular to police.

5. *Regulatory agencies:* there has been no comparable inquiry into the so-called regulatory agencies, but it would be wrong to leave this part of the discussion without reference to their activities. The above discussion of prosecutorial review cannot, it seems, be transferred directly to the role of the regulatory agencies. They bring relatively few prosecutions, and it is assumed that considerations of public interest have already been taken into account by the reluctance to prosecute save in clear and necessary cases. However, those who have conducted research into these agencies have pointed out that some prosecutions are brought readily, in response to a single incident that has

[57] Daw, above n. 23, at 909, responding to Ashworth and Fionda, above n. 23, 903.

received publicity (perhaps through deaths, serious injuries, or an outbreak of food poisoning) and that has revealed failure to comply with legal standards. Such prosecutions could be examples of a form of 'public interest' reasoning hinted at above: that, where serious harm has resulted, it is important to have a public airing of the issues and a decision taken in a public forum about the appropriate disposal of the case. On the other hand, they also demonstrate the danger of identifying the 'public interest' too closely with newsworthiness. One consequence could be 'that safety matters are given disproportionate attention at the expense of occupational health problems, where deaths may in fact be far more numerous'.[58] This brings back into focus the general question of equality of response to similarly harmful and culpable conduct, pointing out that the question is raised not just by the different practices of the police and regulatory agencies but also by practices within regulatory agencies.

5. The Role of the Victim

What role victims actually play in prosecutorial review is not clear. Crown Prosecutors are unlikely to meet victims as part of the review process, and are therefore reliant on what is contained in the papers. There are research findings from the early years of the CPS suggesting that it is willing to defer to the wishes of 'important' victims such as local businesses, at least to the extent of not discontinuing cases that appear to fulfil the criteria.[59] Recent research by Moxon and Crisp shows that some 13 per cent of discontinuances were attributable to the victim's reluctance to proceed—which usually makes it difficult to pursue the case, since the victim's evidence is likely to be crucial—and that a further 6 per cent of discontinuances stemmed from the offender's agreement to compensate the victim.[60]

What role for the victim is recognized in the Code for Crown Prosecutors? Paragraph 6.7 states that the CPS 'acts in the public interest, not just in the interests of any one individual'. However, it goes on to emphasize that 'Crown Prosecutors must always think very carefully about the interests of the victim, which are an important factor, when deciding where the public interest lies'. The use of the word 'interests' rather than 'wishes' is deliberate, and Crown Prosecutors are expected to make themselves aware of the victim's

[58] Hawkins, *The Uses of Discretion* (1992), at 37, referring to K. Hawkins, 'FATCATS and Prosecution in a Regulatory Agency: A Footnote on the Social Construction of Risk' (1989) 11 *Law and Policy* 370.

[59] See McConville, Sanders, and Leng, *Case for the Prosecution* (1991), 114.

[60] As reported in RCCJ, *Report*, para. 4.36.

views but to take account only of their interests.[61] This is the correct approach in theory, it is submitted,[62] but no research findings cast light on whether it is the approach taken in practice by the CPS of the 1990s. One sphere of victims' interests is whether they are likely to receive compensation from the offender: on the one hand it is not possible to have an enforceable right to compensation unless the case is prosecuted (although under the Crime and Disorder Bill 1998 this will be available when young offenders receive a final warning), but on the other hand the Code suggests that in some circumstances the voluntary payment of compensation by an offender may tell against pursuing a prosecution. Paragraph 6.5g suggests that this is a reason against prosecution, but adds that 'defendants must not avoid prosecution simply because they can pay compensation'. The Explanatory Memorandum adds that 'these cases are not easy', and that Crown Prosecutors 'should exercise a discretion against prosecution with some care in these cases'.[63] This may be taken as a further indication of the difficulty in reconciling elements of reparative justice with the English system.

In one type of case, the victim's wishes are highly likely to prevail, and that is where the victim declines to give evidence and wants the prosecution dropped. Many such cases simply cannot proceed without the victim-complainant's evidence, and so have to be dropped. Particularly sensitive are cases of 'domestic' violence, where the complainant later wishes to withdraw her complaint. Among the reasons are that she wishes to be reconciled to her partner, fear of losing children or a desire to keep the family together, or fear of reprisals.[64] As we saw in Chapter 5, some CPS areas require the complainant to go to court in order to withdraw the complaint, as some kind of crude safeguard against unwilling retractions; but the problem can hardly be solved in that way, and it seems unlikely that the CPS can contribute greatly to its solution.

The Victim's Charter makes certain promises about how the CPS will respond to victims. In cases where death has been caused, the CPS will (on request) meet the victim's family in order to explain its decision on prosecution.[65] The CPS representative should introduce herself or himself to the victim before evidence is given in court, should give an explanation of procedures (unless the Witness Service is able to do that), and should explain any delays.[66] To what extent the flow of information to victims has improved, and victims' needs at court are better met, remains to be evaluated.

---

[61] CPS, *Explanatory Memorandum*, above n. 14, para. 4.42.   [62] See Ch. 2.3(b) above.

[63] CPS, above n. 14, para. 4.39.

[64] See the Leicestershire survey by D.Lockton and R. Ward, *Domestic Violence* (1997), 140.

[65] Home Office, *The Victim's Charter* (2nd edn., 1996), 3.   [66] *Ibid.* 4.

6. Delay

Delay in the conclusion of criminal proceedings can have several disadvantageous consequences: witnesses may forget or become unavailable, prolonged anxiety may be caused to the victim and/or to the defendant, and the public impact of the trial may be diluted by its distance from the events to which it relates. In some cases the prosecution may cause delays, whether through incompetence or neglect. Reasons of this kind presumably underlie the provisions against delay in the European Convention on Human Rights.[67] However, there are also cases in which delay may work in favour of the defence, if it is prosecution witnesses that are likely to forget their story, or if there is enough time for the defendant to become established in a more settled or 'respectable' way of life. Delays should be minimized, whether they are attributable to defence tactics or to prosecution indiscipline.

In order to achieve this, however, it is necessary to arrive at a definition of delay. There must be some lapse of time between arrest, first court appearance, and final disposal: the question concerns what is reasonable and what is unreasonable. To determine this one has to set periods of time as the norm for certain stages in the process of a case. This may be accomplished by comparisons of the time taken in different parts of the country at similar stages of the process, with due regard to variations in types of case.[68] Some relevant national guidelines have been promulgated by the Working Group on Pre-Trial Issues,[69] and the Efficiency Commission is also studying the possibilities for reducing delay.

Section 22 of the Prosecution of Offences Act 1985 empowers the Secretary of State to make regulations on time-limits for the maximum time taken by the prosecution at certain stages when a defendant is on remand in custody. Failure to comply with a time-limit results in the defendant being treated as if acquitted, but there is provision for the prosecution to apply for an extension. The court should only grant this if satisfied that 'there is good and sufficient cause for doing so' and that 'the prosecution has acted with all due expedition'. The Divisional Court has had many opportunities to review the application of these tests.[70] Quite apart from the time-limits applicable in custody cases, delay in bringing any case to court may also be challenged through the doctrine of abuse of process. In the leading decision of *Attorney-General's*

---

[67] See above, Ch. 3.3.11.
[68] P. Morgan and J. Vennard, *Pre-trial Delay: The Implications of Time Limits*, HORS 110 (1989); see also Council of Europe, *Delays in Criminal Justice System* (1992).
[69] *Action Plan*, 41–7.
[70] For discussion, see A. Samuels, 'Custody Time Limits' [1997] *Crim. LR* 260.

Reference (No. 1 of 1990),[71] Lord Lane CJ held that proceedings may be stayed for unjustifiable delay, but only in exceptional circumstances. No stay should be granted if there has been fault by the defendant or if the delay stems from the complexity of the case, and generally fault should be shown on the part of the prosecution. The defendant must also show that he or she would suffer serious prejudice to the extent that a fair trial could no longer take place. This decision constitutes a narrowing of the previous jurisprudence.[72]

The decision on this Attorney-General's Reference is also notable for the respondent's reliance on Magna Carta, clause 29 of which guarantees that 'we will not deny, or defer, to any man, either justice or right'. The Court of Appeal held that deferment must connote wrongful delay or deferment, and therefore saw no need to discuss the argument further on the facts of the Reference. The argument has been considered fully in the High Court of Australia, where the conclusion was that clause 29 cannot be used as a basis for a right to speedy trial.[73]

7. Accountability

To what authorities and to what extent are prosecutors accountable? The absence of clear and effective lines of accountability for many regulatory agencies was discussed in the previous chapter.[74] The focus here will be chiefly upon the Crown Prosecution Service, in the context of prosecutorial review.

1. *Accountability to Parliament:* the CPS is organized hierarchically, with its local branches, forty-two areas, and a headquarters. Internal lines of account-ability end with the Director of Public Prosecutions. He or she is answerable to the Attorney-General, who has ministerial responsibility for the general policies pursued by the CPS but not in respect of decisions taken in individ-ual cases. As we saw earlier,[75] the Prosecution of Offences Act 1985 imposes on the Director a statutory responsibility to issue a code, and to report annu-ally to Parliament. There is no accountability to Parliament for decisions in individual cases, but it is the practice of Members of Parliament to refer to the Director of Public Prosecutions individual cases brought to their attention by constituents or others. The Director will usually reply by letter, giving some reason for the decision (often, a decision to discontinue a prosecution). The

---

[71] [1992] 1 QB 630.   [72] A. Choo, 'Delay and Abuse of Process; (1992) 108 *LQR* 565.
[73] *Jago* v. *District Court (NSW)* (1989) 63 AJLR 640, discussed by R. G. Fox, 'Jago's Case: Delay, Unfairness and Abuse of Process in the High Court of Australia' [1990] *Crim. LR* 552.
[74] See Ch. 5.4, above.   [75] See above, s. 1.

CPS is also open to scrutiny by the Home Affairs Committee of the House of Commons and by the National Audit Office.[76]

One significant deficiency in accountability is the absence of an inspectorate. The prisons, the police, and the probation service are all subject to an inspectorate which has a kind of independence within the Home Office. There is no inspectorate of the judiciary, but that is hardly an argument against external inspection of an organization such as the CPS which is at best quasi-judicial. The CPS itself, recognizing the anomaly, has introduced an internal inspectorate in the last two years, but this is no substitute for proper external scrutiny. The Glidewell Review ought to recommend the introduction of a properly-funded external inspectorate, preferably under the Lord Chancellor's Department. Furthermore, such an inspectorate ought to cover the prosecution decisions and procedures of the regulatory agencies too. To make the latter recommendation is not within the terms of reference of the Glidewell Review, but the Government ought to consider it if there is to be the necessary fairness in prosecution policy. It is also important that there be regular externally-conducted research into the CPS and other prosecuting agencies: although the CPS has funded research projects by outside researchers in recent years, there is a need to recognize more formally the contribution to accountability that properly conducted research can make, especially when there are no constraints on the publication of the findings.

2. *Accountability to the courts:* for some years the courts have expressed a willingness to review certain prosecution decisions, and recent years have seen striking developments. It was established in the first *Blackburn* case[77] that the courts would be prepared judicially to review a general policy not to prosecute for certain classes of offence, for example, all thefts with a value below £100. In the third *Blackburn* case[78] Lord Denning MR suggested that the courts would also be prepared to review an individual decision not to prosecute, and this dictum has received recent judicial support.[79] The primary basis for judicial review would be that either the policy or the individual decision was unreasonable in a *Wednesbury* sense, that is, was such that no reasonable prosecuting authority would have adopted the policy or taken the decision.[80] It seems that few people who feel aggrieved at a decision not to prosecute embark on judicial review: the government dismissed the idea of appealing to a magistrates' court for review of a decision not to prosecute,[81] and preferred

---

[76] National Audit Office, *Crown Prosecution Service* (1997).

[77] *R. v. Metropolitan Police Commissioner, ex p. Blackburn* [1968] 2 QB 118.

[78] *R. v. Metropolitan Police Commissioner, ex p. Blackburn (No. 3)* [1973] 1 QB 241.

[79] *R. v. General Council of the Bar, ex p. Percival* [1990] 3 All ER 137.

[80] The scope of the leading case of *Associated Provincial Pictures Houses* v. *Wednesbury Corporation* [1948] 1 KB 223 is discussed by P. P. Craig, *Administrative Law* (3rd edn., 1994), Ch. 11.

[81] Home Office, *An Independent Prosecution Service* (HMSO, 1983).

to allow continued reliance on the power to bring a private prosecution. This requires considerable strength and persistence, usually from the victim or victim's family, but there are examples of such prosecutions succeeding.[82]

Would it be possible to obtain judicial review of a decision to prosecute that was thought unfair? The Divisional Court took this step, with great caution, in *R. v. Chief Constable of Kent and another, ex parte L.* (1991).[83] The Court accepted that an individual decision to prosecute could be subject to judicial review if it was clearly contrary to a settled policy of the Director of Public Prosecutions, i.e. the Code for Crown Prosecutors. However, the particular case involved a juvenile, and the court was careful to confine its remarks to cases involving juveniles, where there is a strong public policy of avoiding court appearances. Notwithstanding this caution, Stuart-Smith LJ in the Divisional Court in *R. v. Inland Revenue Commissioners, ex parte Mead* (1993)[84] accepted that judicial review of a decision to prosecute would also be possible where the applicant was an adult; the other member of the court, Popplewell J, disagreed with this. Stuart-Smith LJ expressed the opinion that successful review would be less likely for adults since the public policy in favour of diversion is less strong than for juveniles. However, the Code for Crown Prosecutors contains a number of clear policies in respect of adult offenders, and it seems perfectly possible that a decision to continue the prosecution of an adult despite that person's age or the staleness of the offence might result in judicial review. The *Mead* case involved the Inland Revenue Commissioners, and this shows that judicial review of decisions taken by other prosecuting authorities would be available if they had declared criteria for prosecution that were sufficiently detailed. Judicial review of decisions to prosecute would be based either on the failure to follow a declared policy, or on the failure to take account of a relevant consideration in reaching the decision.

The doctrine of abuse of process has been invoked against prosecutors in recent years in two main classes of case.[85] First, the court may exercise its power to stay proceedings if there has been delay in the bringing of proceedings that would seriously prejudice the fairness of the trial. The effects of delay are well known, and the European Convention holds that there must be trial 'within a reasonable time'.[86] In the leading case of *Attorney-General's Reference*

[82] Perhaps the most remarkable in recent years is the case that became *Attorney-General's Reference (No. 3 of 1989)* (1990) 90 Cr.App.R. 358, in which the CPS had declined to prosecute for a more serious offence than careless driving.

[83] (1991) 93 Cr.App.R. 416; see the discussion by S. Uglow *et al.*, 'Cautioning Juveniles: Multi-agency Impotence' [1992] *Crim. LR* 632.

[84] [1993] 1 All ER 772; see the discussion of this and other authorities above, pp. 163–5.

[85] For detailed analysis, see A. Choo, *Abuse of Process and Judicial Stays of Prosecution* (1993), chs. 1 and 2.

[86] See Ch. 3.3.11; cf. also para. 8(3) of the Code for Crown Prosecutors relating to 'stale offences', discussed above, section 3.

(No. 1 of 1990),[87] discussed in Section 5 above, the Court of Appeal emphasized that stays of proceedings on grounds of delay would be exceptional, especially if there were no fault on the part of the prosecution. The second class of case is where the defendant is being placed in double jeopardy by the present proceedings, having already been acquitted or convicted on substantially the same facts.[88] However, the Divisional Court has stated that the doctrine of abuse of process is not limited to these two classes of case. In *R. v. Croydon Justices, ex parte Dean* (1993)[89] the police had told a young man who was a fringe participant in a major crime that he would not be prosecuted if he gave evidence against the major participants. However, he was subsequently prosecuted for the crime of assisting offenders, one of the few offences for which the decision to prosecute lies with the CPS rather than the police. The Divisional Court stayed the prosecution, accepting that there had been an abuse of process stemming from the promise of non-prosecution given by the police, even though the police did not have the power to prosecute for this offence. That decision was followed in *Bloomfield* (1997),[90] where the Court of Appeal quashed a conviction in a case which the CPS had declared its intention to drop at a Plea and Directions Hearing, only for the prosecution to be continued when the case came into the hands of a different prosecuting counsel. Likewise in *Townsend, Dearsley and Bretscher* (1998)[91] the Court of Appeal applied the doctrine of abuse of process in quashing a conviction after a person who had been induced to believe that he would not be prosecuted and would instead be called as a prosecution witness in another trial was then prosecuted. In this case, however, the Court did state that breach of a promise not to prosecute would not necessarily give rise to an abuse of process, a dictum which will doubtless be considered in future cases. It need hardly be added that the same principles apply where the promise not to prosecute was given by a regulatory or other prosecuting agency.[92]

These increases in the accountability of prosecutors may be welcomed as supplying the necessary counterbalance to the considerable discretion that exists in the sphere of prosecutorial review. State officials and others are entrusted with great power over the lives of citizens, and the exercise of this power should be open to scrutiny on grounds of fairness. Whether judicial review is the most suitable approach, and whether the three doctrines considered—*Wednesbury* unreasonableness, failure to apply a stated policy,

---

[87] (1992) 95 Cr.App.R. 296.　　[88] The leading case is *Connelly* v. *DPP* [1964] AC 1254.
[89] [1993] 3 All ER 129.　　[90] [1997] 1 Cr.App.R. 135.
[91] [1998] *Crim. LR* 126.
[92] See, e.g., *Postermobile plc* v. *Brent LBC*, *The Times Law Report*, 8 Dec. 1997 (abuse of process for local authority to prosecute after giving assurance that planning permission not required).

and abuse of process—cover the ground adequately and appropriately is a subject for continuing inquiry.

8. Prosecutorial Ethics

In its present form the Code for Crown Prosecutors says nothing about the ethical orientation of prosecutors. No doubt each Crown Prosecutor, as a solicitor or barrister, would claim to be governed by the ethical code of the relevant professional organization. But there is a need to settle the distinctive ethical principles on which the CPS should operate.

In Chapter 3 we reviewed the various formulations of the prosecutor's role, as a kind of 'Minister of Justice' concerned with obtaining convictions without unfairness to defendants.[93] The role has been expressed similarly in the US Supreme Court: the prosecutor

> is in a peculiar and very definite sense the servant of the law, the twofold aim of which is that guilt shall not escape or innocence suffer . . . It is as much his duty to refrain from improper methods calculated to produce a wrongful conviction as it is to use every legitimate means to bring about a just one.[94]

The importance of these statements lies in their endorsement of the argument, developed in Chapter 3 above, that the protection of rights should be regarded as part of the law, and not as standing in opposition to the proper role of police or prosecutors. Whilst it is true that defence lawyers have the primary task of securing the defendant's rights, prosecutors should neither indulge in nor condone unlawful or unethical practices. They should show no less respect for fairness, as embodied in principles such as those set out in Chapter 2, than for the obtaining of convictions of the guilty.

The CPS's Statement of Values and Purpose declares that 'we will do everything in our power to ensure that all defendants are dealt with fairly, and if a case proceeds, that they have a fair trial'.[95] What are the implications of these fine words for practice? One obvious implication concerns the bringing of prosecutions based on tainted investigative procedures. If the CPS discovers that evidence has been obtained in breach of the PACE Codes or other rules, should it 'let the court decide' on admissibility or discontinue the case itself? The answer to the question can be fudged, and the Explanatory Memorandum

---

[93] See above, 69–70.   [94] *Berger* v. *United States* (1935) 294 US 78, at 88 per Sutherland J.
[95] CPS, *Statement of Purpose and Values*, 10; cf. also, at 8: 'Our decisions are informed by, but independent of, the police. This process acts as an important safeguard for the suspect.'

comes close to this when it states that 'often the issue will not be clear cut and Crown prosecutors must consider carefully whether it is more appropriate for the issue to be determined in court'.[96] Even the most casual reading of appellate decisions in the last seven years shows that many prosecutions have been brought in cases of manifest departure from central provisions of the Codes of Practice. The CPS ought to take a more robust ethical stand on respect for fair procedures. There is a need for a clear set of ethical principles, supported by examples of types of case in which they may apply. This means recognizing, rather than denying, the existence of shared values with the police among certain prosecutors, and it requires clear statements of the ethical grounds for discontinuing weak cases, for insisting that Bail Act requirements are fulfilled if applications for remand in custody are to be made (rather than accepting the police view), and so forth. To have a chance of making an impression in practice, such a declaration of principles would need to be accompanied by a well-planned drive to convince Crown Prosecutors that the principles are well founded and ought to be followed, and to dispel the rival notions of 'crime control' and 'prosecuting with one hand tied behind one's back'.[97]

9. Conclusions

In this chapter a number of questions about CPS practice have been raised. The Glidewell Review will deliver its recommendations too late for this book, but we have seen that on many key issues there is a dearth of well-conceived and up-to-date independent research. On the other hand, there are some recent projects, notably John Baldwin's 1995 research, which assist in identifying problems in the CPS. What we need to know, however, is the extent to which the various policies and commitments made in the Code and other CPS documents are implemented in practice—not only those discussed above, but others relating to non-discrimination and extra protection for the vulnerable.

There are also normative questions about the responsibilities of the CPS. At the end of the last chapter, the possibility of conferring on the CPS overall responsibility for prosecutions and diversion was considered. At present the police possess both a dispositive function (decisions on cautioning) and a prosecutorial function (decisions on charging). These are more in the nature of judicial or quasi-judicial functions than tasks for investigators. Should not England and Wales move towards the separation of investigative from these

---

[96] CPS, above n. 14, para. 4.20. [97] See above, Ch. 3.8.

other functions that obtains, more or less, in almost all other European jurisdictions? The 1981 Royal Commission was concerned:

> to secure that after a clearly defined point during the preparation of a case for
> trial and during its presentation at trial someone with legal qualifications makes
> the variety of decisions necessary to ensure that only properly selected, pre-
> pared and presented cases come before the court for disposal; and to do that
> without diminishing the quality of police investigation and preliminary case
> preparation and without increasing delays.[98]

That Royal Commission decided not to overthrow the whole of previous practice and instead proposed that the decision to charge be left in the hands of the
police, bringing in the CPS at the subsequent stage. The 1993 Royal Commission
likewise made no recommendations for structural change of this kind. Its most
far-reaching recommendation in this sphere was that the CPS be given the
power to impose prosecutor fines, adapting the Scottish model.[99] Whatever the
merits of this proposal in isolation, it raised many questions about the division
of responsibilities for diversion that were not tackled in the Commission's
Report, thus leaving even greater confusion in this area. The elementary question of the relationship between cautioning and prosecutor fines was not put, let
alone answered. The proposition that a single agency should deal with dispositive decisions was not properly considered. There would, of course, be problems
of ensuring that such decisions are taken on the basis of sufficient information
from the various sources, but that is a consequential rather than a fundamental
issue. Taken together with the 1993 Royal Commission's curt dismissal of the
proposal that the CPS should decide on the mode of trial of offences triable
either way[100]—a proposal that also reflects the Scottish system—it seems that
the path of reform is blocked either by a lack of confidence in the CPS or by the
power of the police or by a combination of the two.

The 1993 Royal Commission also neglected the question of the proper relationship between the policies of the CPS and those of other agencies with the
power to prosecute, including the regulatory agencies. There are fundamental issues of social fairness here that need to be confronted urgently: otherwise, it looks as if the criminal justice system is intended to bear down
unequally on people committing offences in different circumstances, even
where those offences are of roughly equivalent seriousness. There is a need for
decisions on the proper policies to be pursued, and also for a new system of
accountability that applies the same standards to the CPS and other agencies.
If equality before the law and equal treatment are to be realistic aspirations,
this glaring anomaly must no longer be left unchallenged.

---

[98] RCCP, *Report*, para. 7.6.   [99] RCCJ, *Report*, paras. 5.62 and 5.63.
[100] RCCJ, *Report*, para. 6.12: it 'would not be acceptable here at least for the time being'.

7   Remands before Trial

THE bail/custody decision raises some of the most acute conflicts in the whole criminal process. On the one hand there is the defendant's interest in remaining at liberty until the trial has taken place. On the other hand there is a public interest in obtaining protection from crime. Some practitioners, politicians, and others have concluded that the way to deal with this conflict is in each case to balance the defendant's rights with the interests of society. However, the vague notion of 'balancing' that is usually advanced in this context is manifestly inadequate. No judgement of balance can be properly reached until there is a clear appreciation of what rights defendants (and actual or potential victims) have at this stage, and fuller analysis of the content and legitimacy of the claimed public interests. It will be evident during the course of this chapter that there is a wide range of relevant considerations, combined with a dearth of practical information at some crucial stages. The view might well be taken that no set of rules and exceptions could be framed to deal satisfactorily with all or even most cases—unless the rule itself contained several value-judgements which were left for interpretation in the courts. That remains for discussion. But the issues are too important to leave to wide expanses of little-regulated discretion, whether in the hands of police officers, magistrates, or judges. The focus in this chapter will be on the issues of principle raised by the law and practice.[1]

Questions of remand on bail or in custody arise at various stages in the criminal process. First, there is the question of police bail, pending the first court appearance. Secondly, there is the decision on remand between the first and the final court appearance. Thirdly, there is the question of remand pending an appeal against verdict or sentence, which is the subject of a Practice Direction.[2] And fourthly, there is the question of remand after conviction and before sentence is passed, for example in order to allow time for the preparation of a report on the defendant. In order to keep the discussion within reasonable bounds, the third and fourth decisions will not be discussed here,

---

[1] For a full account of the law and practice, see Paul Cavadino and Bryan Gibson, *Bail: The Law, Best Practice and the Debate* (1993).

[2] *Practice Direction: Bail Pending Appeal* [1983] 1 WLR 1292.

and there will be only a few references to police bail. The principal focus is upon the court's decision whether to remand on bail or in custody between first appearance and trial.

1. Remands and Rights

What rights of a defendant are at stake here? The fundamental right of an innocent person not to be convicted is not called directly into question by a custodial remand, but the presumption of innocence ought to entail a principle that the criminal process should cause the minimum of inconvenience to suspects and defendants. Custodial remands take away liberty. Indeed, one of the reasons why the right not to be wrongly convicted is described as fundamental is the value of liberty. The significance of taking it away is heightened when it is connected to the presumption of innocence: since we are discussing remands before trial, there has been no conviction and the defendant is entitled to be presumed innocent unless and until it is proved otherwise at a trial. As we have seen in Chapter 2, Article 6(2) of the European Convention on Human Rights affirms the presumption of innocence, Article 5(1)(c) provides that a person may be deprived of liberty on reasonable suspicion for the purpose of bringing him or her before a court, and Article 5(3) provides that such a person should be brought promptly before a court and entitled to trial within a reasonable time or to release pending trial.[3] Thus the European Convention lacks a cutting edge on this issue, unless the courts develop the presumption of innocence or the entitlement to release pending trial. Nonetheless, there have been several successful applications to the European Court of Human Rights on the ground that the legal systems of certain other countries occasionally lead to delays as long as three to five years in some cases.[4] In *Tomasi* v. *France* (1992)[5] a delay of over five years was held to breach Article 5(3), and there have been constant calls within France for changes to a system that results in lengthy pre-trial detention.[6]

In principle, it is quite wrong that anyone, including agents of law enforcement, should be able to make an arrest, bring a charge, and then, without

---

[3] J. E. S. Fawcett, *Application of the European Convention on Human Rights* (2nd edn., 1987) argues that there is a need for some redrafting of the various parts of Art. 5 in order to clarify the principles relevant to remand pending trial (88).

[4] For collected cases—including one case in which a delay of 4 years was held not to breach Art. 5(3)—see D.J. Harris, M. O'Boyle, and C. Warbrick, *Law of the European Convention on Human Rights* (1995), 143–4. There are also cases brought under Art. 6.1 for 'trial within a reasonable time', where any prolonged period of inactivity by the prosecutor might lead to a finding of a breach.

[5] (1992) A.241.

[6] H. Trouille, 'A Look at French Criminal Procedure' [1994] *Crim. LR* 735, at 737 and 743.

proving that charge in court, secure the immediate detention of the defendant. Detention without trial is widely regarded as an incident of totalitarianism, or at least an expedient to be contemplated only in an extreme kind of national emergency. It therefore follows that any argument for depriving unconvicted individuals of their liberty in civil society ought to have peculiar strength. Indeed, that point is reinforced when one considers the potential consequences for the defendant of a loss of liberty before trial—not just the deprivation of freedom to live a normal life, often compounded by incarceration under the worst conditions in the prison system, but also restricted ability to prepare a defence to the charge, loss of job, strain on family relations and friendships, and often appearance in court in a deteriorated or demoralized condition. The higher rates of suicide and self-injury for unconvicted rather than convicted prisoners may have much to do with these adversities.[7]

No doubt it was considerations of this kind that led the Supreme Court of the United States to declare:

> this traditional right to freedom before conviction permits the unhampered preparation of a defence and serves to prevent the infliction of punishment prior to conviction. Unless this right to bail before trial is preserved, the presumption of innocence, secured only after centuries of struggle, would lose its meaning.[8]

Yet this statement introduces another concept that needs careful inquiry. If remands in custody are to be permitted at all, can they fairly be described as 'the infliction of punishment'? From time to time it has been alleged that courts have indulged in 'punitive remands', remanding a person in custody when it is known full well that a custodial sentence would not be appropriate on conviction.[9] Remand for those reasons is plainly an abuse. But even in cases where the remand is not punitive, the hardship inflicted on the defendant is undeniable. However, definitions of punishment invariably link the element of hard treatment to conviction of an offence by a court.[10] Remand in custody inflicts hardship, as might a dog-bite or a falling tree in a storm, but it cannot be regarded as punishment. Yet custodial remands do differ in one marked respect from natural disasters: they are intentionally inflicted by a court as a result of a hearing.

The US Supreme Court rejected a challenge to the Bail Reform Act of 1984, which allows a judicial officer to authorize pre-trial detention if there is clear and convincing evidence that 'no condition or combination of conditions of

---

[7] A. Liebling and H. Krarup, *Suicide Attempts and Self-Injury in Male Prisons* (1993), 52.

[8] Per Vinson CJ in *Stack* v. *Boyle* (1951) 342 US 1, at 4.

[9] See e.g. the warning of Lord Hailsham LC against punitive remands in 1971–[1972] *Magistrate* 21.

[10] The classic definition is that of H. L. A. Hart, *Punishment and Reponsibility* (1968), 5.

pre-trial release will reasonably assure the safety of any other person and the community'. Rejecting the argument that the statute was unconstitutional because it imposed punishment before trial, the majority held that a statute on pre-trial detention is 'regulatory, not penal'.[11] The minority retorted that this approach 'merely redefine[s] any measure which is claimed to be punishment as "regulation" and, magically, the Constitution no longer prohibits its imposition'.[12] The reply scores a debating point, but leaves open the justifications for the detention of the mentally disordered, of persons subject to quarantine, of illegal immigrants pending deportation, etc. There surely are circumstances in which the State is justified in depriving a person of liberty even though that person has not been convicted of an offence—indeed, is not even suspected of one. Clearly the justification for this must be strong and pressing, in view of the deprivation of liberty involved. Is there any analogy between the main grounds for custodial remand and those other types of case?[13]

As we will see, one of the three main grounds for refusing bail is that otherwise the defendant is unlikely to stand trial: there is thought to be a significant risk of absconding. The use of the term 'risk' shows that this is a predictive judgement, but so presumably are those that lead to the detention of certain mentally disordered people, illegal immigrants, etc. One central question concerns the relative social importance of ensuring that persons charged with offences attend their trial on the due date. Presumably the police could be dispatched to arrest someone who failed to attend without offering a reasonable excuse, but there might be a greater anxiety over certain defendants who seem likely to flee the country or to hide themselves away. In all cases, the relevant questions concern the evidence of probability on the particular facts, the seriousness of the offence charged (to be set against the risk of the defendant's non-attendance), the possibility of imposing conditions or taking sureties, and thus the degree of risk that must be attained before liberty is taken away. Without concluding this line of argument, one might say that there would be no justification for ordering the detention of persons charged with drunkenness offences simply because they seemed likely to wander off, since the offence is so minor that the public interest in their trial is fairly small; but that there might be ample justification if the defendant were charged with major offences (e.g. violence or serious fraud), and had on previous occasions failed to attend trial, and the court was satisfied that no other method of

---

[11] *United States* v. *Salerno* (1987) 481 US 739. For an accessible discussion, see Lord Windlesham, 'Punishment and Prevention: The Inappropriate Prisoners' [1988] *Crim. LR* 140, at 143–5.

[12] *United States* v. *Salerno*, at 760, per Marshall and Brennan JJ.

[13] Cf. L. M. Natali and E. D. Ohlbaum, 'Redrafting the Due Process Model: The Preventive Detention Blueprint' (1989) 62 *Temple LR* 1225, at 1237–8.

securing attendance at trial would be effective (deprivation of liberty must be a last resort).

A second main ground is the probability of committing offences if granted bail. Again, this is a question of risk and prediction. It is often asserted that there is a public interest in ensuring that people already charged with an offence do not commit offences during the period before their trial. The exact basis for this is unclear. Is it that the State is somehow responsible for the conduct of persons who have been charged but not yet tried, perhaps because it is the slowness of the machinery of criminal justice that creates the opportunities? Otherwise, in what way do remandees differ from, say, people with previous convictions who are walking the streets? Surely it cannot be that anyone who has been charged may be presumed guilty, and for that reason may just as well be likely to commit a further offence if left at large before the formal trial: that reasoning, with its presumption of guilt, would contradict the presumption of innocence. Indeed, this was one of the grounds on which the Irish Supreme Court refused to recognize this as a legitimate ground for pretrial detention, commenting that 'this is a form of preventative justice which . . . is quite alien to the true purpose of bail'.[14] In a subsequent case, the Court added that 'the proper methods of preventing crime are the long-established combination of police surveillance, speedy trial and deterrent sentences'.[15]

A further possibility, raised by the recent enactment of a statutory provision requiring courts to treat the fact that an offence was committed on bail as an aggravating factor in sentencing,[16] is that the period between charge and trial is regarded as a period of special trust, which the 'bail-breaking' offender breaches. Yet this does not explain why the period on bail should be so regarded: is it the idea of State responsibility again or, if not, is there some reason why the defendant should have greater obligations at this time than, say, immediately after the conclusion of a sentence? The latter reason suggests that defendants who are released on bail are granted a privilege that they should not abuse, but if the presumption of innocence and the right to liberty are valued, it is wrong to describe this as a privilege. Questions of this kind are rarely confronted, but it seems clear that considerable significance is attributed to the mere fact that a person has been charged. In so far as this carries any assumption about guilt, it goes against the presumption of innocence. But the Canadian Supreme Court, at least, has concluded that there is an issue of

---

[14] *People (Attorney-General)* v. *Callaghan* [1966] IR 426, per Walsh J at 516.
[15] *Ryan* v. *DPP* [1989] IR 399, per Finlay CJ at 407. These cases are cited by U. ni Raifeartaigh, 'Reconciling Bail Law with the Presumption of Innocence' (1997) 17 *Oxford JLS* 1. In 1996 the Irish Constitution was amended so as to provide for pre-trial detention where reasonably necessary 'to prevent the commission of a serious offence by that person'.
[16] Criminal Justice Act 1993, s. 66(6), substituting s. 29(2) of the Criminal Justice Act 1991.

'public safety' involved here which may justify pre-trial detention.[17] Others might argue that it may be no 'mere fact' that a person has been charged, since the defendant may well have confessed guilt and indicated an intention to plead guilty; but certain well-publicized cases of miscarriage of justice suggest that it would be unwise to build too much on those foundations. It might also be argued that the laying of a charge ought to be attributed significance now that there is a national system of trained prosecutors; but that overlooks the probability that there may have been no real prosecutorial review of the case file at the first remand hearing, and not until some weeks have elapsed since the original charge may the prosecutor be confident that there is a 'realistic prospect of conviction'.[18] The arguments here, then, are much weaker than is commonly supposed.

A third ground is the probability that the defendant might interfere with witnesses or otherwise obstruct the course of justice if released on bail. In some instances the defendant may have been involved in such incidents before, but this ground is of particular importance to the protection of people who have already been victimized. Where a defendant has uttered threats against that person or the court has heard other convincing reasons why the victim fears attack, and a non-custodial remand is unlikely to provide sufficient protection, custody may be justified. This is a particular problem in 'domestic' violence cases.[19] Threats weaken the presumption of innocence and, if it appears to be a choice between the defendant's liberty or the victim's freedom from probable harm, a court may be justified in choosing the latter and ordering a remand in custody. Threats and interference may regarded as attempts to undermine the integrity of the criminal trial, and incarceration may be justified as the only way of protecting the process.

All three grounds for the refusal of bail turn on questions of predicted risk. Risk consists of the probability of an offence being committed if the defendant is granted bail, and the seriousness of any likely offence. A low probability of a very serious offence ought to have more weight than a high probability of a minor offence. Indeed, for non-serious offences, custodial remands should simply be ruled out. If the alleged offence is serious, and if the court is satisfied that there is sufficient evidential basis for the charge and that there is a substantial risk of a serious offence if the person is released on bail (whether with or without conditions), there might be grounds for deprivation of liberty before trial. Where the line should be drawn between serious and non-serious

[17] *Morales* (1993) 77 CCC (3d) 91, holding that on this ground the remand provisions of the Canadian Criminal Code do not breach the Charter of Rights and Freedoms.

[18] See the discussion in Ch. 6.2, above.

[19] House of Commons Home Affairs Committee, Third Report Session 1992–3, *Domestic Violence* (1993), and the Government's Reply, *Domestic Violence*, Cmnd. 2269 (1993), paras. 45 and 69.

is a matter to be taken up at the end of the chapter. The purpose of this introduction has been to demonstrate the relevance of the presumption of innocence, in so far as the various justifications relate to the offence with which the
defendant has been charged. Even if the presumption of innocence is regarded
as irrelevant on the ground that pre-trial detention is not 'punishment',[20]
there remain deep questions about the notion of 'public safety', the problems
of prediction, and deprivation of liberty.

2. The Law Relating to Remands

In this Section of the chapter, we consider the history and current form of the
law relating to remands, first in relation to court remands, and then in relation to remand decisions taken by the police.

1. *Court remands:* both in England and Wales and in the United States the
law relating to remands has developed in two distinct phases. The first phase
in both countries focused chiefly on the problem of securing the attendance
of the defendant at the trial. In *Robinson* (1854), Coleridge J held that this was
the sole point to which the magistrates should give attention.[21] In *Rose*
(1898),[22] Lord Russell stated that 'it cannot be too strongly impressed on the
magistracy that bail is not to be withheld as a punishment but that the
requirements as to bail are merely to secure the attendance of the prisoner at
his trial'. It was not until the 1940s and 1950s that the English courts, with
Lord Goddard as Lord Chief Justice, began to establish that an alternative
ground for remanding in custody is that the defendant is likely to commit an
offence if granted bail.[23] The Home Office took the unusual step of circulat-
ing to all magistrates the text of Lord Goddard's remarks in *Wharton* (1955).[24]
Statutory confirmation came in the provisions of the Criminal Justice Act
1967, an Act which also introduced the possibility of granting conditional
bail.

Two similar phases can be discerned in the American law. Until the 1960s
the law and practice tended to concentrate on the problem of securing the

[20] See also ni Raifeartaigh, above n. 15, for further discussion of this argument.

[21] (1854) 23 LJQB 286. For summaries of the history, see A. K. Bottomley, 'The Granting of Bail:
Principles and Practice' (1968) 31 *MLR* 40, and N. Corre, *Bail in Criminal Proceedings* (1990),
pp. ix–xiv.

[22] (1898) 78 LT 119.

[23] See *Phillips* (1947) 32 Cr.App.R. 47; *Pegg* [1955] *Crim. LR* 308 (the court also mentioning that
D had no answer to the charge); *Wharton* [1955] *Crim. LR* 565 ('unless the justices felt real doubt as
to the result of the case, men with bad criminal records should not be granted bail'); *Gentry* [1956]
Crim. LR 120 (same policy reiterated).

[24] This was pointed out by Bottomley, above n. 21, at 52.

attendance of defendants at trial: surveys showed that courts were mostly using financial bonds (sureties) as the means to this end, and that the result was the pre-trial imprisonment of people too poor to raise the money for such a bond.[25] Congress passed the Federal Bail Reform Act in 1966, legislating for 'release on recognisance' rather than financial bonds as the normal pre-trial order.[26] The second phase was marked by a growing anxiety about the commission of offences by people on bail, a concern that culminated in Congress passing the Bail Reform Act of 1984. Although the Act contains a number of procedural safeguards, its main provision is, as we have seen, based on a prediction of future danger.[27] Many other jurisdictions seem to have arrived at positions broadly similar to the English and American, although the provision in the Canadian Criminal Code still maintains that the primary ground for refusing bail is to secure attendance at the trial. However, the secondary ground (to be considered if the primary ground is inapplicable) refers to 'the protection or safety of the public'.[28]

The relevant law for England and Wales is now contained chiefly in the Bail Act 1976, as amended. In essence, a court has four main alternatives: release on unconditional bail, release on conditional bail, release on bail subject to a surety or security, and remand in custody.

Little needs to be said about unconditional bail. As for conditional bail, the Act makes provision for this in section 3(6). It appears that around one-quarter of defendants granted bail are placed under conditions: Raine and Willson found that the most common condition is residence at a specified address (78 per cent of conditional cases), followed by not contacting named persons (46 per cent), not going to a certain address (24 per cent) curfew (21 per cent), and reporting at a police station (18 per cent).[29] They found that many conditions are proposed by the defence (in the hope of deflecting the court from a custodial remand), rather than by the magistrates themselves. They also found that half their interviewees believed that bail conditions would not be enforced, a perception that clearly weakens the efficacy of conditional bail. The Bail Act also provides that a court may, subject to certain restrictions, require a surety to secure the defendant's attendance at court. It may also require a defendant to give security for surrender to custody before

---

[25] See C. Foote, 'Compelling Appearance in Court: Administration of Bail in Philadelphia' (1954) 102 *U. Pa. LR* 1031, and, on the subsequent research by the Vera Institute that led to the change in federal law, D. J. Freed and P. Wald, *Bail in the United States* (1964).

[26] For a general outline, see P. R. Jones and J. S. Goldkamp, 'Judicial Guidelines for Pre-trial Release: Research and Policy Developments in the United States' (1991) 30 *Howard JCJ* 140.

[27] See n. 11 above and accompanying text.

[28] N. Padfield, 'The Right to Bail: A Canadian Perspective' [1993] *Crim. LR* 510, discussing the provision and its interpretation in the Canadian Supreme Court.

[29] J. Raine and M. Willson, 'The Imposition of Conditions in Bail Decisions' (1996) 35 *Howard JCJ* 256.

release on bail.[30] The danger with financial conditions, as the American experience shows, is that they may tend to exclude the less well-off from bail, and there is English evidence to suggest that some remands in custody occur because the levels of surety set by the courts are unrealistic.[31] This is quite wrong, being unfair discrimination against people of modest means.

The centrepiece of the Act is section 4, which proclaims what has been described as a general right to bail or a presumption in favour of bail. Thus section 4(1) provides that 'a person to whom this section applies shall be granted bail except as provided in Schedule 1 to this Act'. Paragraphs 2 to 6 of part I of that Schedule[32] list a number of 'exceptions to the right to bail', including custodial remands for the defendant's own protection and (more doubtfully) custodial remands because the court does not yet have sufficient information to take a decision on bail. The main provision is paragraph 2, which must be quoted in full:

> The defendant need not be granted bail if the court is satisfied that there are substantial grounds for believing that the defendant, if released on bail (whether subject to conditions or not), would—
>   (a) fail to surrender to custody, or
>   (b) commit an offence while on bail, or
>   (c) interfere with witnesses or otherwise obstruct the course of justice, whether in relation to himself or any other person.

These three grounds correspond broadly with those subsequently incorporated in the Bail Reform Act of 1984 in the United States.[33] The Schedule to the English Act goes on to set out various considerations to which regard should be had when taking bail/custody decisions. Among those is 'the defendant's record as respect the fulfilment of his obligations under previous grants of bail in criminal proceedings', a matter plainly relevant when the court is considering exception (a) to the right to bail.

Another consideration is 'the character, antecedents, associations and community ties of the defendant'. Community ties may be relevant to the probability that a defendant will attend his trial (exception (a)), since it may be argued that a person who is homeless or in temporary accommodation is more likely to abscond than someone with a permanent address (and a

---

[30] For further details, see Cavadino and Gibson, above n. 1, 40–6.

[31] *Ibid.* 170, proposing a legislative provision to require courts to take account of defendants' means and social background.

[32] Pt. II of the Schedule deals separately with non-imprisonable offences, which will not be discussed here.

[33] i.e. serious risk that the defendant will flee or will obstruct justice, or where the case involves a crime of violence (very broadly defined), a major drug offence, or any crime punishable by life imprisonment, or where the case involves a felony charge against someone previously convicted of two offences in the above categories.

family) in the locality. However, it has been urged repeatedly that homelessness should not lead to a custodial remand without thorough exploration of other alternatives.[34] The 'character and antecedents' of the offender may give grounds for a prediction of whether he or she is likely to offend if given bail (exception (b)). This question has attracted surprisingly little legal analysis or empirical inquiry. One oft-quoted statement is that of Atkinson J in the Court of Criminal Appeal in *Phillips* (1947),[35] where he warned courts against granting bail to defendants with a 'record of housebreaking', and added that 'in 19 out of 20 cases it is a mistake [to] release young housebreakers on bail'. Statistical studies suggest that this is a considerable exaggeration.[36]

A further consideration listed in paragraph 9 is 'the nature and seriousness of the offence or default (and the probable method of dealing with the offender for it)'. There is nineteenth-century authority for the view that the seriousness of the offence may have a bearing on the probability of D absconding—the more serious the offence, the greater the incentive to abscond.[37] Again, its statistical basis is untested, and might of its nature be difficult to test. Another interpretation is that this consideration is intended to relate to exception (b), the likelihood of D committing offences if released on bail. In fact it exposes a defect in the wording of exception (b), which nowhere mentions the seriousness of any offences that might be committed. On the face of the Act, and the exceptions to bail that it enumerates, the probability of further minor offences such as shoplifting could justify a custodial remand. For paragraph 9 to mention the probable sentence is insufficient, since the exceptions to bail in the Act fail to make any reference to that at all. The probable sentence would be relevant if exception (b) referred to the likelihood of committing a *serious* offence whilst on bail, as does the law on custodial remands of juveniles, but it does not do so.

In recent years the law on court remands has been toughened. Sections 25 and 26 of the Criminal Justice and Public Order Act 1994 restrict a court's powers to remand on bail two categories of defendant. Any person charged with murder, attempted murder, manslaughter, rape, or attempted rape who already has a conviction for such an offence may not be granted bail.[38] Where a person is charged with an indictable offence which, it appears to the court, was committed at a time when he or she was on bail from an existing charge, the general presumption in favour of bail does not apply.

---

[34] See e.g. Home Office Circular 155/1975, *Bail Procedures*.   [35] (1947) 32 Cr.App.R. 47.
[36] See the discussion of Patricia Morgan's work below, n. 65 and accompanying text.
[37] See the remarks of Coleridge J in *Scaife* (1841) 10 LJMC 144 and later in *Robinson* (1854) 23 LJQB 286.
[38] This mandatory provision is probably in breach of Article 5.1(c) and 5.3 of the ECHR, which require courts to assess the dangers in each individual case.

2. *Police remands:* the powers of the police to remand persons whom they have interviewed and may wish to interview again, and persons whom they have charged, pending their first court appearance, are contained in the Police and Criminal Evidence Act 1984, as amended by the Criminal Justice and Public Order Act 1994. The principal change in the 1994 Act was to confer on the police the power to grant bail with conditions: previously, they were only able to grant unconditional bail or to keep the suspect in custody overnight pending court appearance. One danger of granting such a power, well known to criminologists, is that it will be used in a net-widening manner. That is, a power intended to reduce the number of remands in custody will actually be used in cases where unconditional bail was previously allowed. In Raine and Willson's research at six police stations towards the end of 1995 this seems to have been the result. The introduction of conditional bail led to a small over-all reduction in overnight detention of suspects by the police, but a significant drop in cases of unconditional bail. Where conditional bail was granted, the most frequent conditions were to keep away from a named place or a named person, sometimes for the protection of a witness or complainant. In view of the relatively slight drop in overnight detentions followed by court proceedings, it appears that the change has not contributed to a reduction in costs to the extent that was anticipated.[39] Raine and Willson also found that in some cases the police were using their bail powers as bargaining chips in their dealings with suspects, a finding that is hardly surprising but which raises again the question whether such extensive powers over the liberty of individuals should be granted to the police.

3. The Treatment of Unconvicted Defendants

The vast majority of cases in magistrates' courts do not involve any remand of the defendant, whether on bail or in custody, although the figures show a drift towards dealing with fewer cases at the first appearance. Thus in 1986, the percentages of defendants dealt with at first hearing (and thus not remanded at all) were 97 for summary motoring offences, 92 for other summary offences, and even 47 for indictable offences; by 1996 the figures had fallen somewhat to 89 per cent for summary motoring offences, 82 for for other summary offences, and 36 for indictable offences. About a third of those indictable defendants had been summoned rather than arrested.[40] Turning to those not dealt with on first appearance, there has been a steady increase both in the

[39] J. Raine and M. Willson, 'Police Bail with Conditions' (1997) 37 *BJ Crim.* 593.
[40] *Criminal Statistics, England and Wales 1996*, Tables 8.4 and 8.1.

proportion bailed and in the proportion remanded in custody. In particular, custodial remands of those charged with indictable offences who were ultimately dealt with in a magistrates' court have increased from 7 per cent in 1986 to 10 per cent in 1996. Among those committed by magistrates for trial in the Crown Court, the proportion remanded in custody has risen from 22 per cent in 1986 to 27 per cent in 1996. Research over a decade ago by Jones (1985) revealed wide variations in the use of custodial remands by courts in different areas, with Bedfordshire (7 per cent), Gwent (8 per cent), Merseyside, and the Metropolitan Police District (both 12 per cent) among the lowest, and with a group of predominantly rural areas having the highest custody rates (North Yorkshire 37 per cent, Dorset 31 per cent, Wiltshire and Devon and Cornwall both 29 per cent).[41] More recent research by Hucklesby tends to confirm the continued existence of local cultures on this issue.[42]

What is the position in the prisons? Remand prisoners have always tended to be placed in the most overcrowded conditions in the system, since they are sent to local prisons. In the 1980s the number of remand prisoners increased at a far higher rate than the number of convicted prisoners, and when the Woolf Inquiry reported on conditions in Strangeways and other prisons which had seen disturbances in 1990, a considerable proportion of the report was devoted to improving the lot of remand prisoners—unconvicted, but bearing the brunt of poor conditions.[43] This was certainly inconsistent with the proper treatment of people who have not yet been convicted, even if it was not formally in breach of the presumption of innocence. The steep rise in the numbers of unconvicted prisoners was traced to a sharp increase in the numbers committed to the Crown Court for trial (often at the instigation of liaison judges who advised magistrates to send more cases 'up'), which in turn led to a lengthening of waiting times before Crown Court trial, and hence to longer periods spent in prison by those remanded in custody.[44] In the 1990s, efforts have been made to deal with the problem of high numbers of remandees in prison. The overall remand population is now 20 per cent of the prison population, lower than in the late 1980s, and the average time spent in prison awaiting trial was fifty-three days in 1996, down from fifty-seven days in the early 1990s. Average waiting times before trial in a magistrates' court were

---

[41] P. Jones, 'Remand Decisions at Magistrates' Courts', in D. Moxon (ed.), *Managing Criminal Justice* (1985); see also M. Winfield, *Lacking Conviction: The Remand System in England and Wales* (1984).

[42] A. Hucklesby, 'Court Culture: An Explanation of Variations in the Use of Bail by Magistrates' Courts' (1997) 36 *Howard JCJ* 129.

[43] *Prison Disturbances April 1990: Report on an Inquiry by Rt. Hon. Lord Justice Woolf and His Honour Judge Tumim* (Cm 1456 of 1991), particularly ch. 10.

[44] For fuller analysis, see R. Morgan and S. Jones, 'Bail or Jail?', in E. Stockdale and S. Casale (eds.), *Criminal Justice under Stress* (1992), and the first edn. of this work at 205–7.

seven weeks, and as low as 9.5 weeks for Crown Court trial—a significant reduction from earlier years. There has been a significant increase in the number of persons remanded to prison after conviction and before sentence in the 1990s, but that is not our concern here. The figures for remands pending trial are: in 1986, an average daily population of 8,288 out of 45,241 males, and 361 out of 1,648 females. In 1996, the corresponding figures were 8,004 out of 53,019 males, and 371 out of 2,262 females.[45] Thus the figures have been controlled at a time when changes to the law of bail in 1993 and 1994 were distinctly in the direction of the greater use of custodial remands.

This evidence that the growing numbers held in prison awaiting trial have been 'controlled' should not be taken to suggest that there is no problem. After all, even from the perspective of prison management, one can look back to the year immediately preceding the Bail Act 1976, when only 8 per cent of the prison population was on remand. So the question arises—and the question is more poignant from the point of view of individual liberty—whether it is necessary to have as many as 8,000 people in prison at any one time awaiting trial. One way of examining this issue is to consider the outcomes of the cases against those remanded in custody. According to the *Prison Statistics 1996*, 24 per cent of both male and female remandees were either acquitted or had their cases discontinued. For males, 48 per cent received custodial sentences and 28 per cent non-custodial disposals. For females, 31 per cent received custodial sentences and 45 per cent non-custodial disposals.[46]

These figures raise a number of serious questions. In the cases of those remanded in custody and subsequently acquitted or not proceeded against, the loss of liberty is particularly hard on the individuals concerned. It could be argued that these are not necessarily cases of malfunction in the criminal justice system: if a conscientious judgement was made about the probability that, if not remanded in custody, they would fail to attend trial, commit offences whilst on bail, or interfere with witnesses, none of those matters bears directly on the probability of conviction. It is true that paragraph 9 of Schedule 1 to the Bail Act states that the strength of the evidence should be considered, but it is by no means clear which exception to the right to bail it relates to, and in many cases the court may find it difficult to assess the strength of the evidence at a remand hearing. The European Convention on Human Rights states, in Article 5(5), that 'everyone who has been the victim of arrest or detention in contravention of the provisions of this Article shall have an enforceable right to compensation'. Again, this cannot apply literally

---

[45] *Prison Statistics 1996*, ch. 3.

[46] These figures do not correspond precisely with the figures set out in the *Criminal Statistics, England and Wales 1996*, those figures being sub-divided according to those tried by magistrates, those tried at the Crown Court, and those committed to the Crown Court for sentence.

if there was reasonable suspicion and if a court ordered the pre-trial deten-tion. But several European countries provide State compensation for those acquitted after a custodial remand, and this is logical since the remand could only be justified on the ground that it was in the public interest. However, compensation is not a sufficient answer to the problem. If one-quarter of those remanded in custody are acquitted or not proceeded against, this ought to prompt inquiries into the reasons why they were remanded in custody. Since we have seen that the initial police decision tends to be quite influential, or at least that subsequent decision-makers come to the same conclusion as the police in most cases, we need to investigate the origins and foundations of these police views. It is also important to know why cases were dropped, where that was the outcome, and why this could not have happened at an ear-lier stage. At the very least, the figures suggest that the pain of custodial remand, felt so acutely by those subject to it, does not weigh so heavily with those who take decisions in respect of defendants.

What about those who receive non-custodial sentences after being remanded in custody? This is the outcome for over a quarter of males and nearly one half of all females remanded in custody before trial. Does it mean that they were unnecessarily remanded in custody in the first place?

At least four lines of argument cast doubt on this. The first is the one that most sentencers hasten to offer: that a court passing sentence must recognize the fact that the offender has already spent time in custody, and that a court may properly take this into account and impose a non-custodial sentence in a case where, if there had been no custodial remand, it would probably have imposed custody. The magistrates who pass sentence will rarely be the same individuals who refused bail and ordered the custodial remand, so the sen-tencing decision will be taken entirely *de novo*. There can be no objection to the court taking account of what has already happened: indeed, this may allow the court to adopt a more constructive approach than it might other-wise have felt able to do, by making a community order rather than impos-ing a custodial sentence. The implication of this argument is that the imposition of a non-custodial sentence does not necessarily suggest that the custodial remand was wrong, since in many cases if there had not been a custodial remand there would have been a custodial sentence. In theory this argument seems plausible. It is difficult, however, to determine how much substance it has in practice, since no research has been carried out into the reasoning of magistrates when sentencing offenders who have been in cus-tody on remand. No one knows what proportion of the cases resulting in a non-custodial sentence are a response to the custodial remand, and what proportion imply that there need have been no custodial remand in the first place.

Moreover, this first argument may prove rather more than was intended. If it is true that sentencers tend to take account of the fact that an offender has spent time in custody on remand, it may be the case that some of those given custodial sentences are sentenced in that way simply so as to facilitate their immediate release. If the court learns that an offender has been in prison for two months awaiting trial, it may feel that he or she has already been punished quite sufficiently (or even too heavily) for the offence, and may therefore impose a sentence of four months' imprisonment so as to ensure immediate release.[47] Otherwise, the court might have chosen some kind of community order as a suitable sentence. It is not known how many courts would react in this way—some might grant a conditional discharge or other sentence in these circumstances. But the point is that the numbers of people remanded in custody who are subsequently given custodial sentences by magistrates' courts may also include some cases (we know not how many) where the court would not have imposed custody if there had been no custodial remand. To take the further step and assert that the numbers of those given non-custodial sentences who would have received custody but for the custodial remand are far greater than the numbers of those given custodial sentences who would have received non-custodial sentences but for the custodial remand is to advance into the realms of speculation. The proportions are not known.

A second argument against taking the figures at face value is that the criteria for granting or withholding bail are not directly related to the probability of a custodial sentence. The three criteria in paragraph 2 of the Schedule to the Bail Act focus only on the period between first court appearance and trial. It is true that paragraph 9 of that Schedule suggests that courts should also have regard to 'the nature and seriousness of the offence and the probable method of dealing with the offender for it', but, as argued above, this does not match any of the substantive criteria. Moreover, many remands in custody are not based on this ground. Where a defendant is remanded in custody because there are substantial grounds for believing that otherwise he or she may not attend the trial, or for believing that otherwise witnesses may be threatened, these reasons have nothing to do with the likely sentence in the case. The statistics are not sharp enough to determine the relative proportions of cases: in the Home Office's 1978 survey, the probability of committing an offence was given as a reason in 63 per cent of cases, and the probability of the defendant absconding was given as a reason in 51 per cent of cases. Exactly how many cases depended only on one or the other reason is unclear, but some evidently bear no relationship to the probability of a custodial sentence on conviction.

---

[47] This is said to be the approach of some courts in other European countries: see e.g. W. Heinz, 'The Problems of Imprisonment', in R. Hood (ed.), *Crime and Criminal Policy in Europe: Proceedings of a European Colloquium* (1989).

A third argument, arising from the provisions of the Criminal Justice Act 1991, is that there is now a clear disjunction between remand criteria and sentencing criteria. The 1991 Act states that a court may only impose a custodial sentence if it is of opinion either that the offence(s) are so serious that only a custodial sentence can be justified, or that (where the offence is a violent or sexual offence) only a custodial sentence would be adequate to protect the public from serious harm.[48] No such restrictions are to be found in the Bail Act,[49] and the gap between the two statutes is only narrowed slightly by the provisions of the Criminal Justice Act 1993 on previous convictions and multiple offences.

A fourth argument raises questions about whether the remand decisions taken in court really are considered and rounded determinations. Research by Jones many years ago showed that there was a strong correlation between police decisions on bail or custody and subsequent court decisions.[50] More recent research by Burrows, Henderson, and Morgan[51] and by Anthea Hucklesby[52] confirms that this is still a reality in the vast majority of cases. Thus Hucklesby found that the vast majority of remand hearings were uncontested: only in 9 per cent of cases was there a different view advanced by prosecution and defence. In most cases the CPS did not oppose bail, and in almost half of the cases where bail was opposed the defence did not contest this. At least two processes appear to be at work here. One is the influence of the police: if they grant bail from the police station, it is highly unlikely that a court is going to find that a custodial remand is needed, and the CPS would have difficulty in sustaining such an argument.[53] The other is the influence of court culture, which sustains different rates of remand in custody in different courts over prolonged periods of years.[54] Both influences tend to suggest that in some cases the CPS does not make the recommendation it might think appropriate, and Hucklesby's finding that generally nearly nine out of ten CPS recommendations are accepted by the court[55] shows that the CPS makes different recommendations on similar cases because they are to be heard in different courts, or even by differently-constituted benches. Moreover, this process of anticipating the decisions of other parties is also evident in the

---

[48] For analysis, see Ashworth, *Sentencing and Criminal Justice* (2nd edn., 1995), 228–31 and 163–7.

[49] Although there are some similar restrictions in respect of juvenile remands: see n. 38 above.

[50] P. Jones, 'Remand Decisions at Magistrates' Courts', in D. Moxon (ed.), *Managing Criminal Justice* (1985).

[51] J. Burrows, P. Henderson, and P. Morgan, *Improving Bail Decisions: The Bail Process Project* (1994).

[52] A. Hucklesby, 'Remand Decision Makers' [1997] *Crim. LR* 269.

[53] Burrows *et al.*, above n. 51, 15.   [54] Hucklesby, above n. 42.

[55] Hucklesby, above n. 52, at 276.

approach of some defence solicitors, who admit both to adapting their representations to the particular bench (sometimes not applying for bail if it would be 'hopeless' in view of the constitution of the bench), and to using various tactics or coded language in order to distinguish bail applications which they believe in from those which they make purely because the client has insisted. This is a clear example of unethical behaviour, with defence lawyers failing to do their best to advance a defendant's case or, as Hucklesby puts it, ranking 'their credibility and status with the court above the interests of their clients'.[56] Hucklesby found that the CPS usually failed to give reasons for its representations: indeed, in 60 per cent of cases where the CPS requested a custodial remand, no reasons were stated, and even in cases where the defence contested the hearing the CPS failed to give its reason (e.g. by referring to a reason in the Bail Act) in many cases.[57] These findings constitute a clear demonstration of the way in which apparently open and formal processes mask the reality of informal decision-making, anticipation of the decisions of others, and the drive to maintain professional respect. In the present context, the implication is that decisions result from possibly tacit or even unconscious local coalitions between police practice and bench traditions, with the CPS and defence solicitors operating in a way that sees them anticipating the decision of others in many cases and only rarely standing up for a view that differs from that of other key participants. Of course, a high rate of concordance in decisions does not conclusively prove undue influence, since it remains possible that the police, the CPS, and then the courts are applying the same criteria independently and reaching the same conclusions, but the evidence of the criminal justice practitioners interviewed by Hucklesby strongly suggests otherwise.[58]

Consideration of the four lines of argument against a face-value interpretation of the statistics on trial and sentence therefore demonstrates a pervasive uncertainty about the use of bail and of remands in custody. We lack the detailed research necessary to establish which explanations account for what percentage of cases. What does seem to be clear, however, is that the terms of the law on remands ought to be re-examined. In principle the strength of the case ought to be a primary factor, although in practice this creates difficulties in some cases, where the full evidence may not have arrived by the first (or even subsequent) remand hearing, especially if the results of a forensic science test are being awaited. In principle, too, the probable penalty, if the defendant is convicted as charged, ought to be a factor. The Bail Act should either require the court to be satisfied that a custodial sentence would be appropriate, if the case were proved as alleged, or it should state expressly that there should be

---

[56] *Ibid.* 279.　　[57] *Ibid.* 280–1.　　[58] Hucklesby, above n. 42, at 137–40.

no remand in custody unless there is a substantial risk of serious offences being committed if the defendant were left at liberty.[59] If dangerousness is to be a criterion, there must be legislative guidance not only on the seriousness of the probable offence but on the degree of risk and the basis for inferring it. Any reform should also address the question of the information on which magistrates may be expected to reach such a decision. Without information, or with information only from one source, it is hardly surprising if the CPS and the courts fail to give proper weight to all relevant issues. This calls into question the procedure for taking remand decisions, to be taken up in Section 5 below: how can their promptness be preserved whilst their information base is broadened?

4. The Treatment of Victims and Potential Victims

This is a provocative heading, intended to raise starkly the question whether the public in general or victims in particular have received any benefit from having larger numbers of defendants in custody at any one time. It would be almost impossible to trace any effects on the crime rate, largely because (1) the 'crime rate' is itself an elusive phenomenon which even surveys of victims (which are more complete than official records) have difficulty in charting,[60] and (2) even if we had a reliable measure of the number of crimes committed each year, it would necessarily be a product of several interacting influences, and it would rarely be possible to attribute particular trends to particular causes. But the question can be approached from other angles. One is to inquire into the volume of offences committed by persons who have been granted bail, perhaps with a view to suggesting that either too few people or the wrong people are remanded in custody. Another is to inquire into the proportion of those remanded in custody who are subsequently given non-custodial sentences, with a view to suggesting that it was unnecessary to order their pre-trial detention to secure public protection.

The most direct sense of public protection is to protect someone who has been threatened with violence by the defendant or who has a well-grounded fear of violence. Such issues may arise in neighbourhood disputes or intra-family offences. The *Victim's Charter* states that any victim worried about attack should tell the CPS, which is to inform the court. The police are then

---

[59] The 1996 amendment to the Irish Constitution insists on risk of a serious offence (see n. 15 above), whereas the Canadian provision refers broadly to 'public safety'.

[60] See e.g. P. Mayhew and N. A. Maung, *Surveying Crime: Findings from the 1992 British Crime Survey* (1992).

required to inform the victim if the suspect is released on bail, what conditions (if any) have been imposed, and what the victim can do if the conditions are broken.[61] If the court is satisfied that the only way to remove the threat of violence is to remand the defendant in custody, then this should be done, for the reasons outlined earlier. However, only recently has a prosecution right of appeal been introduced: the prosecution may appeal against a decision to grant bail to someone charged with an offence punishable with a maximum sentence of at least five years.[62]

Turning to public protection in a more general sense, let us begin by considering possible bail failures. Of those bailed to appear at court in 1996, some 13 per cent failed to appear on the due date at a magistrates' court, and some 6 per cent at the Crown Court.[63] These may be regarded as wrong decisions in the sense that the court evidently thought that there were no substantial grounds for believing that they would fail to surrender to custody. However, no such grounds may have been apparent at the time, and in any event the courts could be said to have decided correctly in the vast majority of cases. It is not known whether the small percentage of absconders have any features in common which might be used as as basis for prediction.

Of greater public concern are those defendants remanded on bail who are found to have committed offences during the period of remand. A Home Office survey in 1978 suggested that offences on bail are committed by about 7 per cent of those remanded to appear in a magistrates' court and about 9 per cent of those remanded to appear in the Crown Court.[64] During 1992 there was increased public anxiety about offending by defendants, often young men, who had been released on bail. Senior police officers made statements which suggested that the situation was becoming intolerable, in that a small number of people on bail were responsible for a large number of offences being committed. From a study of the statistics on which these claims were based, Patricia Morgan argued that there had been little change in the rate of offending on bail since the earlier Home Office survey.[65] Depending on the definition and the counting rules, the figure was in the range from 10 to 12 per cent, although it could become 17 per cent if offences resulting in a caution and offences taken into consideration were included. Recent Home Office research has found that 12 per cent of those bailed by the police and 15 per cent of those bailed by a court committed at least one offence on bail. Taking police and court bail together, some 24 per cent of all defendants committed

[61] Home Office, *The Victim's Charter* (1996 edn.), 10.
[62] Bail (Amendment) Act 1993, discussed below, s. 7.
[63] *Criminal Statistics, England and Wales 1996*, Table 8.10.
[64] Home Office, *Report of the Working Group on Magistrates' Courts* (1982)
[65] P. M. Morgan, *Offending while on Bail: A Survey of Recent Studies* (1992).

one or more offences, 4 per cent committing three or more offences. The longer the period on bail, the more likely defendants were to offend. Defendants under 18 were much more likely to offend (38 per cent) than those over 18 (18 per cent).[66] Provisions in the Crime and Disorder Bill 1998 for 'fast-tracking' court proceedings for certain young defendants are intended to address the last two points.

The Home Office study also shows that the people most likely to offend on bail are those charged with theft of or from a vehicle (44 per cent), shop theft (40 per cent), and burglary (38 per cent), many of whom will be young defendants.[67] If public protection is to be an important purpose of the bail/custody decision, then it needs to be asked whether we can predict with sufficient accuracy which offenders are more likely to offend on bail than not. If we could do so, the next question would be whether their offences would be so serious that only custody could be justified for them, to adopt the wording of section 1 of the Criminal Justice Act 1991. If not, then it would be necessary to devise an order that could be made in bail cases which would impose some obligations on the defendant. A measure of public protection might be possible without custody, perhaps through a more precisely targeted form of conditional bail.[68] A determination to increase the number of people remanded in custody might not bring any noticeable difference in offending whilst on bail unless it were targeted on the right people. However, the Association of Chief Police Officers and the Government, in statements in early 1992, seemed to argue not in favour of remanding more people in custody but in favour of remanding the right people. What they failed to make clear was the criterion to be applied in practice.[69]

Having considered the failure of remands on bail, we should now turn to the failures of remands in custody. Is it necessary to remand so many people in custody for so long, as a measure of public protection? There are immediate difficulties with the concept of public protection here. One might say that the public is protected if the commission of any crime is avoided by means of a custodial remand, whether that crime is minor in nature or not. On this view, remands in custody of persons with a record of shop thefts might be justified as protecting the public. To defeat that proposition, it must be argued either (1) that public protection is not an absolute value but rather a benefit to be weighed against disbenefits such as increased costs of imprisonment and increased incursions

---

[66] D. Brown, n. 67 below.

[67] D. Brown, *Offending on Bail and Police Use of Conditional Bail*, Home Office Research Findings No. 72 (1998); compare the differently calculated figures of Morgan, above, n. 65.

[68] Although the research by Raine and Willson (see n. 29 above and text) gives few grounds for optimism about the efficacy of conditional bail.

[69] For discussion, see Morgan and Jones above n. 44, 41–4, and NACRO, *Legislation on Bail: What should be Done?* (1992).

on the liberty of defendants, or (2) that the concept of public protection ought to be confined (in this context as in sentencing) to the protection of the public from violent or sexual offences of a serious nature.[70] This argument will be taken up in the concluding part of the chapter. For the present, we need only recall the discussion in Section 3 of this chapter, where it was shown that one-quarter of those remanded in custody are not convicted, and that around one-third receive non-custodial sentences. For the reasons there discussed, this raises serious questions about the need, from the point of view of public safety, to remand so many people in custody before trial.

5. Procedural Justice and Remand Decisions

We now move on to consider four aspects of procedure relevant to the fairness of remand decisions; the speed of court hearings, the problem of obtaining information, the limitations on fresh argument at subsequent hearings, and appeals.

1. *Speed and delay*: in the 1960s and early 1970s it was the police who dominated remand hearings. A frequent argument was that the defendant should be remanded in custody so that the police could pursue further inquiries, and courts responded to this. The Bail Act 1976 removed this as a reason for refusing bail, but until the mid-1980s almost all remand hearings involved representations from a police officer. The officer would inform the magistrates of any police objections to bail, and then there would be an opportunity for the defendant or (if represented) his solicitor to make representations. Several studies had suggested that the police exerted considerable influence on the outcome of these proceedings, with magistrates following their suggestions in the vast majority of cases.[71] In 1986 the Crown Prosecution Service took over the task of staffing the remand courts, and it was thought that one result would be that greater attention would be paid to the legal criteria in the Bail Act than to the convenience of the police (who might wish to make further inquiries with the defendant 'out of the way'). However, Stone's early research found that there had been no significant change in the substance of the representations made to magistrates.[72] This is hardly surprising, for in practice the Crown Prosecutor is likely to receive a large pile of case files on arrival at work in the morning (consisting of 'overnight arrests' by the police) and will have to present these cases to the court that very morning. In those circumstances

---

[70] The new sentencing law provides some definitions of these terms: see Criminal Justice Act 1991, ss. 1(2)(b), 2(2)(b), and 31. See also above, n. 33 and accompanying text.

[71] See A. K. Bottomley, *Decisions in the Penal Process* (1973).

[72] C. Stone, *Bail Information for the Crown Prosecution Service* (1988).

the most likely course of events is for the prosecutor to rely on the notes appended by the police to each file. Prior to the remand hearing there is unlikely to be much time for a detached review of the nature of the case, as we saw in Chapter 6, and it cannot realistically be expected that the evidential test for bringing a prosecution will be met at the first (or even second) remand hearing. This is an unsatisfactory aspect of the system, and Hucklesby's finding that the CPS rarely gives any specific reason for opposing bail (where it does so), let alone refer the court to the relevant provisions of the Bail Act, suggests that little has improved.[73] During the hearing, speed seems to be of the essence. Although there is no recent evidence of this, Doherty and East's Cardiff study in 1981 found that cases were processed in court with great rapidity, the clerk setting the tone by rattling through the necessary words. Even in cases where defendants were remanded in custody, some 38 per cent were concluded within two minutes and 87 per cent within ten minutes.[74] No doubt some of the former were remands of persons already in prison, whereas most of those taking longer than ten minutes were probably first hearings; no doubt, also, matters have improved in many courts. Nevertheless, it is important to signal the full seriousness of taking away liberty, and to insist on an inquiry as searching as is feasible at that stage. Hucklesby's finding that courts gave reasons for a custodial remand in only 47 per cent of custody cases, when this is a legal requirement in all such cases, confirms that proper safeguards for individual liberty are not being observed.[75]

People who work in the courts may argue that speed is essential: it is in the defendant's interest to have the question of remand dealt with at the earliest opportunity, and magistrates often have large numbers of cases to hear. But these arguments sometimes divert attention away from the issues at stake. For example, courts may not have sufficient information relating to each of the three criteria in the Bail Act—the probability of absconding, the probability of offending, and the probability of interfering with witnesses. The defendant may be unrepresented or, even if legally represented, the solicitor may have had little time to make background inquiries that address the relevant statutory criteria. We have seen that the Schedule to the Bail Act permits a court to remand a person in custody because there is insufficient information to reach a decision. In principle this is an unsatisfactory state of affairs, and two improvements must be made. First, the Schedule should be amended to ensure that a court should first consider conditional bail, and that if this is not suitable it should order the minimum remand period that is feasible (i.e. not

---

[73] Hucklesby, above n. 52, and text thereat.
[74] C. Doherty and R. East, 'Bail Decisions in Magistrates' Courts' (1985) 25 *BJ Crim.* 251; cf. A. Hucklesby, 'Unnecessary Legislative Changes' (1993) 143 *NLJ* 233.
[75] Hucklesby, 'Bail or Jail? The Practical Operation of the Bail Act 1976' (1996) 23 *JLS* 213.

seven days routinely, but no more than two or three days unless there are special circumstances). Secondly, there should be greater funding for bail information schemes, described below, which may both avoid unnecessary custodial remands and enable magistrates to take better-informed decisions.

2. *Bail information schemes*: the problem of obtaining relevant and verified information for remand courts has been recognized for some time. The Vera Institute of Justice began programmes in the United States in the early 1960s, aimed at supplying courts with some objective data on which they could base their decisions, in particular data about the defendant's 'community ties'.[76] This theme was much discussed in England and Wales in the mid-1970s, when bail reform was under consideration, but the innovative Home Office circular on bail in 1975 did no more than state that the Government would be 'grateful' if courts and the Probation Service would 'consider the introduction' of schemes to gather information on community ties for presentation to remand courts. Such schemes as were set up in the mid-1970s were short-lived, apparently because of lack of funds and waning enthusiasm,[77] but the idea behind them was revived in the late 1980s. The Home Office circular of 1988 referred again to the importance of information,[78] but most of the pioneering work in this revival was carried out by the London office of the Vera Institute of Justice.[79] Bail information schemes now appear to be gaining acceptance in the English system. Some of the schemes are based in prisons, helping with information for those already remanded in custody, but the vast majority of schemes operate at magistrates' courts.[80] A probation officer is installed as a bail information officer, with the task of obtaining (and, so far as possible, verifying by telephone) information on an address at which the defendant could stay, on employment, on family ties, etc. The information has to be gathered quickly, usually on the morning of the first remand hearing, but there seems to be general satisfaction with the reliability of the information obtained.[81] In those cases where the defendant seems in danger of being remanded in custody largely because of the absence of an address to stay at, the bail information officer may need to make an attempt to find a place in a bail hostel. This may take time, and may require a case to be put back in the list for hearing. Hucklesby found that very little extra information was available to courts, beyond that given by the CPS and the defence.[82]

---

[76] Jones and Goldkamp, above n. 26, 140–4.
[77] C. Lloyd, *Bail Information Schemes: Practice and Effect*, Home Office RPU Paper 69 (1992).
[78] Home Office Circular 25/1988, *Bail*, para. 5.   [79] Stone, above n. 72.
[80] See Lloyd, above n. 77.
[81] HM Inspectorate of Probation, *Bail Information: Report of a Thematic Inspection in 1992* (1993).
[82] Above, n. 75, at 221–5.

One feature of the current schemes in England and Wales is that the information is not presented directly to the court. The reasoning is that courts might assume that, if no information had been prepared in a case (because the schemes are inevitably selective), there was nothing favourable to say. The American experience, however, is that involving the courts in the introduction and organization of the schemes is an important element in gaining acceptance for them.[83] In England the information is usually made available both to the Crown Prosecution Service and to the defence. Research suggests that in some areas the CPS treats it as an important component in its decision-making, whereas in other areas it regards it as primarily relevant for the defence rather than the prosecution.[84] The latter point is perhaps understandable, because bail information schemes only transmit information favourable to the defendant,[85] but an ethical approach to prosecuting suggests that Crown Prosecutors should be equally interested in information that leads them not to make representations against the grant of bail. The task of the CPS should not be simply to advance the police view, or to put forward a 'modified police view', but to take a broader 'Minister of Justice' approach.[86] It is unfortunate that the Code for Crown Prosecutors says nothing about bail applications.

Bail information schemes seem likely to make some difference in practice.[87] However, their limited bearing on remand decisions should not be overlooked. Their primary relevance is to the first ground for refusing bail, that the defendant is likely to abscond and not attend the trial. Information about 'community ties' might show that he is less likely to abscond. A place at a bail hostel will ensure accommodation for the period before trial. If by these means we can avoid putting people in prison simply to ensure that they attend their trial, this would be a great advance. But it remains the case that the reason behind the majority of decisions to remand in custody is the second statutory ground, the likelihood that the defendant would commit an offence whilst on bail. Bail information schemes are not concerned principally with this ground or this group of defendants, and are therefore unlikely to have much effect on large numbers of cases.

3. *Fresh argument*: the procedural rules surrounding applications for bail also raise important issues. In *Nottingham Justices, ex parte Davies* (1981),[88] the Divisional Court held that the justices were right to adopt a policy of not reconsidering a remand decision unless the defence could show a change of

---

[83] Jones and Goldkamp, above n. 26.

[84] Lloyd, above n. 77.

[85] See the discussion by Cavadino and Gibson, above n. 1, 98–100.

[86] See Ch. 3.10, above.

[87] See generally the essay by G. Mair and C. Lloyd in F. Paterson (ed.), *Understanding Bail in Britain* (1996).

[88] [1981] QB 38.

circumstances or adduce new considerations. Although in many cases it is possible for a defendant denied bail to appeal to the Crown Court, the practical effect of the *Nottingham Justices* ruling was that many defendants did not apply for bail at the first hearing, so as to enable a full argument to be put together by defence lawyers in time for the second hearing. Otherwise there was a risk that a denial of bail after one argued application would preclude argument at a subsequent hearing unless a change of circumstances could be shown. Brink and Stone found that between a half and three-quarters of all those remanded in custody at their first appearance had not asked for bail—exposing at once the extraordinary power of a single Divisional Court ruling, and its potential for injustice.[89] Perhaps in response to Brink and Stone's research, the Government promoted what became section 154 of the Criminal Justice Act 1988, which took effect as an amendment to Schedule 1 of the 1976 Act. Paragraph 2 states that: 'At the first hearing after that at which the court decided not to grant the defendant bail he may support an application for bail with any argument as to fact or law that he desires (whether or not he has advanced that argument previously).' After that, a court is not bound to hear arguments that it has heard previously. The intention was widely thought to be to allow defendants 'two bites at the cherry', in other words two argued applications for bail. Yet the drafting of the 1988 amendments left some uncertainty about this,[90] and all that can be said is that no disputed ruling on the matter has yet reached the Divisional Court.

4. *Appeals and reapplications*: when a court refuses bail or attaches conditions to it, there is an obligation to state the ground(s) on which the court relies and to give reasons for bringing the case within that ground.[91] If the charge is murder or attempted murder, manslaughter, or rape or attempted rape, a court which grants bail in the face of representations by the prosecution must give reasons for doing so.[92] A defendant who is refused bail by a magistrates' court may make a reapplication to a judge in chambers. Correspondingly, the Bail (Amendment) Act 1993 grants the prosecution the power to appeal to a judge against the grant of bail by a magistrates' court in the face of representations by the prosecution, so long as the charge relates to an offence punishable with five years' imprisonment or more, or is an offence of taking a conveyance without authority or aggravated vehicle-taking. This new power has been criticized, persuasively on the ground that the reference to the offences of taking cars is a political response to a 'moral panic' but unconvincingly on the ground that it is wider than the prosecution's powers

---

[89] B. Brink and C. Stone, 'Defendants who do not Ask for Bail' [1988] *Crim. LR* 152.
[90] On which see *Archbold 1998*, para. 3.18.   [91] Bail Act 1976, s. 5(3).
[92] Criminal Justice Act 1988, s. 153, amending Schedule 1 of the Bail Act.

in relation to allegedly lenient sentences.[93] In principle, the power constitutes a fair and proper counterbalance to the defence right of reapplication, unless it comes to be used oppressively. The case for allowing decisions for and against bail to be appealable is one of natural justice. The argument for restricting the court's powers to grant bail to persons accused of certain offences is a separate one, and trades on political popularity and 'public opinion' as constructed by the media, to the neglect of the European Convention on Human Rights.[94]

6. Equal Treatment in Remand Decisions

To what extent do remand decisions appear to discriminate against certain sections of the population? To what extent do they fail to recognize the special needs of certain groups? These questions warrant considerable discussion in their own right, and it is possible only to give some general indications here.

The findings of research into the impact of race on remand decisions prompt questions about discrimination. In his study of over 3,000 cases Roger Hood found that a higher proportion of defendants from an Afro-Caribbean background (26 per cent) than whites (20 per cent) were remanded in custody pending trial and that, even after taking account of variations in the key facts of individual cases, some apparent discrimination remained.[95] The average number of females in prison on remand was around 360–70 in both 1986 and 1996, although it decreased in the early 1990s and has recently returned to this level. None the less, some 3,000 females are remanded in custody each year. Since women tend to be convicted of less serious offences than men, this total needs careful scrutiny: some of the women will be charged with drug-smuggling offences which might result in substantial prison sentences, but others may be repeat small-time property offenders. The Holloway Prison bail unit may have improved conditions,[96] but the most significant problems stem from court decisions. Research by Mary Eaton follows other research in suggesting that women who do not occupy the traditional role of wife and mother are at greater risk of custodial remand, and goes on to suggest that the control exerted by

---

[93] See Cavadino and Gibson, above n. 1, 162–5.

[94] As argued in n. 38 above, the provision in s. 25 of the Criminal Justice and Public Order Act 1994 is incompatible with Article 5 of the ECHR.

[95] R. Hood, *Race and Sentencing* (1992), 146–50; see generally M. Fitzgerald, *Ethnic Minorities and the Criminal Justice System*, RCCJ Research Study 20 (1993), 19–21.

[96] See Cavadino and Gibson, above n. 1, 102–4.

family life on women may, in effect, be treated as 'comparable to that offered by the prison system' when considering whether or not to remand a female defendant in custody.[97] Thus the apparently benevolent emphasis on a defendant's 'community ties' may have disturbing implications for women in differing situations. More thorough research is needed to examine the issue of custodial remands for women: we saw earlier that only 31 per cent of women remanded in custody receive custodial sentences, and this raises acute questions about the justifications for depriving them of their liberty in the first place.

Special arrangements for the remand of mentally disordered defendants were introduced by the Mental Health Act 1983. However, the power to remand defendants to hospital for a psychiatric report, rather than to prison, appears not to have been widely used. Courts still remand defendants to prison for reports in larger numbers. A further power to remand defendants to hospital for treatment has hardly been used at all.[98] The Reed Committee recommended the broadening of these statutory powers, together with restrictions on the power of courts to remand defendants to prison for the primary purpose of medical assessment.[99] This has not been done. In practice, considerable numbers of mentally disturbed defendants are still remanded in custody. A study by Robertson and others in 1989 found that many custodial remands were made in cases where the offence was minor and the defendant had no fixed address. There were then delays before an assessment by an outside psychiatrist could take place, and often delays in hospital admission thereafter, although about a half of those seen by psychiatrists were offered a hospital bed. The authors comment that 'remands in custody [are] not only an inhumane, but an ineffective way of securing help and care for disturbed people'.[100] A 1993 survey by Kennedy and others confirmed that many mentally disturbed people remanded in custody did not have stable housing arrangements, and the authors argue that at least one-fifth of them could and should be accommodated in probation hostels rather than placed in prison.[101] At the very least, there should be a clear set of statutory steps for

[97] M. Eaton, 'The Question of Bail', in P. Carlen and A. Worrall (eds.), *Gender, Crime and Justice* (1987), 95, at 107; the previous research cited is that by D. Farrington and A. Morris, 'Sex, Sentencing and Reconvictions' (1983) 23 *BJ Crim.* 229.

[98] P. Fennell, 'Diversion of Mentally Disordered Offenders from Custody' [1991] *Crim. LR* 333, at 337–40.

[99] Department of Health and Home Office, *Review of Health and Social Services for Mentally Disordered Offenders and Others Requiring Similar Services*, Cm 2088 (1992).

[100] G. Robertson, S. Dell, A. Grounds, and K. James, 'Mentally Disordered Remand Prisoners' (1992) 32 *Home Office Research Bulletin* 1.

[101] M. Kennedy, C. Truman, S. Keyes, and A. Cameron, 'Supported Bail for Mentally Vulnerable Defendants' (1997) 36 *Howard JCJ* 158.

courts to consider in such cases, if necessary awaiting evidence rather than committing a defendant to custody.[102]

There are also special arrangements for the remand of juvenile defendants. In essence, the court has three alternatives if it decides not to remand a juvenile on bail: remand to local authority accommodation, remand to local authority accommodation with conditions attached, and remand to a prison or remand centre.[103] The last-mentioned alternative is hedged about with restrictions to ensure that the power is only used for sexual, violent, or other serious charges, for juveniles who have absconded persistently from local authority accommodation and have committed a serious offence whilst unlawfully at large, and for those in respect of whom only a custodial remand is adequate to protect the public from serious harm.[104] Despite these restrictions, it appears that this new power has been used in significantly more cases than the previous power.[105] This is worrying: it was widely accepted that Prison Service establishments are not suited to the care of the young, and the 1991 Act made provision for the ultimate abolition of these remands for defendants aged under 17, but the Crime and Disorder Bill 1998 seems to be moving in the opposite direction.

7. Reducing the Problems

In the concluding Section of this chapter there will be further discussion of the justifications for depriving individuals of their liberty before trial, and the length of that deprivation. Here, some ways of dealing with the problem of unnecessary custodial remands will be outlined briefly—bail hostels, electronic monitoring, time-limits for prosecution, and new arrangements to determine mode of trial. The contribution of bail information schemes has already been discussed.

1. *Bail hostels*: we have seen that one of the main problems is ensuring that defendants attend their trials. To imprison someone simply in order to secure this result is to adopt an extremely strong measure. Facilities for placing defendants in hostels have therefore been developed, and there appear to be around 2,000 available places. Since many defendants will spend weeks rather than months in these hostels, their contribution in relieving the prisons is probably much greater than those figures suggest. However, one abiding dif-

---

[102] See the diversion schemes discussed in Ch. 5, at pp. 147–9.
[103] For fuller discussion, see Cavadino and Gibson, 135–8 and 210–13.
[104] Criminal Justice Act 1991, s. 62.   [105] Cavadino and Gibson, above n. 1, 141–3.

ficulty with any such measure of 'diversion from custody' is whether courts might not be using bail hostels for defendants who would not have been sent to prison if bail hostels had not existed. Hostels do impose restrictions on liberty, and there is some research suggesting that such a 'malfunction' exists in relation to their use.[106]

2. *Electronic monitoring*: another expedient, which might succeed both in ensuring that a defendant attends trial and in preventing (or at least detecting) the commission of offences during the period before trial, would be to introduce the electronic monitoring of defendants thought to be at risk. Once again this might be contemplated as a means of 'diversion from custody', by identifying people who might otherwise be remanded in custody but for whom the machinery of 'tagging' might allow them to be returned to the community. There was a field trial at three courts in 1989: in fact, the courts seemed reluctant to use this alternative, and out of the fifty defendants for whom electronic monitoring was used there were eighteen breaches of conditions and eleven offences committed.[107] Although the researchers found that courts were using it only for defendants who would otherwise have been remanded in custody (i.e. no evidence of the expected 'malfunction'), the low usage and apparently high failure rate meant that little was heard of this alternative for several years. However, it was revived in 1995 for offenders, and further trials in three areas have proved 'successful' in the sense that there have been few equipment failures and a breach rate of only around 20 per cent.[108] It is said that the Government is considering a reintroduction of electronic monitoring as a condition of bail. There remain, however, strong ethical objections to electronic monitoring, on the grounds that it is degrading and an invasion of privacy,[109] and these objections are not diminished by the 'anything but prison' approach.

3. *Time-limits*: since 1987 there have been limits on the length of time that a person may be kept in custody before trial. It is not proposed to enter into the details of the limits here,[110] since they appear not to have exerted any significant influence on waiting times so far, chiefly because courts have often acceded to prosecution requests for extensions. However, the use of time-limits is one strategy for controlling the duration of pre-trial remands in

---

[106] H. Lewis and G. Mair, *Bail and Probation Work, ii: The Use of London Probation Bail Hostels for Bailees*, Home Office Research and Planning Unit Paper 50 (1989).

[107] G. Mair and C. Nee, *Electronic Monitoring: The Trials and their Results*, HORS 120 (1990).

[108] E. Mortimer and C. May, *Electronic Monitoring of Curfew Orders: the Second Year of the Trials*, Home Office Research Findings No. 66 (1997).

[109] For discussion, see Ashworth, above n. 48, 265–6.

[110] See Cavadino and Gibson, above n. 1, 50–4, summarizing the case law, and P. Henderson, *Monitoring Time Limits on Custodial Remands*, Home Office Research and Planning Unit Paper 69 (1991).

custody, as has also been recognized in the United States.[111] There are now sufficient decisions of the Divisional Court on what constitutes a 'good and sufficient cause' for extending the law to provide the foundation for clearer and tighter guidelines.[112] The Crime and Disorder Bill 1998 will alter the sanction for non-compliance with time limits from an acquittal to a stay of the proceedings, and it also contains other provisions relating to time limits.

4. *Mode of trial*: it was observed earlier that one reason for the steep increase in the number of persons in custody awaiting trial during the 1980s was the higher proportion of defendants committed for trial to the Crown Court. Waiting times for Crown Court trials have always been longer than those for the magistrates' courts, although the difference in 1996 was relatively small (9.5 weeks compared with seven weeks). There have been several recent changes in respect of mode of trial, and these are discussed in Chapter 8 below.

8. Conclusions

To deprive someone of liberty before trial and conviction is *prima facie* an incursion into that individual's rights, and in principle any burden on an individual at this stage (let alone the deprivation of liberty) needs to be justified.[113] The only way to construct a justification for doing so is to argue that either there is a distinct risk to the rights of another citizen, or there are overwhelming reasons of public interest. A distinct risk to the rights of another citizen might arise if the defendant had already been charged with assaulting a person and there was evidence to suggest a risk of further violence. Alternatively it might arise where there is reason to believe that the defendant will threaten someone, especially a victim-complainant or witness. It might also be said to arise where there is a risk of the defendant committing offences if granted bail, since many offences infringe the rights of individuals. On this last point, however, it is important to be more specific about the kinds of rights to be violated. Since the issue is whether or not the deprivation of liberty before trial can be justified, and since we are discussing probabilities rather than the certainty of infringing another's rights, this ought to be confined to crimes of a particular level of seriousness—that is, at least those crimes likely in themselves to lead to a custodial sentence for the perpetrator.

---

[111] See generally J. Vennard, 'Court Delay and Speedy Trial Provisions' [1985] *Crim. LR* 73.

[112] A. Samuels, 'Custody Time Limits' [1997] *Crim. LR* 260.

[113] R. A. Duff, *Trials and Punishments* (1986), 140, arguing that in principle custodial remands are utterly inconsistent with respect for individual citizens as rational agents.

The second possible justification refers to overwhelming reasons of public interest. One of these might be the public interest in ensuring that defendants who have been charged attend their trials. Although it would be difficult to deny some such interest, it is questionable whether it is strong enough to justify taking away a person's liberty, particularly when absconding is not a certainty but a greater or lesser probability. This is, *par excellence*, a sphere in which non-custodial methods of securing attendance should be developed. It may be argued that the public interest in ensuring that someone is tried becomes greater as the crime charged becomes more serious, and so the seriousness of the charge should be a relevant factor. Once again, however, a court should surely satisfy itself that the Crown Prosecution Service believes that there is sufficient evidence to continue with the charge (recognizing the practical difficulties of this).[114] Moreover, the court should satisfy itself that the offence as alleged is 'worth imprisonment', before there is any question of imprisoning someone so as to ensure that the trial takes place. Expressed in the form that the court should have regard to the punishment to be expected on the basis of the available evidence, this principle would ensure a proper sense of proportion in pre-trial detention.[115]

Another form of public interest may be that of minimizing the number of offences committed by persons on bail. The foundations of this interest were discussed critically in Section 1 of this chapter, but the recent enactment of a provision requiring courts to treat offending on bail as an aggravating factor in sentencing demonstrates the political force of this concern.[116] It is particularly strong when there is reason to believe that a defendant has already committed one serious offence and is likely to commit others. Yet we should recall the fallibility of predictions of dangerous behaviour: at the very least, the law should specify the type and level of behaviour, the prediction of which might justify a custodial remand.[117] The Bail Act's reference simply to committing 'an offence' whilst on bail is much too weak. It should also be insisted that, before a custodial remand is ordered, the prosecution set out the main elements of their case, so that the court can be satisfied (so far as is possible at this early stage) that there is cogent evidence against the defendant. It is well known that this would create practical problems: but the starting point should be that an individual should not be deprived of liberty just because the police or CPS have a hunch that the person may well be guilty. Out of proper respect for the presumption of innocence, the court system must do better

---

[114] See Ch. 6.2 above.

[115] See the judgment of the Bundesgerichtshof in Germany to this effect, quoted at length by Fawcett, *Application of the European Convention* (1987), 111–13.

[116] Criminal Justice Act 1993, s. 66(6), substituting s. 29(2) of the Criminal Justice Act 1991.

[117] See, e.g., the argument by J.F. Williams, 'Process and Prediction: A Return to a Fuzzy Model of Pretrial Detention' (1994) 79 *Minnesota LR* 325.

than that. If a court is asked to remand in custody before there is substantial evidence, it should pause long, and should allow only a short remand. The problem of delays in obtaining forensic science evidence should be tackled separately and urgently. Such a change would also provide some kind of safeguard against the detention of someone likely to be acquitted. There should be a similar safeguard against the detention of someone unlikely to be given a custodial sentence for the offence(s) alleged, as stated in the previous paragraph.

It should also be shown that it is more likely than not that this defendant will commit an offence likely to result in imprisonment if granted bail: this requires a database for the prediction of offending, the like of which appears not to exist in England and Wales. There is a database for the probability of keeping the conditions of parole if released from prison, and there are some data on the probability of certain offenders committing so-called 'dangerous' offences. But here, unlike in the United States,[118] there is no database that can be used to predict offending, let alone serious offending, whilst on bail. The American research by Goldkamp and Gottfredson does contain some useful pointers—for example, that reoffending and non-appearance at trial are highly correlated so that to predict one is usually to predict the other; and that bailees are more likely to offend the longer the period awaiting trial[119]—but it remains true that the numbers of false positives would be high. The scattered research in England suggests the same, as we saw above: it is easy to say that people charged with taking cars are the group most likely to offend on bail, but most of them are not in fact detected in law-breaking whilst on bail. It is easy to claim that courts should have greater regard to objections to bail advanced by the police, but the vast majority of those to whom the court grants bail in the face of police objections are not detected in law-breaking whilst on bail.[120] As Gottfredson and Gottfredson remark, referring to several pieces of American research, 'the results of these studies cast serious doubt on current abilities to predict with great accuracy the statistically rare events of failure to appear at trial and pre-trial crime'.[121]

None of these observations breaks new ground, and yet their significance for bail has been accorded little attention. Thousands of people are being deprived of their liberty every year on the basis of predictions. These have no statistical foundation, and all the criminological evidence in analogous fields points to the likelihood of considerable over-prediction. Even if it were emphasized that the primary concern is to prevent the commission of serious

---

[118] See J. Goldkamp and M. R. Gottfredson, *Policy Guidelines for Bail: An Exercise in Court Reform* (1985), based on research in Philadelphia courts.

[119] *Ibid.*   [120] See above, n. 67 and accompanying text.

[121] Gottfredson and Gottfredson, *Decision-Making in Criminal Justice* (1988), 93.

crimes in the period between arrest and trial, that does not make the problem any easier. Serious crimes are harder to predict than law-breaking in general, and the rate of false positives may well be very high. The only possible justification here is that, where the crime is so serious that a substantial custodial sentence is likely to result, pre-trial imprisonment is less of an unwarranted imposition on the guilty (but not the innocent) defendant.[122]

At a time when governments have shown an attraction to tougher policies on remands, it is essential to reassert fundamental principles: there should be a strong presumption in favour of liberty; this ought not to be displaced unless the court is satisfied that there is sufficient evidence to continue with the charge, a test which should become stricter as time progresses and should require careful judgements by the Crown Prosecution Service; the charge, if proved at the trial, should be likely to result in the imposition of a custodial sentence; and, even in such cases, the presumption ought not to be displaced unless remand in custody is necessary because either (1) the defendant appears unlikely to attend the trial and non-custodial measures such as the imposition of conditions or the taking of sureties appear unlikely to be successful in securing his or her attendance; even if the court is satisfied on that ground, it should consider whether the defendant might be remanded to a bail hostel rather than to prison; or (2) the defendant appears likely to commit an offence serious enough for custody if granted bail, whether subject to conditions or not;[123] or (3) the defendant appears likely to threaten witnesses or otherwise to interfere with the course of justice.[124]

In order to translate the principles into practice, some thought should be devoted to the idea of developing bail guidelines as a basis for magistrates' decision-making and training. Guidelines have been introduced in Philadelphia with a measure of success.[125] One precondition would be thorough research into the characteristics of remand cases, their disposal at present, and the subsequent conduct of remandees. This would provide the necessary database. Guidelines would then be constructed, and it would remain necessary to insist on improvements in the availability of information relating to defendants. It would remain open to courts to depart from the

---

[122] This is not to overlook the disadvantages of custodial remands mentioned at the beginning of the chapter—the poor prison conditions, the effect on a person's morale and physical appearance, the inhibitions of preparing the defence, etc.

[123] It should be noted that French law has a presumption in favour of custody where the alleged offence is a crime rather than a mere délit: L. Leigh and L. Zedner, *A Report on the Administration of Criminal Justice in the Pre-trial Phase in France and Germany*, RCCJ Research Study 1 (1992), 23.

[124] Cf. the Canadian provision discussed by Padfield, above n. 28, 510, which refers only to 'the commission of an offence' without any express reference to seriousness, although it does use the phrase 'necessary in the public interest or for the protection or safety of the public'.

[125] Gottfredson and Gottfredson, above n. 121, 105–10.

guidelines on giving reasons, but this would surely be a more sensitive approach to the problems of remand decisions than legislative restrictions.

Several points emerge from the foregoing. First, bail/custody decisions are generally predictive, and the evidence for making these predictions is rarely strong. That counsels great caution. Secondly, much turns on the seriousness of the charge. Rather than simply stating that courts should 'balance' this factor against others, more attention should be paid to the deep significance of depriving someone of liberty and to the probability of a prison sentence being imposed if the facts alleged are proved. That requires the court to make a prediction of a different kind, but one that should be possible if there is coherent guidance on sentencing. This leads on to the third factor: there must be greater willingness among decision-makers to question the decisions taken previously in each case, and to re-appraise the evidence and the approach to be taken. In particular, the CPS must be prepared to conduct a meaningful review of the police conclusion, and the court to conduct a meaningful review of the CPS recommendation. Defence lawyers, too, must be prepared to offer a 'full and fearless' defence rather than trying to curry favour with the court or CPS. Such changes will require alterations to the system, since decision-makers cannot be expected to reach different decisions without (a) time and (b) fresh information. Fourthly, there is the need for cogent evidence of guilt before a person is remanded in custody. Such a requirement is likely to cause considerable difficulties in practice: can the police or prosecution be expected to marshall their evidence quickly? To what extent should account be taken of the probable line of defence, and the evidence for it? (Yet if both these hurdles could be surmounted, would not a decision to remand in custody tend to create a presumption of guilt when the case subsequently comes to trial—and unfairly so, since any previous determination will have incorporated few safeguards?) Fifthly, assuming that the Bail Act were to be revised to take account of the proposed changes, a culture of legality should be introduced into remand hearings. Hucklesby's findings about the rarity of references to the 1976 Act suggest a rather cavalier approach.

In those cases where a custodial remand is held to be necessary for one of the reasons above, efforts must be made to keep its duration to a minimum. The question of unnecessary delay in bringing cases to court must be reconsidered at the highest level—not merely because people who should have the benefit of the presumption of innocence are losing days, weeks, and months of their lives, but also because longer waiting times in prison cost the State money. Time-limits and their exceptions should be tightened, and there should be fresh consideration of the need for twenty-eight-day remands in some cases. For those who are remanded in custody, the conditions in which they are held must be improved urgently. Lord Windlesham has argued powerfully for the separate treatment of individuals on remand,[126] and the Woolf Report placed particular emphasis on this,[127] resulting in a Prison Service statement of principles on unconvicted prisoners in 1992. Further attention must also be given to the creation of a new middle path between custodial remand and conditional bail. This might take the form of release upon undertakings, with properly funded supervision from the Probation Service. If successful, it could avoid loss of liberty and show proper respect for the rights of defendants and victims.

[126] Windlesham, above n. 11, 140.   [127] See Morgan and Jones, above n. 44.

8   Mode of Trial

THIS chapter deals with decisions on mode of trial. In England and Wales criminal cases may be tried either at the Crown Court or in a magistrates' court, depending on the legal classification of the offence and sometimes also on the decision of a magistrates' court or of the defendant. The choice of mode of trial has a number of possible implications—the length of delay before trial, the probability and duration of remand in custody, the degree of support for witnesses, the degree of anxiety for defendants, the probability of acquittal, the severity of sentence if convicted, the cost to the public, etc. Decisions on mode of trial can be influenced or even controlled through the charging and discontinuance practices of the prosecution, but one of the central recommendations in the report of the Royal Commission on Criminal Justice raised again the question whether and to what extent defendants can be said to have a right to trial by jury.

The chapter begins with an outline of the existing statutory framework. We then turn to the operation of the system in practice, considering decisions by defendants and decisions by magistrates. The powers of the Crown Prosecution Service are then discussed, before going on to examine some key issues of policy and principle relating to mode of trial. The implications of the present system for victims and of certain ethnic minorities are examined, and in particular the likely effects of the changes brought about by the Criminal Procedure and Investigations Act 1996 are discussed.

1. The Statutory Framework

English law divides offences into three categories.[1] The first consists of offences triable only on indictment. Among these are the most serious offences in the criminal calendar, such as murder, manslaughter, rape, and

[1] The law is contained in pt. II of the Criminal Law Act 1977. Those statutory provisions resulted from the recommendations of the James Committee, some of which are discussed in s. 3 of this chapter.

wounding with intent, together with a number of other offences such as blackmail. These offences are triable only in the Crown Court: if the case is contested, trial is by judge and jury. The third category consists of offences triable summarily only. Among these are the least serious types of offence, such as non-payment of the television licence fee and many road traffic offences. These offences are triable only in a magistrates' court, and trial is usually by a bench of lay magistrates advised by a clerk.[2]

It is the second category of offences that gives rise to most discussion. These are offences 'triable either way', that is, they may be tried in the Crown Court or at a magistrates' court. Broadly speaking, this category includes offences of intermediate seriousness or of variable seriousness. It includes several of the most frequently committed offences, such as theft, handling stolen goods, obtaining by deception, and burglary. The procedure here is that the mode of trial must be decided in a magistrates' court, but with an important recent change. Section 49 of the Criminal Procedure and Investigations Act 1996, implemented in October 1997, introduced a system of 'plea before venue'. In other words, the defendant is asked whether the intended plea is guilty or not guilty, before the issue of mode of trial is raised. If the defendant signifies an intention to plead guilty, the magistrates are required to assume jurisdiction. The magistrates then determine the seriousness of the offence, and may either pass sentence themselves or commit the case to the Crown Court for sentence.[3] Where the defendant signifies a plea of not guilty, the procedure is as in former years. Thus, in the first place, the law confers on the magistrates the power to decide whether the case should be tried summarily or should be committed to the Crown Court for trial. Among the circumstances that section 19 of the Magistrates' Courts Act 1980 directs them to consider are the nature of the case, whether the circumstances of the offence give it a serious character, and whether the sentencing powers of a magistrates' court would be adequate. In practice, they are more likely to have regard to the 'Mode of Trial Guidelines', issued with the authority of the Lord Chief Justice and differing in some respects from the legal provisions.[4] Before taking their decision, the magistrates must invite the prosecution and the defence to make representations on mode of trial. If the magistrates decide that the case ought to be committed to the Crown Court for trial, the next step is committal for

---

[2] There are also around 100 stipendiary magistrates, who are legally qualified and sit alone. Their numbers have been increasing in recent years: whereas formerly they were to be found chiefly in large urban areas, they are now scattered more widely across the country.

[3] For discussion, see R. Leng and R. Taylor, *Blackstone's Guide to the Criminal Procedure and Investigations Act 1996*, and A. Edwards, 'The Procedural Aspects' [1997] *Crim. LR* 321, at 329–31.

[4] For discussion of the (unpublished) 1995 version of the Guidelines, see S. White, 'The Antecedents of the Mode of Trial Guidelines' [1996] *Crim. LR* 471.

trial.[5] If, on the other hand, the magistrates decide that the case is suitable for summary trial, they must then ask the defendant whether he or she consents to summary trial or wishes to elect trial in the Crown Court. The defendant thus retains an absolute right to elect Crown Court trial for all either-way offences.

2. Mode of Trial Decisions in Practice

In 1996 some 465,000 persons were prosecuted for offences that were triable either way or on indictment only (the latter group probably amounts to fewer than 20,000). Some 81,000 cases were committed for trial to the Crown Court, which means that over five-sixths of all either-way cases were tried in the magistrates' courts.[6] In general, therefore, the vast majority of mode of trial decisions are in favour of trial in the magistrates' court. Looked at from the Crown Court, however, around four-fifths of its case-load consists of cases triable either way. In 1996 some 68 per cent of these cases were committed because of decisions taken by magistrates, with elections by defendants accounting for less than one-third.[7] These figures show that most of the defendants who could choose Crown Court trial have tended not do so, chiefly because they intend to plead guilty. None the less, the Crown Court is overflowing with cases, and it is hardly surprising that there has been considerable pressure, for reasons of economy and management, to reduce the numbers of either-way cases going there. This was the intention behind the new 'plea before venue' system introduced in 1997, but its effect in practice is still unclear. Many defendants may still respond by indicating a plea of not guilty, in order to secure Crown Court trial, and so we must inquire why those defendants who choose the Crown Court do so. First, however, we should consider the decisions of magistrates' courts to commit defendants to the Crown Court.

(a) Decisions by Magistrates

Under the pre-1997 system, magistrates themselves committed more defendants to the Crown Court than the number of defendants electing that mode of trial. At that time, magistrates might take a decision on mode of trial only

---

[5] These will not be discussed here. In practice, the vast majority of committals are now 'paper committals', not challenged by the defence and not requiring a court hearing of any kind. For further discussion, see *ibid.*, ch. 4.

[6] *Criminal Statistics England and Wales 1996*, ch. 6; the total number of indictable cases in 1986 was similar, at 463,000.

[7] *Criminal Statistics England and Wales 1996*, para. 6.15.

after giving the prosecution and the defence an opportunity to make representations. In fewer than one-half of cases in Riley and Vennard's study where the defendant was legally represented did the defence make any submissions on mode of trial.[8] Since the defendant had an absolute right to elect Crown Court trial, the defence has no need to make representations in favour of this: the defendant will have the opportunity to make that election. But where the defence preferred summary trial and made representations in its favour, while the prosecution argued in favour of committal to the Crown Court, the magistrates accepted the prosecution's view in twenty-seven of the twenty-nine cases. Indeed, in Riley and Vennard's study some 96 per cent of magistrates' decisions were consistent with the prosecutor's representations.[9]

One possible explanation for this high degree of concordance is that the magistrates were failing to exercise independent judgement, and were simply accepting the prosecution's view almost every time. Another possible explanation is that prosecutors and magistrates were independently applying the same criteria, and usually came to the same conclusion. However, the analysis was rendered more complex by the considerable local variations in committals for trial, which might be explained partly by persistent local traditions and, in some areas, by the influence of the local liaison judge.[10] It might have been expected that the promulgation of National Mode of Trial Guidelines in 1991 would have removed local variations, but a report by the Criminal Justice Consultative Council in 1993 was pessimistic about this. It acknowledged that 'local cultures might build up and Crown Prosecutors in framing advice might be influenced by the informal policy of the local bench'.[11] The Council raises some poignant questions about local policies:[12] it is doubtful whether many of these policies could survive scrutiny from the national point of view, but the resilience of local cultures, to which the CPS then adapted their behaviour, was a significant practical problem.

One factor that magistrates had to take into account when deciding on mode of trial, according to section 19(3) of the Magistrates' Courts Act 1980, was whether the maximum penalty they have power to impose would be adequate. The survey by Hedderman and Moxon showed that, of the cases sent to the Crown Court by magistrates, over two-thirds received sentences that lay within the powers of the magistrates' court.[13] This seems to suggest either that magistrates did not regard this as the most important factor, or that magistrates had insufficient information on which to base an accurate prediction of sentence. The latter was probably true, in that magistrates are not told about previous convictions at a mode of trial hearing, and may assume either that

---

[8] Riley and Vennard, n. 16 below, 12.   [9] *Ibid.* 11.
[10] Riley and Vennard, *Triable-Either-Way Cases* n. 16 below, 9–10.   [11] n. 16 below, 8.
[12] *Ibid.* 10 and 20.   [13] Hedderman and Moxon, n. 16 below, ch. 4.

the defendant has them or that the prosecution is representing in favour of Crown Court trial because it knows of them. Mitigating factors are unlikely to come out fully at this stage, and no pre-sentence report is likely to be available. However, a more persuasive explanation is that the likely penalty was not regarded as a sufficiently powerful reason to override some local policies or traditions, such as the policy of committing all residential burglaries to the Crown Court irrespective of the particular facts.[14]

One of the main reasons for the new 'plea before venue' system introduced by the Criminal Procedure and Investigations Act stemmed from the research findings of Hedderman and Moxon, mentioned above, that two-thirds of defendants committed to the Crown Court by magistrates received sentences within the powers of a magistrates' court. The new system removes the vast majority of these cases from mode of trial decisions. If the defendant signifies an intention to plea guilty, the magistrates 'shall' assume jurisdiction. As will be seen in the following paragraph, this may not work to the disadvantage of defendants, inasmuch as Crown Court sentences have tended to be much more severe than those in magistrates' courts for comparable cases. But the unknown factor is how magistrates will deal with these new decisions. Once they have assumed jurisdiction, they must decide whether the case falls within their sentencing powers (six months' imprisonment, or a maximum of twelve months on two or more charges) or should be committed for sentence to the Crown Court. They will receive much more information than on a mode of trial hearing: the prosecution will not only give the facts, but any previous convictions will be made known, and the defence will outline any mitigating circumstances. No doubt they will receive 'advice' from some local liaison judges about which cases to commit for sentence, but it remains probable that they will deal with far more serious cases than they have been accustomed to sentencing. This is not least because they have to take account of the discount for pleading guilty (section 48 of the Criminal Justice and Public Order Act 1994) when deciding whether to deal with the case or commit for sentence. Certainly it was the intention of the Government that the new 'plea before venue' system should cut costs by relieving the Crown Court of some of its case-load: whether the inevitable increase in the number of cases committed for sentence will result in an overall cost saving remains to be seen. Whether magistrates are equipped to pass sentence in more and more serious cases is open to doubt: what is known about local variations, in spite of the Magistrates' Association's own *Sentencing Guidelines*,[15] is hardly encouraging.

---

[14] Referred to by the Criminal Justice Consultative Council, *Mode of Trial Decisions and Sentencing*, 10.

[15] Discussed in A. Ashworth, *Sentencing and Criminal Justice* (2nd edn., 1995), 53–6.

(b) Decisions by Defendants

At least four major research studies in the last twenty years inquired into the reasons why many defendants who could have their cases tried in a magistrates' court chose to go to the Crown Court under the pre-1997 system.[16] The substance of their findings is strikingly similar, although both Gregory and Bottoms and McClean found a significant minority of defendants who seemed not properly to have appreciated the choice they had made.[17] The main finding was that those defendants and their advisers who chose Crown Court trial seemed to lack confidence in the quality of magistrates' justice. They seemed to believe that magistrates' courts favour the prosecution unduly, and that the Crown Court offers a fairer and fuller hearing with a higher chance of acquittal. Indeed, in Hedderman and Moxon's sample some 69 per cent of defendants and 81 per cent of solicitors gave the higher chance of acquittal as a reason.[18] In Riley and Vennard's study the reason given most frequently by defendants who chose the Crown Court was 'previous experience with the courts', a reason not developed by the authors but which may well reflect perceptions of fairness and of acquittal rates.[19] All the studies showed that most of those who intended to plead not guilty choose to be tried in the Crown Court, whereas most of those who intended to plead guilty consented to summary trial if it was offered.

These trends in practice may appear to reflect rational choices. A person who intends to plead not guilty to one or more charges will naturally wish to maximize the probability of acquittal. There is no absolutely reliable comparison of acquittal rates, but Julie Vennard concluded that the acquittal rate in the magistrates' courts was about half that in the Crown Court, some 30 per cent compared with 57 per cent.[20] Penny Darbyshire, using a different calculation, suggests a difference between 40 per cent in Crown Court trials and 22–24 per cent in magistrates' court trials.[21] The rationality of choosing the Crown Court should not, however, be assessed on this basis alone. Consider, for example, the minority of defendants who intended to plead not guilty and yet who consented to trial by magistrates—about one-quarter of the

[16] A. E. Bottoms and J. D. McClean, *Defendants in the Criminal process* (1976); J. Gregory, *Crown Court or Magistrates' Court?* (1976); D. Riley and J. Vennard, *Triable-Either-Way Cases: Crown Court or Magistrates' Court?*, HORS 98 (1988); C. Hedderman and D. Moxon, *Magistrates' Court or Crown Court? Mode of Trial Decisions and Sentencing*, HORS 125 (1992).

[17] Gregory, above n. 16, 10; Bottoms and McClean, above n. 16, 84–5.

[18] Hedderman and Moxon, above n. 16, 20.

[19] Riley and Vennard, above n. 16, 17; cf. also Hedderman and Moxon, above n. 16, 22.

[20] J. Vennard, 'The Outcome of Contested Trials', in D. Moxon (ed.), *Managing Criminal Justice* (1985), at 131.

[21] P. Darbyshire, 'For the New Lord Chancellor—Some Causes for Concern about Magistrates' [1997] *Crim. LR* 861, at 869.

defendants in Riley and Vennard's study who intended to plead not guilty.[22] Predominant among their reasons were the avoidance of delay and the chance of a lighter sentence if convicted. These reasons, if borne out by experience, might well be taken to outweigh the higher probability of acquittal offered by Crown Court trial. In fact, experience supports both reasons. Delays in bringing cases to trial are shorter for trials in magistrates' courts than for the Crown Court trials.[23] Moreover, one study suggests that sentences in the Crown Court for triable-either-way cases are some seven times as severe as they are for comparable cases sentenced by magistrates—custody is three times more likely, and custodial sentences are more than twice the length on average.[24]

This analysis might suggest that, from the defendant's point of view, decisions on mode of trial had an element of roulette. The defendant who opts for the Crown Court gambles on an acquittal, knowing that the delay will be longer and knowing that if the gamble fails the sentence is likely to be far more severe than in a magistrates' court. The defendant who consents to summary trial knows that the chances of acquittal are lower, but has the consolation that the process will be over more quickly and that the sentence will not be as severe. However, the research indicates that the reality of the pre-1997 system was even more complex, since at least five further factors came into play:[25]

(a) *Prison more congenial:* for those defendants who believe that they will receive a prison sentence ultimately, it might be thought beneficial to elect Crown Court trial so as to maximize the time spent on remand. Remand prisoners enjoy more 'privileges' inside prison than sentenced prisoners and, even though they are often held in overcrowded establishments, they are more likely to be held near their home, so that family visits are less difficult.

(b) *Disclosure:* almost one-half of all defendants and solicitors in Hedderman and Moxon's study stated that one reason for electing trial was to obtain more information about the prosecution case.[26] It is possible that this disclosure led to some of the changes of plea (below), but the system of disclosure has changed now as a result of the Criminal Procedure and Investigations Act 1996.[27]

(c) *Late change of plea:* one characteristic of the pre-1997 system was that some two-thirds of those electing Crown Court trial changed their plea to guilty before the trial came on.[28] Thus the 'fuller and

---

[22] P. Darbyshire, 'For the New Lord Chancellor—Some Causes for Concern about Magistrates' [1997] *Crim. LR* 861, 16–17.

[23] See p. 236 above.

[24] Hedderman and Moxon, above n. 16, 36–7.

[25] For fuller discussion on these factors, see 231–3 of the first edn.

[26] Hedderman and Moxon, above n. 16, 20.   [27] For an outline, see Ch. 4.2.18 above.

[28] Riley and Vennard, above n. 16, 19; Hedderman and Moxon, above n. 16, 22–4.

fairer' hearing never takes place, and the advantages of pleading guilty (perhaps with some bargain involved) take precedence.[29]

(d) *Sentence levels:* many defendants who elected trial in the Crown Court were unaware of the large differences in sentence severity between the Crown Court and magistrates' courts.[30] Indeed, 59 per cent of defendants and 38 per cent of solicitors in Hedderman and Moxon's sample expressed the belief that the sentence would be lighter in the Crown Court,[31] a belief which in general is false. As Hedderman and Moxon demonstrated, sentence levels are on average around seven times as severe.

(e) *Legal advice:* about three-quarters of solicitors in Riley and Vennard's study offered advice to their clients on mode of trial, and it seems that that advice usually accorded with the defendant's own preference. 'Only 6 out of 98 defendants initially favouring the magistrates' court were advised to elect, while 23 of the 156 intending to opt for the Crown Court were advised to consent to summary trial'.[32] Solicitors' views on the advantages of the two modes of trial were similar to those of defendants, and it is possible that they too underestimate the high risks of electing trial in the Crown Court. They may underestimate the numbers who subsequently change their plea to guilty, and they may underestimate the much greater severity of Crown Court sentences. Otherwise, it might be argued, they would do their clients a greater service by advising strongly against election in more cases.

These factors also had a bearing on the decision to introduce the new 'plea before venue' system in the Criminal Procedure and Investigations Act 1996. The findings of Hedderman and Moxon's research were so powerful that it was possible to take the view that it would be in the interests not only of the Government (in terms of cost savings) but also of defendants (in terms of sentence length) if those who were going to plead guilty did so at a much earlier stage. The misconceptions of defendants and their legal advisers about sentencing differentials between magistrates' courts and the Crown Court would then be reduced in significance. For these reasons, all defendants who signify an intention to plead guilty to either-way offences are 'dealt with' by the magistrates.

---

[29] Hedderman and Moxon, above n. 16, 23, found that 29% of those who changed their plea did so in exchange for the prosecution dropping or reducing one or more charges.

[30] It is also likely that many of those who consent to summary trial do not realize how favourable to them the difference in sentence is likely to be.

[31] Hedderman and Moxon, above n. 16, 20.   [32] Riley and Vennard, above n. 16, 18.

But it is evident that the advantages for defendants may not come without complications which could, in some cases, undermine them completely. The first point is that defendants will still have to consider their plea at an early stage, when neither they nor their legal advisers may have sufficient knowledge of the prosecution case on which to make an informed decision. This reintroduces a distinct element of roulette: if there has not been sufficient disclosure at the key stage, or if it is last-minute disclosure, the defence will doubtless seek an adjournment. Otherwise, there is a choice between signifying a guilty plea when there may be a flaw in the prosecution case, or indicating a not guilty plea and then (if this is changed later) foregoing some of the sentence discount because the plea was not made at the earliest opportunity. Many defendants will doubtless be advised to delay indicating any plea until the prosecution have made sufficient advance disclosure. A second point is that the magistrates may, in any event, commit the defendant to the Crown Court for sentence rather than using their own powers. If that becomes the norm, either nationally or (at the behest of local judges) in certain areas, then these defendants will be sentenced by the Crown Court in any event.

3. Prosecutorial Powers and Mode of Trial

Whilst English prosecutors do not have the right to determine the level of court in which a case is tried, it is evident that in many cases they have considerable power *de facto*. A concordance rate of 96 per cent between magistrates' decisions and prosecution representations could include a number of cases where prosecutors are merely trying to anticipate magistrates' decisions rather than influence them, but the likelihood is that magistrates are (at least sometimes) influenced by what prosecutors say. However, English prosecutors have more subtle ways of influencing mode of trial, through decisions on the charge(s) to be brought in a particular case. If the prosecutor wishes a case to be heard in the Crown Court, the way to ensure this is to bring a charge that is triable only on indictment. If, on the other hand, a prosecutor wishes a case to be dealt with in a magistrates' court, the way to ensure this is to bring a charge that is triable summarily only.

Of course it would be wrong to suggest that prosecutors have a completely free hand in this matter. Much depends on the nature of the defendant's conduct and the availability of offences that are summary only or (perhaps less easy) indictable only. The criminal law does not offer great choice in some spheres. Much may also depend on the charge originally laid, usually by the police: the Crown Prosecution Service might continue with an either-way charge in order to avoid disappointment to the police and a possible deterioration in working arrangements, even if the case could have been dealt with adequately at a magistrates' court.[33] We have seen, in Chapter 6, that the Crown Prosecution Service has wide powers to drop cases, including the statutory power to discontinue prosecutions in the magistrates' courts, under section 23 of the Prosecution of Offences Act 1985, and a power to drop cases when they are called on at the Crown Court.[34]

Discontinuance can be followed by recharging, although this would be a relatively rare event. The Code for Crown Prosecutors gives three reasons why a prosecution might be re-started: where a review suggests that the original decision was wrong, where significant evidence unexpectedly comes to hand later, or where the CPS discontinues the original prosecution but tells the defendant that it might be re-started when further evidence becomes available.[35] This does not mention the possibility of re-starting a prosecution in order to alter the venue, but paragraph 7.3 of the 1994 Code states that 'Crown Prosecutors should not change the charge simply because of the decision made by the court or the defendant about where the case will be heard'.

Why might the prosecution wish to ensure that a case is tried in a magistrates' court? This question has been discussed by appellate courts in cases where prosecutors have dropped more serious charges in order to ensure summary trial, and where defendants have challenged the decision by seeking to invoke the doctrine of abuse of process.[36] In *Ramsgate Justices, ex parte Warren et al.* (1981)[37] the defendants were charged with various either-way offences as a result of disturbances on the sea-front at Ramsgate. When the defendants elected trial in the Crown Court, the police dropped the either-way charges and instead charged each defendant with a summary offence. In *Canterbury and St Augustine's Justices, ex parte Klisiak* (1981)[38] the defendant was charged with criminal damage at a public house to the value of £414. At this time persons charged with criminal damage had a right to elect Crown Court trial if the damage was valued at more than £200. Klisiak elected trial. The police subsequently wrote to the defendant's solicitors informing them of an intention to amend the charge to damage valued at £155, adding that this, 'as you of course will realise, precludes this case from a Crown Court hearing'.

Declining to accept the submission that the prosecutor's conduct in either case amounted to an abuse of process, Lord Lane CJ, in the Divisional Court,

---

[33] The findings of J. Baldwin, 'Understanding Judge Ordered and Directed Acquittals in the Crown Court' [1997] *Crim. LR* 536, discussed in Ch. 6.2, are consistent with some such practices.

[34] Discussed in Ch. 6.2 and 6.3, above.

[35] Crown Prosecution Service, *Code for Crown Prosecutors* (3rd edn., 1994), para. 10.

[36] See generally A. Choo, *Abuse of Process and Judicial Stays of Criminal Proceedings* (1993).

[37] (1981) 72 Cr.App.R. 250.

[38] *Ibid.*

placed great weight on the fact that the prosecutors could have chosen to prefer the lower charges at the outset. 'It seems to me that to achieve this same result by the procedural course which, in fact, was adopted, cannot be said to have been oppressive or unjust or any abuse of the processes of the court.' He added that there may be good reasons for choosing a lesser charge—e.g. speed of trial, sufficiency of proof, and trial summarily rather than on indictment, perhaps in order to deal swiftly with disorder such as sea-front disturbances during the summer holiday period. Lord Lane added that 'it is, however, to be hoped that, where proper, the lesser charge will be preferred at the outset'.[39]

This judgment has acquired great respect, and the Code for Crown Prosecutors used to refer to it extensively.[40] Yet Lord Lane's discussion of the applicants' main point is unconvincing. He referred to the contention that, when the prosecution reduces the charges from either-way to summary offences, 'the defendant may thereby lose his right to trial by jury if, indeed, it is, on balance, properly to be described as a loss at all'. Lord Lane plainly thought that to speak of losing a right was a ridiculous analysis:

> what the prosecution have done is to lower the nature of the case against the defendant and the possible consequential penalties. We have a Gilbertian result here of applicants complaining that they are now charged with lesser offences than those which they originally had to face.[41]

The allusion to comic opera misses the point. It is not so much that the defendants were complaining that they were likely to receive lower sentences: that would indeed be a nonsensical attitude. Surely their complaint was that they were being deprived of Crown Court trial and the higher chances of acquittal. After all, these are the reasons why most of the defendants electing trial in the Crown Court do so,[42] and the acquittal statistics certainly favour Crown Court trial.[43] As the James Committee recognized:

> What matters to them is the fact of conviction or acquittal. Except in the most serious cases, where the defendant knows that if convicted he will receive a substantial sentence of imprisonment, loss of reputation or loss of livelihood rather than the possible sentence may well be what is uppermost in his mind.[44]

Of course it is fair to say that such a defendant would probably receive a higher sentence if convicted in the Crown Court, but the Lord Chief Justice's reason-

---

[39] (1981) 72 Cr.App.R. at 261.

[40] As we saw in Ch. 6, the 1994 version of the Code relegates 'technical' matters such as this to the CPS Manuals.

[41] *Ibid.* at 259.   [42] See n. 18 above and accompanying text.

[43] See n. 19 above and accompanying text.

[44] James Committee, *The Distribution of Criminal Business between the Crown Court and Magistrates' Courts*, Cmnd. 6323 (1975), para. 59; see also para. 142 on the reasons for electing Crown Court trial in drunk-driving cases in the 1970s.

ing in the *Canterbury* and *Ramsgate* cases overlooks the prior question of conviction or acquittal. The same reasoning was adopted by Leggatt J in the Divisional Court in *Liverpool Stipendiary Magistrate, ex parte Ellison* (1990).[45]

In the *Liverpool* case, Bingham LJ did warn against a prosecutor 'manipulating or using the procedures of the court in order to oppress or unfairly to prejudice a defendant before the court'. The position seems to be that a prosecutor can amend the charges so long as the charge remains an appropriate one on the facts, and so long as there is no bad faith on the part of the prosecutor or unfairness or prejudice to the defendant. The issue of prejudice raises deep questions concerning the nature of the defendant's rights. Since English law does confer on defendants an absolute right to elect Crown Court trial for either-way offences, at what stage does that right crystallize? One difference between the three cases is that in the *Ramsgate* and *Canterbury* cases the magistrates had already held the proceedings for the determination of mode of trial and the defendants had exercised their right to elect trial on indictment, whereas in the *Liverpool* case the charge was amended before the mode of trial decision had been taken. Leggatt J in the *Liverpool* case seemed not to make this distinction when he opined that 'to speak of depriving the applicant of his right to trial by jury is . . . only a pejorative way of making the point that on the reduction of the charge he ceased to be confronted by a charge sufficiently serious to warrant trial by jury'. He also stated that 'until the more serious charge in this case was withdrawn, the applicant enjoyed such a prospective right [to trial by jury], but in relation to the less serious charge he did not'.[46] On the facts of the *Liverpool* case it would be difficult to argue that any substantive right had yet vested in the defendant—both for the principled reason that no election had been made, and for the pragmatic reason that this might otherwise inhibit the prosecution from amending the charges where a review of the evidence or a change in circumstances rendered this advisable. However, once the magistrates have held proceedings for the determination of mode of trial, one might maintain that the right has vested, and therefore any change should require the defendant's consent.

How far the pragmatic reason should be given weight in cases where the defendant has already elected trial on indictment is a difficult matter. In the *Canterbury* case the matter was clouded: the original charge related to property valued at £414 but the prosecution maintained that they then found that they had insufficient evidence of the damage to certain items. If this was true, then the defendant could hardly claim even an embryonic right to elect trial in respect of damage that he could not be proved to have caused. But the suspicion in the *Canterbury* case is that the explanation of 'insufficiency of

---

[45] [1990] RTR 220.   [46] *Ibid.* at 226.

evidence' may have been a device used to ensure that the case did not go to the Crown Court. The point is therefore reduced to one of the prosecutor's motivation. The *Ramsgate* case raises another difficulty. It seems that one reason for preferring summary charges was to ensure that the cases were dealt with more quickly (Crown Court waiting times tend to be longer) in the hope of achieving a deterrent effect during the summer holiday season. Could it be said that that deprives the defendant of an embryonic right? Is the reason given not a proper prosecutorial argument?

These arguments suggest that two questions should be kept distinct. One is the question of proper and improper reasons for prosecutors preferring certain charges. The basic ethical proposition is that the charge should be the one that relates most closely to the facts that the prosecutor has a reasonable prospect of proving. Then there is a need for guidance on the broad range of ethical reasons for departing from this: among the proper reasons might be the need for expedition in dealing with the case, the effect on certain witnesses, and whether the magistrates' sentencing powers for a lesser offence would be adequate; one improper reason might be the improved chances of obtaining a conviction in the magistrates' court. Some such reasons should be stated in guidelines (although these could not be exhaustive), and a system of accountability should be put in place, since these decisions have significant consequences for defendants. A more focused doctrine of abuse of process might be a suitable way of enforcing accountability,[47] but the primary approach would be to articulate clear guidance for prosecutors.

The second question is that of timing, within the present system which grants defendants a right to elect. Whilst it is right that there should be continuing review of case files by prosecutors, it is surely wrong that a change of mind by the prosecution after a defendant has elected trial on an either-way charge should be allowed to remove the case to the magistrates' court, if the defendant is unwilling to agree to that course. This creates a difficulty, since it was argued in Chapter 6 above that the prosecution should have the right to drop a case (and, therefore, to reduce the charge) at any time until the start of the Crown Court trial. Sensible as this is as a matter of prosecution policy, it creates a conflict in cases where the defendant has already elected Crown Court trial. There is a difference between preferring a lesser charge originally, for acceptable reasons as set out in guidelines, and preferring a lesser charge after mode of trial proceedings, for whatever reasons. This difference was recognized in *Brooks* (1985),[48] where the Court of Appeal held that the prosecutor had abused the process of the court by bringing a charge of an indictable-only offence after mode of trial proceedings in which the magis-

---

[47] See the discussion of accountability in Ch. 6.6, above.   [48] [1985] *Crim. LR* 385.

trates did not follow the prosecutor's representations and declined to commit the defendant for trial on an either-way charge. O'Connor LJ held that the prosecutor's decision effectively amounted to overruling or usurping the decision of the magistrates.[49] The same reasoning ought to apply, *pari passu*, to decisions taken by prosecutors after the defendant has exercised the right to elect trial on indictment, and we saw earlier that paragraph 7.3 of the 1994 CPS Code is to this effect.

As it has been argued above that the proper exercise of prosecutors' powers may turn on motivation, can a similar argument be applied to defendants and their rights? We have seen that defendants occasionally elect trial on indictment in order to postpone the time of their conviction, perhaps to gain the privileges of a remand prisoner for a longer time if they believe a custodial sentence to be inevitable. Recent research shows that this strategy carries a high risk, since custodial sentences in the Crown Court are two-and-a-half times as long on average as those in magistrates' courts, although some of these defendants would in any event be committed for sentence to the Crown Court.[50] But it can be argued that this use of the right of election is improper, in that it bears no relation to the reason for granting the right. The James Committee mentioned elections made on the advice of a legal adviser, chiefly (although not explicitly) to obtain higher fees for that legal adviser.[51] Such elections would also be improper, though the impropriety stems from the defence lawyer rather than from the defendant. The most contestable category is that of guilty defendants who elect Crown Court trial in the hope of taking advantage of the tendency of juries to acquit: is this legitimate or not?

4. Some Questions of Principle

For at least twenty years governments have been concerned about mode of trial decisions. Most of this concern seems to have had far more to do with public expenditure and the staffing of the courts than with issues of principle. The report of the Royal Commission on Criminal Justice seemed preoccupied by such policy constraints but did refer to some questions of principle, as we shall see. It would be unrealistic in modern times to suggest that all defendants should have the right to jury trial, whatever their offence.[52] The cost

[49] Cf. *R.* v. *Redbridge Justices and Fox, ex p. Whitehouse* (1992) 156 JPR 293, where Neill LJ held that there might be circumstances in which it might not be an abuse of process for a prosecutor to prefer a higher charge after the completion of mode of trial proceedings in court (at 300).

[50] See above, n. 24 and accompanying text.

[51] James Report, para. 52, '. . . neither proved nor disproved . . .'

[52] Although this does appear to be suggested by M. Mansfield, *Presumed Guilty* (1993), 207–9.

differences between the magistrates' courts and the Crown Court are enormous, with perhaps a tenfold differential. Thus, unless the trial system is to be altered radically—to which possibility we will return later—it seems probable that there will continue to be some offences triable only on indictment, others triable only summarily, and an intermediate group. Even this is not inevitable, however, since in Scotland there is no such division and it is left chiefly to the prosecutor to determine the level of court in which the case will be tried. Decisions on mode of trial also have consequential effects for the running of the criminal justice system. Since committals to the Crown Court are more frequently in custody than remands in magistrates' courts, there is the effect on prison numbers and costs.

In terms of principle, then, what should be the starting point? The Royal Commission quite properly challenged the so-called 'right to jury trial':[53] any thorough inquiry should refuse to accept the labelling of something as a 'right' until the case has been made out. The alleged right to be tried by twelve of one's peers is not mentioned in the European Convention on Human Rights or similar documents. It is difficult to regard it as a constitutional right, since Magna Carta is vague and the Scots have never known such a right.[54] Is it merely a historical curiosity of the English system, or are there strong arguments of principle in its favour? Three issues are selected for brief discussion here—the benefits of jury trial, the right to jury trial, and the criteria for allocating cases to one or other mode of trial.

1. *The benefits of jury trial*: these benefits can only be considered thoroughly in comparison with the benefits of alternative modes of trial. Some research findings that compare the opinions of defendants and their solicitors on jury trial and trial by magistrates were given earlier.[55] They are strongly favourable to Crown Court trial in terms of the fairness of its procedure. The impression given is that the Crown Court looks into cases more thoroughly and allows more time for putting the case and examining the evidence, whereas magistrates' courts operate at too great a speed and tend to give undue weight to the word of police witnesses. These are mere opinions, although they have been reaffirmed by all research projects on the point. One apparent benefit of jury trial for defendants, as explained earlier, is that the acquittal rate is almost twice as high in jury trial as in trial by magistrates.[56] This does not establish that Crown Court trials reach correct verdicts more frequently than magistrates. The explanation for the higher acquittal rate could be that juries are

---

[53] For a more detailed discussion of the Royal Commission's reasoning on mode of trial, see 244–6 of the first edn. of this work.

[54] See P. Darbyshire, 'The Lamp that Shows that Freedom Lives: Is it Worth the Candle?' [1991] *Crim. LR* at 742–3.

[55] See above, nn. 18–23 and accompanying text.

[56] See above nn. 20–1 and accompanying text.

often more gullible than magistrates, particularly when their members are relatively new to the courts; or in some cases juries could be unduly sceptical of police evidence. It is not known which mode of trial is a more 'accurate' tribunal in terms of rectitude of decision-making, but it is known which favours the defence and which favours the prosecution.

Other benefits have been claimed for jury trial, but some of these owe more to rhetoric than to careful analysis. It is sometimes argued that juries operate as a defence against the oppressive use of State power. This may be supported by reference to acquittals in a few famous trials, notably that of Clive Ponting in 1985, but sceptics point out that there are plenty of trials (e.g. the Guildford Four, the Birmingham Six) in which juries have not performed this function.[57] It is also argued that juries can go against the strict letter of the law and apply 'jury equity' where the situation seems to call for it. Again, there may be some examples of this, but it is hard to say exactly what this 'equity' stems from in the cases where it is exercised—an assertion that Parliament was wrong, proper or improper sympathy for the defendant, or an award for the oratory or even the charm of counsel in the case.[58] In any event, jury acquittals are unaccompanied by reasons, and in general one can only speculate about their basis. Certain other benefits claimed for jury trials are even more doubtful: proponents often point to the randomness of juries, overlooking the fact that this can lead to particular juries being grossly unrepresentative.[59] The arguments about the jury are many and complex, and they continue to be suffused with high-sounding claims.[60] Suffice it to say that there is a dearth of hard evidence about the way in which English juries operate, as the Royal Commission recognized and lamented,[61] and that the most important fact is that juries acquit defendants at trials more frequently than magistrates do.

2. *The foundations of the right to jury trial*: although the use of the term 'right' in this context is time-honoured, it is doubtful how far such a notion can be used as a basis for arguing that more or fewer offences should be triable by jury. For a long time some cases have been triable only before magistrates, and there are few voices heard in favour of jury trial for every offence created by the law. Moreover some cases are triable only in the Crown Court and, as Darbyshire argues, to regard those as cases in which the defendant has a right to jury trial is to glorify the compulsion that exists: the defendant

---

[57] See Darbyshire, above n. 54, at 747.   [58] *Ibid.* 750–1.

[59] *Ibid.* 744–5; cf. the new data in M. Zander and P. Henderson, *Crown Court Study*, RCCH Research Study 19 (1993), ch. 8.

[60] For a recent flourish, compare B. Houlder, 'The Importance of Preserving the Jury System and the Right of Election for Trial' [1997] *Crim. LR* 875, and the reply by P. Darbyshire at [1997] *Crim. LR* 911.

[61] RCCJ, *Report*, para. 1.8; cf. the questions asked of individual jurors in the survey by Zander and Henderson, above n. 59, ch. 8.

cannot choose any other mode of trial (unlike, for example, in the United States, where defendants can choose trial by judge alone).[62] Indeed, some would say that it is inaccurate to use the term 'right' for something that a person cannot decide to accept or waive.[63] In his criticism of the Royal Commission's proposals, Lord Taylor was careful to refer to 'our culture and the perception of many that trial by jury is a fundamental right'.[64] For which offences of intermediate gravity, if any, can this properly be described as a right?

It is not difficult to find a historical answer to the question. Defendants in many cases have had the right to choose jury trial for over a century. The James Committee found great support among defendants for this right, and went so far as to conclude that 'there is a real danger that the total removal of the present right of election would undermine the trust and support which the criminal justice system at present commands among the general public'.[65] Whether the last few words would be true of the present day, following the notorious 'miscarriage of justice' cases, may be doubted; but the overall sentiments might still find favour if careful research on the point were undertaken. The James Committee did consider two alternatives. It held that the power should not be given to the prosecution, as it is in Scotland, because England and Wales had no public prosecutor system and it would be wrong 'for the authority that has investigated the offence, apprehended the accused and decided what offence should be charged to decide also the mode of trial'.[66] Since then the Crown Prosecution Service has been introduced, but the 1993 Royal Commission simply stated that to give the power to the Crown Prosecution Service 'would not be acceptable here at least for the time being'.[67] This presumably means that there is not yet thought to be sufficient confidence in the work of the CPS.

It is evident from the *Canterbury, Ramsgate,* and *Liverpool* cases[68] that there are occasions when prosecutors have firm views on where the case should be tried, and that those views may differ from the defendant's. Since magistrates tend to acquit less frequently than juries, prosecutors might be expected to push more cases—or the more doubtful cases—into the lower courts. This would be welcome to the Government for the policy reasons elaborated above, but what of a defendant's right? The basis for asserting that could only be that certain types of case (serious, complex) ought to have a fuller examination than magistrates' courts can provide; that seriousness should be

---

[62] Darbyshire, above n. 54, 743–4.
[63] J. Feinberg, 'In Defence of Moral Rights' (1992) 12 *Oxford JLS* 149, at 155.
[64] Lord Taylor, 'Criminal Justice after the Royal Commission', *The Times*, 28 July 1993.
[65] James Report, para. 60.   [66] *Ibid.*, para. 48.
[67] RCCJ, *Report*, para. 6.12.   [68] See above, nn. 37, 39, and 45.

assessed from the defendant's point of view, since it is his or her future that is in question; and that others such as courts and prosecutors could not be trusted to take this decision from the defendant's point of view, since they have other concerns about speed and cost (and for the prosecutor, probably, winning).[69]

3. *Criteria for allocating cases to one or other mode of trial*: the general method by which the James Committee constructed its recommendations on the classification of offences was to consider sentence levels. If most of those dealt with at the Crown Court received sentences within the powers of magistrates, then the offence would generally be made summary only. This was the approach with drunk driving, which has been triable only in magistrates' courts since 1977.[70] In earlier years these charges had been a fertile field for oratory by defence counsel, addressed to the sympathies of jurors who might themselves have committed the offence, and for the exploitation of 'technicalities' in the law. The Committee hoped that the result of making the offence triable summarily only would be to increase the proportion of guilty pleas, and this seems to have happened. In some other respects, however, the Committee's views have not been followed. For example, it recommended that driving whilst disqualified needed the sterner hand of the Crown Court, but in 1988 this was made summary only. They also recommended that assaulting a police officer, one of the rare offences prior to 1977 that was triable on indictment at the instance only of the prosecution, should become triable either way. However, it recognized that this might cause a great increase in Crown Court trials, and in the event the Government avoided this consequence by reducing the maximum penalty and making the offence triable summarily only. This illustrates one element of compromise in these decisions—that maximum penalties tend to be reduced when offences are made triable summarily only—but it is an element that tells against those who maintain their innocence. As with the 'Gilbertian' argument above, some defendants want a better chance of acquittal rather than a lesser penalty if convicted.

In 1988 Parliament passed a Criminal Justice Act which reduced four offences to the 'summary only' category—driving whilst disqualified, taking a car without the owner's consent, common assault, and criminal damage to a value less than £2,000. The effect of this was to reduce the work-load of the Crown Court by around 6 per cent.[71] In addition, a working party was set up to draft guidelines for mode of trial decisions. A Practice Note issued by the Divisional Court, under the authority of the Lord Chief Justice, sets out

[69] Cf. the discussion of prosecutorial ethics in Ch. 6.7.
[70] Criminal Law Act 1977, pt. II, applying James Report, paras. 146–8.
[71] Criminal Statistics, England and Wales (1989), para. 6.12.

'National Mode of Trial Guidelines'.[72] The expressed purpose 'is to provide guidance not direction'. Presumably another purpose is to do this on a national basis, and to move away from the local variations revealed by the research. The guidelines recall the criteria in the Magistrates' Courts Act 1980, but there was a significant (and unexplained) change between the 1990 and 1995 versions. The prohibition on taking account of previous convictions and personal mitigation has been removed, without any published explanation of the legal justification for this.[73] The guidelines identify certain features of each of some twelve common either-way offences that may render that offence serious enough to be committed for trial. On each page there is a statement urging the magistrates to accept jurisdiction whenever possible. There has been no published study of the practical effects of the guidelines. They are, however, objective criteria (though fairly general and lacking detail) which, if applied in the right spirit and without corruption by local policies, might lead magistrates to accept jurisdiction in more cases. This does not necessarily mean that all those cases would then be tried by magistrates, since the defendant retains the right to elect. The question whether that is justifiable remains. It must be emphasized, however, that there are relatively few cases in which they will now come into play: under the 'plea before venue' system, only in those cases where the defendant indicates a not guilty plea will the question of mode of trial be raised, and in most such cases one assumes that the defendant will wish to elect for Crown Court trial. Relatively rarely will the magistrates need to adjudicate.

There is still a need, however, to resolve the proper approach to awkward types of case such as the small-value theft, deception, or handling. The James Committee grasped this nettle and decided to recommend that they should become triable summarily only. It accepted the argument that the value of the property stolen is not always a good guide to the seriousness of an offence, but concluded that in most cases it would be. It accepted the argument that to draw a monetary line would lead to some invidious distinctions, but pointed out that many other European. American, and Commonwealth jurisdictions have two or more offences of theft divided in monetary terms. It also accepted that a minor theft charge might have a major bearing on a defendant's career, but argued that many other stigmatic offences are triable only summarily (e.g. indecent exposure, soliciting, evasion of public transport fares). Its conclusion was that it is in the wider public interest to reserve the relatively scarce

---

[72] This Practice Note was reported at (1991) 92 Cr.App.R. 142. Unfortunately, and for unexplained reasons, the subsequent version of the National Mode of Trial Guidelines has not been promulgated officially: see generally S. White, 'The Antecedents of the Mode of Trial Guidelines' [1996] *Crim. LR* 471.

[73] See the critique by White, above n. 72.

resource of trial on indictment for cases more serious than minor thefts and minor offences of damage.[74]

The James recommendations on minor damage were accepted and have been expanded to the extent that now any offence of damage valued at less than £5,000 is triable only in a magistrates' court. But the recommendation on minor thefts had only a short-lived effect. The Government included a provision in its Criminal Justice Bill 1976–7 that would have made thefts of property valued at under £20 triable summarily only, but parliamentary opposition led to its withdrawal.[75] Members of Parliament made much of the link between dishonesty, career, and jury trial. Magistrates' courts were simply not thought adequate to the task of evaluating the evidence and applying the law in a case on which a respectable person's career hangs.

The subject reappeared in a Consultation Paper issued by the Government in 1986, where a compromise proposal was aired. This was to create a presumption that offences of dishonesty involving property less than a specified sum be tried summarily only. From the policy point of view a significant reduction of Crown Court work might follow.[76] Magistrates would be able to displace the presumption by committing cases to the Crown Court if they found special circumstances of exceptional gravity. Excluded from the presumption would be cases in which the defendant had no previous conviction for an offence of dishonesty, where there would be an absolute right to elect trial in the Crown Court.[77] This proposal seems to meet the principal thrust of the earlier parliamentary opposition, but it runs into a separate group of objections based on equality of treatment and unfair discrimination. The Royal Commission's recommendation—to the effect that magistrates should make the decision, that one relevant factor would be 'loss of reputation', and that this would 'often be relevant only to first offenders'— attracted criticism for the same reason. Thus Lord Taylor stated: 'I do not accept that a defendant with a criminal record has, by that token, a weaker claim to jury trial. On the contrary, he or she may well feel specially vulnerable. "Round up the usual suspects" may not be just an old joke.'[78] The Lord Chief Justice went on to say that, if it came to a choice between a monetary limit and the 'socially divisive regime that may well result from the Commission's more sweeping proposal', the former should be preferred. 'Insignificance of the offence is a fairer test than insignificance of the offender'. The James Committee used a similar

---

[74] James Report, paras. 78 ff.

[75] For critical discussion of this part of the Bill, see [1977] *Crim. LR* 65 and 125.

[76] RCCJ, *Report*, para. 6.16, notes that removing trial by jury from offences of theft, deception, and handling of property under £100 would reduce the Crown Court work-load by some 10%.

[77] Home Office, *The Distribution of Business between the Crown Court and Magistrates' Courts* (1986).

[78] Taylor, above n. 64.

argument against giving the power to magistrates' courts: magistrates would be required to have regard to the consequences of conviction for the particular defendant, and this might make them appear biased if they committed well-to-do defendants to the Crown Court and retained lower-class defendants for summary trial.[79] This argument about social class becomes closely intertwined with the point about previous convictions, since it is assumed that most middle-class defendants will have no previous convictions. The only way of avoiding the reproach of inequality of treatment is to select an arbitrary limit, probably one of monetary value, and this will revive anxieties about the quality of magistrates' justice—for middle-class defendants.

Under the 'plea before venue' system, defendants will retain their right to elect for Crown Court trial for these offences if they indicate a plea of not guilty. They stand to lose their sentence discount (under section 48 of the Criminal Justice and Public Order Act 1994) if they are found guilty, but the reason for going to the Crown Court is presumably to take advantage of the higher rate of acquittal. Whether the new system will place extra pressure on defendants not to contest a case in which they have an arguable point or where the evidence appears equivocal remains to be tested. But, before matters are allowed to go further, it is important to remedy the deficiency in the Royal Commission's discussion of the problem and to put the focus on magistrates' justice. There is a need for substantial change, from the selection of magistrates, through their training, to courtroom procedures.[80] Unless the quality of magistrates' justice is changed in such a way that justice is being seen to be done far more frequently, defendants and their lawyers will retain feelings of unfairness and Governments will not achieve the shift of business and reduction in costs which appear to be their primary objectives.

5. Implications for Victims

What implications, if any, does the debate about mode of trial have for the rights and interests of victims? Three matters stand out. One is that Crown Court trial usually means a longer delay before the case is dealt with. This may prolong the victim's anxiety, both generally and particularly in cases where the defendant is on bail and the victim is worried about this. A second is that the greater formality of the Crown Court might put the victim in greater awe of the proceedings. There are allied matters such as the waiting facilities, which might be better at some Crown Courts, but many of these factors vary

---

[79] James Report, para. 59.
[80] See the cogent arguments put forward by Darbyshire, above n. 21.

geographically and according to their impact on particular victims. There is now a Witness Service at all Crown Court centres which offers support and familiarization advice to victims and witnesses, but such support is available only at a small number of magistrates' courts. The third factor is much less subjective: it is that victims are far less likely to be awarded compensation in the Crown Court than in magistrates' courts.[81] This is not simply a reflection of the fact that the Crown Court imposes more custodial sentences and compensation orders are rarely combined with custody. Even taking that into account, Crown Court judges appear to be less willing to make compensation orders, despite the requirement in the Criminal Justice Act 1988 that they should consider this in every case involving injury, loss, or damage. The Royal Commission recognized the point but made no recommendation.[82] The proper approach is to seek to eliminate this anomaly by improved training of judges and counsel, emphasizing the prosecutor's responsibility for raising the issue of compensation.[83]

6. Discriminatory Practices

Evidence of different modes of trial for defendants from ethnic minorities is inconclusive. Two studies in Leeds suggest that magistrates commit for trial at the Crown Court a higher proportion of defendants from an Afro-Caribbean background than whites, and one of the studies suggests that Afro-Caribbeans are also more likely than whites to elect.[84] A study in London courts suggests that Afro-Caribbean defendants are significantly more likely to exercise their right to Crown Court trial.[85] This accords with Hood's finding that a higher proportion of Afro-Caribbean defendants plead not guilty in the Crown Court,[86] since presumably those who intend to plead guilty would be much more likely (following the usual pattern) to choose Crown Court trial. Once again, therefore, we find a close connection between plea and mode of trial.

---

[81] Hedderman and Moxon, above n. 16, 32.　　　　　[82] RCCJ, *Report*, para. 6.8.
[83] See now the Statement on the Treatment of Victims and Witnesses by the Crown Prosecution Service, discussed in Ch. 6 above, which affirms this responsibility (para. 14). For judicial authority, see *Panayioutou* (1989) 11 Cr.App.R(S) 535 and *Hartrey* (1993) 14 Cr.App.R(S) 507.
[84] I. Brown and R. Hullin, 'A Study of Sentencing in the Leeds Magistrates' Court: The Treatment of Ethnic Minority and White Offenders' (1992) 32 *BJ Crim.* 41; T. Jefferson and M. Walker, 'Ethnic Minorities in the Criminal Justice System' [1992] *Crim. LR* 83, who suggest that Afro-Caribbeans are more likely to elect. The term 'Afro-Caribbean' is used throughout as a short way of denoting those from an Afro-Caribbean background.
[85] A. Shallice and P. Gordon, *Black People and White Justice* (1990), discussed by M. Fitzgerald, *Ethnic Minorities and the Criminal Justice System*, RCCJ Research Study 20 (1993), 21 and 45.
[86] R. Hood, *Race and Sentencing* (1992).

There is insufficient information on whether magistrates are more likely to commit Afro-Caribbeans to the Crown Court, but the probability that more Afro-Caribbeans choose the Crown Court suggests that abolition of the defendant's right of election might amount to indirect discrimination, and would certainly be so perceived. It would, to put matters crudely, result in many Afro-Caribbeans being tried unwillingly in courts in which the decision-makers are predominantly white and middle class. It may be fair to assume that the proportion of magistrates' courts sitting with one member from an ethnic minority is lower than the 35 per cent of juries that contain at least one member of an ethnic minority,[87] and this may contribute to the greater faith of non-white defendants in trial by jury.

7. Reforming the System for Determining Mode of Trial

It is apparent that the question of mode of trial raises acute conflicts between policy and principle. The fundamental argument of policy is an economic and managerial one, that the country cannot afford to pay for the continuing expansion of Crown Court trial. That must be a matter of political judgement, and one on which opinions may differ. However, there is some political wisdom in accepting that as an inevitable starting-point and then discussing what can be done about it.

The approach discussed so far in this chapter has been to reduce the number of cases committed to the Crown Court, and three ways of achieving this have been discussed. The first, reclassifying some offences to 'summary only' and retaining the existing system otherwise, is a relatively blunt instrument; but it would be likely to achieve the policy objective if it took away from the Crown Court many small-value property offences. The second is the 'plea before venue' system introduced by the 1996 Act, which encourages defendants who intend to plead guilty to declare that intention in the magistrates' court, with the possibility that the magistrates will then assume jurisdiction and pass sentence, although they also have power to commit for sentence to the Crown Court. The third, abolishing the defendant's right of election (along the lines proposed by the Royal Commission), seems rather less likely to achieve the policy objective unless accompanied by new guidelines and new attitudes in the magistrates' courts and, perhaps, in the Crown Prosecution Service. The first and third ways of reducing committals seem to emphasize

---

[87] The latter figure comes from Zander and Henderson, above n. 16, 241.

the seriousness of the offence, whether intrinsically or in its consequences for the defendant, and pay little attention to the complexity of the case as a reason for Crown Court trial.

Whichever approach is adopted, many similar issues arise. Neither Parliament nor the Royal Commission has paid sufficient attention to them. One is the quality of magistrates' justice, about which defendants and solicitors have generally been quite disparaging in the last twenty years. There is a widespread feeling that summary justice is too summary, and that magistrates' courts give insufficient opportunity for a full examination of the case.[88] Any policy of reducing the case-load of the Crown Court must be accompanied by renewed efforts to improve the quality, or at least the appearance of quality, in magistrates' justice. It is a significant reproach of the Royal Commission that it failed to grasp this issue, which is becoming ever more important as magistrates' courts are subjected to fresh scrutiny and new managerial regimes. Of course we cannot tell, because of lack of information, whether the disparity in acquittal rates between the two levels of court derives from the gullibility of juries, a bias in magistrates' courts towards the prosecution, or some other influence. But there may be implications for the presumption of innocence if one effect of any reform is to relegate some defendants to a form of justice that inclines unfairly in favour of conviction.

These implications become doubly serious if it is found that ethnic minority defendants have greater faith in Crown Court trial, not only because of its greater thoroughness but also because of the greater likelihood of finding a member of an ethnic minority on a jury than on a bench of magistrates. This line of reasoning militates in favour of reclassification as the avenue of reform, since at least that is neutral in relation to class, ethnic origin, and other factors. Reclassifying property offences according to monetary value is likely to give rise to cries of arbitrariness—e.g. jury trial if £100 is stolen but summary trial if it is merely £99—but it is fair to say that these have not inhibited the use of monetary limits for criminal damage since 1977.

At present, however, this and other means of reducing the numbers of cases going to the Crown Court have been set aside while the new 'plea before venue' system, introduced in October 1997, is evaluated. From the Government's point of view, the question is whether significant cost savings are produced, and this will turn largely on the number of cases committed to the Crown Court for sentence. From the CPS's point of view, the question is whether it will feel it necessary to alter its charging practices (e.g. by charging

---

[88] It is noteworthy that the Justices' Clerks Society (in its evidence to the 1993 Royal Commission) pressed the argument for allocating cases according to the complexity of the issues rather than purely the seriousness of the case, which suggests a lack of confidence in lay magistrates as a tribunal for dealing with many of the cases that might otherwise come before them.

more indictable-only offences), especially if it finds magistrates passing sentence in some cases which it regards as more appropriate for the Crown Court. From the point of view of defendants, however, there are serious issues about the pressure to enter a plea at an early stage,[89] before proper information on and consideration of the prosecution case, and about the approaches taken by magistrates, whether in passing sentence themselves or in committing to the Crown Court.

All three ways of reducing the number of Crown Court trials assume, however, that the English system should continue with its existing forms of trial, by magistrates and by jury. A strong argument has been advanced by Sean Doran and John Jackson for a third form of trial, notably trial by judge alone.[90] Drawing on their own research into judge-only trials in Northern Ireland and their proposals for improving that system,[91] they show that many other common law systems have introduced the possibility of 'jury waiver', whereby a defendant may opt for trial by judge alone. Whether this would prove attractive to administrators and the Government might be expected to depend on cost calculations. But in principle there are good reasons for introducing this possibility; and, as argued in the next chapter, it might be developed into a model that gives judges more control over cases generally and allows some form of judicial scrutiny of guilty pleas. However, one significant side-effect of the 'plea before venue' system is that fewer guilty plea cases will come before the Crown Court, which turns attention once again to procedures in the magistrates' courts.

---

[89] The Court of Appeal has confirmed that the maximum sentence discount is reserved for those who indicate a guilty plea at the 'plea before venue' stage: *Rafferty, The Times*, April 9, 1998.

[90] S. Doran and J. Jackson, 'The Case for Jury Waiver' [1997] *Crim. LR* 155.

[91] J. Jackson and S. Doran, *Judge without Jury* (1995).

9   Plea

ONE of the key decisions for people who are prosecuted is how to plead. With the exception of special pleas such as *autrefois convict* and *autrefois acquit* in cases where the defendant pleads that he or she has previously been tried for the offence,[1] and the rare plea of not guilty by reason of insanity, defendants have a choice of two: guilty or not guilty. We have seen from the previous chapter that decisions on plea may influence decisions on mode of trial, in so far as most of those wishing to plead not guilty to either-way offences tend to elect Crown Court trial, whereas under the Criminal Procedure and Investigations Act 1996 the 'plea before venue' system ensures that those who indicate an intention to plead guilty are dealt with in the magistrates' courts (subject to the possibility of committal to the Crown Court for sentence). What effect the 'plea before venue' system will have upon the dynamics and the numbers of decisions to plead guilty remains to be seen, but it adds further pressures to those already prominent in English criminal justice.

If the defendant pleads not guilty, the case goes to trial. If the defendant pleads guilty, there is no trial. Instead, the prosecution gives a statement of facts in court and, unless the defence disputes this statement to an extent that requires some form of hearing to resolve the matter,[2] the judge or magistrates will proceed to sentence the defendant. The European Convention on Human Rights declares that 'everyone is entitled to a fair and public hearing', that 'everyone charged with a criminal offence shall be presumed innocent until proven guilty according to law', and that everyone shall have the right 'to examine or have examined witnesses against him'.[3] In some countries these rights are thought so fundamental that they cannot be waived: the unavailability of the guilty plea is regarded as a guarantee of defendants' rights.[4] In France, for example, there is no such thing as a plea of guilty: the court must

---

[1] For discussion, A. Choo, *Abuse of Process and Judicial Stays of Criminal Proceedings* (1993), ch. 2.

[2] See the leading case of *Newton* (1982) 4 Cr.App.R(S) 388, and the discussioin by A. Ashworth, *Sentencing and Criminal Justice* (1992), 281–4.

[3] See Ch.2.4 above.

[4] M. Damaska, 'Evidentiary Barriers to Conviction and Two Models of Criminal Procedure: A Comparative Study' (1973) 121 *U. Pa. LR* 506.

examine the dossier to ensure that there is sufficient evidence of guilt. That rigid approach was called into question by the Delmas-Marty Commission,[5] and it seems possible that some matters may in future be dealt with on a guilty plea. In the Netherlands there seems to be an increasing gap between legal theory and legal practice: the theory is still that the ascertainment of guilt is for public officials to accomplish, not for defendants to concede, and the court must review and check the dossier; in practice there are various possibilities of bargaining, and more summary procedures for those who do not contest their guilt.[6] In Germany there is no guilty plea, but there are forms of 'plea bargain' in which a defendant may confess to the judge in order to gain a reduction in the sentence.[7] In England and Wales there is not even the appearance of a review by the court, although in Crown Court cases the judge may read the papers quickly before dealing with a case on a guilty plea. In essence, the guilty plea constitutes a waiver by the defendant of the right to be tried.

This chapter begins with an inquiry into the percentage of defendants who plead guilty. It then considers some of the principal reasons for changes of plea, looking at charge bargains (where the defendant agrees to plead guilty in exchange for the prosecution reducing the level of the charge or the number of charges), at fact bargains (where the defendant agrees to plead guilty only on the basis that the prosecution will put forward a particular version of the facts), and at plea negotiation (where the change of plea is motivated by considerations of sentence). Various proposals for reform are then evaluated in the light of defendants' rights and the supposed advantages to the system.

1. The Rate of Guilty Pleas

In the magistrates' courts the rate of guilty pleas is well over 90 per cent. Most of these are relatively minor matters, three-quarters being summary offences that almost always end in a fine. A contested trial in a magistrates' court is therefore fairly rare: even among either-way offences heard in magistrates'

---

[5] Commission Justice Pénale et Droits de l'Homme, *La Mise en État des affaires pénales* (1991), 10.

[6] See the discussion by N. Jorg, S. Field, and C. Brants, 'Are Inquisitorial and Adversarial Systems Converging?', in C. Harding *et al.*, *Criminal Justice in Europe* (1995), esp. 47–51.

[7] J. Herrmann, 'Bargaining Justice: A Bargain for German Criminal Justice?' (1992) 53 *U. Pittsburgh LR* 755; L. Leigh and L. Zedner, *A Report on the Administration of Criminal Justice in the Pre-trial Phase in France and Germany*, RCCJ Research Study 1 (1992), 43. H. Jung, 'Plea-Bargaining and its Repercussions on the Theory of Criminal Procedure', (1997) 5 *Eur. J. of Crime, Criminal Law and Criminal Justice* 112.

courts the rate of guilty pleas appears to be around 90 per cent.[8] We saw in the preceding chapter that the acquittal rate in the early 1980s was 30 per cent in magistrates' courts compared with 57 per cent in the Crown Court.[9]

In the Crown Court the rate of guilty pleas stood at 65 per cent in 1996. For several years the statistics have constantly shown a distinct difference in guilty plea rates from circuit to circuit, and this remains evident in the 1996 statistics. Thus the North Eastern circuit has a guilty plea rate of 77 per cent, whereas in the London courts the figure is 49 per cent. No clear explanation for these divergences has been found. The acquittal rate of those who plead not guilty seems to be roughly the same among the various circuits, around 55–60 per cent However, that is a percentage of a much larger number in London than in the North East, and it must not be thought that this is a jury acquittal rate. In 1996 some 47 per cent of acquittals were ordered by the judge and 17 per cent were directed by the judge, so that jury acquittals accounted for just over one-third (36 per cent) of the total.[10] As for regional differences, the cultures of some provincial Bars could be different from that in London: if there are fewer barristers, they may be expected to know one another and to know the limited pool of judges rather well, and may therefore be able to give much more confident predictions of the outcome to their clients.

Why do so many defendants plead guilty and forgo their right to be tried? Some years ago Bottoms and McClean conducted interviews with over 200 defendants who pleaded guilty either at a magistrates' court or at the Crown Court. When they asked why the defendant pleaded guilty, about two-thirds answered that it was because they were guilty. Indeed, some 70 per cent of these admitted to the police from the beginning that they were guilty.[11] The circumstances in which some of the remainder pleaded guilty will be discussed later, but the important point here is that a majority of those who plead guilty accept their guilt without demur.

What about those who change their plea? There is little information about plea-changers in the magistrates' courts,[12] but for the Crown Court there are statistics on what are termed 'cracked trials'. A cracked trial is one that is listed as a not guilty plea, with court time set aside for a contested trial, and in which the defendant changes to a guilty plea after the case has been listed, i.e. at a fairly late stage. Some trials 'crack' on the day of the hearing, others a day or two before. Cracked trials cause considerable concern to administrators, since

---

[8] D. Riley and J. Vennard, *Triable-Either-Way Cases: Crown Court or Magistrates' Court?* HORS 98 (1988), 6.

[9] J. Vennard, 'The Outcome of Contested Trials', in D. Moxon (ed.), *Managing Criminal Justice* (1985).

[10] All the figures are taken from the *Judicial Statistics 1996*, ch. 6.

[11] A. E. Bottoms and J. D. McClean, *Defendants in the Criminal Process* (1976), 115.

[12] J. Baldwin, *Pre-Trial Justice* (1986), 92–7.

they cause listing difficulties (even though there are usually one or two other trials waiting to come on) and consequently they may cause a wastage of scarce resources, namely court time, judicial time, and public money. They also cause unnecessary inconvenience and even anxiety to victims and other witnesses who are brought to court on what turns out to be a fruitless journey. The scale of the problem was evident from the findings of the Crown Court survey in the early 1990s: of the 65 per cent of cases that were guilty pleas, only 39 per cent were originally listed as guilty pleas and the remaining 26 per cent were made up of 'cracked trials' which were originally listed as not guilty pleas.[13] Some 31 per cent were listed as not guilty pleas and did go to trial, which confirms that the rate of 'cracking' of cases that begin as not guilty pleas is little short of one-half (i.e. 26 per cent compared with 31 per cent). That was a national figure, however, and other research suggests that it masked considerable variations between regions.[14] Statistics for 1996 show that the proportion of Crown Court trials that 'cracked' is declining, if rather slowly: of the 65 per cent of cases that were guilty pleas, about a third (just under 20 per cent of the total) stemmed from 'cracked trials'.[15] No doubt the figures for 1998 will be much different, if the new system of 'plea before venue' achieves its objectives. However, there is still good reason to enquire: why do so many defendants who apparently start out with the intention of contesting their guilt subsequently change their minds and admit it?

2. Pleading Not Guilty

We have seen that a small minority of defendants in magistrates' courts plead not guilty throughout, but that in the Crown Courts it is around 35 per cent who exercise their right to be tried. More do so in London, fewer in the North-East. Why do they persist in their pleas of not guilty, whilst others change their pleas? Once again, the most obvious answer is that they maintain that they are not guilty. It seems that around 60 per cent of defences involve a denial of the basic facts:[16] around one in six of these are alibi defences, and perhaps one-quarter are claims of mistaken identification.[17] The other 40 per cent of defences accept the basic facts but contest guilt on the basis of justification or

---

[13] M. Zander and P. Henderson, *Crown Court Study*, RCCJ Research Study 19 (1993), 95–6; the study probably under-recorded the numbers originally listed as guilty pleas, since the national average rate of guilty pleas was around 70 rather than 65%—see *ibid.* 248.

[14] P. Robertshaw, ' "Cracked Trials": What is Happening?' [1992] *Crim. LR* 867; to similar effect, the Seabrook report.   [15] *Judicial Statistics 1996*, Tables 6.7 and 6.8.

[16] Zander and Henderson, above n. 13, 121.   [17] *Ibid.* 75 and 92.

lack of culpability. Some three-quarters of these seem to amount to a denial of *mens rea*, and almost all the remaining one-quarter claim self-defence.

Just as it seems likely that some people who are innocent eventually plead guilty, so it also seems likely that some who are guilty plead not guilty. They may do so for a variety of personal reasons, ranging from over-confidence to shame at the offence and an unwillingness to admit it publicly in any circumstances (e.g. with serious sexual offences). It is possible, though, that some defendants are alive to the possibility that they have a chance of gaining an acquittal if prosecution witnesses fail to attend court to give evidence. It is recognized that some defendants who change their pleas to guilty on the day of the trial do so because they see that the prosecution witnesses are at the court. Presumably there are others who, seeing that the prosecution witnesses have not arrived, persist in their plea of not guilty, with the result that the case collapses. While no study has identified the numbers involved, it seems entirely plausible that some defendants do benefit from windfalls of this kind.[18] To what extent such practices will alter as a result of the 'plea before venue' system for either-way offences is hard to gauge, but one effect is to place considerable pressure on people to indicate a guilty plea at an early stage, so as to obtain the maximum sentence discount.

3. Charge Bargains

The term 'charge bargaining' is used here to encompass two distinct kinds of case. The first is where a defendant faces two or more charges and signifies an intention to plead not guilty to them. It is then possible for the prosecution to drop one or more of the others, in return for a plea of guilty to one charge. Either the prosecution or the defence may suggest this way of resolving the matter. Many of these are cases where several distinct offences are alleged, but some will be cases in which the prosecution has charged a person with both theft and handling stolen goods in the expectation that there would be a conviction of only one offence. The second kind of case is where the defendant faces a serious charge and signifies an intention to plead not guilty to it. It may be possible for the prosecution to drop the serious charge in exchange for a plea of guilty to a less serious charge. Much depends on the criminal law. At some points the law seems to be ready-made for this kind of charge bargain: for example, a defendant might intend to plead not guilty to grievous bodily harm with intent, contrary to section 18 of the Offences Against the Person Act 1861, but might be willing to plead guilty to the lesser offence of grievous

---

[18] Cf. the reasons for prosecution decisions to discontinue cases and for directed acquittals, in Ch. 6.2, above.

bodily harm contrary to section 20 of the same Act. The same applies if the original charge is under section 20, and the defendant is willing to plead to the lesser offence under section 47. It is not unknown for defendants charged with murder to offer a plea of guilty to manslaughter: this is often done in cases of diminished responsibility, but may also be done on other grounds. With other serious offences such as rape and robbery the law itself does not provide an apparent lesser alternative, but there might be circumstances in which rape is reduced to indecent assault or robbery to theft. The Code for Crown Prosecutors formerly cited as a common example 'burglary reducing to theft by virtue of a denial of the element of trespass'.[19]

In what proportion of cases do charge bargains of these kinds take place? Most of the research focuses on the Crown Court, but charge bargains are by no means uncommon in magistrates' courts. Thus both Baldwin[20] and Mulcahy[21] found plenty of evidence of charges being reduced in number or in seriousness, followed by a change of plea to guilty. Such practices may be the result of a pre-trial review, whereby the defence lawyer discovers the likely strength of the prosecution case; or they may emerge by the usual processes of interaction between prosecution and defence lawyers, either around the court or even by telephone contact. Mulcahy's interviews with a small number of defence and prosecution lawyers working in magistrates' courts led to the conclusion that trial-avoidance is thought desirable on both sides: if this is a fair representation of the general working culture,[22] to which there may be a few exceptions, then it is likely that there will be considerable pressure on defendants in magistrates' courts to plead guilty.

Turning to the Crown Court, as many as seventy-seven of the 112 defendants in McCabe and Purves's sample who changed their plea at a late stage pleaded guilty to only part of the original indictment,[23] whereas in Baldwin and McConville's sample it was only eleven out of 121 late guilty pleaders[24] and in Bottoms and McClean's sample only three out of sixty-eight.[25] Most of the recent research on cracked trials does not provide details of the nature of any negotiation that took place, but some 51 per cent of those in Hedderman and Moxon's sample who changed their plea stated that they did so in the

---

[19] Crown Prosecution Service, *Code for Crown Prosecutors* (1992 edn.), para. 11. Most of the references in this Ch. will be to the 1992 version, since one of the consequences of putting the latest (1994) version into 'ordinary English' is that many informative policy statements have been removed from public view.   [20] J. Baldwin, *Pre-Trial Justice* (1986).

[21] A. Mulcahy, 'The Justifications of "Justice": Legal Practitioners' Accounts of Negotiated Case Settlements in Magistrates' Courts' (1994) 34 *BJ Crim.* 411.

[22] See also M. McConville *et al.*, *Standing Accused* (1994), 194–8 and M. Travers, *The Reality of Law* (1997) ch. 5, on defence solicitors.

[23] S. McCabe and R. Purves, *By-Passing the Jury* (1972).

[24] J. Baldwin and M. McConville, *Negotiated Justice* (1977), ch. 2.

[25] Bottoms and McClean, above n. 11, 126–7.

expectation that some charges would be dropped or reduced, resulting in a lighter sentence.[26] It may therefore be assumed that one or other form of charge bargain is a fairly frequent phenomenon.

What are the advantages and disadvantages for the prosecution? The chief benefit is that they are assured of at least one conviction, and do not have to risk the hazards of trial, more particularly in the Crown Court with an over-all acquittal rate of around 57 per cent. In view of the possibility that witnesses may fail to turn up or may alter their story, or that the jury will be swayed by some non-legal factor, it is tempting for the prosecution to settle for a certain conviction. The disadvantage is that the resulting conviction may not give a proper reflection of the gravity of the offending behaviour. In principle this is to be avoided, although the 1992 version of the Code for Crown Prosecutors did not recommend this approach in undiluted form:

> The overriding consideration will be to ensure that the court is never left in the position of being unable to pass a proper sentence consistent with the gravity of the defendant's actions . . . Administrative convenience in the form of a rapid guilty plea should not take precedence over the interests of justice, but where the court is able to deal adequately with an offender on the basis of a plea which represents a criminal involvement not inconsistent with the alleged facts, the resource advantages both to the Service and to the courts generally will be an important consideration.[27]

Shorn of its double negatives, this seems to suggest that it is proper to accept a plea of guilty to a lesser offence if the maximum sentence for that offence is not too low compared with the seriousness of what the defendant did. Thus, for example, if in the Crown Court a defendant enters a plea of not guilty to a charge of causing grievous bodily harm with intent (which carries a maximum sentence of life imprisonment), and the defendant then offers to plead guilty to the lesser offence of inflicting grievous bodily harm (which carries a maximum sentence of five years' imprisonment), the prosecutor should reflect on whether the five-year maximum is appropriate for what was done. In practice, courts hardly ever pass sentences approaching five years for this offence, and sentences longer than three years are rare.[28] Assuming that the prosecutor believes that there are reasonable prospects of establishing that the grievous bodily harm was caused with intent—and that belief should be held, otherwise the charge ought to be reduced without any question of bargain-ing—he or she must decide whether a sentence in the three- to four-year

---

[26] C. Hedderman and D. Moxon, *Magistrates' Court or Crown Court?*, HORS 125 (1992), 24.

[27] Code for Crown Prosecutors, para. 11.

[28] Cf. *McLoughlin* (1985) 7 Cr.App.R(S) 67 (three years too long when plea of guilty to s. 20, not s. 18), with *Moore* (1991) 13 Cr.App.R(S) 130 (three years upheld, fortunate not to have been charged with s. 18 offence).

range would be adequate. It might be argued that, since many sentences for the more serious offence of causing grievous bodily harm with intent are in the three- to four-year range too, the only effect of accepting the plea may be that a less serious conviction is entered on the offender's criminal record. However, the Court of Appeal has stated that a sentencer must have regard to the fact that the plea of guilty is only to the lesser offence and must not sentence on a different basis.[29] In so far as this is true, and a plea to a lesser offence invariably leads to a lesser sentence, this should mean that many offenders receive a sentence lower than they would have done if the prosecution had proved the higher offence at trial. In addition to this, of course, the defendant would receive a sentence discount for pleading guilty, which would not have been granted on conviction after a trial. Similar plea negotiations might take place in a magistrates' court at the lower level of a section 20 charge (unlawful wounding) being reduced to a section 47 charge (actual bodily harm). The prosecution might argue that some offenders are therefore sentenced less severely than they deserve, whereas others might question whether the original charge was not too high or, at least, optimistic and designed to facilitate later negotiation.

What are the advantages and disadvantages from the defendant's point of view? These depend on whether the defendant has committed an offence and, if so, what offence(s). It is easy to say that, if the defendant has really committed the higher offence, a plea of guilty to a lesser offence brings a benefit to the defendant in terms of a lower sentence. What is more debatable is the kind of case in which the defendant may be said to have been overcharged in order to put pressure on him or her to plead guilty to the lesser charge. Research has not focused on the extent to which such cases occur: prosecutors tend to deny that they do, whereas defendants and lawyers acting for the defence are confident that this does happen from time to time. Overcharging is contrary to the Code for Crown Prosecutors,[30] as one might expect of an official document, but whether supervision within the Crown Prosecution Service is sufficiently active to ensure that such cases are rare aberrations is hard to assess. One could certainly see that it might operate to the defendant's disadvantage in certain cases where an injury is caused that fulfils the definition of a wound. If the prosecution charge the defendant with wounding with intent, the defence might succeed in having it reduced to unlawful wounding. But if the original charge was unlawful wounding, the defence in the magistrates' court might succeed in having it reduced to assault occasioning actual bodily harm. The starting-point may therefore matter.

The position is even worse for the defendant who maintains innocence of all charges. A massive institutional temptation is held out, stemming from

---

[29] e.g. *McLoughlin* (1985) 7 Cr.App.R(S) 67; *Stewart* (1990) 12 Cr.App.R(S) 15.
[30] *Code for Crown Prosecutors* (3rd edn., 1994), para. 7.2.

three sources—pleading guilty to a lesser charge should result in a lower sentence for the lesser offence, plus a further discount for pleading guilty, and if the defendant indicates a guilty plea when brought before the magistrates on an either-way charge the early plea may result in the magistrates passing sentence or at least committing the case to the Crown Court for sentence with a full discount. Thus if counsel's advice is that pleading guilty to a lesser charge is likely to result in a non-custodial sentence whereas conviction after a trial might result in custodial sentence, a defendant may succumb to the pressure to forgo a perfectly reasonable defence. The dependence of the defendant on his or her legal representatives is considerable, and this brings issues of professional ethics to the fore.

4. Fact Bargains

Relatively little attention has been devoted to this class of case, which may be said to lie half-way between charge bargains and the straightforward plea bargains to be discussed in the next section. There is, however, evidence that in some cases there has been an agreement by the defendant to change the plea to guilty on the faith of a promise by the prosecution to state the facts of the case in a particular way. An agreement not to mention a particular aggravating feature, for example, or not to mention the part played by another (such as a friend or spouse) may be sufficient to persuade the defendant to plead guilty. Again, the principal advantage for the prosecution is that it secures a conviction in the case, even though the 'public interest' may be said to lose because the sentence is based on facts less serious than those that actually occurred. There is also the discount for pleading guilty, which will lower the sentence further. The defendant, on the other hand, stands to benefit from these sentence reductions—although it can only be counted as a benefit if he or she is actually guilty of a more serious version of the offence than that put to the court.

The 1992 Code for Crown Prosecutors dealt not with this type of case but with the opposite situation, stating that 'having accepted a plea, the Crown Prosecutor must not then open the case on the basis that what the defendant actually did was something more serious than appears in the charge'.[31] Though formally unregulated, the practice of stating the facts more favourably to the accused can have implications for victims. In the Victim's Charter it is stated that prosecutors 'must be ready to intervene to correct any

---

[31] Code for Crown Prosecutors, para. 11.

misleading speech in mitigation, particularly where attempts are made to denigrate the character of the victim'.[32] However, in one widely publicized 1993 case this plainly did not happen. The complainant in a rape case discovered that, although the offender had pleaded guilty, he pleaded guilty only on the basis that she consented to intercourse when it began and subsequently changed her mind. On inquiring how this version of facts was put forward, she learnt that this was the basis on which the plea of guilty was negotiated—in effect, to a version of the offence which was much less serious, and which in her view was a travesty of the true facts. Presumably the prosecution was concerned to avoid a trial, perhaps because of a belief that the victim would not attend court to give evidence or might not be a convincing witness, or possibly in order to spare the victim the distress of having to give evidence.

It might be added that, where there is a dispute about the factual basis of a guilty plea, there is provision for the judge to hold a post-conviction hearing to determine the issue. Known as *Newton* hearings,[33] these involve the hearing of evidence from both sides, in general applying the same rules of evidence as would apply at trial. The judge then determines the issue, and this becomes the basis for sentence. It might therefore be possible for a defendant who is not offered a fact bargain by the prosecution to plead guilty with a view to contesting the prosecutor's version of the facts in a *Newton* hearing. This, of course, is more hazardous than relying on the prosecutor to present the facts favourably in the first place.

5. Plea Bargains

One of the main reasons for dealing first with charge bargains and fact bargains is that it leaves for separate consideration those cases in which the defendant intends to plead not guilty to the charge and then, at a late stage, alters the plea to guilty. These are cases where there is no question of reducing the number or level of the charges, and no bargain about the factual basis on which the case will be put forward. The essence seems to be that the defendant trades a chance of acquittal for a lower sentence than would have been received in the event of a conviction. There are four major sources of incentive for the defendant to plead guilty: the sentence discount, the 'plea before venue' system, Plea and Directions hearings, and lawyer's advice. Each of

---

[32] Home Office, *Victim's Charter* (1990), 17–18: the whole thrust of those paragraphs is that the defence may seek to minimize the defendant's role. Cf. now Crown Prosecution Service, Statement on the Treatment of Victims and Witnesses (1993).

[33] The leading case is *Newton* (1982) 4 Cr.App.R(S) 388.

these must be examined in turn, but together they amount to formidable pressure. Most of the discussion here relates to the Crown Court, but the recent emphasis on granting the 'guilty plea discount' in magistrates' courts suggests that plea bargains, as well as charge bargains, may also be significant there.

1. *The sentence discount:* the Royal Commission on Criminal Justice recommended that the graduated sentence discount for pleading guilty should be clearly stated.[34] Section 48 of the Criminal Justice and Public Order Act 1994 now does so, although in rather circumlocutory terms which necessitate reference to the case law:

(1) In determining what sentence to pass on an offender who has pleaded guilty to an offence before that or another court a court shall take into account:
(a) the stage in the proceedings for the offence at which the offender indicated his intention to plead guilty; and
(b) the circumstances in which this indication was given.

(2) If as a result of taking into account any matter referred to in subsection (1) above the court imposes a punishment on the offender which is less severe than it would otherwise have done, it shall state in open court that it has done so.[35]

The section avoids stating the amount of the discount, which judicial precedents set at up to one-third;[36] and it avoids stating the principle that an earlier plea attracts a greater discount, although this is well established.[37] Its circumspect wording does leave open the possibility that exceptions to the principle may be made, and there are some recent authorities suggesting that no discount, or only a small discount, need be given where the offender was caught 'red-handed', and therefore had no option but to plead guilty.[38] However, the section does make it clear that it applies to all courts (including magistrates' courts) and to all forms of sentence (including fines and community sentences). Evidence shows that the overall differences in the Crown Court are considerable: thus in 1996 some 72 per cent of adult males pleading not guilty who were convicted received custodial sentences, compared with 61 per cent of those pleading guilty, and the average lengths of custodial sentences were thirty-six months and twenty-one months respectively.[39] This is an even wider differential than Roger Hood found in his sample of 3,000

---

[34] Royal Commission on Criminal Justice (1993), paras. 7.45 to 7.47.

[35] The section now has a third sub-section, added by the Crime (Sentences) Act 1997, which is omitted here.

[36] *Buffrey* (1993) 14 Cr.App.R(S) 511.

[37] For discussion of the case law, see A. Ashworth, *Sentencing and Criminal Justice* (2nd edn., 1995), 136–40.

[38] Compare *Landy* (1995) 16 Cr.App.R.(S) 908 with *Fearon* [1996] 2 Cr.App.R.(S) 25.

[39] From *Criminal Statistics England and Wales 1996*, 158–9.

Crown Court cases, but it is important to note that the 1996 figures are gross figures which take no account of previous convictions or mitigating factors. When Hood took account of the usual variables in analysing his data, a difference of ten months was reduced to one of three months.[40] However, the 1996 figures are intriguing in other ways, since they show that for some offences the average sentence on a plea of guilty was *higher* than on conviction after a trial.

What may be the explanation for the higher sentences for those who plead guilty to causing death by dangerous driving and for indecent assaults, and the small difference for 'other woundings'? The commentary in the *Criminal Statistics* suggests that some of the guilty pleas might be late pleas, or the offences may be more serious, or the offenders may have more previous convictions than those who go to trial. Those are all possible factors, and Hood's findings (above) show that if all factors are taken into account the differences tend to diminish. The commentary adds that 'it is likely that for some offences, such as other woundings and indecent assault on a female, those pleading guilty may originally have been charged with more serious offences (wounding or rape in these examples) and are, therefore, at the more serious end of the offences within the class shown'.[41] This is plausible, and could also account for the figures for indecent assault on a male (an offence that could be reduced from rape or buggery). But a different explanation is required for the startling figures for causing death by dangerous driving. Perhaps it is that those who plead guilty are persuaded that there is really no point in contesting the case because the offence was such a bad one, whereas those who do contest it are those whose offence is at the lower end of the scale, just above the boundary between dangerous and careless driving.

The result of this discussion is that there is both statutory authority for, and broad empirical confirmation of, a significant discount for pleading guilty. In so far as the discount is known to defendants or is brought to their attention by lawyers, it is likely to exert a considerable pressure towards pleading guilty. That, of course, is the purpose of the relevant law. It was formerly thought that the sentence discount did not apply in magistrates' courts, but section 48 makes the position clear and each page of the Magistrates' Association's *Sentencing Guidelines* now reminds benches that a timely plea should result in a sentence reduction.

2. *Plea before venue:* a second standing incentive to plead guilty stems from the 'plea before venue' system described in Chapter 8 above. It should be recalled that this only applies to those charged with triable-either-way

---

[40] R. Hood, *Race and Sentencing* (1992), 125.
[41] *Criminal Statistics England and Wales 1996*, 159.

Table 9.1 Males aged 21 and over sentenced for indictable offences at the Crown Court: plea rates and custodial sentencing for selected offences

England and Wales 1996

Offence[1]	Pleaded guilty (%)	Custody rate (%)		Average sentence length (months)	
		Guilty	Not guilty	Guilty	Not guilty
Violence against the person					
Causing death by reckless driving	57	73	81	35.9	29.1
Wounding or other act endangering life	57	84	94	42.9	54.4
Threat or conspiracy to murder	74	57	70	26.4	(33.4)
Other wounding, etc.	78	52	60	14.3	15.1
All	73	58	73	21.9	32.5
Sexual offences					
Rape	39	95	98	74.7	83.8
Indecent assault on a female	67	64	83	25.3	23.7
Indecent assault on a male	72	68	84	30.5	29.1
All	64	69	88	33.7	46.2
Burglary					
In a building other than a dwelling	87	67	64	16.6	21.3
In a dwelling	91	80	83	21.1	26.8
All	91	77	78	20.4	25.6
Theft and handling stolen goods					
Other theft or unauthorised taking	80	56	55	11.4	17.4
Handling stolen goods	81	45	55	12.6	15.0
Theft from the person of another	82	51	54	11.9	15.0
Theft by an employee	85	58	54	11.5	(12.4)
Theft from shops	85	40	31	8.9	(7.4)
All	83	51	53	12.0	15.0
Fraud					
Other forgery	81	52	71	12.7	18.0
Other fraud	83	54	65	15.4	22.6
All	83	53	65	15.1	21.5
Criminal damage					
Arson	85	66	92	32.4	42.1
All	87	45	70	28.4	39.1
Drug offences					
Trafficking	83	71	90	27.2	54.7
Possession	93	23	35	11.3	(21.2)
All	84	63	86	27.0	52.3

(1) Only those offences where at least 100 pleaded guilty or not guilty are shown separately.
() Based on less than 50 cases.

offences, who may have been committed by magistrates to the Crown Court for trial or may have elected themselves. It is estimated that the total numbers of either-way cases committed in recent years is around 60,000 out of the total of 80,000 (the others being indictable-only offences, to which the 'plea before venue' system does not apply). Of those 60,000 perhaps 18,000 may be expected to plead guilty, leaving around 40,000 cases on which the 'plea before venue' system may bite. As we saw in Chapter 8, the defendant is put to a decision at an early stage before magistrates, and that is the time (presumably) at which the maximum sentence discount for pleading guilty is available.[42] The purpose of the system is to avoid late changes of plea and to have more cases dealt with cheaply in the magistrates' courts. But one effect may be increase the pressure on defendants to plead guilty.

3. *Pre-trial hearings:* since the early 1980s some magistrates' courts have held pre-trial reviews of contested cases, with a view to facilitating an exchange of information between prosecution and defence, identifying issues so as to save time and perhaps bring about pleas of guilty.[43] Following the spread of advance disclosure in the late 1980s some courts ceased to hold pre-trial reviews, but others have persisted with them in the 1990s. It seems that they may have modest advantages in cost-benefit terms: Brownlee, Mulcahy, and Walker found that they had little overall effect on the speed of case disposition, and resulted in relatively few changes of plea to guilty, but they still argue that there were overall cost-savings because the reviews were relatively inexpensive.[44] There is no legal framework for pre-trial reviews, the form of which varies according to the locality, and it is not known how many court areas still hold them. Turning to the Crown Court, one of the Royal Commission's recommendations was that there should be some kind of hearing before the trial at which counsel is asked about the defendant's plea, in the hope of eliciting earlier guilty pleas (especially those so late as to result in a 'cracked trial'). Although the full set of Royal Commissions proposals on this was not accepted, Plea and Directions hearings are now a feature of Crown Court procedure.[45] They are meant to take the defendant's plea, and if the plea is guilty the judge should proceed to sentencing wherever possible. Where the defendant indicates a not guilty plea, prosecution and defence are expected to assist the judge in identifying the key issues in the case, and to provide any other information relevant to the proper listing of the case. In all cases counsel for the defence is required to complete a 'Judge's Questionnaire' about the case, and it should be noted that question 1(b) asks counsel whether the

---

[42] See now *Rafferty, The Times,* 9 April 1998.

[43] See Baldwin, above n. 20.

[44] I. Brownlee, A. Mulcahy, and C.P. Walker, 'Pre-Trial Reviews, Court Efficiency and Justice: A Study in Leeds and Bradford Magistrates' Courts' (1994) 33 *Howard JCJ* 109.

[45] *Practice Direction: Plea and Directions Hearings* [1995] 1 WLR 1318.

defendant's attention has been drawn to section 48 of the Criminal Justice and Public Order Act 1994 (set out above). Thus those who maintain a plea of not guilty are made well aware of the law's considerable incentives to change their plea. This point is taken up in the next paragraph.

4. *The Turner rules:* the strong impression of one researcher into pre-trial practice in the Crown Court was that the identity and sentencing reputation of the judge or recorder are key factors in decisions on plea.[46] It therefore follows that, where the sentencer's reputation is not known, defence counsel may wish to discover the judge's preliminary view about the likely sentence. In the leading decision of *Turner* (1970),[47] the Court of Appeal laid down various rules to govern the conduct of judges and counsel in these matters. The first rule is that defence counsel should be free to give advice to the defendant, if necessary in strong terms, about the best approach. The second is that defendants should have freedom of choice, having heard the advice. The third is that defence counsel should be able to see the judge, and vice versa, on matters relating to trial and sentence, but that this should only be done when really necessary. And fourthly, the judge should never indicate the likely sentence, except to say that the sentence will take the same form whether the defendant pleads guilty or is convicted.

The warning by Lord Parker CJ in *Turner* that visits by counsel to the judge's private room should be kept to a minimum has not been heeded. There is a long series of Court of Appeal decisions quashing convictions for breaches of the rules. Twice in 1990 the Court of Appeal lamented the frequency of such visits, with Lord Lane CJ stating that 'no amount of criticism, no number of warnings, and no amount of exhortation seems to be able to prevent that happening'.[48] The principal difficulty is that, if counsel discloses to the defendant that he or she has been to see the judge, any advice then given to the defendant may appear to be based on what the judge said. In *Pitman*[49] the judge indicated that if the defendant changed his plea to guilty as charged there would be substantial mitigation, even though the defendant wished to argue that he was guilty not of reckless driving but of the less serious offence of careless driving. In *Turner* counsel stated or implied that the judge had indicated that the sentence on the defendant would be non-custodial if he pleaded guilty, but custodial if convicted after a trial.[50] In both cases the Court of Appeal held that this placed improper pressure on the defendant in deciding on plea. The problems were of a different kind in *Smith*, where counsel

---

[46] J. Bredar, 'Moving up the Day of Reckoning: Strategies for Attacking the Problem of "Cracked Trials" ' [1992] *Crim. LR* 153.

[47] [1970] 2 QB 321.

[48] *Pitman* [1991] 1 All ER 468; the second case was *Smith* (1990) 90 Cr.App.R. 413, per Russell LJ. See also the strong words of Lord Mustill in *Preston* (1994) 98. Cr.App.R. 405 at 425–6.

[49] [1991] 1 All ER 468.   [50] [1970] 2 QB 321.

said that the judge had undertaken to give a non-custodial sentence in the event of a guilty plea but the judge recollected no such undertaking. The Court of Appeal insisted that there should be a tape recorder or shorthand writer for any such meetings.[51] This would at least prevent disputes about what was said, but the deeper problem is whether such meetings should take place at all. Bypassing the trial may also mean bypassing the rights of certain parties.

However, it would be wrong to assume that the reported appellate decisions convey a full picture of daily practice. A survey in the early 1990s found that some judges were clearly doing what the Court of Appeal said they should not do, while other judges refused to see counsel for this purpose.[52] It appears that practice is variable, and this is manifestly unsatisfactory in terms of equality of treatment of like cases. The Seabrook Report maintained that some judges were not honouring the principle that a guilty plea should attract mitigation of one-quarter or one-third,[53] and the Table of 1996 Statistics (above) does raise questions about this. The practice of the Bar may also have a bearing on plea decisions: in the survey by Zander and Henderson some 70 per cent of those who changed their plea met the trial counsel only on the day of the trial.[54] Some 94 per cent of those who received legal advice on plea and who changed their minds followed the advice they received, often because it conformed with their own view, but sometimes because of persuasion by counsel.[55] One of the purpose of Plea and Directions hearings is to bring forward the time of meetings with counsel, although it is not known in what proportion of cases the same counsel deal with both PDH and any later trial.

What is the balance of advantages of plea bargains for the State? They contribute to the smooth running of the system by bringing speed and a reduction of the cost and resources needed to deal with the cases. They ensure a conviction, and avoid the hazards of trial which in 1996 produced an overall acquittal rate of 58 per cent in the Crown Court. In the present system these advantages come at the price of a sentence reduction: it could be claimed that offenders who benefit from the sentence discount are receiving a lower sentence than they deserve (on the basis of harm and culpability), purely for reasons of speed and cost. Those who believe that sentencing should be based on preventive grounds, such as deterrence or incapacitation, would also regard the discount as detracting from its primary purpose. It would be difficult to calculate whether these losses to the system are justified by the advantages, because that would also involve a calculation of how many defendants

---

[51]   (1990) 90 Cr.App.R. 413.
[52]   JUSTICE, *Negotiated Justice: A Closer Look at the Implications of Plea Bargains* (1993), 3.
[53]   Seabrook Report, 12.   [54]   Zander and Henderson, above n. 13, 55.
[55]   *Ibid.* 96–8.

would persist in a not guilty plea if there were no sentence discount for pleading guilty.

What is the balance of advantages for victims? In general guilty pleas spare victims the anxiety of having to give evidence in court, and the unpleasantness of hearing all the details of the crime analysed at length in public. For those victims who do give evidence (a minority, because of the large numbers of guilty pleas), the process is often stressful.[56] But the advantage of avoiding this anxiety is purchased at the price of sentence reductions, and victims may share some of the disquiet about undeserved mitigation or reduced protection described in the previous paragraph.

What is the balance of advantages for defendants? The primary benefit is the discount for pleading guilty, which in general promises a substantial reduction in the length of a custodial sentence and (as suggested earlier)[57] may in some cases result in the passing of a non-custodial rather than a custodial sentence. Such sentence reduction may be magnified by the defence lawyer's speech in mitigation: in general, it is much easier to construct a convincing mitigation for someone who has pleaded guilty than for someone who has contested guilt. It used to be said that a further advantage was that a defendant who was remanded in custody and who intended to plead guilty could delay the plea in order to benefit from being imprisoned closer to home, but the recent emphasis on larger discounts for early pleas may have lessened the attraction of this course.

These, however, are only advantages for the guilty defendant. From the point of view of other defendants, these are disincentives that pull against a justifiable challenge to the prosecution case, which might be said to be embodied in the presumption of innocence. Among these are innocent defendants who feel pressure to plead guilty, because they may not obtain an acquittal and it might appear best to 'cut their losses' in the hope of receiving a non-custodial sentence. Estimates of the number of innocent defendants who take this course vary: Zander and Henderson's figures suggest that up to 11 per cent of guilty pleaders claim innocence,[58] and earlier research suggested that as many as 18 per cent of guilty pleaders were 'possibly innocent' of one or more charges.[59] There is an important question of definition here, since a person may have an arguable defence and yet be advised that running the defence is not worth the loss of discount. If so, this raises squarely the issue

[56]   e.g. J. Morgan and L. Zedner, *Child Victims* (1992), 141–3; J. Shapland, J. Willore, and P. Duff, *Victims in the Criminal Justice System* (1985), 63–7.
[57]   See the statistics cited at 278–9 above.
[58]   Zander and Henderson, above n. 13, 138–42; cf. the dispute over these figures between M. Zander, 'The "Innocent"(?) Who Plead Guilty' (1993) 143 *New LJ* 85, and M. McConville and L. Bridges, 'Pleading Guilty Whilst Maintaining Innocence' (1993) 143 *New LJ* 160.
[59]   Bottoms and McClean, above n. 11, 120.

of whether a defendant may be said to have a right to have the prosecution case proved in court and, if so, whether the sentence discount does not impose an unfair disincentive to exercising this right. Moreover in practice there may be problems over the accuracy of counsel's advice to the defendant, for we have seen that the sentencing practice of judges is somewhat variable and may not be easy for counsel to predict.

6. Official Proposals for Reform

There is much that is unsatisfactory in current rules and practices. Charge bargains are an unavoidable aspect of any system that includes graduated criminal offences (more serious, less serious) and that allows multiple charging. Graduated offences are right in principle,[60] and it is often justifiable to charge more than a single offence. But the result is to place pressure on defendants to plead guilty to something as a kind of compromise. Fact bargains seem to have arisen through the absence of controls on the way in which the prosecution states the facts before sentence on a guilty plea: if the statement is unfairly adverse to the defendant it can be challenged, but if it is unfairly favourable, there seems to be no check. Plea bargains in the Crown Court appeared to operate in a kind of half-light, with some judges prepared to see counsel in order to give an indication of sentence and others not, and with a difficulty of predicting the sentence in any individual case. To what extent Plea and Directions hearings have altered the dynamics has not yet been studied. Defendants may be given advice by their counsel, sometimes in strong terms, but the basis of this may not be completely accurate. In effect, there is an element of gambling in the defendant's decision-making here: the roulette wheel has taken the place of the rule of law. From the defendant's point of view, all three forms of bargain raise fundamental questions about the implications of the presumption of innocence and about the privilege against self-incrimination. They also raise questions about the quality of defence lawyering: what ought in theory to be 'full and fearless defence' within an adversarial system can become, in some courts and with some sets of lawyers, a series of negotiations based on mutual respect and without always putting the client's interests first. From the public point of view, these practices enable some defendants who are guilty to 'play the system', for example by waiting until the day of trial in order to see whether key witnesses attend before signifying plea, in a manner that raises questions about the public interest in law enforcement.

---

[60] For elaboration, see A. Ashworth, *Principles of Criminal Law* (2nd edn., 1995), ch. 3, esp. 86–90.

We have seen that the system has changed significantly in the 1990s. The 'plea before venue' system for triable-either-way offences was introduced in October 1997, in an attempt to keep many cases out of the Crown Court, at least for purposes other than sentence. Plea and Directions hearings have been introduced, as recommended by the Royal Commission, and the numbers of 'cracked trials' have begun to decline. The guilty plea discount on sentence was put into statutory form in 1994, but the Royal Commission's further recommendation that judges be required to state how much discount has been given was not pursued, in the face of objections from the higher judiciary. Judges are traditionally sensitive about making their sentence calculations explicit, and probably resisted this proposal on the 'thin end of the wedge' argument, since discounts for guilty pleas are often quantified by the Court of Appeal.

On the Royal Commission's main recommendation in relation to pleas and cracked trials, the 'sentence canvass', there has been little movement. If counsel are to be able to advise their lay clients properly on the likely sentence, rather than simply stating the existence of the discount, they need to overcome the difficulty of predicting sentence without knowledge of the judge's approach and of all the necessary facts. The Royal Commission, broadly following the Seabrook Report, recommended that the judge should give an indication of the highest sentence on a guilty plea, if approached by defence counsel. This would involve a reversal of one of the cardinal principles in *Turner*, but the Royal Commission was encouraged by the support of 88 per cent of defence barristers, 86 per cent of prosecution barristers, and 67 per cent of judges for a reform that would 'permit full and realistic discussion between counsel and the judge about plea and especially sentence'.[61] Most defendants in the Crown Court seemed to know about the sentence discount,[62] but the Royal Commission started from the proposition that defendants are more interested in 'the actual sentence and in particular whether it will be custodial or not'.[63] Their proposal for a procedure of 'sentence canvass' has five main elements. First, it should take place only at the request of defence counsel on instructions from the defendant. Secondly, it may take place at the preparatory hearing, at a hearing called specially for the purpose, or during the trial. Thirdly, both sides should be represented and either a recording or a note should be made. Fourthly, the only question the judge may answer is, 'what would be the maximum sentence if my client were to plead guilty at this stage?' Fifthly, the judge may decline to answer the question where this might be especially difficult or might prejudice others, such as co-defendants.

---

[61] Zander and Henderson, above n. 13, 145.   [62] *Ibid.* 146 (62%).
[63] RCCJ, *Report*, para. 7.49.

Eschewing points of detail, we may consider two possible problems with this approach. One is the difficulty that judges may experience in making these predictions. The Royal Commission goes some way towards resolving this, by emphasizing that the indication is only of the 'maximum' sentence that would be given and by providing that each counsel should make a brief statement of facts and mitigation before the judge decides. Under the Criminal Justice Act 1991 the pre-sentence report will be important in many cases and is unlikely to have been prepared if the defendant has signified the intention of pleading not guilty. The effect of the pre-sentence report might be to lead the court towards a community sentence rather than a custodial sentence. In the absence of this, both the judge and the defendant may be handicapped in their decision-making. The other possible problem concerns the degree of voluntariness in the defendant's decision. This will be analysed further in the next section, but the Royal Commission's proposals did leave the matter in some doubt. The Royal Commission accepted 'that to face defendants with a choice between what they might get on an immediate plea of guilty and what they might get if found guilty by the jury does amount to unacceptable pressure'.[64] Yet their proposal was, in effect, that defendants would be told the judge's view of what the highest sentence on a guilty plea would be. They were then likely to ask counsel to predict what the sentence would be on a conviction after a trial, knowing that the sentence on a guilty plea would be significantly lower. In *Turner* the court held that: 'a statement that on a plea of guilty he would impose one sentence but that on a conviction following a plea of not guilty he would impose a severer sentence is one that should never be made'.[65] This, the court held, would constitute undue pressure on the accused. Thus the pressure would be unacceptable if the judge gave a view on both eventualities but was acceptable if the judge gave one and counsel the other. The Royal Commission seemed to agree with this. No doubt counsel would perform the duty of advising the defendant not to plead guilty if he or she is not guilty, but this advice might well be overshadowed by the other considerations pressing forward.

7. Deeper Principles

The proposals just considered are unsatisfactory. One of the Royal Commission's most conspicuous omissions was its failure to discuss the rights of defendants in any principled fashion, let alone in the context of the

---

[64] RCCJ, *Report*, para. 7.50.   [65] [1970] 2 QB 321, at 327.

European Convention on Human Rights. There is also little evidence that it thought more widely and more deeply about the relationship between the trial-avoidance mechanisms, now so dominant in English criminal justice, and the whole adversarial rhetoric of the system.

This is no mere academic quibble. From the vantage-point of Scotland, Sheriff-Principal Nicholson writes that 'it would be quite unacceptable that, in a legal system which presumes innocence and which permits every person to go to trial, a person who was found guilty after trial should be punished more severely simply because he had not pleaded guilty'.[66] The same point was made by the Lord Justice-Clerk in *Strawhorn* v. *McLeod*: referring to the sentence discount, he held that 'in our opinion no such inducement should be offered to accused persons. In this country there is a presumption of innocence and an accused person is entitled to go to trial and have the Crown to establish his guilt if the Crown can.'[67] Yet English law calmly and openly breaches this principle, now to the extent of legislating (in section 48 of the 1994 Act) in favour of the sentence discount for pleading guilty. The 'sentence canvass' system proposed by the Royal Commission, were it ever to be introduced, would reinforce the conflict with principle. What, then, are these deeper principles, and what is the authority for them?

1. *The presumption of innocence*: we have already noted that Article 6(2) of the European Convention on Human Rights declares that 'everyone charged with a criminal offence shall be presumed innocent until proved guilty according to law'.[68] One implication of this seems to be that a defendant has a right to put the prosecution to proof. No one should be recorded as guilty of an offence until the prosecution has proved that guilt, and 'any doubt should benefit the accused'.[69] There is no objection to an informed waiver of the right to be tried, but one can argue that the voluntariness of the waiver should be ascertained by the court, with reference to the case file.[70] If waiver of the right to be tried is permitted, and if we are serious about the presumption of innocence, anything that represents a standing incentive to waive the right would seem to contradict or weaken the presumption of innocence. It is one thing to allow defendants to choose whether or not to be tried; it is quite another thing to try to buy out their insistence on being tried. Yet this is exactly what the discount for pleading guilty is designed to do—to act as an incentive to forgo one's right to be tried and to have the prosecution prove guilt. In the United States the Supreme Court has taken the view that a sentence discount for

---

[66] C. G. B. Nicholson, *The Law and Practice of Sentencing in Scotland* (1st edn., 1981), 219.
[67] 1987 SCCR 413, at 415.   [68] Ch. 2.4.
[69] *Barbera, Messegue and Jabardo* (1989) A. 146 33; see generally Jung (above n. 7) at 117–21.
[70] Such an approach is discussed below, at pp. 295–7. However, it would not be easy to adapt it to magistrates' courts, unless qualified clerks were given some powers of this kind.

pleading guilty does not undermine the Fifth Amendment right not to plead guilty: although in *United States* v. *Jackson* (1968) the Court held that the objectives of the Government 'cannot be pursued by means that needlessly chill the exercise of basic constitutional rights'; subsequent decisions have held that the sentence discount falls outside this ban, doubtless influenced by the belief that plea bargaining is essential to the smooth functioning of American criminal justice.[71]

Another argument against the sentence discount is this. If there is a fundamental right to be presumed innocent until proved guilty, it is surely wrong that exercise of this right by someone who is subsequently convicted at the trial should result in a sentence that is higher than would have been the case on a guilty plea. The Court of Appeal described the present English position beautifully in an early sentencing decision: 'This court feels that it is very improper to use language which may convey that an accused is being sentenced because he has pleaded not guilty or because he has run his defence in a particular way.'[72] Improper as it may be to use such language, the effect of the discount for pleading guilty is that the person convicted after a trial does receive a longer sentence for that reason. Whether or not one expresses it in terms of forgoing mitigation, the exercise of the right to be tried has its cost. Indeed, if one accepts that the discount may be as much as one-third, this means that a person convicted after a trial may legitimately receive a sentence 50 per cent longer than someone who pleads guilty. No wonder that Sheriff-Principal Nicholson described the system as unacceptable.

The Royal Commission might defend itself by arguing that it took a pragmatic view. Cracked trials have to be reduced, as a matter of administrative necessity, and talk of defendants' rights does nothing to ease this pressing problem. Certainly it would be wrong for the advocates of rights to argue that it behoves us to take every possible step to ensure that innocent persons are never convicted. That would result in an immense investment of resources into criminal trials that might cripple the economy. But to dismiss that extreme position is not enough. As Dworkin argues, there is a strong case for maintaining that at all points in criminal justice our procedures should put the proper value on the fundamental harm of wrongful conviction.[73] What is the proper value may be a matter of debate, but the argument here is that to hold out a substantial sentence discount as a standing incentive for defendants to waive their right to trial goes too far. It fails to take the presumption of innocence seriously. The strongest counter-arguments are the 'cultural block'

[71] See *Brady* v. *US* (1970) 397 US 742, and *Corbitt* v. *New Jersey* (1978) 439 US 212.

[72] *Harper* [1968] 2 QB 108.

[73] R. M. Dworkin, 'Principle, Policy, Procedure', in C. Tapper (ed.), *Crime, Proof and Punishment* (1981), 212.

view, which is that the discount is so ingrained in our culture that taking it away might well alter behaviour significantly, and the 'unfair advantage' view, which is that defendants may be encouraged to insist on trial in the hope that witnesses may fail to attend or forget or change their story, with the result that guilty persons would benefit from a windfall that was unfair on society (including any victim of the offence). These points are pursued below.

2. *The privilege against self-incrimination*: this privilege finds a place in the US Constitution but not, as such, in the European Convention on Human Rights. However, in the decision in *Funke, Cremieux and Miailhe* v. *France*[74] the European Court recognized the link between the presumption of innocence in Article 6(2) and this privilege, referring to 'the right of anyone charged with a criminal offence to remain silent and not to incriminate himself'. In subsequent decisions the Court described the privilege against self-incrimination as a 'generally recognized international standard' which lies 'at the heart of the notion of fair procedure under Article 6'.[75] The implications of this for the post-1994 English law on adverse inferences from silence were considered in Chapter 4 above, but there are further implications. The Royal Commission did recognize that there is now considerable literature on the phenomenon of false confessions.[76] A majority of the Commission took the view that existing safeguards under the Police and Criminal Evidence Act 1984 are sufficient, whilst three members of the Commission insisted that a conviction should never be based on a confession unless there is supporting evidence.[77] The Commission as a whole accepted the terms of section 76 of the 1984 Act, that a confession should not be admitted if it was obtained in consequence of anything said or done which was likely, in the circumstances existing at the time, to render it unreliable. Setting aside the criticism that this test needs amendment,[78] one might argue that *pari passu* a plea of guilty should not be upheld if it was obtained in consequence of what might be described as a substantial inducement; indeed, the argument would be that the legal system should not provide such an inducement.

The Royal Commission came even closer to self-contradiction when its approach to the right to remain silent under police questioning is considered. Once again, its members divided on the question whether it would be right for the law to permit a jury or magistrates to draw an adverse inference from the defendant's failure to answer questions or to mention a point subsequently relied upon in defence. A minority of two thought that courts should

---

[74] (1993) A. 256.
[75] In *Murray* v. *UK* (1996) 22 EHRR 29 and in *Saunders* v. *UK* (1997) 23 EHRR 313.
[76] RCCJ Report, para. 4.32. [77] *Ibid.* paras. 4.85–4.87.
[78] J. Jackson, 'The Royal Commission on Criminal Justice: The Evidence Recommendations' [1993] *Crim. LR* 817, at 826–8.

be invited to draw appropriate inferences (the view accepted by the then Government and enshrined in the 1994 Act), whereas the majority held 'that the possibility of an increase in the convictions of the guilty is outweighed by the risk that the extra pressure on suspects to talk in the police station and the adverse inferences invited if they do not may result in more convictions of the innocent'.[79]

Consistency would require that the Royal Commission took the same stance on the discount for pleading guilty, since it is intended to, and probably does, exert extra pressure on defendants at the stage of deciding on plea. But the Royal Commission said little about this, once it had made the point that its own survey results may overestimate the numbers of innocent people pleading guilty.[80] The Report states:

> Provided that the defendant is in fact guilty and has received competent legal advice about his or her position, there can be no serious objection to a system of inducements designed to encourage him or her so to plead. Such a system is, however, sometimes held to encourage defendants who are not guilty of the offence charged to plead guilty to it nevertheless . . . This risk cannot be wholly avoided and, although there can be no certainty as to the precise numbers . . . it would be naive to suppose that innocent persons never plead guilty because of the prospect of the sentence discount.[81]

The only relevant point made subsequently is that 'against the risk that defendants may be tempted to plead guilty must be weighed the benefits to the system and to defendants of encouraging those who are in fact guilty to plead guilty. We believe that the system of sentence discounts should remain.'[82] This kind of 'balancing' argument, which appears to assign no particular weight to the presumption of innocence or the privilege against self-incrimination, is quite unacceptable.[83] The Royal Commission did accept that particular care should be taken during plea negotiations with vulnerable defendants who would be entitled to the support of an 'appropriate adult' at a police station[84]—rather a weak gesture towards this group, but at least an acknowledgement that the analogy with confessions is a fair one.

The Commission's general assumption appeared to be that counsel would safeguard the defendant's interests, but leave may be taken to doubt this. Even the *Turner* rules allow that counsel may give his or her advice, if necessary, in strong terms. That might easily be perceived as pressure by a defendant, especially one unfamiliar with the Crown Court. The decision in *Turner* distinguishes between statements believed to come directly from the judge, which were thought to exert unfair pressure, and counsel's own 'best advice', which

---

[79] RCCJ, *Report*, paras. 4.20–4.25.   [80] *Ibid.* para. 7.43.   [81] *Ibid.* para. 7.42.
[82] *Ibid.* para. 7.45.   [83] See the discussion of 'balancing' at Ch. 2.2 above.
[84] *Ibid.* para. 7.51.

was not thought unfair.[85] The findings of Baldwin and McConville's research in the 1970s were that over half of those who changed their plea to guilty at a late stage were responding to what they perceived as pressure from their barrister.[86] In the absence of fuller research—and it is fair to point out that far more research has been done into false confessions than into decisions to change plea—little should be made of this distinction. After all, the 'person in authority' requirement in the law of confessions was abandoned in 1984: it no longer matters where the 'things said or done' come from, so long as they tend to render the confession unreliable.

3. *The right to be treated fairly and without discrimination*: we have seen that Article 14 of the European Convention on Human Rights insists that the rights in the Convention 'shall be secured without discrimination on any ground such as sex, race, colour'. Would this principle be breached, either in the letter or in the spirit, if it were found that the operation of the criminal justice system routinely discouraged members of a particular ethnic minority from disputing their guilt?

Consider the available evidence in England and Wales. All studies that have included data on defendants' plea show that both persons from an Afro-Caribbean background and those from an Asian background tend to plead not guilty at a higher rate than whites. It also appears that Afro-Caribbeans are more likely to be acquitted, which may be regarded as vindicating their pleas.[87] Roger Hood found that not only do Afro-Caribbeans tend to plead not guilty more frequently than whites but that, when convicted, they tend to receive longer sentences largely because they have forfeited the discount for pleading guilty.[88] This can be regarded as a form of indirect discrimination: a general principle (the sentence discount) has a disproportionate impact on members of ethnic minorities simply because they exercise a right (the right to be tried and to be presumed innocent until convicted). The Royal Commission seemed to recognize this, but merely expressed its support for 'the recommendation made by Hood that the policy of offering sentence discounts should be kept under review'.[89] In fact, Hood argued that 'it is time [i.e. now] to consider all the implications of a policy which favours so strongly those who plead guilty'.[90] The Commission went on to state that careful ethnic monitoring of sentences was needed to detect whether there are sentencing patterns that are unfavourable to particular minority groups.

[85] [1970] 2 QB 321.

[86] Baldwin and McConville, above n. 24, 28; cf. also Bottoms and McClean, above n. 11, 79 and 130; J. Morison and P. Leith, *The Barrister's World* (1992), 132–7; and Travers, above n. 22, ch. 5.

[87] For a useful summary, see M. Fitzgerald, *Ethnic Minorities and the Criminal Justice System*, RCCJ Research Study 20 (1993), 26.

[88] Hood, *Race and Sentencing* (1992), 125.   [89] RCCJ, *Report*, para. 7.58.

[90] Hood, above n. 88, 182.

However, Hood has established that there are such patterns, and he raised the issue of principle—should we persist with the sentence discount? It is unfortunate that the Commission tackled neither of the key issues here.

4. *The right to a 'fair and public' hearing.* Article 6(1) of the European Convention declares that 'everyone is entitled to a fair and public hearing', and goes on to describe the limited situations in which 'the press and public may be excluded from all or part of the trial'. One characteristic of cases in which there is a guilty plea is that there is no real public hearing. An added characteristic of cases in which there is a plea bargain is that the crucial negotiation takes place in the absence not only of the public but also of the accused. The High Court of Australia has spoken strongly against these private meetings between judge and counsel, disapproving even the limited contact allowed by the *Turner* rules on the ground that this is inconsistent with 'the common law rule which requires a court to administer justice in public'.[91] While plea negotiation involving counsel and/or the judge may or may not infringe the European Convention, it certainly detracts from the spirit of Article 6(1). A defendant's fate is determined by words spoken in private, of which only some are relayed to the defendant by counsel. In some American jurisdictions a change of plea is only accepted if the defendant meets the judge and is questioned about the motivation behind the change, so that the judge is satisfied that it is a voluntary change. That, too, takes place in private, but at least it involves the defendant in person.

8. Conclusion

From the point of view of principle there are powerful arguments in favour of abolishing the sentence discount for those who plead guilty. It is certainly against the spirit of four fundamental rights and freedoms recognized under the European Convention on Human Rights—the presumption of innocence, the privilege against self-incrimination, the right to equality of treatment, and the right to a fair and public hearing—and is probably against the letter of two of them. It treats the question of sentence as a negotiable commodity—not directly, in England and Wales, since judge and counsel would rarely discuss specific sentences, but indirectly to the extent that the sentence may reflect not the harm and culpability of the defendant's conduct but the outcome of negotiations. Some of these points of principle have been recognized in Germany, although the Federal Constitutional Court appears not to have faced the arguments squarely.[92]

[91] R. v. *Tait and Bartley* (1979) 24 ALR 473, at 488.   [92] Herrmann, above n. 7, at 767–8.

It is unfortunate that the Royal Commission on Criminal Justice saw no reason to re-examine the justifications for the sentence discount for pleading guilty. Presumably it adopted the widespread view among practitioners that abolition of the discount is unthinkable because of its probable consequences. Courts would soon be overwhelmed by defendants exercising their right to trial, and the system would grind expensively to a halt. But this has not happened elsewhere. Scotland has survived without any general principle that a guilty plea merits a reduced sentence. Other European countries operate satisfactorily without the discount, although there are suggestions that in practice a defendant who signifies a willingness to admit guilt may reap some benefit from this.[93] In Philadelphia, the fourth largest city in the United States, there is no principle of sentence discount for pleading guilty. The result is that most defendants in felony cases do opt for trial, many of these being 'bench trials' by judge alone, which can be dealt with fairly quickly. This shows that, even in a country in which plea bargaining has come to be regarded as endemic, it is in fact merely a policy choice.[94] It could be eliminated or reduced substantially. That might entail costs, but that throws down the challenge to simplify criminal procedure generally. The US Federal Guidelines were designed to reduce the discount for pleading guilty and to place controls on plea negotiation: Schulhofer and Nagel conclude, as a result of ongoing research, that in the vast majority of cases (some 65 to 80 per cent) there is compliance with the guidelines and plea negotiations are not used as a means of circumventing them.[95] Alschuler, who has studied plea bargaining in the United States extensively over a long period, argues that changes in criminal procedure could make for a fairer system that afforded the opportunity of trial to every defendant.[96] Such judicial examinations may be relatively brief—the more searching they are, the longer and more expensive they become—but there are strong reasons of principle in favour of experimenting with this approach. They would certainly be a better use of court time than the questioning of complainants who wish to withdraw.[97] It is time to consider radical alternatives in England and Wales, bearing in mind the interests of victims and the strains of giving evidence.

[93] See the authorities cited in n. 7 above.

[94] S. Schulhofer, 'Is Plea-Bargaining Inevitable?' (1984) 97 *Harv. LR* 1037.

[95] S.J. Schulhofer and I.H. Nagel, 'Plea Negotiations under the Federal Sentencing Guidelines: Guideline Circumvention and Its Dynamics in the Post-*Mistretta* Period' (1997) 91 *Northwestern ULR* 1284.

[96] Among his many writings, see particularly A. Alschuler, 'Implementing the Criminal Defendant's Right to Trial' (1983) 50 *U. Chi. LR* 931.

[97] Cf. the finding of A. Cretney and G. Davis, 'Prosecuting "Domestic' Assault" [1996] *Crim. LR* 162, at 169, that some courts insist on the complainant responding to the court's questions.

A starting-point would be to reconsider the guilty plea itself. Rarely has it been considered whether we should remove the possibility of a guilty plea from, say, indictable cases. It may be true that some other European countries are beginning to see the merits of guilty pleas in certain types of case, but there is little evidence that serious consideration has ever been given in England to the arguments for abolishing guilty pleas in some cases. Is judicial scrutiny of the factual basis of a case thought unnecessary, or beneficial only in an ideal world, or simply prohibitively expensive? Have the foundations for each of these views been examined? Then it would be necessary to examine the justification for the sentence discount itself. Apart from the reasons already given, it is no argument that the possibility of charge reduction would be unaffected by any abolition of the discount. That is true, and will remain as an incentive to certain innocent defendants to 'cut their losses'. But that is an argument in favour of judicial scrutiny of guilty pleas; and, in any event, the existence of some unavoidable compromises of principle does not absolve one from avoiding those that can be avoided. Any fundamental re-examination ought also to extend to aspects of sentencing. There would be a need for more sentencing guidelines for particular offences, and it would be necessary to assess the impact on sentence levels of abolishing the discount. There would be no reason for raising sentence levels overall, but the size of current differences between sentences after guilty pleas and those after trials makes it important to consider where the new levels should be set.

The sentence discount is not the only structural incentive to plead guilty. There is also the 'tit-for-tat' rule in cross-examination of a defendant who gives evidence: if the defence attack the character of one or more witnesses for the Crown, the prosecution may in turn attack the defendant's character.[98] In practice this means that if the defence questions a police officer with a view to suggesting that he or she attributed to the defendant words that were not spoken ('verbals') or 'planted' evidence on the defendant, this opens the way for the defendant to be cross-examined about any previous convictions. It is a rule that may inhibit defendants with previous convictions from attacking Crown witnesses and from giving evidence (subject, now, to the further disadvantage that adverse inferences may be drawn), leaving them with a choice of tactics that is bound to involve some sacrifice. If this is combined with the sentence discount, the effect may be to create strong pressure to plead guilty.

Proper respect for the fundamental freedoms declared by the European Convention on Human Rights, now incorporated into English law, requires the abandonment of the sentence discount for pleading guilty, and the re-

---

[98] Criminal Evidence Act 1898, s. 1(f)(ii), discussed by A.A.S. Zuckerman, *The Principles of Criminal Evidence* (1989), ch. 13.

appraisal of the whole system of guilty pleas. In the past, Royal Commissions and many others have declined to take this approach seriously, fearing that it is bound to lead to organizational and financial disaster. Of course there would be tremendous difficulties in such a great cultural change, and it does not follow that because something works in Scotland it would work in England and Wales if the system were altered. Altering the system would cause resistance, since many people believe that the discount is a right or a necessity and might well act accordingly. However, it was argued above that case settlements and plea negotiations ought to be abandoned, and Stephen Schulhofer has advanced the same view in powerful terms:

> Contractual exchange, under appropriate conditions, can leave both parties better off. But the converse is also true. When the conditions necessary for welfare-enhancing transactions are not met, contractual exchange can leave both parties worse off. In criminal justice, pervasive structural impediments to efficient, welfare-enhancing transactions have produced just this situation. With trials in open court and deserved sentences imposed by a neutral factfinder, we protect the due process right to an adversarial trial, minimize the risk of unjust conviction of the innocent, and at the same time further the public interest in effective law enforcement and adequate punishment of the guilty. But plea negotiation simultaneously undercuts all of these interests. The affected parties are represented by agents who have inadequate incentives for proper performance; prospects for effective monitoring are limited or non-existent; and the dynamics of negotiation can create irresistible pressure for defendants falsely to condemn themselves. As a result, plea agreements defeat the public interest in effective law enforcement at the same time that they deny defendants the benefits of a vigorous defence and inflict undeserved punishment on innocents who could win acquittal at trial.[99]

Of course these words were written in an American context, and the somewhat optimistic description of trials might be overdone. Indeed, this point is taken up by Robert Scott and William Stuntz, who ask whether it is really desirable to to push more innocent people to trial, on the basis that some of them will be convicted and will then receive harsher sentences than they would have done if they had pleaded guilty:

> This result stands every known theory of distributional justice on its head. We would think it common ground that losses, equally unjust losses, are better spread than concentrated, all else being equal. Schulhofer, like most critics of plea bargaining, seems to prefer a few innocent defendants serving long prison terms to a larger number serving a few years apiece.[100]

---

[99] S.J. Schulhofer, 'Plea Bargaining as Disaster' (1992) 101 *Yale LJ* 1979 at 2008–9.
[100] R.E. Scott and W.J. Stuntz, 'A Reply: Imperfect Bargains, Imperfect Trials and Innocent Defendants' (1992) 101 *Yale LJ* 2011, at 2013.

Their view is certainly contestable: if all known theories of distributional justice point in the direction of more convictions for the innocent, then that is a good reason for not subscribing to them. From the rights perspective, the right of innocent persons not to be convicted ought to be recognised as a strong right, not to be traded. But Scott and Stuntz would insist that, in a world where there are going to be convictions of innocent people, we must face the choice to which they refer, and not avoid it. Their approach, in the leading article on which Schulhofer was commenting, is to eschew both extremes—to argue both against the existing system of plea negotiation, and against the abolition of all plea negotiations—and to press the case for refiguring the bargaining process in order to make it fairer. They start from the position that modern criminal justice systems are so demanding of resources that, in most countries, there is an 'inability to test innocence claims at acceptable cost'.[101] They therefore make several proposals for reforming the system, mostly aimed at US jurisdictions. Adapted to England and Wales, their proposals would include greater information for the defendant on the choice to be made, and clearer sentencing guidance to enhance predictability (although not minimum sentences, since flexibility would be helpful). Even as an interim position, however, this ought not to be followed in this country unless the size of the discount were significantly reduced. At present, the pressure is simply too great, and the effect on innocent defendants (especially those from certain racial minorities) is unacceptable.

Defendants should not only be given more accurate information, but they should receive proper advice and protection. The aim should be to alter the culture of the professions and the courts, notably by re-asserting the adversarial nature of defence lawyers rather than the collaborative and compromising approach which is too common in current practice. Research projects at different times and in different parts of the country refer to the strongly co-operative and non-adversarial nature of much case settlement,[102] and there is no shortage of examples in the study of defence lawyers by McConville, Hodgson, Bridges, and Pavlovic.[103] It is not suggested that this change could be achieved easily, especially in firms receiving relatively modest rewards for their legal aid work, but it is an approach that has not been properly tried.

The Seabrook Committee's proposal that judges should signify the effect of the discount on a particular sentence should also be followed, notwithstanding the hoped-for reduction in the amount of discounts. The best reason for allowing any discount to remain on the day of the trial is to spare those

---

[101] R.E. Scott and W.J. Stuntz, 'Plea Bargaining as Contract' (1992) 101 *Yale LJ* 1909, at 1951.

[102] See, e.g., Brownlee, Mulcahy, and Walker, above n. 44, at 120, and A. Mulcahy, 'The Justifications of "Justice" ' (1994) 34 *BJ Crim.* 411, at 421–3.

[103] M. McConville *et al.*, *Standing Accused* (1994), 188–98.

victims who have been damaged psychologically or who are afraid from having to give evidence. The Royal Commission's proposal for 'sentence canvass' should be rejected on the ground that it would intensify pressure on defendants to plead guilty. The Commission's reasoning did, however, draw attention to the problems in the present system of predicting what sentence a court might give, problems not confined to the Crown Court. For so long as any variation on the existing structure remains, this will inject an element of roulette into a system already loaded against the defendant who wishes to plead not guilty. Thus in his research report on serious fraud, Levi castigated the bargaining practices that came to his attention:

> The haphazard structure under which discussions sometimes take place in camera without solicitors (including in-house SFO lawyers), police or defendant being present gives rise to enormous problems, maximises incoherence, and generates no precedent for dealing consistently and fairly with cases.[104]

It is therefore essential to increase the amount of sentencing guidance available both to Crown Court judges and to the magistracy, a policy that has greater advantages than assisting defendants in their decision-making. As already argued, the amount of the sentence discount must be reduced significantly, and judges required to state the exact effect that the discount had upon the sentence they pass. Changes such as these might smooth the transition to an altered system of criminal procedure that does not rely on tempting defendants to forgo their rights.

---

[104] M. Levi, *The Investigation, Prosecution and Trial of Serious Fraud*, RCCJ Research Study 14 (1993).

Part III

Conclusions

10   Criminal Process Values

CHAPTERS 4 to 9 of the book have discussed six key stages of decision-making in the criminal process, making reference to issues of policy and principle in the relevant law and practices. It is time now to reflect more generally upon the values that appear to dominate the English criminal process, the values that ought to dominate it, and how change might be brought about.

1. The Avoidance of Criminal Trials

Early in the first chapter a distinction was drawn between three types of decision at the pre-trial stage—processual decisions, which are concerned with the progress of the case from arrest through to court, or as far as the case goes; dispositive decisions, which divert a case from the process of prosecution and trial and which may impose a kind of penalty; and the temporizing decision, remand, which determines whether or not the defendant should be at liberty between first court appearance and trial. While there is often a tendency to regard these decisions as discrete rational determinations, it will have become apparent that they cannot be assessed properly without having regard to the system or process of which they form part. Thus, for example, each decision is shaped by the flow of information to the decision-maker and by the way in which 'facts' and opinions are selected, constructed, and communicated. Additionally, each decision-maker may be not only subject to rules or guidelines, as the case may be, but also influenced by an occupational culture and by the expectations of others both within and outside the system. It is therefore important not to neglect the serial view of decisions, noting that decisions by the public and by ordinary police officers or by the personnel of regulatory agencies may have considerable implications for later determinations; that decisions on charge may have implications for mode of trial; that decisions on mode of trial may have implications for remand and for plea; and so forth. As a result of the exploration of decision-making in the chapters above, it should be clear that central concepts such as 'the facts', 'innocence', and 'guilt' are sometimes not objective phenomena (as often assumed), but rather compromises or value-judgements emanating from the practices and pressures of the process.

Little has been said, in the foregoing chapters, about the differences between accusatorial and inquisitorial systems of criminal justice. The English criminal process is fundamentally accusatorial in orientation, eschewing the idea of an impartial inquiry into the case by a neutral official in favour of the notion that a fair result emerges from an adversarial process in which the prosecution constructs a case for convicting the defendant and he or she attempts to undermine or discredit that case. One reason for not dwelling on this contrast is the complexity of the adversarial/inquisitorial division, both in theory and in practice. That, in itself, deserves a full study.[1] Another reason may be found in what may be termed the 'theory of convergence'—suggesting that the trend in Europe has been away from a clear dichotomy of approaches and towards a unified framework.[2] The convergence is said to have been assisted by the European Convention on Human Rights and the judgments of the Court: the Convention emphasizes the rights of the individual defendant, in a way that typifies accusatorial systems (for example, the various rights enumerated in Article 6, included the right to confront each witness), but it also promotes some principles associated with an inquisitorial approach, such as equality of arms and the duty of disclosure. It may be added that, quite apart from any influence exerted by the European Convention, the 'ideal type' of an accusatorial or an inquisitorial criminal procedure is hard to find in Europe. The example of forms of plea bargaining in Germany was given in Chapter 9, and the introduction of adversarial elements into the Italian system in 1989 is another example.[3] However, care must be taken in the interpretation of these and other trends. So much depends on the legal traditions and social culture of different countries that there can rarely be any simple comparison between the elements of two different criminal justice systems.

It has also become evident that, whereas the rhetoric of criminal procedure tends to place emphasis on trial by jury according to the laws of evidence, the practice is otherwise. Most cases are heard in magistrates' courts, not in the Crown Court with a jury. The vast majority of cases—over 90 per cent in magistrates' courts and some two-thirds in the Crown Court—proceed on a plea of guilty, which means that no trial of guilt ever takes place. In no sense is this

---

[1] As in the well-known work by M. Damaska, *The Faces of Justice and State Authority* (1976).

[2] e.g. N. Jorg, S. Field and C. Brants, 'Are Inquisitorial and Adversarial Systems Converging?', in C. Harding, P. Fennell, N. Jorg, and B. Swart (eds.), *Criminal Justice in Europe* (1994).

[3] See V. Grevi, 'The New Italian Code for Criminal Procedure: a Concise Overview', in A. Pizzorusso (ed.), *Italian Studies in Law* (1994), ii.

a 'natural' or 'unavoidable' phenomenon: the system is structured so as to produce it. There are incentives towards the avoidance of trials, incentives that do not exist in some other legal systems. The most notable of these is the sentence discount for a plea of guilty, up to one-third off the sentence that would otherwise be given for the offence. In recent years there have been increasing fiscal pressures towards having fewer cases dealt with in the Crown Court and more in the magistrates' courts, manifested (for example) in the reclassification of certain offences as 'summary only' in 1988 and the introduction of the 'plea before venue' system in 1997. However, in addition to these structural factors there are also cultural influences pulling in the same direction. We have noted evidence that defence lawyers and prosecutors may act co-operatively at some stages, particularly in plea negotiations. What ought to be different ethical orientations may sometimes become submerged in the working practices and occupational cultures of the local groups of professionals.

It is not only for cases that are pursued to conviction that the system tends strongly towards trial-avoidance. The trend towards diversion is designed to take cases out of the formal criminal process and to dispose of them separately. Predominant among these dispositive decisions are the police caution, the different forms of 'caution plus', the various warnings and compounded penalties used by the 'regulatory' agencies, and discontinuances by the Crown Prosecution Service that are followed by a caution. The Crime and Disorder Bill 1998 is set to introduce a more rigid statutory regime for the diversion of offenders under 18. The foundations of the movement towards diversion may be located in different theoretical considerations: the painful consequences of being prosecuted may themselves be too severe a response to some forms of wrongdoing; encounters with the court system may create stigma and disadvantage; and diversion is far less expensive than court proceedings. Although some may suspect that considerations of cost weigh most heavily in inclining policy-makers towards diversion, the advantage on this occasion is that economic savings may also result in procedures that achieve a more proportionate response to non-serious law-breaking.

It would be wrong, however, to overlook the disadvantages. On a general plane, a widely used discretion not to prosecute may be regarded as undermining the principle of legality and the idea of the rule of law, and serious consideration should be given to the decriminalization of some forms of conduct. On a more specific plane, existing methods of diversion are often inseparable from incentives for the suspect or defendant to accept them. Rather like the discount for pleading guilty, the incentive to accept a caution—combined, of course, with a statement that the suspect must not admit to anything that he or she did not do—may prove a powerful practical inducement to terminate one's involvement with the criminal justice system quickly and without the anxiety of a court appearance. However, the European Court has insisted and English law generally provides that anyone who does not wish to accept diversion can decline and invite the prosecution to bring the case before a court.[4] Now that cautions (together with reprimands and final warnings) are recorded nationally and are liable to be cited in court if the defendant is subsequently convicted of an offence, the possibility of challenge is particularly important. In practice, however, this requires a certain self-confidence and resilience. If diversion is to remain as a feature of the criminal process (which it certainly should do), suspects should be provided with safeguards, such as access to legal advice and a principle that any sentence the court passes on a finding of guilt should not be more onerous than the penalty voluntarily rejected by the defendant.

These remarks are at a general level, and the practical operation of the system may vary to some extent according to the type of crime alleged. At various stages in the text we have noted the special difficulties arising in cases of child abuse and 'domestic' violence, and separate studies have highlighted the particular problems and the different procedures adopted.[5] Much more could have been said about pre-trial procedures for these offences and for others such as rape, serious fraud, terrorist crimes, and so on. Indeed, some might argue that there is now no single system but a broad framework encompassing a number of sub-systems. Going hand in hand with this have been arguments, indeed assumptions, that the special requirements of investigating a particular type of crime justify derogations from the rights of suspects, an approach criticized in Chapter 2.5 above. More generally, we have noted the absence of any overall strategy in pre-trial justice. There is no aspiration to treat like cases alike, that most elementary proposition of justice, and different agencies continue to operate in different ways. The police and the CPS have their different powers and their different spheres, although the National Standards for cautioning are closely parallel to the Code for Crown Prosecutors. The regulatory agencies follow their differing paths and priorities. These variations, not to mention the discretionary power within each of them, leave open the possibility of practices that discriminate on irrelevant grounds such as class, social position, race, and gender. There is no common starting-point, no conception that people who commit offences of similar seriousness should receive similar responses (unless there are strong grounds for doing otherwise), and no real attempt to provide guidance on the relative

---

[4] See the ECHR references above, p. 150, n. 29.

[5] On 'domestic' violence, for example, see S. Grace, *Policing Domestic Violence in the 1990s* (1995); A. Cretney and G. Davis, 'Prosecuting "Domestic" Assault' [1996] *Crim. LR* 162; and D. Lockton and R. Ward, *Domestic Violence* (1997).

seriousness of the various types of offence. Like sentencing, diversion decisions are dispositive. Unlike sentencing, there are no open hearings and the principles relating to specific types of offence are hardly developed at all.

The absence of an aspiration to treat like cases alike is also manifest in local variations of policy. National Standards on cautioning were issued as such in 1990 and 1994, but we saw in Chapter 5 that research shows the persistence of variations among police force areas, most of which follows longstanding patterns. To what extent statutory change in the Crime and Disorder Bill 1998 (introducing reprimands and final warnings for young offenders) can expect to penetrate these local cultures is a question for future research. National Mode of Trial guidelines were promulgated in 1991 and 1995, but it is not clear whether these have succeeded in removing or even reducing the sturdy independence of some local liaison judges, justices' clerks, and benches.[6] Local variations in remand decisions, in plea rates, and in the practices of some regulatory agencies are also long-standing. However, it would be inadvisable to attempt to stifle all local variation, particularly when several worthwhile innovations in the criminal process have originated in local schemes (e.g. bail information schemes, Public Interest Case Assessment schemes). But it is no less wrong to tolerate what, in effect, are declarations of local independence in matters of criminal justice policy. It is unjust that a person who is (rightly or wrongly) suspected of a certain offence in one area should be treated in a significantly different way from a person in a similar person in another area. Local variations in practice should be monitored and local variations in policy should only be permitted if clear justifications can be found: this would expose the unwarranted whilst enabling experimental schemes to be introduced.

Both processual and dispositive decisions, as we have seen, tend towards the avoidance of trials. One feature of pre-trial processes that has become evident from the foregoing chapters is the tendency of some decisions to be taken in anticipation of the decisions of other agencies. There are, in fact, several influences flowing in different directions. Almost all the 'input' received by the CPS comes from the police, who therefore exert considerable practical influence through their construction of case files. We have seen how some of the working practices of the CPS (in relation to bail and mode of trial decisions, for example) may be shaped by local magistrates or justices' clerks or the local judiciary. Equally some defence solicitors will tailor their approach on bail and other matters to the particular prosecutor, justices' clerk, or bench of magistrates. Magistrates may defer to the police or to the CPS rather than applying their judgement independently on remands or mode of trial. It is not

---

[6] These local 'cultures' were mentioned as recently as 1993 by the Criminal Justice Consultative Committee, *Mode of Trial Decisions and Sentencing* (1993), 8; see above, Ch. 8.2.

always easy to be sure of the existence of undue influence in these relation-ships: it is sometimes theoretically possible that two different parties are applying the same test and reaching the same conclusion, but the research cited on prosecutions (Chapter 6), on remands (Chapter 7), and on mode of trial (Chapter 8) is strongly suggestive of other, less ethical approaches.

One person who perhaps does not have the central role that would be appropriate is the defendant. Under existing practice in both the Crown Court and magistrates' courts, the defendant is excluded from plea negotia-tions themselves and has to depend on the mediated words of legal represen-tatives.[7] Direct information for the defendant is relatively rare, and this places much emphasis on the quality of legal representation. There is growing evi-dence that this is variable, and that it is not always motivated by a desire to secure the defendant's rightful advantages but is sometimes diluted by a desire to curry favour with the police, or to obtain the maximum fee for the mini-mum work, or not to 'pull the stops out' for a client deemed unworthy.[8] At Plea and Directions hearings in the Crown Court the defendant is entitled to be present, whereas those magistrates' courts that operate some form of pre-trial review do not admit defendants (or magistrates), and confine attendance to prosecuting and defending lawyers and the justices' clerk. In the face of strong structural and cultural pulls towards trial avoidance and negotiated outcomes, an independent and ethical approach from the defence lawyer is vital to protect the suspect-defendant. One who cannot rely on his or her legal representatives for full support and good advice is, given the other disadvan-tages outlined in Chapter 4 and elsewhere, in a particularly vulnerable posi-tion.

2. The Principled Approach

The scourge of many debates about criminal justice policy is the concept of 'balance'. As it is often expressed, notably by the 1993 Royal Commission, the 'balancing' of conflicting interests is presented as if there is no particular weighting of or priority among the interests. They are all matters to be taken into consideration, and somehow a 'balance' emerges. Sometimes the process is given an apparent respectability by quoting probabilities that a certain con-sequence will ensue—for example, the low risk of innocent people being con-victed. The existence of a low risk on one side of the equation may be thought

---

[7] J. Baldwin, *Pre-Trial Justice* (1986); A. Mulcahy, 'The Justifications of Justice' (1994) 34 *BJ Crim.* 411.

[8] M. McConville *et al.*, *Standing Accused* (1994), 273 and 281.

to tip the scales in that direction. However, as argued in Chapter 2 above, this would be to short-circuit the course of reasoning and to ignore the strength of certain rights. It is time, now, to re-state the argument in the light of the material in the intervening chapters.

The principled approach to criminal justice differs from that embodied in Packer's famous models. They are, after all, merely models by which to interpret the criminal process; and, even if they were adequate models, they do not indicate a particular conclusion. The principled approach, on the other hand, is explicitly normative. It sets out various rights and principles that ought to be safeguarded. One consequence of the Human Rights Bill 1998 will be to bring rights into a central position. The European Convention on Human Rights will be available to, and will to a considerable extent govern the adjudications of, the criminal courts. Public authorities, including all the major criminal justice agencies, will also have to conform to the requirements of the European Convention. This is likely to usher in a new legalism, with suspects, defendants, and convicted offenders attempting to invoke the various Convention rights in the hope of persuading courts not to follow certain precedents or even to declare certain statutory provisions incompatible with the ECHR. If defence lawyers are willing to take on and to press these claims, there could be significant changes in respect of adverse inferences from silence when questioned by the police, the provisions of disclosure of evidence, the use of various forms of electronic surveillance to gather evidence, and even the discount for pleading guilty.

None of this is to suggest that the ECHR should be regarded as a solution to the ills of the pre-trial criminal process. Both in Chapter 2 and subsequently, attention has been drawn to various shortcomings of the Convention. Its coverage of rights is incomplete and patchy: if one were drawing up such a document for the new millenium, there are several obvious candidates for inclusion that find no place in the 1950 Convention—for example, victims' rights, protection for witnesses, fault requirements for criminal convictions, and so on. It might also be said that the ECHR rights are, for the most part, broadly stated and therefore likely to prove blunt instruments. That, however, would be to ignore the case law of the European Court of Human Rights, which has led to the sharpening of several provisions, for example those on access to a court to determine the duration of detention (Article 5), the doctrine of equality of arms (Article 6), and the apparently broad 'prevention of crime' exceptions to the right of privacy (Article 8). British courts have an obligation, under the Human Rights Bill 1998, to take account of decisions of the European Court. To what extent they will follow them, or will themselves take the opportunity to sharpen the often blunt wording of the ECHR, remains to be seen.

A further point, emphasized in Chapter 2 above, is that the ECHR does yield a certain weighting of human rights. Some are absolute, others are strong rights from which derogation may be made for limited reasons, and still others are subject to circumscribed exceptions on the face of the Convention. No doubt critics would protest that, unless and until we know the interpretation placed on a particular Article in relation to a particular fact situation, this powerful side of the ECHR will be little felt. But that is an unduly pessimistic view, which in any event ignores the European Court's case law. The human rights argument was always far more powerful than the deeply unsatisfactory approach of the Royal Commission on Criminal Justice in 1993, with its scandalous failure to take any notice of the ECHR. Since the Human Rights Bill 1998, it has become both powerful and unavoidable.

3. Discrimination and Non-discrimination

The principle of equality before the law, or non-discrimination, is often declared to be a fundamental element in the administration of justice. Article 14 of the ECHR declares a right not to be discriminated against in the exercise of Convention rights, but we noted in Chapter 2 that this is an unduly restrictive formulation of the principle. It also tends to overlook the case for special treatment of certain groups—positive discrimination, aimed at insulating the vulnerable from pressures with which they cannot fairly be expected to cope. We have seen that there is a strong case for special procedures to protect the mentally disordered, and also for special assistance for those who do not understand the English language well enough. These and other claims for positive discrimination must be kept under constant review. Moreover, lip-service to the rather pallid principle of non-discrimination alluded to in section 95 of the Criminal Justice Act 1991 must not cause a neglect of research and other inquiries into whether the practice conforms to the law. The recent introduction in England and Wales of a system for the collection of evidence on certain of these matters should not lead us to forget the evidence that people from an Afro-Caribbean background may be disadvantaged in decisions to prosecute or caution, decisions on mode of trial, and in the process of plea negotiation. Increases in the number of people from ethnic minorities in the legal profession and the various criminal justice agencies are necessary, but they are unlikely to solve the above problems, at least in the short term. The extent of discrimination on grounds of sex is unclear, but studies of sentencing suggest that it would be unwise to take at face value the apparently lenient treatment of women and girls.

In relation to young suspects and defendants, a case for positive discrimination has long been recognized. However, the trend of proposals from governments of both parties in the 1990s has been towards a more punitive approach to the young. The 1997 White Paper, *No More Excuses*, adopts forms of rhetoric about young defendants which seem at odds with the emphasis in the United Nations Declaration on the Rights of the Child on the primacy of the best interests and welfare of the child. This is a regrettable turn in criminal justice policy.

In discussions of discriminatory practices, it is important not to ignore discrimination according to factors connected with social class or wealth. It is evident from Chapters 5 and 6 that any systematic examination of the prosecution policies of the police compared with those of the so-called regulatory agencies would reveal a diversity of approaches, amounting in general to a less formal, less public, and less severe response to law-breaking by employers, taxpayers, and others in established ways of life. It is hardly surprising that statistics about the social background of offenders show a predominance of those from the lower socio-economic groups when the enforcement process is skewed against those groups and in favour of those from the higher occupational categories. However, dealing with this presents a structural problem of immense proportions. Those who adopt a desert or retributive approach would probably argue that the first task should be to decide on the relative seriousness of all these offences, whether 'white-collar', 'normal', 'financial', 'commercial', 'domestic', or however they may be labelled. The second task might then be to ensure that the criminal law is invoked at a certain level of seriousness, whatever the context of the offence, and not below that level. This would represent an attempt to achieve equality before the law, preventing the use of the criminal process for relatively minor offences by impecunious or poorly connected defendants when at the same time corporate or wealthy defendants benefit from a less vigorous approach. That enterprise would not be easy to achieve, however, for many reasons. Among those reasons are the ways in which certain regulatory offences are drafted, and the possibility that wealthy or corporate 'deviants' might deploy their considerable resources to devise means of 'creative compliance' with the law.[9]

An alternative approach, which rejects desert as the leading principle in favour of a form of restorative justice, would be to cease the search for equivalent measures of punishment and instead to require corporations who offend to make due reparation to those harmed by their offending behaviour.[10] This approach is premised not only on a rejection of the retributive

---

[9] D. McBarnet and C. Whelan, 'The Elusive Spirit of the Law: Formalism and the Struggle for Legal Control' (1991) 54 *MLR* 848.

[10] See, e.g., B. Fisse and J. Braithwaite, *Corporations, Crime and Accountability* (1993).

paradigm for punishment but also on the difficulty and expense involved in holding companies responsible according to traditional criminal procedures and doctrines. Thus Braithwaite and Fisse argue that companies should be served with a notice that presumes liability and requires them to state what remedial measures they propose to take, in respect of both any individual victims and the wider community. The goal is that this would enable other law enforcement agencies to devote more resources to fairness in dealing with other forms of crime, for which the authors also have proposals.[11]

Important as it is to tackle unfair discrimination in the criminal law, in the enforcement process, and in criminal procedure, one cannot overlook the difficulty of doing so within a society many of whose institutions and practices may be said to lean towards unfair discrimination. So far as policing is concerned, for example, 'the young "street" population has always been the prime focus of police order maintenance and law enforcement work. The processes of racial disadvantage in housing, employment and education lead young blacks to be disproportionately involved in street culture.'[12] This demonstrates the folly of regarding the criminal process as something separate from wider social issues and capable of separate treatment. It also demonstrates the folly of regarding issues of race as separate from other issues of general social policy. Similar arguments could be made about gender. This is not to deny the importance of efforts to remove discrimination from the criminal process, but it is to argue that there are structural factors that make it likely that some discriminatory effects might be found even if the law and its enforcers were scrupulously fair in their own actions.

4. Promoting the Principles

How should the principled approach outlined in Chapter 2 and in this chapter be put into practice? Lawyers would tend to look to a network of rules or to a system of legal regulation as the means of advancing the desired principles. It has often been remarked that many stages in the criminal process are characterized by wide swaths of little-regulated discretion, from which it is assumed that the path of reform involves restrictions on or the complete removal of discretion. However, this would be naïve. It would be to assume that the existence of rules eliminates the practices that discretion allows. There are plenty of examples of rules being circumvented or neutralized, for

---

[11] J. Braithwaite and P. Pettit, *Not Just Deserts: A Republican Theory of Criminal Justice* (1990); cf. A. von Hirsch and A. Ashworth (eds.), *Principled Sentencing* (2nd edn., 1998), ch. 7.

[12] R. Reiner, *The Politics of the Police* (2nd edn., 1992), 169.

instance by the police (Chapter 4), by Crown Prosecutors (Chapter 6), and by counsel and judges (Chapter 9). From the point of view of observance, it is doubtful that rules enacted in primary legislation will necessarily be more successful than guidelines within or outwith the ambit of secondary legislation.

We saw in Chapter 1 that the origins of many of the miscarriage of justice cases of recent years lie in the early parts of the criminal justice system, particularly the stage of investigation by police and forensic scientists. One of the most welcome developments has been the creation of the Criminal Cases Review Commission: although the fruits of its labours have not come greatly into the public arena at the time of writing, it is an important step away from the previous arrangements for dealing with evidence of miscarriages of justice. It is, however, a remedial rather than a preventive mechanism, and it remains necessary to focus attention on the working practice of the police and other law enforcement agencies, and also the Crown Prosecution Service and defence lawyers, at the early stages in the process. Not to be overlooked, also, is the effect of criminal procedure and the laws of evidence on these early stages. The attrition rate is a cause for concern, and may embody miscarriages of justice of a different kind inasmuch as guilty people are not prosecuted or are acquitted because the system is organized in a way that fails to prevent that result. Thus there is a need to review procedures for the giving of evidence by live video link (available only for child witnesses at present), the giving of evidence in court from behind a screen, limits on the scope of questions in cross-examination, and a whole host of other issues. The European Court of Human Rights has shown itself willing to approve some such adaptations of the traditional model of a criminal trial, whilst guarding the rights of accused persons under Article 6,[13] but this is in response to member states that have introduced changes of this kind. The ECHR does not mandate particular systems.

The principle of 'equality of arms' must also spread further into these early decisions: some steps have been taken, in the shape of lay visitors to police stations, legal aid, access to legal advice in the police station, duty solicitor schemes, and so forth, but it is essential to lay greater emphasis on what occurs at these early stages and on the quality of legal advice available to defendants when they make what may turn out to be crucial choices. One essential part of achieving change would be to alter the fee structure in the legal aid system to provide greater rewards for preparation and early advice. However, it must be said that recent changes and proposals in respect

---

[13] *Doorson* v. *The Netherlands* (1996) 22 EHRR 330; *Van Mechelen* v. *The Netherlands* [1997] HRCD 431.

of criminal legal aid seem driven more by short-term cost cutting than by enhancement of protection of the rights of suspects and defendants.[14]

What should happen when a breach of one or more pre-trial procedures is uncovered? Much has been made, both by academics[15] and even by some British judges,[16] of the 'integrity principle'. The argument is that the integrity of the court, or more widely of the criminal justice system, would be compromised if it were to act on evidence that had been obtained as a result of a departure from proper procedure. At one level the argument is persuasive, and the imagery of 'tainting' or 'the fruit of the poisoned tree' seems apposite. Yet in other respects the integrity principle leaves certain questions unanswered.[17] Should every departure from procedure, no matter how small or inconsequential, be regarded as calling into question the integrity of a court or the whole system? If not, by what criteria can we tell whether integrity is compromised? Questions of this kind raise a doubt whether the integrity principle can be a satisfactory operating standard for the courts: attractive as it is in clear and gross cases, it needs considerable refinement if it is to be suitable for the general run of situations.[18] The disciplinary principle cannot withstand careful scrutiny, since the actions or remarks of judges have no formal disciplinary consequences for the police or other investigative authority in general, or for the particular investigator. Professional discipline is and should be the concern of tribunals constituted for that purpose, as mentioned above. In practice the disciplinary principle amounts to nothing more than a principle of public censure, a symbolic practice of criticizing the conduct of an investigator or investigative agency in court, often bolstered by reporting in the mass media. More relevant to the objective of promoting a principled approach to criminal justice is the protective principle: that a court should not act on evidence if that would deprive the defendant of a protection that should have been assured. In other words, a deviation from procedures may only be overlooked if it can be regarded as 'technical', not because it is intrinsically small but rather because it has not prejudiced, or, alternatively, has not prejudiced significantly, the defendant. The defendant should not be disadvantaged by an investigator's non-observance of the procedures.

---

[14] For a wide-ranging discussion, see R. Young and D. Wall, *Access to Criminal Justice* (1996).

[15] e.g. A. A. S. Zuckerman, *The Principles of Criminal Evidence* (1989), A. Choo, *Abuse of Process* (1993).

[16] Notably the speech of Lord Lowry in *R. v. Horsferry Road Magistrates' Court, ex p. Bennett* [1993] 3 WLR 90.

[17] One question, raised above in Ch. 2.5.2, but not pursued here, is whether the concept of integrity incorporates the social value placed on the conviction of the guilty, as certain American judges have maintained.

[18] See Ch. 2.5.2 above, and compare A.A.S. Zuckerman, *Principles of Criminal Evidence* (1989), 350–2, with P. Mirfield, *Silence, Confessions, and Unfairly Obtained Evidence* (1997), ch. 23–8.

It will be apparent that, even if the appropriateness of the protective principle is accepted, its implementation depends on a considerable value-judgement if the term 'significant' is introduced into its formulation. A strong version of the principle would exclude any such qualification, and is to be preferred if rights are to be respected fully. However, in terms of practical politics there may be some pressure to qualify the principle so as to avoid losing 'good' convictions for a procedural departure that really had little effect on the defendant's exercise of rights. That would require some kind of judgement to be reached, but it is clearer what is at stake when dealing with ordinary cases under the protective principle than under the integrity principle. What neither the protective principle nor the principle of integrity settles is the most appropriate consequences of breach. Rarely is it suggested that there should be a complete defence to criminal liability (although this has been argued to be appropriate for entrapment[19]), but in many cases a decision to stay the prosecution on the ground of abuse of process will have a similar effect, whereas the better-established remedy of excluding evidence is less powerful and may occasionally leave room for a conviction based on other admissible evidence.[20] One might then ask why the prevention of conviction is regarded as the benchmark of appropriateness if the protection of the defendant from unfair disadvantage is the rationale. Ideally, the strength of the response should be in some way proportionate to the degree of disadvantage to the defendant (which, to re-emphasize, is not the same as the degree of the departure from proper procedure).

The promotion of a principled approach therefore requires not only the provision of training, guidance, and supervision but also sufficient and appropriate remedies in cases where the principles are not put into practice. No doubt it would be argued that there are professional organizations to take care of such matters, and the Law Society's Advocacy Code and the Bar Council's Code of Conduct will be cited. The Royal Commission on Criminal Justice formed the view that the 'last-minute culture' of the criminal Bar, under which briefs are returned late and counsel has little opportunity for thorough preparation or proper discussion with client, victim, or witnesses, would be difficult to dislodge. Whether the proper solution is to try to break the culture or to try to reshape it,[21] fuller investigation should be made of the possibility that prosecutions and defendants are disadvantaged by the criminal Bar's approach. The confidence expressed by most barristers in their ability to deal with preparations satisfactorily at the last minute, even though

---

[19] See Ch. 4.2.1.

[20] Choo, above n. 15, ch. 4; see also s. 76(4) of PACE, which allows a court to admit evidence of matters discovered in consequence of an inadmissible confession.

[21] Compare RCCJ, *Report*, para. 7.36, with the Note of Dissent by Professor Zander, para. 47.

supported by many other professionals,[22] should be taken as the starting-point for further research rather than as grounds for concluding that all is well.

However, the discussion of occupational cultures which began in Chapter 3 and continued in subsequent chapters makes it plain that there is, at the very least, a risk that simply changing the rules will fail. The risk of failure would be greatest where the particular occupational culture is adverse and strong. It is therefore necessary to attempt to reshape the occupational cultures of some of those working within the criminal process. Ethical principles need to be drawn up which spell out the role responsibilities of prosecutors and defence lawyers, and the constraints on their pursuit of these goals. The ethical principles should ideally be supported by examples of situations in which they are intended to bite. This would be a means of challenging occupational cultures in a direct way. In order to do that, of course, it would be necessary to have a reasonably accurate impression of the operation of occupational cultures in practice, and the available research (discussed in foregoing chapters) provides plenty of evidence of some unethical practices (without suggesting that all members of the various groups follow these practices). Ideas such as 'society expects us to fight crime with our hands tied behind our backs' must be carefully and persuasively unpicked. A further necessary step is to incorporate into training the reasons for respecting rights, and reorienting professional goals and official performance indicators in a way that reveres and rewards respect for rights over the mere obtaining of convictions.

None of this means that convicting the guilty is unimportant; rather, it emphasizes that this worthy goal should be achieved by fair processes. This is not just a matter of ensuring that this country upholds the European Convention on Human Rights, although that is constitutionally important after the Human Rights Bill. There is also evidence that people in general regard fair procedures as an essential element in a criminal justice system. To set against the belief of some politicians that public confidence in the system would be threatened by thoroughgoing respect for human rights (not that it is often thus expressed) are the findings of social psychologists such as Tom Tyler, which insist that the fairness of procedures is no less valued and may be more highly valued than the outcomes of those procedures.[23] Tyler found that people 'focus more on their opportunities to state their case than they do on their influence over decisions',[24] and even went so far as to claim that 'if people receive fair procedures, outcome is not relevant to their reactions. If they do not, it is.'[25]

---

[22] M. Zander and P. Henderson, *Crown Court Study*, RCCJ Research Study 19 (1993), paras. 2.4.8, 2.4.13, 2.5.4, and 2.5.13.

[23] T. R. Tyler, *Why People Obey the Law* (1990).   [24] *Ibid.* 126.   [25] *Ibid.* 101.

5. The Criminal Process of the Future

In this chapter some reformist proposals have been advanced in relation to the selected stages of the criminal process discussed earlier in the book. The proposals have been made, self-evidently, from a limited perspective. For example, they have not taken account of the possibility that the criminal justice system may move significantly towards a restorative paradigm in the coming years. Experiments with restorative justice are already beginning in certain areas, and the provisions of the Crime and Disorder Bill on warnings for young offenders will bring them into a more central position. However, although there is a small number of schemes for restorative justice that apply to adult offenders and to moderately serious cases, the principal thrust of the movement is towards young offenders and non-serious offences.[26] There are potential problems with such developments, such as the safeguarding of defendant's rights, the possibility of pressure on victims, and the likelihood of unequal burdens on offenders, but it is right that forms of restorative justice should be tried so as to enable an evaluation of the benefits and disadvantages.

Any set of detailed proposals such as those in this book is likely to have a modest effect if other aspects of the criminal justice system remain little changed, and any changes in the criminal justice system may have a modest effect if various social structures and policies remain little changed. Moreover, considerations of cost and public expenditure must be taken into account by anyone who forsakes the cover of academic discussion to venture some policy proposals. Recognizing cost as a constraint does not, however, argue against fundamental change. The Report of the 1993 Royal Commission was a missed opportunity in criminal justice reform. It was—inevitably, as the Commissioners would doubtless argue—pervaded by managerial and fiscal concerns, but its approach was largely to consider expenditure in relation to discrete stages in the process. The annual budget of the whole system—including police, prosecutors, courts, legal aid, prisons, and so forth—is immense. A different approach would be to consider a five-year reorientation of expenditure which would enhance human rights to the greatest extent without increasing the overall budget. Rather than discussing a 'balance' at each stage of the process, the approach would be to meet the challenge of ensuring or maximizing respect for rights with a minimum loss of convictions

---

[26] For further discussion, see, e.g., the ch. by J. Dignan 'Reintegration through Reparation: A Way Forward for Restorative Justice?' in R.A. Duff, S. Marshall, R.E. Dobash, and R.P. Dobash (eds.), *Penal Theory and Practice* (1994); J. Dignan and M. Cavadino, 'Towards a Framework for Conceptualising and Evaluating Models of Criminal Justice from a Victim's Perspective' (1996) 4 *International Review of Victimology* 153, and the selection of readings in von Hirsch and Ashworth (eds.), above n. 11, ch. 7.

of the guilty, looking critically at the roles of the various professional groups, at their powers, and at their practices. In addition to debating the rights of victims, the approach would be to examine methods of preventing crime that promise fewer victims (and fewer offenders), such as the wider availability of pre-school education, improved housing, and other changes in social policy. The inquiry thus strays into spheres of expenditure other than criminal justice, but this is inevitable and proper. Even if the debate could be confined within criminal justice, this approach would place the benefits of, say, pre-trial legal representation in a proper perspective rather than simply seeing it as an extra expense.

It is necessary to think the unthinkable, and to attempt to break free from some traditional modes of thought. The European Convention on Human Rights may to some extent light the way, even though it is a conservative document. It provides a reason for initiating an unprejudiced assessment of the abolition of the guilty plea discount and of the drawing of adverse inferences from failure to answer police questions, to give two examples of changes indicated by the ECHR. Some would doubtless wish to see more fundamental changes in the criminal justice system, and indeed it has been argued above that there should be a greater emphasis on fairness (particularly in respect of diversion from the criminal process), that a clearer ethical lead should be given to those working within the system, and that no set of changes is likely to be successful in the absence of wider changes in social policy, education, and housing. In all these matters, the priority should be to determine the desirable reforms, to create strategies for ensuring that they are properly received by those within the system who are likely to have to operate them, and then to try to ensure that they are not undermined by ill-informed and adverse reportage in the mass media.

Appendix
Parts of the European Convention on Human Rights incorporated by the Human Rights Bill 1998

The Governments signatory hereto, being Members of the Council of Europe,

Considering the Universal Declaration of Human Rights proclaimed by the General Assembly of the United Nations on 10 December 1948;

Considering that this Declaration aims at securing the universal and effective recognition and observance of the Rights therein declared;

Considering that the aim of the Council of Europe is the achievement of greater unity between its Members and that one of the methods by which the aim is to be pursued is the maintenance and further realization of Human Rights and Fundamental Freedoms;

Reaffirming their profound belief in those Fundamental Freedoms which are the foundation of justice and peace in the world and are best maintained on the one hand by an effective political democracy and on the other by a common understanding and observance of the Human Rights upon which they depend;

Being resolved, as the Governments of European countries which are like-minded and have a common heritage of political traditions, ideals, freedom and the rule of law to take the first steps for the collective enforcement of certain of the Rights stated in the Universal Declaration;

Have agreed as follows:

Article 1

The High Contracting Parties shall secure to everyone within their jurisdiction the rights and freedoms defined in Section I of this Convention.

Section I

Article 2

1. Everyone's right to life shall be protected by law. No one shall be deprived of his life intentionally save in the execution of a sentence of a court following his conviction of a crime for which this penalty is provided by law.

2. Deprivation of life shall not be regarded as inflicted in contravention of this Article when it results from the use of force which is no more than absolutely necessary:

(*a*) in defence of any person from unlawful violence;

(*b*) in order to effect a lawful arrest or to prevent the escape of a person lawfully detained;

(*c*) in action lawfully taken for the purpose of quelling a riot or insurrection.

Article 3

No one shall be subjected to torture or to inhuman or degrading treatment or punishment.

Article 4

1. No one shall be held in slavery or servitude.

2. No one shall be required to perform forced or compulsory labour.

3. For the purpose of this Article the term 'forced or compulsory labour' shall not include:

(*a*) any work required to be done in the ordinary course of detention imposed according to the provisions of Article 5 of this Convention or during conditional release from such detention;

(*b*) any service of a military character or, in case of conscientious objectors in countries where they are recognized, service exacted instead of compulsory military service;

(*c*) any service exacted in case of an emergency or calamity threatening the life or well-being of the community;

(*d*) any work or service which forms part of normal civic obligations.

Article 5

1. Everyone has the right to liberty and security of person. No one shall be deprived of his liberty save in the following cases and in accordance with a procedure prescribed by law;

(*a*) the lawful detention of a person after conviction by a competent court;

(*b*) the lawful arrest or detention of a person for non-compliance with the lawful order of a court or in order to secure the fulfilment of any obligation prescribed by law;

(*c*) the lawful arrest or detention of a person effected for the purpose of bringing him before the competent legal authority on reasonable suspicion of having committed an offence or when it is reasonably considered necessary to prevent his committing an offence or fleeing after having done so;

(*d*) the detention of a minor by lawful order for the purpose of educational supervision or his lawful detention for the purpose of bringing him before the competent legal authority;

(*e*) the lawful detention of persons for the prevention of the spreading of infectious diseases, of persons of unsound mind, alcoholics or drug addicts, or vagrants;

(*f*) the lawful arrest or detention of a person to prevent his effecting an unauthorized entry into the country or of a person against whom action is being taken with a view to deportation or extradition.

2. Everyone who is arrested shall be informed promptly, in a language which he understands, of the reasons for his arrest and of any charge against him.

3. Everyone arrested or detained in accordance with the provisions of paragraph 1(*c*) of this Article shall be brought promptly before a judge or other officer authorized by law to exercise judicial power and shall be entitled to trial within a reasonable time or to release pending trial. Release may be conditioned by guarantees to appear for trial.

4. Everyone who is deprived of his liberty by arrest or detention shall be entitled to take proceedings by which the lawfulness of his detention shall be decided speedily by a court and his release ordered if the detention is not lawful.

5. Everyone who has been the victim of arrest or detention in contravention of the provisions of this article shall have an enforceable right to compensation.

Article 6

1. In the determination of his civil rights and obligations or of any criminal charge against him, everyone is entitled to a fair and public hearing within a reasonable time by an independent and impartial tribunal established by law. Judgment shall be pronounced publicly but the press and public may be excluded from all or part of the trial in the interest of morals, public order or national security in a democratic society, where the interests of juveniles or the protection of the private life of the parties so require, or to the extent strictly necessary in the opinion of the court in special circumstances where publicity would prejudice the interests of justice.

2. Everyone charged with a criminal offence shall be presumed innocent until proved guilty according to law.

3. Everyone charged with a criminal offence has the following minimum rights:

- (*a*) to be informed promptly, in a language which he understands and in detail, of the nature and cause of the accusation against him;
- (*b*) to have adequate time and facilities for the preparation of his defence;
- (*c*) to defend himself in person or through legal assistance of his own choosing or, if he has not sufficient means to pay for legal assistance, to be given it free when the interests of justice so require;
- (*d*) to examine or have examined witnesses against him and to obtain the attendance and examination of witnesses on his behalf under the same conditions as witnesses against him;
- (*e*) to have the free assistance of an interpreter if he cannot understand or speak the language used in court.

Article 7

1. No one shall be held guilty of any criminal offence on account of any act or omission which did not constitute a criminal offence under national or international law at the time when it was committed. Nor shall a heavier penalty be imposed than the one that was applicable at the time the criminal offence was committed.

2. This article shall not prejudice the trial and punishment of any person for any act or omission which, at the time when it was committed, was criminal according to the general principles of law recognized by civilized nations.

Article 8

1. Everyone has the right to respect for his private and family life, his home and his correspondence.
2. There shall be no interference by a public authority with the exercise of this right except such as is in accordance with the law and is necessary in a democratic society in the interests of national security, public safety or the economic well-being of the country, for the prevention of disorder or crime, for the protection of health or morals, or for the protection of the rights and freedoms of others.

Article 9

1. Everyone has the right to freedom of thought, conscience and religion; this right includes freedom to change his religion or belief, and freedom, either alone or in community with others and in public or private, to manifest his religion or belief, in worship, teaching, practice and observance.
2. Freedom to manifest one's religion or beliefs shall be subject only to such limitations as are prescribed by law and are necessary in a democratic society, in the interests of public safety, for the protection of public order, health or morals, or for the protection of the rights and freedoms of others.

Article 10

1. Everyone has the right to freedom of expression. This right shall include freedom to hold opinions and to receive and impart information and ideas without interference by public authority and regardless of frontiers. This article shall not prevent States from requiring the licensing of broadcasting, television or cinema enterprises.
2. The exercise of these freedoms, since it carries with it duties and responsibilities, may be subject to such formalities, conditions, restrictions or penalties as are prescribed by law and are necessary in a democratic society, in the interests of national security, territorial integrity or public safety, for the prevention of disorder or crime, for the protection of health or morals, for the protection of the reputation or rights of others, for preventing the disclosure of information received in confidence, or for maintaining the authority and impartiality of the judiciary.

Article 11

1. Everyone has the right to freedom of peaceful assembly and to freedom of association with others, including the right to form and to join trade unions for the protection of his interests.
2. No restrictions shall be placed on the exercise of these rights other than such as are prescribed by law and are necessary in a democratic society in the interests of national security or public safety, for the prevention of disorder or crime, for the protection of health or morals or for the protection of the rights and freedoms of others. This Article shall not prevent the imposition of lawful restrictions on the exercise of these rights by members of the armed forces, of the police or of the administration of the State.

Article 12

Men and women of marriageable age have the right to marry and to found a family, according to the national laws governing the exercise of this right.

Article 14

The enjoyment of the rights and freedoms set forth in this Convention shall be secured without discrimination on any ground such as sex, race, colour, language, religion, political or other opinion, national or social origin, association with a national minority, property, birth or other status.

Article 15

1. In time of war or other public emergency threatening the life of the nation any High Contracting Party may take measures derogating from its obligations under this Convention to the extent strictly required by the exigencies of the situation, provided that such measures are not inconsistent with its other obligations under international law.
2. No derogation from Article 2, except in respect of deaths resulting from lawful acts of war, or from Articles 3, 4 (paragraph 1) and 7 shall be made under this provision.
3. Any High Contracting Party availing itself of this right of derogation shall keep the Secretary-General of the Council of Europe fully informed of the measures which it has taken and the reasons therefore. It shall also inform the Secretary-General of the Council of Europe when such measures have ceased to operate and the provisions of the Convention are again being fully executed.

Article 16

Nothing in Articles 10, 11 and 14 shall be regarded as preventing the High Contracting Parties from imposing restrictions on the political activity of aliens.

Article 17

Nothing in this Convention may be interpreted as implying for any State, group or person any right to engage in any activity or perform any act aimed at the destruction of any of the rights and freedoms set forth herein or at their limitation to a greater extent than is provided for in the Convention.

Article 18

The restrictions permitted under this Convention to the said rights and freedoms shall not be applied for any purpose other than those for which they have been prescribed.

Protocol

First Protocol: Enforcement of Certain Rights and Freedoms not included in Section I of the Convention

The Governments signatory hereto, being Members of the Council of Europe,

Being resolved to take steps to ensure the collective enforcement of certain rights and freedoms other than those already included in Section I of the Convention for the Protection of Human Rights and Fundamental Freedoms signed at Rome on 4th November, 1950 (hereinafter referred to as 'the Convention'),

Have agreed as follows:

Article 1

Every natural or legal person is entitled to the peaceful enjoyment of his possessions. No one shall be deprived of his possessions except in the public interest and subject to the conditions provided for by law and by the general principles of international law.

The preceding provisions shall not, however, in any way impair the right of a State to enforce such laws as it deems necessary to control the use of property in accordance with the general interest or to secure the payment of taxes or other contributions or penalties.

Article 2

No person shall be denied the right to education. In the exercise of any functions which it assumes in relation to education and to teaching, the State shall respect the right of parents to ensure such education and teaching in conformity with their own religious and philosophical convictions.

Article 3

The High Contracting Parties undertake to hold free elections at reasonable intervals by secret ballot, under conditions which will ensure the free expression of the opinion of the people in the choice of the legislature.

Select Bibliography

Altschuler, A. (1983), 'Implementing the Criminal Defendant's Right to Trial', *U. Chi. LR*, **50**: 931.

Ashworth, A. (1993), 'Victim Impact Statements and Sentencing', *Crim. LR*, 498.

—— (1993), 'Some Doubts about Restorative Justice', *Criminal Law Forum*, **4**: 277.

—— (1995), *Sentencing and Criminal Justice*, 2nd edn., London: Butterworths.

—— (1995), *Principles of Criminal Law*, 2nd edn., Oxford: Oxford University Press.

—— (1998), 'Should the Police be Allowed to Use Deception?', *Law Quarterly Review*, **114**: 108.

——, and Fionda, J. (1994), 'The New Code for Crown Prosecutors: Prosecution, Accountability and the Public Interest', *Crim. LR*, 894.

Audit Commission (1993), *Tackling Crime Effectively*, London: Audit Commission.

—— (1996), *Misspent Youth: Young People and Crimes*, London: Audit Commission

Baker, E. (1998), 'Taking European Criminal Law Seriously', *Crim. LR*, 361.

Baldwin, J. (1985), *Pre-Trial Justice*, Oxford: Oxford University Press.

—— (1992), *The Role of Legal Representatives at Police Stations*, Royal Commission on Criminal Justice Research Study No. 3, London: H.M.S.O.

—— (1992), *The Supervision of Police Investigations in Serious Criminal Cases*, Royal Commission on Criminal Justice Research Study No. 4, London: H.M.S.O.

—— (1997), 'Understanding Judge Ordered and Directed Acquittals in the Crown Court', *Crim. LR*, 536.

——, and McConville, M. (1977), *Negotiated Justice*, Oxford: Martin Robertson.

Baldwin, R., and Hawkins, K. (1984), 'Discretionary Justice: Davis Reconsidered', *Public Law*, 570.

Barclay, G. C. (1995), *Digest 3: Information on the Criminal Justice System in England and Wales*, London: Home Office.

Beetham, D. (1991), *Legitimacy and Power*, London: Macmillan.

Bennion, F. (1986), 'The Crown Prosecution Service', *Crim. LR*, 4.

Bingham, Sir T. (1993), 'The European Convention on Human Rights: Time to Incorporate', *Law Quarterly Review*, **109**: 390.

Bittner, E. (1967), 'The Police on Skid Row: a Study in Peace-Keeping', *American Sociological Review*, **32**: 699.

Blagg, H. (1997), 'A Just Measure of Shame? Aboriginal Youth and Conferencing in Australia', *BJ Crim.*, **37**: 481.

Blair, I. (1985), *Investigating Rape: a New Approach for the Police*, London: the Police Foundation.

Blake, M., and Ashworth, A. (1998), 'Some Ethical Issues in Prosecuting and Defending Criminal Cases', *Crim. LR*, 16.

Block, B., Corbett, C., and Peay, J. (1993), *Ordered and Directed Acquittals in the Crown Court*, Royal Commission on Criminal Justice Research Study No. 15, London: H.M.S.O.

Bottomley, A. K. (1968), 'The Granting of Bail: Principles and Practice', *MLR*, **31**: 40.

—— (1973), *Decisions in the Penal Process*, Oxford: Martin Robertson.

Bottoms, A. E., and McClean, J. D. (1976), *Defendants in the Criminal Process*, London: Routledge.

Braithwaite, J. (1989), *Crime, Shame and Reintegration*, Cambridge: Cambridge University Press.

—— (1997), 'Conferencing and Plurality: reply to Blagg', *BJ Crim.*, **37**: 502.

——, and Pettit, P. (1990), *Not Just Deserts: a Republican Theory of Criminal Justice*, Oxford: Oxford University Press.

Bredar, J. (1992), 'Moving up the Day of Reckoning: Strategies for Attacking the Problem of Cracked Trials', *Crim. LR*, 153.

Brink, B., and Stone, C. (1988), 'Defendants who do not ask for Bail', *Crim. LR*, 152.

Brown, D., Larcombe, K., and Ellis, C. (1993), *Changing the Code*, Home Office Research Study 129, London: H.M.S.O.

Brown, I., and Hullin, R. (1992), 'A Study of Sentencing in the Leeds Magistrates' Court: the Treatment of Ethnic Minority and White Offenders', *BJ Crim.*, **32**: 41.

Brownlee, I., Mulcahy, A., and Walker, C. P. (1994), 'Pre-Trial Reviews, Court Efficiency and Justice: a Study in Leeds and Bradford Magistrates' Courts', *Howard JCJ*, **33**: 109.

Bucke, T., and Brown D. (1997), *In Police Custody: police powers and suspects' rights under the revised PACE codes of practice*, Home Office Research Study 174, London: Home Office.

Burney, E., and Pearson, G. (1995), 'Mentally Disordered Offenders: Finding a Focus for Diversion', *Howard JCJ*, **34**: 291.

Burrows, P., Henderson, P., and Morgan, P. (1994), *Improving Bail Decisions: the Bail Process Project*, London: Home Office Research and Planning Unit.

Carlen, P., and Worrall, A., eds. (1987), *Gender, Crime and Justice*, Milton Keynes: Open University Press.

Carson, D. (1989), 'Prosecuting People with Mental Handicaps', *Crim. LR*, 87.

Cavadino, M., and Dignan, J. (1997), *The Penal System: an Introduction*, 2nd edn., London: Sage.

Cavadino, P., and Gibson, B. (1993), *Bail: the Law, Best Practice and the Debate*, Winchester: Waterside Press.

Christie, N. (1977), 'Conflicts as Property', *BJ Crim.*, **17**: 1.

Clare, I., and Gudjonsson, G. (1993), *Devising and Piloting an Experimental Version of the 'Notice to Detained Persons'*, Royal Commission on Criminal Justice Research Study No. 7, London: H.M.S.O.

Clarkson, C., Cretney, A., Davis, G., and Shepherd, J. (1994), 'Assaults: the Relationship between Seriousness, Criminalisation and Punishment', *Crim. LR*, 4.

Clayton, R., and Tomlinson, H. (1987), *Civil Actions against the Police*, London: Sweet & Maxwell.

Choo, A. (1993), *Abuse of Process and Judicial Stays of Criminal Proceedings*, Oxford: Oxford University Press.

Corre, N. (1990), *Bail in Criminal Proceedings*, London: Fourmat.

Council of Europe (1985), *The Position of the Victim in the Framework of Criminal Law and Procedure*, Strasbourg: Council of Europe.

Cranston, R. (1979), *Regulating Business*, Oxford: Oxford University Press.

Cretney, A., and Davis, G. (1996), 'Prosecuting "Domestic" Assault', *Crim. LR*, 162.

——, ——, Clarkson, C., and Shepherd, J. (1994), 'Criminalising Assault: the Failure of the "Offence against Society" Model', *BJ Crim.* **34**: 15.

Criminal Law Revision Committee (1972), *Eleventh Report: Evidence (General)*, Cmnd. 4991, London: H.M.S.O.

Crisp, D., and Moxon, D. (1995), *Case Screening by the Crown Prosecution Service: How and Why Cases are Terminated*, Home Office Research Study 137, London: H.M.S.O.

——, Whitaker, C., and Harris, J. (1995), *Public Interest Case Assessment Schemes*, Home Office Research Study 138, London: H.M.S.O.

Damaska, M. (1973), 'Evidentiary Barriers to Conviction and Two Models of Criminal procedure: a Comparative Study', *U. Pa. LR*, **121**: 506.

—— (1976), *The Faces of Justice and State Authority*, New Haven: Yale University Press.

Darbyshire, P. (1991), 'The Lamp that Shows that Freedom Lives: is it worth the candle?', *Crim. LR*, 740.

—— (1997), 'For the New Lord Chancellor: Some Causes for Concern about Magistrates', *Crim. LR*, 861.

Davies, F. G. (1995), 'CPS Charging Standards: a Cynic's View', *Justice of the Peace*, **159**: 203.

—— (1997), 'Ten Years of the Crown Prosecution Service: the Verdict', *Justice of the Peace*, **161**: 207.

Daw, R. (1994), 'The CPS Code – a Response', *Crim. LR*, 904.

Dennis, I. (1995), 'Instrumental Protection, Human Right or Functional Necessity? Reassessing the Privilege against Self-Incrimination', *Cambridge LJ*, **54**: 342.

Dignan, J. (1994), 'Reintegration through Reparation: a Way Forward for Restorative Justice', in Duff, Marshall, Dobash and Dobash, q.v.

——, and Cavadino, M. (1996), 'Towards a Framework for Conceptualising and Evaluating Models of Criminal Justice from a Victim's Perspective', *International Review of Victimology*, **4**: 153.

Dine, J. (1993), 'European Community Criminal Law', *Crim. LR*, 246.

Doran, S., and Jackson, J. D. (1997), 'The Case for Jury Waiver', *Crim. LR*, 155.

Duff, P. (1993), 'The Prosecutor Fine and Social Control', *BJ Crim.*, **33**: 481.

——, and Meechan, K. (1992), 'The Prosecutor Fine', *Crim. LR*, 22.

Duff, R. A., Marshall, S. E., Dobash, R. E., and Dobash, R. P., eds. (1994), *Penal Theory and Practice*, Manchester: Manchester University Press.

——, and Simmonds, N. E., eds. (1984), *Philosophy and the Criminal Law*, Hanover: Springer Verlag.

Dunnighan, C., and Norris, C. (1995), 'A Risky Business: Exchange, Bargaining and Risk in Recruitment and Running of Informers by English Police Officers' (unpublished).

Dworkin, R. (1977), *Taking Rights Seriously*, London: Duckworth.

Easton, S. (1991), *The Right to Silence*, Aldershot: Avebury.

—— (1991), 'Bodily Samples and the Privilege against Self-Incrimination', *Crim. LR*, 18.

Eaton, M. (1987), 'The Question of Bail', in Carlen and Worrall, q.v.

Edwards, A. (1997), 'Criminal Procedure and Investigations Act 1996: the Procedural Aspects', *Crim. LR*, 321.

Evans, R. (1993), *The Conduct of Police Interviews with Juveniles*, Royal Commission on Criminal Justice Research Study No. 8, London: H.M.S.O.

—— (1993), 'Evaluating Young Adult Diversion Schemes in the Metropolitan Police District', *Crim. LR*, 490.

——, and Ellis, R. (1997), *Police Cautioning in the 1990s*, Home Office Research Findings No. 33, London: Home Office.

Ewing, K., and Gearty, C (1990), *Freedom under Thatcher*, Oxford: Oxford University Press.

Farrington, D., and Morris, A. (1983), 'Sex, Sentencing and Reconvictions', *BJ Crim.*, 23: 229.

Fawcett, J. E. S. (1987), *Application of the European Convention on Human Rights*, 2nd edn., Oxford: Oxford University Press.

Feeley, M. (1979), *The Process is the Punishment*, New York: Russell Sage Foundation.

Feinberg, J. (1992), 'In Defence of Moral Rights', *Oxford JLS*, 12: 149.

Fennell, P. (1991), 'Diversion of Mentally Disordered Offenders from Custody', *Crim. LR*, 33.

Fenwick, H. (1995), 'Rights of Victims in the Criminal Justice System: Rhetoric or Reality?', *Crim. LR*, 843.

Field, S., and Thomas, P. A., eds. (1994), *Justice and Efficiency*, Oxford: Blackwell.

Fisse, B., and Braithwaite, J. (1993), *Corporations, Crime and Accountability*, Sydney: University of Sydney Press.

Fitzgerald, M. (1993), *Ethnic Minorities and the Criminal Justice System*, Royal Commission on Criminal Justice Research Study No. 20, London: H.M.S.O.

Foote, C. (1954), 'Compelling Appearance in Court: the Administration of Bail in Philadelphia', *U. Pa. LR*, 102: 1031.

Fox, R. G. (1990), 'Jago's Case: Delay, Unfairness and Abuse of Process in the High Court of Australia', *Crim. LR*, 552.

Freed, D. J., and Wald, P. (1964), *Bail in the United States*, New York: Vera Institute of Justice.

Galligan, D. (1988), 'More Scepticism about Scepticism', *Oxford JLS*, 8: 249.

—— (1988), 'The Right to Silence Reconsidered', *Current Legal Problems*, 80.

Gearty, C., ed. (1997), *European Civil Liberties and the European Convention on Human Rights*, Amsterdam: Kluwer.

Grace, S. (1995), *Policing Domestic Violence in the 1990s*, Home Office Research Study 139, London: H.M.S.O.

Greer, S. (1990), 'The Right to Silence: a Review of the Current Debate', *MLR*, 53: 709.

Gregory, J., and Lees, S. (1996), 'Attrition in Rape and Sexual Assault Cases', *BJ Crim.*, 36: 1.

Grevi, V. (1994), 'The New Italian Code of Criminal Procedure: a Concise Overview', in Pizzarusso, q.v.

Gudjonsson, G. (1992), *The Psychology of Interrogations Confessions and Testimony*, London: Wiley .

——, Clare, I., Rutter, S., and Pearse, J. (1993), *Persons at Risk during Interviews in Police Custody: the Identification of Vulnerabilities*, Royal Commission on Criminal Justice Research Study 12, London: H.M.S.O.

Harding, C., Fennell, P., Jorg, N., and Swart, B., eds. (1995), *Criminal Justice in Europe: a Comparative Study*, Oxford: Oxford University Press.

Harris, D. J., O'Boyle, M., and Warbrick, C. (1995), *The Law of the European Convention on Human Rights*, London: Butterworths.

——, and Joseph, S., eds. (1995), *The International Covenant on Civil and Political Rights and United Kingdom Law*, London: Butterworths

Hart, H. L. A. (1968), *Punishment and Responsibility*, Oxford: Oxford University Press.

Hawkins, K. (1984), *Environment and Enforcement*, Oxford: Oxford University Press.

——, ed. (1992), *The Uses of Discretion*, Oxford: Oxford University Press.

——, and Thomas, J., eds. (1984), *Enforcing Regulation*, Oxford: Oxford University Press.

Hayes, J., and O'Higgins, P., eds. (1990), *Lessons from Northern Ireland*, Belfast: SLS Publications.

Hedderman, C., and Hough, M. (1994), *Does the Criminal Justice System Treat Men and Women Differently?*, Home Office Research Findings No. 10, London: Home Office.

——, and Moxon, D. (1992), *Magistrates' Court or Crown Court? Mode of Trial Decisions and Sentencing*, Home Office Research Study 125, London: Home Office.

Heinz, W. (1989), 'The Problems of Imprisonment', in Hood, q.v.

Henderson, P. (1991), *Monitoring Time Limits on Custodial Remands*, Home Office Research and Planning Unit Paper 69, London: Home Office.

Herrmann, J. (1974), 'The Rule of Compulsory Prosecution and the Scope of Prosecutorial Discretion in Germany', *U. Chi. LR*, 41: 468.

—— (1992), 'Bargaining Justice: a Bargain for German Criminal Justice?', *U. Pittsburgh LR*, 53: 755.

Heydon, J. D. (1980), 'Entrapment and Unfairly Obtained Evidence in the House of Lords', *Crim. LR*, 129.

Hilson, C. (1993), 'Discretion to Prosecute and Judicial Review', *Crim. LR*, 639.

Hodgson, J. (1997), 'Vulnerable Suspects and the Appropriate Adult', *Crim. LR*, 785.

Holdaway, S. (1983), *Inside the British Police*, Oxford: Blackwell.

Home Office (1983), *An Independent Prosecution Service for England and Wales*, Cmnd. 9074, London: H.M.S.O.

—— (1989), *Report of the Working Group on the Right of Silence*, London: Home Office.

—— (1991), *Custody, Care and Justice*, Cmnd. 1647, London: H.M.S.O.

—— (1996), *The Victim's Charter*, London: Home Office.

—— (1997), *Rights Brought Home: the Human Rights Bill*, Cmnd. 3782, London: Home Office.

—— (1997), *No More Excuses: a New Approach to Tackling Youth Crime in England and Wales*, London: Home Office.

Hood, R. G., ed. (1989), *Crime and Criminal Policy in Europe: Proceedings of a European Colloquium*, Oxford: Centre for Criminological Research.

—— (1992), *Race and Sentencing*, Oxford: Oxford University Press.

Hough, M. (1987), 'Thinking about Effectiveness', *BJ Crim.*, 27: 70.

Houlder, B. (1997), 'The Importance of Preserving the Jury System and the Right of Election for Trial', *Crim. LR*, 875.

Hoyano, A., Hoyano, B., Davis, G., and Goldie, S. (1997), 'A Study of the Impact of the Revised Code for Crown Prosecutors', *Crim. LR*, 556.

Hucklesby, A. (1996), 'Bail or Jail? The Practical Operation of the Bail Act 1976', *Journal of Law and Society*, 23: 213.

—— (1997), 'Remand Decision Makers', *Crim. LR*, 269.

—— (1997), 'Court Culture: an Explanation of Variations in the Use of Bail by Magistrates' Courts', *Howard JCJ*, 36: 129.

Hughes, G., Pilkington, A., and Leistan, R. (1998), 'Diversion in a Culture of Severity', *Howard JCJ*, 37: 16.

Humphreys, C. (1955), 'The Duties of Prosecuting Counsel', *Crim. LR*, 739.

Hunt, A., and Young, R. (1995), 'Criminal Justice and Academics: Publish and Be Ignored?', *Holdsworth Law Review*, 17: 193.

Hutter, B. (1988), *The Reasonable Arm of the Law*, Oxford: Oxford University Press.

—— (1989), 'Variations in Regulatory Enforcement Style', *Law and Policy*, 11: 153.

Ipp, D. A. (1998), 'Lawyers' Duties to the Court', *LQR*, 114: 63.

Irving, B., and Hilgendorf, L. (1980), *Police Interrogation: the Psychological Approach*, Royal Commision on Criminal Procedure Research Study No. 1, London: H.M.S.O.

——, and Dunnighan, C. (1993), *Human Factors in the Quality Control of CID Investigations*, Royal Commission on Criminal Justice Research Study No. 21, London: H.M.S.O.

Jackson, J. D. (1986), 'The Insufficiency of Identification Evidence based on Personal Impression', *Crim. LR*, 203.

—— (1991), 'Curtailing the Right of Silence: Lessons from Northern Ireland', *Crim. LR, 404*.

—— (1993), 'The Evidence Recommendations', *Crim. LR*, 817.

—— (1994), 'The Right of Silence: Judicial Responses to Parliamentary Encroachment', *MLR*, **57**: 270.

——, and Doran, S. (1995), *Judge without Jury*, Oxford: Oxford University Press.

Jackson, S. (1998), 'Family Group Conferences in Youth Justice? The Issues for Implementation in England and Wales', *Howard JCJ* **37**: 34.

Jefferson, T., and Walker, M. (1992), 'Ethnic Minorities in the Criminal Justice System', *Crim. LR*, 83.

Jones, P. R. (1985), 'Remand Decisions at Magistrates' Courts', in Moxon, q.v.

——, and Goldkamp, J. S. (1991), 'Judicial Guidelines for Pre-Trial Release: Research and Policy Developments in the United States', *Howard JCJ*, **30**: 140.

Jung, H. (1993), 'Criminal Justice: a European Perspective', *Crim. LR*, 237.

—— (1997), 'Plea-Bargaining and its Repercussions on the Theory of Criminal Procedure', *European Journal of Crime, Criminal Law and Criminal Justice*, **5**: 112.

JUSTICE (1993), *Negotiated Justice: a Closer Look at the Implications of Plea Bargains*, London: JUSTICE.

Kamisar, Y. (1987), 'Comparative Reprehensibility and the Fourth Amendment Exclusionary Rule', *Michigan LR*, **86**: 1.

Kennedy, M., Truman, C., Keyes, S., and Cameron, A. (1997), 'Supported Bail for Mentally Vulnerable Defendants', *Howard JCJ*, **36**: 158.

King, M. (1981), *The Framework of Criminal Justice*, London: Croom Helm.

Lacey, N. (1996), 'Community in Legal Theory: Idea, Ideal or Ideology', *Studies in Law, Politics and Society*, **15**: 105.

Langbein, J. (1974), 'Controlling Prosecutorial Discretion in Germany', *U. Chi. LR*, **41**: 439.

Law Commission (1997), *Criminal Law: Consents to Prosecution*, Consultation Paper No. 149, London: H.M.S.O.

Leigh, L. H., and Zedner, L. (1992), *A Report on the Administration of Criminal Justice in the Pre-Trial Phase in France and Germany*, Royal Commission on Criminal Justice Research Study No. 1, London: H.M.S.O.

Leng, R. (1993), *The Right to Silence in Police Interrogation*, Royal Commission on Criminal Justice Research Study No. 10, London: H.M.S.O.

—— (1994), 'A Recipe for Miscarriage: the RCCJ and Informal Interviews', in McConville and Bridges (eds.), q.v.

—— (1995), 'Losing Sight of the Defendant?', *Crim. LR*, 704.

——, and Taylor, R. (1996), *The Criminal Procedure and Investigations Act 1996*, London: Blackstone Press.

Lensing, H., and Rayar, L. (1992), 'Notes on Criminal Procedure in the Netherlands', *Crim. LR*, 623.

Lester, A. (1984), 'Fundamental Rights: the U.K. Isolated?', *Public Law*, 46.

Levi, M. (1993), *The Investigation, Prosecution and Trial of Serious Fraud*, Royal Commission on Criminal Justice Research Study No. 14, London: H.M.S.O.

Lidstone, K., Hogg, R., and Sutcliffe, F. (1980), *Prosecutions by Private Individuals and Non-Police Agencies*, Royal Commission on Criminal Procedure Research Study No. 10, London: H.M.S.O.

Liebling, A., and Krarup, H. (1993), *Suicide Attempts and Self-Injury in Male Prisons*, Cambridge: Institute of Criminology.

Lloyd, C. (1992), *Bail Information Schemes: Practice and Effect*, Home Office Research and Planning Unit Paper 69, London: Home Office.

Lockton, D., and Ward, R. (1997), *Domestic Violence*, London: Cavendish.

McBarnet, D., and Whelan, C. (1991), 'The Elusive Spirit of the Law: Formalism and the Struggle for Legal Control', *MLR* 54: 848.

McCabe, S., and Purves, R. (1972), *By-Passing the Jury*, Oxford: University of Oxford Penal Research Unit.

McConville, M. (1992), 'Videotaping Interrogations: Police Behaviour on and off Camera', *Crim. LR*, 532.

——, and Baldwin, J. (1981), *Prosecution, Courts and Conviction*, Oxford: Oxford University Press.

——, and Bridges, L. (1993), 'Pleading Guilty Whilst Maintaining Innocence', *New LJ*, **143**: 160.

——, ——, Hodgson, J., and Pavlovic, A. (1994), *Standing Accused*, Oxford: Oxford University Press.

——, and Hodgson, J. (1993), *Custodial Legal Advice and the Right of Silence*, Royal Commission on Criminal Justice Research Study No. 16, London: H.M.S.O.

——, Sanders, A., and Leng, R. (1991), *The Case for the Prosecution*, London: Routledge.

——, and Bridges, L., eds. (1994), *Criminal Justice in Crisis*, London: Edward Elgar.

McKenzie, I., Morgan, R., and Reiner, R. (1990), 'Helping the Police with their Inquiries: the Necessity Principle and Voluntary Attendance at the Police Station', *Crim. LR*, 4.

McMahon, M. (1990), 'Net-Widening: Vagaries in the Use of a Concept', *BJ Crim.*, **30**: 121.

Maguire, M., and John, T. (1996), 'Covert and Deceptive Policing in England and Wales: Issues in Regulation and Practice', *European Journal of Crime, Criminal Law and Criminal Justice*.

——, and Norris, C. (1993), *The Conduct and Supervision of Criminal Investigations*, Royal Commission on Criminal Justice Research Study No. 5, London: H.M.S.O.

——, Morgan, R., and Reiner, R., eds. (1997), *Oxford Handbook of Criminology*, 2nd edn., Oxford: Oxford University Press.

Mair, G., and Nee, C. (1990), *Electronic Monitoring: the Trials and their Results*, Home Office Research Study 120, London: H.M.S.O.

Malleson, K. (1993), *Review of the Appeal Process*, Royal Commission on Criminal Justice Research Study No. 17, London: H.M.S.O.

—— (1995), 'The Criminal Cases Review Commission: How will it Work?', *Crim. LR*, 929.

Manning, P. (1977), *Police Work*, Cambridge, Mass: MIT Press.

Mansfield, G., and Peay, J. (1985), *The Director of Public Prosecutions*, London: Routledge.

May, R. (1997), 'The Legal Effect of a Police Caution', *Crim. LR*, 491.

Mayhew, P., Elliott, K., and Dowds, L. (1989), *The 1988 British Crime Survey*, Home Office Research Study 111, London: H.M.S.O.

——, and Maung, N. A. (1992), *Surveying Crime: Findings from the 1992 British Crime Survey*, Home Office Research Study 132, London: H.M.S.O.

Miers, D. (1992), 'The Responsibilities and Rights of Victims of Crime', *MLR*, 55: 482.

Mirfield, P. (1997), *Silence, Confessions and Improperly Obtained Evidence*, Oxford: Oxford University Press.

Morgan, D., and Stephenson, G., eds. (1994), *Suspicion and Silence*, Oxford: Blackwell.

Morgan, J., and Zedner, L. (1992), *Child Victims*, Oxford: Oxford University Press.

Morgan, P. (1992), *Offending While on Bail: a Survey of Recent Studies*, London: Home Office Research and Planning Unit.

——, and Vennard, J. (1989), *Pre-Trial Delay: the Implications of Time Limits*, Home Office Research Study 110, London: H.M.S.O.

Morgan, R., and Jones, S. (1992), 'Bail or Jail?', in Stockdale and Casale, q.v.

Morison, J., and Leith, P. (1992), *The Barrister's World*, Oxford: Oxford University Press.

Morris, A., Maxwell, G, and Robertson, J. P. (1993), 'Giving Victims a Voice: a New Zealand Experiment', *Howard JCJ*, 32: 304

Morris, N., and Tonry, M. (1990), *Between Prison and Probation*, New York: Oxford University Press.

Mortimer, E., and May, C. (1997), *Electronic Monitoring of Curfew Orders: the Second Year of the Trials*, Home Office Research Findings No. 66, London: Home Office.

Moston, S., and Stephenson, G. (1993), *The Questioning and Interviewing of Suspects outside the Police Station*, Royal Commission on Criminal Justice Research Study No. 22, London: H.M.S.O.

Mott, J. (1983), 'Police Decisions for Dealing with Juvenile Offenders', *BJ Crim.*, 23: 249.

Moxon, D., (ed.) (1985), *Managing Criminal Justice*, London: H.M.S.O.

Mulcahy, A. (1994), 'The Justifications of Justice: Legal Practitioners' Accounts of Negotiated Case Settlements in Magistrates' Courts', *BJ Crim.*, 34: 411.

Munday, R. (1996), 'Inferences from Silence and European Human Rights Law', *Crim. LR*, 370.

Natali, L. M., and Ohlbaum, E. D. (1989), 'Redrafting the Due Process Model: the Preventive Detention Blueprint', *Temple LR*, 62: 1225.

National Audit Office (1997), *The Crown Prosecution Service*, London: National Audit Office.

Newburn, T., and Merry, S. (1990), *Keeping in Touch: Police-Victim Communication in Two Areas*, Home Office Research Study 116, London: H.M.S.O.

Newton, T. (1998), 'The Place of Ethics in Investigative Interviewing by Police Officers', *Howard JCJ*, 37: 52.

Nissman, C. M., and Hagen, E. (1982), *The Prosecution Function*, Washington: Lexington.

Nobles, R., and Schiff, D. (1997), 'The Never Ending Story: Tragic Choices in Criminal Justice?', *MLR*, 60: 293.

O'Connor, P. (1992), 'Prosecution Disclosure: Principle, Practice and Justice', *Crim. LR*, 464.

Packer, H. (1968), *The Limits of the Criminal Sanction*, Stanford, CA: Stanford University Press.

Padfield, N. (1993), 'The Right to Bail: a Canadian Perspective', *Crim. LR*, 510.

Palmer, C. (1996), 'Still Vulnerable after all these Years', *Crim. LR*, 633.

Parker, H., Sumner, M., Jarvis, G. (1989), *Unmasking the Magistrates*, Milton Keynes: Open University Press.

Pattenden, R. (1991), 'Should Confessions be Corroborated?', *LQR*, **107**: 319.

—— (1995), *English Criminal Appeals, 1844–1994*, Oxford: Oxford University Press.

Philpotts, G. J. O., and Lancucki, L. B. (1979), *Previous Convictions, Sentence and Reconvictions*, Home Office Research Study 53, London: H.M.S.O.

Pizzarusso, A., ed. (1994), *Italian Studies in Law, vol. II*, Dordrecht: Martinus Nijhoff.

Pollard, C. (1994), 'A Case for Disclosure?', *Crim. LR*, 42.

—— (1996), 'Public Safety, Accountability and the Courts', *Crim. LR*, 152.

Raifertaigh, U. ni (1997), 'Reconciling Bail Law with the Presumption of Innocence', *Oxford JLS*, **17**: 1.

Raine, J., and Willson, M. (1996), 'The Imposition of Conditions in Bail Decisions', *Howard JCJ*, **35**: 256.

—— (1997), 'Police Bail with Conditions', *BJ Crim.*, **37**: 593.

Reiner, R. (1992), *The Politics of the Police*, 2nd edn., Hemel Hempstead: Wheatsheaf.

—— (1993), 'Investigative Powers and Safeguards for Suspects', *Crim. LR*, 808.

Richardson, G. (1987), 'Strict Liability for Regulatory Crime', *Crim. LR*, 295.

Richardson, G., Ogus, A., and Burrows, P. (1982), *Policing Pollution*, Oxford: Oxford University Press.

Riley, D., and Vennard, J. (1988), *Triable-Either-Way Cases: Crown Court or Magistrates' Court?*, Home Office Research Study 98, London: H.M.S.O.

Roberts, P. (1996), 'What Price a Free Market in Forensic Science Services? The Organisation and Regulation of Science in the Criminal Process', *BJ Crim.*, **36**: 37.

——, and Willmore, C. (1993), *The Role of Forensic Science Evidence in Criminal Proceedings*, Royal Commission on Criminal Justice Research Study No. 11, London: H.M.S.O.

Robertshaw, P. (1992), 'Cracked Trials: what is happening?', *Crim. LR*, 867.

Robertson, G. (1994), 'Entrapment Evidence: Manna from Heaven or Fruit of the Poisoned Tree?', *Crim. LR*, 805.

——, Dell, S., Grounds, A., and James, K. (1992), 'Mentally Disordered Remand Prisoners', *Home Office Research Bulletin*, **32**: 1.

Robinson, P. H. (1988), 'Legality and Discretion in the Distribution of Criminal Sanctions', *Harvard Journal on Legislation*, 25: 393.

Roording, J. (1996), 'The Punishment of Tax Fraud', *Crim. LR*, 240.

Royal Commission on Criminal Justice (1993) (chair: Viscount Runciman), *Report*, Cmnd. 2263, London: H.M.S.O.

Royal Commission on Criminal Procedure (1981) (chair: Sir Cyril Phillips), *Report*, Cmnd. 8092, London: H.M.S.O.

Rozenberg, J. (1993), 'Miscarriages of Justice', in Stockdale and Casale (1993), q.v.

Rutherford, A. (1993), *Criminal Justice and the Pursuit of Decency*, Oxford: Oxford University Press.

Samuels, A. (1997), 'Custody Time Limits', *Crim. LR*, 260.

Sanders, A. (1985), 'Class Bias in Prosecutions', *Howard JCJ*, 24: 176.

—— (1988), 'The Limits to Diversion from Prosecution', *BJ Crim.*, 28: 513.

—— (1997), 'From Suspect to Trial', in Maguire, Morgan, and Reiner (1997), q.v.

Sanders, A., and Bridges, L. (1990), 'Access to Legal Advice and Police Malpractice', *Crim. LR*, 494.

——, and Young, R. (1995), *Criminal Justice*, London: Butterworths.

Schiff, D., and Nobles, R. (1996), 'Criminal Appeal Act 1995: the Semantics of Jurisdiction', *MLR*, 59: 573.

Schulhofer, S. (1984), 'Is Plea Bargaining Inevitable?', *Harv. LR* 97: 1037.

—— (1992), 'Plea Bargaining as Disaster', *Yale LJ*, 101: 1979.

——, and Nagel, I. (1997), 'Plea Negotiations under the Federal Sentencing Guidelines', *Northwestern ULR*, 91: 1284.

Scott, R. E., and Stuntz, W. J. (1992), 'Plea Bargaining as Contract', *Yale LJ*, 101: 1909.

——, —— (1992), 'A Reply: Imperfect Bargains, Imperfect Trials and Innocent Defendants', *Yale LJ*, 101: 2011.

Shapland, J., Duff, P., and Willmore, J. (1985), *Victims in the Criminal Justice System*, Aldershot: Gower.

Sharpe, S. (1997), *Judicial Discretion and Criminal Investigation*, London: Sweet & Maxwell.

Skolnick, J. (1966), *Justice without Trial*, New York: Wiley.

——, and Leo, R. (1992), 'The Ethics of Deceptive Interrogation', *Criminal Justice Ethics*, 11: 3.

Smith, D., and Gray, J. (1983), *Police and People in London*, London: Policy Studies Institute.

Smith, J. C. (1995), 'The Criminal Appeal Act 1995: Appeals against Conviction', *Crim. LR*, 920.

Smith, L. (1989), *Concerns about Rape*, Home Office Research Study 106, London: H.M.S.O.

Soothill, K., Francis, B., and Sanderson, B. (1997), 'A Cautionary Tale: the Sex Offenders Act 1997, the Police and Cautions', *Crim. LR*, 482.

Spencer, J. R., and Flin, R. (1993), *The Evidence of Children*, 2nd edn., London: Butterworths.

——, ed. (1989), *Children's Evidence in Legal Proceedings*, Cambridge: University Faculty of Law.

Sprack, J. (1997), *Emmins on Criminal Procedure*, 7th edn., London: Blackstone Press.

—— (1997), 'The Duty of Disclosure', *Crim. LR*, 308.

Stavros, S. (1994), *The Guarantees for Accused Persons under Article 6 of the European Convention on Human Rights*, Amsterdam: Martinus Nijhoff.

Stockdale, E., and Casale, S., eds. (1993), *Criminal Justice under Stress*, London: Blackstone Press.

Stone, C. (1988), *Bail Information for the Crown Prosecution Service*, London: Vera Institute of Justice.

Tak, P. J. P. (1986), *The Legal Scope of Non-Prosecution in Europe*, Helsinki: HEUNI.

Tapper, C., ed. (1981), *Crime, Proof and Punishment*, London: Butterworths.

Travers, M. (1997), *The Reality of Law*, Aldershot: Ashgate.

Trouille, H. (1994), 'A Look at French Criminal Procedure', *Crim. LR*, 735.

Twining, W. L. (1987), *Theories of Evidence: Bentham and Wigmore*, London: Weidenfeld and Nicolson.

Tyler, T. (1990), *Why People Obey the Law*, New Haven, CT.: Yale University Press.

Uglow, S. (1984), 'Defrauding the Public Purse', *Crim. LR*, 128.

——, Dart, A., Bottomley, A., and Hale, C. (1992), 'Cautioning Juveniles—Multi-Agency Impotence', *Crim. LR*, 632.

United Nations (1985), *Basic Principles of Justice for Victims of Crime and Abuse of Power*, New York: United Nations.

Van Ness, D. (1993), 'New Wine and Old Wineskins: Four Challenges of Restorative Justice', *Criminal Law Forum*, **4**: 251.

Von Hirsch, A. (1993), *Censure and Sanctions*, Oxford: Oxford University Press.

——, and Ashworth, A., eds. (1998), *Principled Sentencing: Readings in Theory and Policy*, 2nd edn., Oxford: Hart Publishing.

Walker, C. P., and Starmer, K., eds. (1992), *Justice in Error*, London: Blackstone Press.

White, S. (1996), 'The Antecedents of the Mode of Trial Guidelines', *Crim. LR*, 471.

Williams, J. F. (1994), 'Process and Prediction: a Return to a Fuzzy Model of Pre-Trial Detention', *Minnesota LR*, **79**: 325.

Windlesham, Lord (1988), 'Punishment and Prevention: the Inappropriate Prisoners', *Crim. LR*, 140.

Young, R., and Wall, D. (1996), *Access to Criminal Justice*, London: Blackstone Press.

Zander, M. (1977), 'The Criminal Process: a Subject ripe for a Major Inquiry', *Crim. LR*, 249.

—— (1993), 'The Innocent (?) who Plead Guilty', *New LJ*, **143**: 85.

—— (1993) 'Where the Critics got it Wrong', *New LJ* **143**:1338.

——, and Henderson, P. (1993), *Crown Court Study*, Royal Commission on Criminal Justice Research Study No. 19, London: H.M.S.O.

Zuckerman, A. A. S. (1989), 'Trial by Unfair Means', *Crim. LR*, 855.

—— (1989), *The Principles of Criminal Evidence*, Oxford: Oxford University Press.

Index